This is the first comprehensive introduction to the works and social contexts of women writers in early modern Britain, a period when it was considered unfeminine to write and yet women were the authors of many poems, translations, conduct books, autobiographies, plays, pamphlets and other texts. Drawing together the pioneering work of feminist literary critics and historians, this survey examines ways in which the idea of woman was constructed in the sixteenth and seventeenth centuries, and women's role in and access to literary culture; it then focuses on women writers and their output across the spectrum of genres from courtly romance to Quaker prophecy. A unique chronology offers a woman-centred perspective on historical and literary events, and there is a guide to further reading. *Women and Literature in Britain, 1500–1700* explores the history of women's part in the development of literary culture, while revealing how paradoxical that history can be.

WOMEN AND LITERATURE IN BRITAIN
1500–1700

WOMEN AND LITERATURE IN BRITAIN, 1500–1700

EDITED BY

HELEN WILCOX

University of Groningen

CAMBRIDGE
UNIVERSITY PRESS

Published by the Press Syndicate of the University of Cambridge
The Pitt Building, Trumpington Street, Cambridge CB2 1RP
40 West 20th Street, New York, NY 10011–4211, USA
10 Stamford Road, Oakleigh, Melbourne 3166, Australia

First published 1996

Printed in Great Britain at the University Press, Cambridge

A catalogue record for this book is available from the British Library

Library of Congress cataloguing in publication data

Women and literature in Britain, 1500–1700 / edited by Helen Wilcox.
p.   cm.
Includes bibliographical references and index.
ISBN 0521 46219 3 (hardcover). ISBN 0 521 46777 2 (paperback)
1. English literature – Early modern, 1500–1700 – History and
criticism.   2. Women and literature – Great Britain – History – 16th
century.   3. Women and literature – Great Britain – History – 17th
century.   4. English literature – Women authors – History and
criticism.   I. Wilcox, Helen.
PR113.w65   1996
820.9′9287′09031 – dc20   95–51404 CIP

ISBN 0 521 46219 3 hardback
ISBN 0 521 46777 2 paperback

Contents

Contributors

Ros BALLASTER teaches English Literature at Mansfield College, Oxford University. She is the author of *Seductive Forms: Women's Amatory Fiction, 1684–1740* (1992), editor of Delarivier Manley's *New Atalantis* for Penguin Classics (1992), and has published several articles on seventeenth- and eighteenth-century writing by women.

MARGARET W. FERGUSON has taught at Yale and Columbia Universities and is now Professor of English at the University of Colorado. The author of *Trials of Desire: Renaissance Defenses of Poetry* (1983), she has co-edited *Rewriting the Renaissance: the Discourses of Sexual Difference in Early Modern Europe* (1986) and *Postmodernism and Feminism* (1994). She is currently completing a book on female literacy and literary production in early modern France and England.

ELSPETH GRAHAM is Principal Lecturer in Literature and Cultural History at Liverpool John Moores University. She edited (with Hilary Hinds, Elaine Hobby and Helen Wilcox) *Her Own Life: Autobiographical Writings by Seventeenth-Century Englishwomen* (1989) and has published articles on seventeenth-century autobiography and women's writing, Bunyan and Milton, and feminist literary theory.

HELEN HACKETT is Lecturer in English at University College, London. She is the author of *Virgin Mother, Maiden Queen: Elizabeth I and the Cult of the Virgin Mary* (1994) and of articles on Mary Wroth's *Urania*. She is currently working on a book on women and romance in the Renaissance.

ELIZABETH H. HAGEMAN is Professor of English at the University of New Hampshire. She is, with Suzanne Woods, co-general editor of the series Women Writers in English, 1350–1850, published by Oxford University Press. She is currently working with Andrea Sununu on an edition of Katherine Philips (1631/2–1664) for that series.

JACQUELINE PEARSON is Lecturer in English Literature at the University of Manchester. She is the author of two books on Renaissance and Restoration drama, most recently *The Prostituted Muse: Images of Women and Women Dramatists, 1642–1737* (1989) and a number of articles on seventeenth-century women writers. She is now completing *A Dangerous Recreation: a Literary History of Women's Reading from 'The Female Quixote' to 'Scotch Novel Readers'*.

BRONWEN PRICE is Lecturer in English at Portsmouth University. Her doctorate, which she obtained from the University College of Cardiff, was on seventeenth-century poetry. She has published articles on Herrick and Lovelace and is currently working on studies of Cavendish's *The Blazing World* and seventeenth-century women's poetry.

HILDA L. SMITH is an Associate Professor in the Department of History at the University of Cincinnati and served as Director of the university's Center for Women's Studies from 1987 to 1993. She has a dual interest in the field of women's history and the intellectual and social development of seventeenth-century England. She is the author of *Reason's Disciples: Seventeenth-Century English Feminists* (1982) and co-author (with Susan Cardinale) of an annotated bibliography entitled *Women and the Literature of the Seventeenth Century* (1990).

ANN THOMPSON is Professor of English and Head of the English Department at the Roehampton Institute, London. She is one of the general editors of the new Arden Shakespeare series (Arden 3), and general editor of a series of books on feminist criticism of Shakespeare for Routledge. She has published widely on Shakespeare, including *Shakespeare's Chaucer*, *Shakespeare, Meaning and Metaphor* (with John O. Thompson) and an edition of *The Taming of the Shrew*.

BETTY S. TRAVITSKY was formerly Research Librarian of the Billy Rose Theatre Collection of the New York Public Library for the Performing Arts. She is editor of *The Paradise of Women: Writings by Englishwomen of the Renaissance* (1981; reprinted 1989), and co-editor of *The Renaissance Englishwoman in Print: Counterbalancing the Canon* (1990), *Women in the Renaissance: an Interdisciplinary Forum* (1991) and *Attending to Women in Early Modern England* (1994).

SUZANNE TRILL is Lecturer in Renaissance Literature at the Queen's University of Belfast. Her research focuses on women's use of Scripture in the early modern period. She is the co-editor, with William Zunder, of *Writing and the English Renaissance* (1996).

VALERIE WAYNE is Professor of English at the University of Hawaii at Manoa. She has edited *The Matter of Difference: Feminist Criticism of Shakespeare* (1991), Edmund Tilney's *The Flower of Friendship: a Renaissance Dialogue Contesting Marriage* (1992), and Thomas Middleton's *A Trick to Catch the Old One*, which appears in *The Collected Works of Thomas Middleton* (1995) for which she served as an associate general editor.

HELEN WILCOX is Professor of English Literature at the University of Groningen, The Netherlands. Her research and publications concern early modern women's writing, seventeenth-century devotional poetry and Shakespeare. She has co-edited *Teaching Women: Feminism and English Studies* (1989), *Her Own Life: Autobiographical Writings by Seventeenth-Century Englishwomen* (1989), *The Body and the Text* (1990) and *George Herbert: Sacred and Profane* (1995).

Acknowledgements

Many people have contributed towards the making of this book. I should first like to thank all the contributors for their co-operation in, and abiding enthusiasm for, the project, as well as their innovative scholarship. I should particularly like to acknowledge the advice given by Ann Thompson and Valerie Wayne in the preparation of the introductory materials. Josie Dixon at Cambridge University Press has been patient, encouraging and an astute reader, for which many thanks are due. Lastly, I should like to take this opportunity to dedicate the book not only to the memory of the early modern women whom it celebrates, but also in gratitude to my modern and long-suffering family – Allan, Thomas and Joseph – who have been an unfailing source of inspiration and support.

A note on references

Page numbering

Some early modern manuscripts (mss) and printed books do not have pages numbered according to the modern convention. In cases where a number refers to a sheet of paper, both back and front, then these two sides are distinguished in references as 'r' (recto, meaning the front, i.e. the right-hand half of a double open page) and 'v' (verso, meaning the reverse or back of the sheet).

In some early printed books there are no numbers at all but signs such as a printer's mark or a letter at the bottom of the first page of a new section of the book. In these cases, the reference A3v, for example, means the back of the third (right-hand) page of the section marked A; if the beginning of this section was page 1 of the book, then A3v would be page 6 in modern numbering.

Abbreviations

Some publications are referred to in this book by means of abbreviations, as follows:

ANQ	American Notes and Queries
DLB	Dictionary of Literary Biography
DNB	Dictionary of National Biography
EC	Essays in Criticism
ELH	English Literary History
ELN	English Language Notes
ELR	English Literary Renaissance
EMS	English Manuscript Studies
HLQ	Huntington Library Quarterly
JEGP	Journal of English and Germanic Philology
JEH	Journal of Ecclesiastical History
MLQ	Modern Language Quarterly

MP	*Modern Philology*
MQ	*Musical Quarterly*
PMLA	*Proceedings of the Modern Language Association of America*
RD	*Renaissance Drama*
RES	*Review of English Studies*
SB	*Shakespeare Bulletin*
SC	*The Seventeenth Century*
SCJ	*Sixteenth Century Journal*
SCR	*South Central Review*
SEL	*Studies in English Literature*
SP	*Studies in Philology*
SQ	*Shakespeare Quarterly*
SS	*Shakespeare Survey*

Chronology: women and literature in Britain, 1500–1700

	Event	Text (publication unless stated to the contrary)
1501		Margery Kempe, *Short Treatyse of Contemplacyon*
1504		Lady Margaret Beaufort, translation of *The Imitation of Christ* (Thomas a Kempis)
1509	Henry VIII's accession to the English throne	
1521		Christine de Pisan, *Boke of the Cyte of Ladyes* published in English
1524		Margaret (More) Roper, translation of *A Devout Treatise Upon the Pater Noster* (Erasmus)
1529		Juan Luis Vives, *The Instruction of a Christian Woman* (1523) published in English
1533	Catherine of Aragon divorced by Henry VIII	
1534	Reformation consolidated in England Henry VIII made 'supreme head' of the Church of England	
1536	Execution of Anne Boleyn Wales annexed to the English crown	
1536–9	Henry VIII closes convents and monasteries	
1538	Destruction of shrine of Virgin Mary at Walsingham	
1540		Sir Thomas Elyot, *Defence of Good Women*
1541	Henry VIII declared King of Ireland	
1545		Anon., *The Scholehouse of Women* (attributed in 1548 to Edward Gosynhyll)
1546	Execution of Anne Askewe	Katherine Parr, *Prayers or Meditacions*
1547	Edward VI's accession	
1548	(approximately)	Anne (Cooke) Bacon, translation of *Sermons of Bernadine Ochine of Sena*
1550		Jane Lumley, manuscript translation of Euripedes' play *Iphigenia in Aulis*
1553	Mary's accession as first Queen Regnant of England since the disputed rule of Matilda (twelfth century)	

Date	Historical events	Literary works
1554	Execution of Lady Jane Grey (who reigned briefly in 1553 as the Protestant alternative to Mary)	
1558	Elizabeth I's accession	John Knox, *First Blast of the Trumpet against the monstrous regiment of women*
1560		Ann Lok, translation of Calvin's *Sermons* with her own sonnet cycle appended
1563		First English edition of Foxe's *Book of Martyrs* (*Actes and Monuments*)
1564		Anne (Cooke) Bacon, translation of *An Apologie in defence of the Churche of England* (official translation of John Jewel's text on church doctrine)
1573		Isabella Whitney, *A sweet Nosegay, or pleasant Posye*
1574		Elizabeth Tyrwhit, *Morning and Evening Prayers*
1575–6	Statute passed (18 Elizabeth) withdrawing benefit of clergy from those who raped by force	
1578		Margaret Tyler, translation of *The Mirrour of Princely deedes and Knighthood* (secular romance by Diego Ortunez de Calahorra)
1582		Thomas Bentley, ed., *The Monument of Matrones*
1584		Anne Wheathill, *A Handfull of holesome (though homelie) hearbs*
1586	Execution of Margaret Clitherow; Treaty of Berwick between Scots and English	William Camden, *Britannia*
1587	Execution of Mary Queen of Scots	
1588	Queen Elizabeth's Tilbury speech; Spanish Armada defeated	
1589		*Jane Anger, her protection for Women*; Anne Dowriche, *The French Historie*
1592		Mary Sidney, Countess of Pembroke, translation of *Antonius* (tragedy by Robert Garnier); Philip Stubbes, *A Christall Glasse, for Christian Women* (on his late wife Katherine)

	Event	Text (publication unless stated to the contrary)
1599		Mary Sidney presents manuscript of psalms in verse transition to Queen Elizabeth
1603	Death of Elizabeth I Accession of James VI of Scotland to English throne Witchcraft made a punishable offence in English law	Lady Anne Clifford begins her *Diary* Elizabeth Melville, Lady Culross, *Ane Godlie Dreame* (in Scots dialect; printed in English *c.* 1606)
1604		Elizabeth Grymeston, *Miscelanea*
1605		Elizabeth (Cooke) Russell, translation of *A Way of Reconciliation* (John Poynet)
1609		Robert Filmer, *Patriarcha*
1611	Lady Arbella Stuart attempts to escape to the continent with William Seymour	'Authorised Version' (otherwise known as the 'King James Bible') Aemilia Lanyer, *Salve Deus Rex Judaeorum*
1613	Marriage of Elizabeth Stuart (daughter of James I and Queen Anne) to Frederick the Elector Palatine	Elizabeth Cary, *The Tragedie of Mariam*
1615	Trial of Frances Howard	Helkiah Crooke, *Microcosmographia: a Description of the Body of Man*, first English medical text to mention the clitoris (identified in Venice in 1559 as the 'seat of woman's delight') Joseph Swetnam, *The Arraignment of Lewd, idle, froward and unconstant women*
1616		Dorothy Leigh, *The Mothers Blessing*
1617		Rachel Speght, *A Mouzell for Melastomus* Ester Sowernam, *Ester hath hang'd Haman* Constantia Munda, *The Worming of a Mad Dogge*

Year	Events	Works
1620		Anon, *Swetnam the Woman Hater Arraigned by Women* Anon, *Hic Mulier, Haec Vir*
1621	King James pronounces on women wearing men's apparel	Lady Mary Wroth, *The Countesse of Montgomeries Urania* Rachel Speght, *Moralities Memorandum*
1622		Elizabeth Clinton, *The Countesse of Lincolnes Nurserie*
1623		M. R., *The Mother's Counsell*
1624		Elizabeth Joceline, *The Mothers Legacie*
1625	Charles I's accession	
1626		Lady Eleanor Douglas, *A Warning to the Dragon*
1629		Helen Livingston, Countess of Linlithgow, *Confession and Conversion*
1631		William Livingstone, *Conflict in Conscience* (narrative of Bessie Clerksone)
1632		T. E., *The Lawes Resolutions of Womens Rights* Martha Moulsworth writes her autobiographical poem 'My Name was Martha'
1633		Alice Sutcliffe, *Meditations of Man's Mortalitie*
1634		Jane Owen, *Antidote against Purgatory*
1640		Mary Tattlewell and Joan Hit-him-home, *The Women's Sharpe Revenge*
1641	Relaxation of publishing laws	
1642	Women petition parliament in London, led by Anne Stagg, 'Gentlewomen and Brewer's Wife' Outbreak of civil war Public theatres closed (until 1660)	
1645		Katherine Chidley, *A New-Yeares Gift and Good Counsel to the Petitioners* Elizabeth Richardson, *A Ladies Legacie to her Daughters*
1648		Elizabeth Poole, *A Vision … the disease and cure of the kingdome*
1649	Execution of Charles I; declaration of Commonwealth	
1651		Anna Weamys, *A Continuation of Sir Philip Sidney's 'Arcadia'* Mary Cary, *A New and More Exact Mappe*

	Event	Text (publication unless stated to the contrary)
1652	'Pacification' of Ireland by Cromwellian army	
1653		An Collins, *Divine Songs and Meditations* Margaret Cavendish, Duchess of Newcastle, *Poems and Fancies* and *Philosophicall Fancies*
1654		Anna Trapnel, *The Cry of a Stone* Arise Evans, *A Message from God, By a Dumb Woman* (Elinor Channel's prophecy)
1656		Margaret Cavendish, *Nature's Pictures*
1658		Sarah Jinner, *An Almanack or Prognostication for Women*
1659		Anna Maria van Schurmann, *The Learned Maid* published in English
1660	Restoration of the monarchy; Charles II's accession	
1661		Hannah Wolley, *The Ladies Directory*
1662	Royal patent that women should play female roles on public stage	*The Life and Death of Mrs Mary Frith, Commonly Called Mal Cutpurse* Margaret Cavendish, *Playes*
1663		Mary Carleton, *An Historicall Narrative* Katherine Philips's translation of *Pompey* (Corneille) performed in Dublin
1664		Katherine Philips, *Poems*
1666		Margaret Fell Fox, *Womens Speaking Justified*
1667	Margaret Cavendish visits Royal Society	*Poems by Mrs Katherine Philips, the Matchless Orinda* Dorothy Pakington, *Causes of the Decay of Christian Piety*
1669		Frances Boothby, *Marcelia: or the Treacherous Friend* performed in London by the King's Company
1670		Aphra Behn, *The Forc'd Marriage* and Elizabeth Polwhele, *The Faithful Virgins* performed in London by the Duke's Company

1671	Lucy Hutchinson, *Memoirs of the Life of Colonel Hutchinson* completed (in manuscript until 1806)
	Jane Sharp, *The Midwives Book*
1673	Bathsua Makin, *Essay to Revive the Antient Education of Gentlewomen*
	Susanna Bell, *The Legacy of a Dying Mother*
1677	Anne Wentworth, *A Vindication*
1679–80	Midwife Elizabeth Cellier tried for alleged involvement in the 'Meal-Tub Plot' (a supposed Catholic plot to assassinate Charles II)
1683	Jane Lead, *Revelation of Revelations*
1685	James II's accession
1688	Aphra Behn, *Oroonoko*
	Lord Halifax, *The Lady's New-Years Gift: or, Advice to a Daughter*
	Elizabeth Cellier, *To Dr——An Answer to his Queries*
1689	'Glorious Revolution'; accession of William and Mary
	Account of the Travels, Sufferings and Persecutions of Barbara Blaugdone
1691	Mary Astell, *A Serious Proposal to the Ladies*
1694	Catherine Trotter, *Agnes de Castro*
1695	Delarivier Manley, *The Royal Mischief*
1696	Judith Drake, *An Essay in Defence of the Female Sex*
	Mary Pix, *The Beau Defeated*
1700	Posthumous publication of Mary Mollineaux, *Fruits of Retirement, or Miscellaneous Poems*
1702	

Introduction

Helen Wilcox

> But when some of those thoughts are sent out in words, they give the
> rest more liberty to place themselves in a more methodical order:
> marching more regularly with my pen on the ground of white
> paper. But my letters seem rather as a ragged rout than a well
> armed body. For the brain being quicker in creating than the hand
> in writing or the memory in retaining, many fancies are lost, by
> reason they oft-times outrun the pen. Where I, to keep speed in the
> race, write so fast as I stay not so long to write my letters plain:
> insomuch as some have taken my handwriting for some strange
> character.
>
> (Margaret Cavendish, Duchess of Newcastle, 'A True
> Relation of my Birth, Breeding and Life')[1]

Margaret Cavendish's account of the exhilarating process of writing,
taken from her autobiography published in 1656, seems an appropriate
passage with which to begin our consideration of women and literature
in Britain in the sixteenth and seventeenth centuries. For her words
express many of the paradoxes associated with women, writing and early
modern history. Cavendish, literate and relatively leisured, was bursting
with creative energy, as is suggested in her description of the quickness
(literally, 'aliveness' as well as speed) of the brain, the impression of her
thoughts queuing up to be 'sent out in words', and the image of the
tumbling 'ragged rout' of letters on the page. But Cavendish's choice of
metaphors is a vivid reminder of the gendered world in which such a
woman lived and wrote. She wrote from a feminine perspective and
achieved a freedom of style all her own; but in her description of the
writing process her words become drilled, 'marching' as a masculine
army, aspiring to become a 'well armed body' dominating the page. This
is ironic, since as a writer she entered a world of genres and traditions,
muses and authors, in which the woman was constructed as the inspiration rather than the creator, the subject of fascination rather than the

speaking or controlling subject. The 'ground of white paper' (on which Cavendish radically hoped to place her own mark) was a prevailing Renaissance image of the woman herself, waiting in silent chastity to receive the imprint of the male.[2] Margaret Cavendish, author and female subject, was trapped between two worlds. Perhaps it is no surprise, then, that she went on to create her own *New Blazing World*.[3]

Cavendish's account of imaginative composition, one of the earliest known detailed records of the writing process, highlights the complexities of creativity and constraint experienced by a woman writer in the early modern period. The passage goes on to consider the process of transferring imaginative 'fancies' (which 'run' so fast that they leave the pen behind) into written and readable form. This conversion from concept to text was no easy business, not only because the resultant hasty handwriting was so untidy as to risk being mistaken for, as Cavendish ruefully notes, 'some strange character'. It was also, more significantly, not straightforward for a woman to circulate or publish her own writings in the early modern era; to do so was a bold, much criticised and frequently isolated action. When Cavendish used her private means to publish 'A True Relation of my Birth, Breeding and Life' (from which the above extract is taken) as part of a collection called *Nature's Pictures Drawn by Fancy's Pencil to the Life* (London, 1656), she was the first British woman to publish her own secular autobiography. When the second edition of *Nature's Pictures* came out in 1671 (while Cavendish was still alive) her autobiography was, for reasons never explained, no longer included. Even those female 'fancies' that reached print could subsequently be 'lost'. To quote Cavendish's own words with poignant irony, the communal 'memory' often has difficulty in 'retaining' the output of the woman writer, as intervening literary history has undoubtedly shown.[4]

The interplay of imagination and language, and the tensions between expression and reception, all seen here in miniature in the extract from Cavendish's autobiography, have to be kept in mind as we attempt fully to appreciate the history of women and literature. As well as discovering, reading, analysing and enjoying the works of early modern British women writers, we need to become familiar with the religious, social and literary culture of which they were a part. That is why this book is entitled 'women and literature' and not simply 'women writers'. It is designed as an introduction to contexts as well as texts, so that the texts may be read and understood for all their richness. What could, and did, these women write? For whom did they write? What were their models and sources, if any? How did their writings change and develop during the sixteenth and seventeenth centuries? By what means were they enabled to write, or discouraged or deflected from their desire to express themselves? Is it a hopelessly anachronistic idea to think of writing in the early modern period as 'expressing oneself'? These are the kinds of questions that this book as a whole seeks to begin to answer.

The first tool that this volume offers is a chronological table of Britain in the sixteenth and seventeenth centuries, indicating some familiar landmarks of history such as the Reformation, the accession of queens and kings, and the English Civil War. What makes the chronology different, and of special relevance to this study, is that it also shows historical events of particular relevance to women, such as the execution of female martyrs, the women's petition to parliament, and the decree allowing women to act in public theatres. Alongside the historical events is a column giving some key publications by or about women during this period. In addition to showing at a glance just what (and how much!) was written, when, and by whom, the chronology also makes it possible for readers to look up texts mentioned during the course of this book, and to set them in their precise historical framework.

The main body of the book is divided into two sections. The first, 'Constructing Women', sets out some of the most important contexts for an understanding of women and their lives in early modern Britain. What were the influences and traditions, the philosophies and prejudices, that formed Renaissance ideas of woman? The first three chapters examine the role and nature of humanist education, religious contexts and the tradition of advice books for women. As these discussions make clear, the social construction of femininity was rarely a simple, and certainly not an exclusively male, activity; as the account of conduct books (chapter 3) shows, advice came from mothers as well as patriarchs. The other three chapters in the first section examine further questions of cultural formation: what did women read; how were they represented on the stage; and to what extent might women in themselves represent alternative modes of knowing, particularly when challenged with the rise of scientific thought?

The discussion of feminine knowledge and its exploration by the writer Margaret Cavendish (chapter 6) stands at the borderline of the two halves of the book and leads directly into the subject of the second section, 'Writing Women'. After an opening chapter that considers Renaissance concepts of the 'woman writer' (mirroring the enquiry into the Renaissance concept of woman, with which the first section begins), the second section then proceeds to examine groups of texts by early modern British women writers. Their writings are clustered by tradition, subject or genre: the chapters treat, in turn, courtly writing, poetry, autobiographical writing, prose and drama. The overall sequence of textual kinds makes chronological sense – there was a higher proportion of courtly texts in the earlier part of our period, and a greater flourishing of playwrights in the concluding decades – but within each chapter there is a wide-ranging consideration of the output of British women writers over two centuries.

The centuries in question were thrilling ones in terms of new achievements by women writers. They contain the publication date of the first autobiography (male or female) in English (Margery Kempe, 1501), the first English publication of a secular text translated by a woman (Margaret Tyler, 1578), the first original play known to have been written by a woman (Elizabeth Cary, 1613), the first secular autobiography to be published by a woman (Margaret Cavendish, 1656), the first woman to earn her living by writing (Sarah Jinner), and the first play scripted by a woman to be performed on a British stage (Katherine Philips, 1663). Such firsts, however, have always to be set against the backdrop of women's severely constrained social and legal position. In law, women had no status whatsoever but were only daughters, wives or widows of men; according to the church they were to be silent and listen to the advice of husbands or pastors; in religious and cultural patterns of thought, they were daughters of Eve with a continuing proneness to temptation and a disproportionate burden of guilt.[5]

As we approach these women and their texts from our late twentieth-century perspective, it is all too easy to simplify the lines of history and mutual identification. We need to remind ourselves, for example, of the pervasiveness of religion, as practice, as controversy, as restraint, as means of expression, as life's calling or as life's threat, for early modern women. We also need to avoid the assumption that patriarchal culture was upheld only by men; many of the tropes of misogynist thinking were deeply absorbed and reproduced by women themselves.[6] The distinction between men and women in the sphere of literature may also be misread; not all texts with a female name attached to them were necessarily by women, just as most 'women' on the stage were not, in fact, women at all. It is vitally important that we recognise these uncertainties and asymmetries if we are to read the early modern period accurately. Such instability is also to be found in the notion of 'Britain' in the sixteenth and seventeenth centuries. The discussions in this book make reference to women in the history and culture of Scotland, Ireland and Wales as well as England, even though the majority of the texts stem from England. But the very concept of Britain itself was problematic in this period; Wales was annexed to the English crown in 1536, and in 1541 Henry VIII was declared King of Ireland. The poetry of Mary Queen of Scots is appropriately studied here, as are the pronouncements of her son, James VI and I, who came from Scotland to the throne of England in 1603 and spoke out not only against witchcraft (in 1603) but also against women wearing men's apparel (in 1620). It may be anachronistic to refer to James as a homosexual, but his life, reigns and opinions form a vivid emblem of the unstable boundaries of gender and nationality in this period.

The juxtaposing of women and men, poetry and politics, texts and contexts and many other binaries in the following chapters is intended ultimately to blur the distinctions between these sometimes overstressed opposites. It is also our hope that this book as a whole will enable readers to experience something of the unique excitement, controversy and creativity of early modern women and their era. Readers who are led to explore the original works themselves, and/or more detailed critical or historical studies of the period, are advised to consult the reading list that follows on from the final chapter. The scholarship and insights of all those who have contributed to this book have been inspired by the work of the many other critics mentioned or noted in the chapters, but particularly those whose writings or editions appear in the list. One of the most refreshing features of the study of early modern British literature in the last two decades has been painstaking rediscovery and re-presentation of women's writing and of ideas concerning women in the sixteenth and seventeenth centuries. This book is a tribute to that work, as well as an introduction to its significance.

Readers of this book will encounter many memorable early modern women and their even more distinctive works in the pages that follow. May it be said of these writing women, as Margaret Cavendish wrote of her own 'fancies', that 'it is as great a grief to leave their society, as a joy to be in their company'.[7]

NOTES

1. Elspeth Graham, Hilary Hinds, Elaine Hobby and Helen Wilcox, eds., *Her Own Life: Autobiographical Writings by Seventeenth-Century Englishwomen* (London: Routledge, 1989), p. 94.
2. See, for example, *Othello* IV.ii.72–3: 'Was this fair paper, this most goodly book, / Made to write "whore" upon?' For a fine discussion of gendered metaphors for writing, see Susan Gubar, '"The Blank Page" and the Issues of Female Creativity', anthologised in Elaine Showalter, ed., *The New Feminist Criticism: Essays on Women, Literature and Theory* (London: Virago, 1986), pp. 292–313. See also pp. 84–5 below.
3. In 1666 Cavendish published *Observations upon Experimental Philosophy*, which included her vision of a 'New Blazing World'. This text is now available in Kate Lilley, ed., *The Blazing World and Other Writings* (Harmondsworth: Penguin, 1994).
4. See Joanna Russ, *How to Suppress Women's Writing* (London: Women's Press, 1984).
5. See in particular the first three chapters of this volume.
6. See, for example, the discussion of the complexities of Aphra Behn's position at the end of Margaret W. Ferguson's chapter, 'Renaissance concepts of the "woman writer"'.
7. Graham, *et al.*, eds., *Her Own Life*, p. 94.

PART I

Constructing women in early modern Britain

CHAPTER I

Humanist education and the Renaissance concept of woman

Hilda L. Smith

Women, or 'woman' to use language more familiar to sixteenth and seventeenth century authors, composed a group that early modern writers felt obliged both to define and to advise. Women existed more clearly as a category in the minds of Renaissance authors than as disparate individuals. This chapter will focus on understanding what the category 'woman' meant during the Renaissance, and what values and social realities placed women there. What qualities most defined them? What realities clearly constrained them? Which social classes mattered (and which did not) in developing this concept of woman? Such questions emerge from issues embedded within 'woman' as Renaissance concept, and they aid us in understanding major early modern texts which treat women.

Sixteenth-century humanism, whose authors produced the most important Renaissance works on women, was an educational and philosophical movement that criticised the limited academic universe of late medieval scholasticism. Humanism, originating in fourteenth-century Italy, spread throughout the educated classes of early sixteenth-century England and continued its influence into the seventeenth as well. This chapter will focus on the broad outlines of Renaissance humanism, its treatment of women, and its growth and ultimate decline. Sixteenth-century humanism, as exemplified in the works of Thomas More, Thomas Elyot and Juan Luis Vives, offered an educational and linguistic programme for those who wished to pursue the 'New Learning'. Humanists claimed that medieval scholasticism, which involved a series of dialogues concerning philosophic and scientific concepts, was an overly structured intellectual exercise, far removed from the actual texts on which such exercises were based. Humanism's new learning was grounded in a critique of scholasticism, and favoured precise knowledge of classical languages, heightened emphasis on the study of Greek, and a return to an earlier, and more accurate, version of the Scriptures

stripped of commentary by the church fathers. Personal ethics, spirituality and civic responsibility were the lessons to be gleaned from authenti-
cated Scriptures and the best of ancient thinkers. Insisting on a solid
knowledge of classical languages and a serious university education,
humanists applied the principles learned from such education to the
public and private duties of individuals.

While women were a part of the intellectual and social changes tied to
the spread of humanist ideas, they were always on the periphery. In
theory, humanism was an education that had as much to offer women as
men, but in practice it was situated in universities, from which women
were excluded, and applied to the governance of families and to public
office, positions outside their responsibility. Although women were
placed on the periphery by Renaissance authors, they were not totally
excluded from the humanist programme. Humanism, especially the
Northern Humanism associated with Erasmus and More, embraced
Christian values on the grounds that humanist scholarship promoted a
more informed and serious brand of Christianity. Thus the traditional
emphasis on female piety blended well with the emphasis on Christian
beliefs and biblical truths, and women's learning was encouraged by
Vives and More but never at the same level or for the same purposes as
that of gentlemen.[1]

Humanist authors offered an educational continuum that allowed
men of the middling classes to progress through boarding school and
university to professional positions where they could either preach or
teach the new learning. Boys were introduced to its principles through
properly trained schoolmasters and clerics; humanist education created
better public and private men through learning and concepts of civic
virtue. Their training urged Renaissance gentlemen to apply the moral,
political and rhetorical lessons gained from the ancients and the Christian insights elicited from Scripture to the governance of their families,
their local magisterial and judicial responsibilities and their service to a
prince.[2]

The humanist educational programme continued into the late sixteenth and early seventeenth centuries and underlay the educational
revolution of 1580–1640 that provided a classical and civic education for
greater numbers of men from a wider class spectrum. The massive
increase in grammar schools and numbers of students from commoner
families at Oxford and Cambridge fostered an education that offered
males advice about their duties to God and country. Much of their
curriculum echoed the new learning of the early sixteenth century. Thus

through the 1630s that tie between education and public duty favoured by the earlier humanists flourished, and women continued to be omitted. Renaissance humanism was then closely tied to a gentleman's (or socially mobile commoner's) career because education framed his values and directed his actions as head of a family, holder of a local political or legal office, or member of the royal government. However, what relevance did such an education, especially in its applied setting, hold for women? Was there anything that could truly be termed a Renaissance notion of woman? Or did Renaissance thinkers simply create a pastiche of ideas, symbols and values gleaned from ancient and scriptural texts concerning women's nature? In other words, was there anything original in what English humanist authors wrote about women?[3]

Humanist texts such as Sir Thomas More's *Utopia* (1516, Latin; 1551, English), Baldassare Castiglione's *The Courtier* (1531, Italian; 1561, English), Thomas Elyot's *The Governour* (1531), and Niccolo Machiavelli's *The Prince* (1560, Italian; 1640, English) provided political guidance to educated men. Although Castiglione's programme for proper behaviour at court and Machiavelli's guide for a prince were Italian works, they were highly influential in the development of civic virtue in sixteenth-century England. Each of these authors counselled the ruler and governing classes on practical and ethical questions. It is, above all, this utilitarian nature of humanist writings, and their limited audience, that excluded women from an educational programme for which they were otherwise entirely eligible. Most humanists admitted that women had the ability to learn; it was simply a question of what they would do with such learning and whether it might interfere with their more important responsibilities as wives and mothers.[4]

Humanism flourished within England from 1515 to 1550 and continued to have significant influence into the later sixteenth and early seventeenth centuries and beyond. For women, the most important humanist works appearing during that period were Juan Luis Vives's *Instruction of a Christian Woman* (1529), as well as his *Plan of Study for Girls* (1523); Roger Ascham's *The Schoolmaster* (1570); Thomas Elyot's *Defence of Good Women* (1540); and John Aylmer's defence of Elizabeth's rule, *A Harbour for Faithful and True Subjects* (1959), against John Knox's attack on women rulers, *The First Blast of the Trumpet against the monstrous regiment of women* (1558). Henricus Cornelius Agrippa's work *A Treatise of the Nobility of Womankind* (1542) was translated into English and formed a model, along with Boccaccio's *Concerning Famous Women* (1359; first English translation, 1963), for those works that presented linguistic and historical/mythical examples of women's superiority. Agrippa, for instance, argued that 'Eve', as standing for soul, was linguistically superior to 'Adam', associated with the earth. Authors such as Edward Gosynhyll wrote on both sides of the issue; he praised women's intelligence and character in *The Praise of all Women* (1542?) and ridiculed women's learning in *The Scholehouse of Women* (1541). Writers such as Gosynhyll revealed that the controversy surrounding women's learning promised financial gain and did not require ideological consistency. It was a popular and profitable subject, and a debate that seemed to produce endless broadsides and tracts along with longer works.[5]

Although these works differed on specific points, they all carried two common themes. First, they made clear that the humanist educational and social programme preparing independent men for learning and responsible positions did not apply to women, and second, that women remained more imbued with the Christian virtues associated with the medieval world than did their male counterparts. Men were expected to remain true Christians, but they were to incorporate secular knowledge from the ancients with Christianity. Demands for morality and chastity constrained women and narrowed their existence. Ruth Kelso noted this distinction in her ground-breaking work of 1956, *Doctrine for the Lady of the Renaissance*. 'The moral ideal for the lady is essentially Christian, ... as that for the gentleman is essentially pagan. For him the ideal is self expansion and realization... For the lady the direct opposite is prescribed. The eminently Christian virtues of chastity, humility, piety, and patience under suffering and wrong, are the necessary virtues.'[6]

In the seventeenth century, tracts concerning women's nature took on a scurrilous tone during the early reign of James I, and evinced puritan overtones later on in the 1620s. At the beginning of the seventeenth century authors debated whether women were in league with the devil and whether men could beat their wives, and produced tracts on a range of sexually provocative topics. Following 1620, advice literature concerning women adopted a more puritan tone in William Gouge's description *Of Domesticall Duties* (1622) and in conduct books such as Richard Brathwaite's, *The English Gentlewoman* (1631). While such works avoided the misogynist tone of Joseph Swetnam's *The Arraignment of Lewd, idle, froward and unconstant women* (1615), a characteristic of James's early reign, they advocated restricted, domestic lives for women. Other authors identified the best qualities in women who lived in other times and places; Thomas Heywood in *The General History of Women* (1657) provided lists and descriptions of outstanding women from the past. Ancient history,

Scripture and mythology provided the raw data for such works and, while certainly positive, these writings held little relationship to real women in the past, or inspiration for women in the present. Such authors were followed, later in the century, by those who wished to ally themselves with either Queen Mary or Queen Anne, or other important women who could serve as patrons. Their works were quite similar to Agrippa's linguistic and cultural arguments from the sixteenth century or Heywood's discussion of exceptional women. Two of the most important were Nahum Tate's *A Present for the Ladies* (1693), modelled heavily on Agrippa, and William Walsh's *A Dialogue Concerning Women, being a Defence of the Sex* (1691), which held much in common with Thomas Elyot's earlier *Defence of the Female Sex* (as did Henry Care's translation of Agrippa in 1670).[7]

Evidencing little integration between broad humanist principles and specific writings on women, authors treated them separately. No humanist author placed women within the utilitarian core of humanist training and vocation. That women were intended as wives proved the single most important restriction on what they should learn and how they could use that learning. To grasp fully humanist arguments concerning women it is important to place them within general humanist ideals, which, rather than equalling universal principles directed to a broad audience, were restricted both by class and gender to a small minority of Englishmen.

Recent scholarship on women during the Renaissance has offered much valuable information about the complexity of humanist views toward questions of gender, but it has provided less insight on the general nature and gender-specific quality of classic humanist texts. One cannot understand what humanists were saying about women without considering what they were saying specifically to men in their supposedly general works. As Ruth Kelso established nearly forty years ago, to understand thoroughly what Renaissance authors had in mind for women's education one also has to consider what they intended for men's. Slighting such works ignores what humanists believed were the central lessons to be gleaned from humanist training.

Lively scholarship has emerged over the last two decades concerning the treatment of women by Renaissance authors, as well as attention to the writings of Renaissance women. For historians, the essay that launched much of this interest was Joan Kelly Gadol's 'Did Women Have a Renaissance?', which raised doubts about women's inclusion in Renaissance progress. It was followed in 1980 with Ian Maclean's monograph *The Renaissance Notion of Woman*. Maclean's work is strongly grounded in a range of philosophic, medical and social literature from the sixteenth and seventeenth centuries and offers the most systematic overview of Renaissance attitudes on the nature of the female sex. By the mid to late 1980s (as well as 1990 to 1992), a number of book-length works emerged including *Rewriting the Renaissance* (1986), a collection organized around the unifying theme of gender definition; Margaret King's *Women of the Renaissance* (1991); *Renaissance Feminism* (1990) by Constance Jordan; and *The Invention of the Renaissance Woman* (1992) by Pamela Joseph Benson.[8] While innumerable articles have appeared in both historical and literary journals on the topic in recent years, literary scholars have dominated the field. Both monographic and article-length studies explore the questions of humanism's impact on women, the lives of individual women intellectuals, the role of sexuality in defining women in the sixteenth century and jointly seek a gendered paradigm that can help to explain women's partial inclusion in the Renaissance's reach. On the whole they are more positive than the scenario outlined by Joan Kelly almost twenty years ago, but all recognise the problematic nature of women within Renaissance discourse.

The three recent book-length studies by King, Jordan and Benson find things to admire in Renaissance authors. King, the lone historian, treats women in the family, in religion and in the realm of high culture. Her work is useful for those students seeking an overview of recent scholarship on women's intellectual and social existence within the Renaissance; but it lacks a clear unity, dipping briefly into a range of writings and usually finding more to praise than to condemn. Constance Jordan entitles her work *Renaissance Feminism*, yet in the introduction she is not always clear about the feminism emerging from Renaissance sources. For her, feminism seems to be best characterised as 'a representation of the world from a woman's point of view'. Also she writes:

the feminism of Renaissance texts represents a (roughly) uniform and consistent theory of knowledge, recognized and recognizable as a theory or a point of view, by which to justify feminist assumptions of the virtue of women and, conversely, to call into question patriarchal assumptions of their inferiority.[9]

Not merely is this a fairly unclear definition of Renaissance feminism, it is also difficult to apply when determining the extent of a text's feminist content. Jordan offers stronger negative arguments for Renaissance feminists, especially in their rejection of Aristotelian views, but is weaker in developing positive reasons for their being considered feminists. Ian

Maclean, whose work remains the most impressive intellectual overview, also posed the question: 'is there a Renaissance "feminist" movement?' He mostly responds 'no', and argues that 'the main causes for stasis in the notion of woman which emerge from this study are, in different contexts, the desire to foster and preserve the scholastic synthesis, and the influence on thought of the institution of matrimony'.[10] This certainly seems a fair conclusion and helps to explain the lack of originality or individuality among Renaissance thinkers regarding women.

Pamela Joseph Benson, in attempting to explore *The Invention of the Renaissance Woman*, sets Renaissance writings about women into a broader rhetorical context. She argues that Renaissance humanists followed two alternatives for the model woman; either the 'justice' model, which contended women could possess the cardinal virtues along with men, or the 'care' model, which glorified women's superior moral nature and natural virtue. Humanist rhetoric, she contends, often led authors to employ dialogues between regressive and progressive spokesmen on women's abilities, and such dialogues limited their taking progressive views to their logical conclusions. Authors gave as much time, and often as much respect, to views they were theoretically opposing as to their own positions.[11] Yet was it because humanists were enmeshed in a rhetorical exercise that they did not pursue the logical conclusion of their arguments for women's rational soul and equal or complementary abilities? Much more to the point was the reality that supposedly universal humanist principles were only intended for a certain class of independent men; if one treats the discussion of women as gender specific and humanism's intellectual and political programme as gender neutral, one misses the ways in which the general applied only to men.

Another limitation in these recent studies is their conflation of women, femininity, sexuality and feminine qualities attached to non-human entities such as fortuna, when assessing the positive nature of an author's views of women. Almost anything that Renaissance authors said concerning topics related to women's nature, the softer side of creation, less controllable or predictable natural phenomena, or the emotional rather than the rational, is used to document their views on the potential and actual lives of women. Such judgements seem problematic, especially when situated within humanist values of scholarship and social utility. As Kelso stated, a Renaissance woman could pursue her talents 'as leisure and opportunity and necessity allow'. But she continued, 'There were none, however, to argue that she should have equal opportunity and equal reward for her effort. The real feminist was still to be born'. Recent scholars seem not so much to have refuted her position, as to have embraced a broader sense of feminism, or perhaps sidestepped the distinction she posed in 1956.[12]

ENGLISH HUMANISM AND WOMEN'S LEARNING

One cannot overemphasise the importance of Juan Luis Vives in laying the groundwork for humanism's limited vision of women's potential. His work, more than any other, established the parameters of women's learning in the first half of the sixteenth century. He was the most widely read and influential author, and his *Instruction of a Christian Woman* saw numerous printings following its appearance in 1523 in Latin and its translation into English by Richard Hyrde, a member of Thomas More's household, in 1529. Even so, it was a limited and even a contradictory vision of the proper education for women. Only nine pages were devoted to the actual education of women. Most of the book treated manners and family, especially how a wife should establish respect toward her husband and his relatives. Also, it was directed to aristocratic ladies and not to a wide range of English families. In his 'Plan of Study for Girls', Vives developed an educational programme for Mary Tudor, the royal princess. He encouraged learning for women, but not learning that invited or prepared them to delve into complex matters such as theology and philosophy. Vives offered training that aided women to become well-informed and charming companions to their husbands, pious and good Christians, and individuals able to deal easily and sympathetically with Scripture and catechism.[13]

When speaking to women directly, Vives was often negative; he stressed that their desires to learn beyond their needs was wrong and to go abroad was at the detriment of their reputations and those of their husbands. However, in his work directed to husbands, *The Duty of a Husband*, he was much more positive, urging husbands not to neglect their wives' educations and reminding them that women were rational creatures created by God. His restrictions contrasted women's intellectual needs with men's, highlighted women's inability to teach, and stressed the necessity for strict female chastity.

Vives noted that 'though the precepts for men be innumerable; women yet may be informed with few words'. Again, hearkening back to humanist bonds between learning and vocation, he explained this dictum by the fact that 'men must be occupied both at home and abroad, both in their own matters and for the common weal'. But for women, their responsibility was tied to 'honesty and chastity' and when knowledgeable there, they were 'sufficiently appointed'. Secondly, women, because of Eve's failings, were not to teach lest they 'bring others into the same error' as individuals 'of weak discretion, and that may lightly be deceived'. Finally, a woman's domestic life left little time for learning, nor 'unstable' thought given to 'wandering out from home'. In his *Instruction of a Christian Woman*, Vives revealed that he advocated educating women because he feared their learning: women's education must be closely supervised so that it would not encourage their raising questions beyond their capabilities or take them out of the home into unseemly public discourse.[14]

While most current scholars see Vives's views concerning women's education as seriously flawed, less criticism is directed against other sixteenth-century authors who significantly restrict women's learning and public role. Two important thinkers provide guidance. They are Thomas Elyot, through his humanist classic *The Governor* and his lesser known work *The Defence of Good Women*, and Richard Mulcaster, with his general educational treatise including a brief chapter on the need to educate girls. Again, one must not treat these works as general treatises that apply to all, or as specialised works applying only to women. The general treatises are as gender restricted as the latter; they simply do not reflect those restrictions in their titles.

In *The Governour*, Thomas Elyot offers an early work on education published in English. It appeared in 1531 and was intended to make his views more widely accessible and to demonstrate that abstract and expert disciplines could be expressed in English. Latin was, of course, the universal language of learned men; but had the work been a domestic guide for women, Elyot's innovative choice of the vernacular would have seemed commonplace. *The Governour* was dedicated to Henry VIII, and its intent was to define a commonweal and to establish the proper education and duties of those belonging to the state.[15] For Elyot 'a public weale' was a body resting upon 'a compact' and 'made of sundry estates and degrees of men, which is disposed by the order of equity and governed by the rule and moderation of reason'. But he noted that commonweal was not an appropriate term because it supposed 'that every thing should be to all men in common, without discrepancy of any estate or condition', and such a non-hierarchical society without clear lines of command would lead to 'perpetual conflict'. Other than supporting Tudor corporate ideas of government based on a well-ordered body,

Elyot in this work reflected humanist proclivities to discuss issues of social standing without regard to gender. The democratic nature of governments is evaluated only on the classes of men who are allowed public involvement; the exclusion of women is ignored.[16]

After contending that the best form of rule was royal governance, Elyot acknowledged the need for 'inferior governors' or magistrates, and much of his educational programme was intended for this class. In book I his discussion touched upon the 'bringing up of the child [boy] of a gentleman, which is to have authority in a public weale'. Such education was quite broad, including music, dancing, painting; but by the age of fourteen the pupil needed to concentrate on logic and rhetoric, especially by hearing Cicero read aloud, and at fourteen and fifteen he was ready for the study of law since it was the age at which 'time springeth courage'. By sixteen he should be devoting more of his studies to philosophy and government. This education as a whole should instil grace, valour and reason and, in particular, judgement. Elyot offered advice about those ancients most useful to the Renaissance gentleman and encouraged poetry for its lessons in reason, courage and human emotions. Each of the subjects was grounded upon the boy's development, so that age as well as class dictated what subjects were to be taught. And again, such stages of maturation that carried with them an appropriate curriculum, occurred only among males. It is thus this blending of the external needs of government and the internal nature of boys' development that dictated their graduated educational course.[17]

Elyot's *Defence of Good Women* lacked the systematic structure of the *Governour*. It was written in dialogue form, modelled on Greek debates, and organized around the life of Lady Zenobia, a woman interested in learning. Most of the argument was carried on by two debaters, Cannius and Candidus, who disputed whether Aristotle's view of women as being different and imperfect was true and should prevent them from pursuing learning. Cannius accepted Aristotle's position, and Candidus opposed him insisting that women did have the ability to pursue serious education. Perhaps most significant was the timidity of Candidus' defence. When he was joined by Zenobia, she defined the goals for her education in ways that did not interfere with her subordinance to her husband. Elyot envisioned an education that would fill the youth of noble women, one not tied to the humanist programme that prepared men for independent judgement and broad-based knowledge.

Candidus noted that women were much blamed for their inconstancy, but this had not been his experience. In response, Cannius linked his opponent to poets who admired women and wrote erotic verse, not to those philosophers who seriously debated the relative merits of the sexes. Candidus offered the typical ancient heroines, most of whom sacrificed all for husband or children, and quoted Aristotle in support of complementary skills in men and women to make the household function. He utilised such arguments to demonstrate that because patience and conservation (women's duties) require more skill than strength and acquisition (men's responsibilities), women possessed greater reason.[18]

Zenobia, who was Queen of Palymyra (in Syria) but now a widow and prisoner of the Emperor Aurelian (who pursued scholarship and taught her children), joined them for dinner. Candidus noted her knowledge of Latin and Greek as well as 'the Egyptian language', and was assured that she would demonstrate to Cannius 'that in women is both courage, constancy and reason'. She pledged that her early education in moral philosophy only made her a better wife.[19]

without prudence and constancy, women might be brought lightly into error and folly, and made therefore unmeet for ... assistance and comfort to man through their fidelity, ... I also found that Justice teacheth us women to honour our husbands next after God, which honour resteth in due observance.[20]

Her current interest in scholarship and any public discourse evolving from it were emblems of her widowhood, 'For during the life of my noble husband of famous memory, I ... never [did] say or do any thing, which might not content him, or omit anything which should delight him, such circumspection good learning ministered to me'. The work, though, credited her political leadership along with her serious education. She told of her leadership of her kingdom, which was under threat from the Romans and thieves from Arabia, but always in a modest way with her children present and acknowledging the great accomplishments of her dead husband. It would be difficult to imagine a more circumscribed defence of women's learning and their public rule. Yet Elyot is often credited with the courage to defend Catherine of Aragon through this work. Certainly, his *Defence of Good Women* in no way incorporated women's education into humanist values.[21]

The work of Richard Mulcaster is of special interest in comparison to the previous discussions of Elyot and Vives. He wrote later in the century, during Elizabeth's reign, and, as a master of the Merchant Taylor's Company, he had a more practical and broader reach than his predecessors. His *Positions [–] necessarie for the training up of children, either for skill in their booke or health in their body* (1581) was primarily a work outlining a boy's education. It emphasised what the state and the economy could gain through educating the young. Yet while advocating learning for boys and girls from the urban artisanry, Mulcaster showed greater similarity to his aristocratic predecessors on issues of gender than on issues of class.[22]

A master of his own school, Mulcaster thought more systematically about the daily curriculum for middle-class children than did most educational writers during the sixteenth century. Although he discussed girls' education, he devoted only one of forty-five chapters to the subject. Four arguments grounded his defence of girls' training: (1) it was customary to educate girls at least to the primary level; (2) since they would eventually become mothers, it behoved society to attend to their minds and bodies; (3) they had ability to learn as rational creatures; and (4) learned ladies had demonstrated that such education was not wasted. He pointed to Queen Elizabeth and other scholarly ladies of her age to demonstrate the latter point.

Unlike those writing only for upper-class audiences, Mulcaster distinguished among the needs for women's education based on their future vocation. Those intended for marriage should be trained in obedience and housewifery, but if it were necessary for a woman to make a living then she had to be taught a trade. The group, however, that was to have the broadest education was that at the apex of the social scale. 'The greater born ladies and gentlewomen, as they are to enjoy the benefit of this education most' should have 'the best teachers, and greatest helps; neither abridged in time but to play all at full'.[23]

Yet in this comparison of women's needs with men's, class played a lesser role than gender. Mulcaster contended that most attention should go to males as learning was 'first framed for their use and most properly belonging to them'. Women should not be omitted, but responsibility for educating them evolved 'only out of courtesy and kindness'. He strayed little from the humanist view that men's education was 'without restriction either as regards subject-matter or method' because of their work being 'so general', while women's lives were limited and 'so must their education be also'. Thus, even this more pragmatic educator from the later sixteenth century, who saw learning as something from which both state and individual could gain, accepted the humanist continuum of education fitting only within the lives of men (or royal women) who needed knowledge to perform well upon the public and household stage.[24]

As noted earlier, although humanist ideas were spread in England during the early 1500s, they still held sway into the seventeenth century. It is thus important to understand how humanist values, and ideas concerning women's education, varied from the sixteenth to the seventeenth century. In looking at the advice of Sir Thomas More (early sixteenth century) and George Savile, Lord Halifax (later seventeenth century) concerning their daughters' educations, one can gain some sense of the changes in such views from the beginning of the sixteenth century to the conclusion of the seventeenth.

MORE AND HALIFAX

Much of the writings of the sixteenth and seventeenth centuries concerning female education was men's advice to their daughters, or advice to tutors or teachers concerning the proper education for girls. In assessing the evolution of humanist ideas concerning women's education, I have chosen two representative works from an earlier and later period: Thomas More's correspondence with his daughters and their tutors written from 1522 to 1535, and George Savile, Lord Halifax's *The Lady's New Years Gift; or, Advice to a Daughter*, published in 1688.[25]

Thomas More wanted to encourage his daughters' serious scholarship and took great pride in corresponding with Bishop Fisher and others about their learning. He was not convinced, however, that women were men's intellectual equals, but argued that if they were – or even if they were not – (and then especially so), they needed a solid education. More wanted his children to be neither 'puffed up with the vain praises of men, nor dejected by any slander of disgrace' while gaining 'the solid fruits of learning'. The qualities he stressed were 'piety towards God, charity towards all men, modesty and Christian humility in themselves'. More rejected the popular view that 'woman's brain be of its own nature bad, and apter to bear fern than corn'. He thought that there was no 'difference in harvest time, whether he was man or woman, that sowed first the corn; for both of them bear the name of a reasonable creature equally'. Yet even accepting women's intellectual inferiority, through serious instructions 'the defect of nature may be redressed by industry'.[26]

This advice appeared in More's correspondence instructing his tutor William Gonell on how to direct his daughters' education. After supporting his views on women's intellect with reference to St Jerome and St Augustine, who gave such difficult texts to young female minds that 'scarcely our old and greatest professors of divinity can well read them, much less be able to understand them perfectly', More sets out the proper curriculum for his daughters, whom he terms 'my young wenches'. Work most diligently, Gonell is instructed, to root out pride before it can take root in young minds and 'hammer it into their heads' that 'vain glory is abject, and to be despised, neither any thing to be more worthy or excellent, than that humble modesty, which is much praised by Christ'. Thus, they should read 'the wholesome precepts' of the church fathers; the Scriptures; and those ancient authors, though heathen, who laid down sound moral principles.[27]

The correspondence with his children makes it clear that More cared much for their scholarship and was continually testing them so that they achieved linguistic and rhetorical perfection. The letters show a loving, affectionate concern, but one tinged with fatherly supervision and inspection that must have filled his daughters with dread. He expressed the pleasure, when his daughters were travelling, that their letters maintained appropriate standards: 'You have not ... omitted any thing of your custom of exercising yourselves, either in making of declamations, composing of verses, or in your logick exercises'. Such care demonstrated 'that you dearly love me' for 'you have so great a care to please me by your diligence'. He praised his children's letters as 'being full of fine wit, and of a pure Latin phrase'. However, he singled out the correspondence of his son John, who was younger than his sisters Margaret and Elizabeth, in ways that again highlighted an atmosphere filled with both affection and apprehension. John's letter was longer and 'took more pains'; he revealed accuracy and elegance, and 'he playeth also pleasantly with me, and returneth my jests upon me again very wittily; and this he dothe not only pleasantly, but temperately withal, shewing that he is mindful with whom he jesteth, to wit, his father, whom he endeavoureth so to delight, that he also afeared to offend'. He then tells his daughters they must write him a letter each day and no excuses will be accepted, and concludes 'when having nothing to write of, you write as largely as you can of that nothing, than which nothing is more easy for you to do, especially being women, and therefore prattlers by nature'.[28]

More can be forgiven for jesting with his daughters because he seems to have held genuine affection for them, and he is one of a handful of Renaissance thinkers who either gave an equal education to daughters or advocated such. However, his educational programme was hardly without stress for his children, and he seems not to have realised that there might have been greater tolerance for male than female offspring to jest with fathers. Yet, in many ways, his was the most positive voice among male humanists during the sixteenth century in England.

While More highly praised Vives's writings on women's education, and was said to have been planning a translation of *Instruction of a Christian Woman* before Hyrde took up the challenge, still they sound quite different when discussing the subject. It might have been a difference of temperament, or perhaps More's concern for his daughters, that separated these two influential humanists. Each limited the ends of women's education to the family circle, but More urged training in positive, affectionate language, while Vives's tone was more wary. More reflected in both his life and writings the humanist integration of scholarship and public duty, and it was the goal he established for a follower of the new learning, but not for his daughters. His serious intellectual goals for them were not to interfere with their natural piety or submission to husbands. Therefore, it is not so much what More advocated that leaves a positive picture for current scholars, but rather its expression of genuine warmth and affection. In many ways it was all that separated him from Juan Luis Vives.

Underpinning More's complicity in humanist limitations on female education were his general works directed to male readers. As with other humanists, he assumed that the seat of progressive scholarship would be the universities. 'Humanistic education is the chief, almost the sole reason why men come to Oxford; children can receive a good education at home from their mothers, all except for cultivation and book learning'. Men's learning was contrasted with education by a mother in the home; although exceptional women (such as his daughter Margaret) could be included in serious tutoring at home, they were as excluded as other women from the humanist continuum that prepared boys and men for public roles. Either in universities where, in the words of More, 'academics, delivered from the necessity of earning their daily bread, might there pursue the liberal arts,' or among courtiers and public servants discussed most thoroughly in Elyot's *The Governour*, humanist blueprints for life and learning never contemplated women. Humanist education simply did not aim to transform women's lives as it did for apt boys and men exposed to the new learning.[29]

In his 1688 advice to his daughter, Halifax, perhaps recognising the great increase in learned women and women writers after 1640, felt some obligation to justify his rather hard words. 'You must take it well to be prun'd by so kind a Hand as that of a Father ... Some inward resistance there will be, where Power and not Choice maketh us move; but where a Father layeth aside his Authority, and persuadeth only by his Kindness, you will never answer to Good Nature, if it hath not weight with you'.

Like More, Halifax began with the need for serious education to buttress one's Christian faith. However, reflecting the increasing role of rational Christianity, he favoured a faith grounded in reason and not superstition. For his daughter's education, he maintained that 'the first thing to be consider'd is Religion; it must be the chief Object of your Thoughts'. Religion must be drawn close to one before other distractions dilute its appeal, but it must be religion for an adult. 'Religion doth not consist in believing the Legends of the Nursery, where Children with their Milk are fed with the Tales of Witches, Hobgoblins, Prophecies and Miracles'. Also, reflecting the values of 'the Trimmer', he favoured toleration: 'It is not true Devotion, to put on our angry zeal against those who may be of a different Persuasion'.[30]

While Halifax's advice stressed the importance of tolerance and rationality seldom mentioned in More's instructions to tutors or children, it lacked the serious intellectual content of More's words. Rather, he was concerned more with social custom in preparing his daughter for her responsibilities as an adult and gave the bulk of space in his 134-page treatise to relations between husband and wife. The work focused on a pleasant, almost rarefied mix of reason and faith and used more practical language and romantic imagery than that found in the work of his sixteenth-century predecessor. In defining the nature of religion, he reveals this mix: 'religion is exalted Reason, refin'd and fitted from the grosser part of it: it dwelleth in the Upper Region of the Mind, where there are few Clouds and Mists to darken or offend it'. While the language reveals the greater commercialisation of the late seventeenth century and its attraction to science, the role he outlined for his daughter's married life seems quite similar to More's, though with less evidence of room for serious scholarship.[31]

Halifax, in discussing her faith in preparation for marriage, utilised scientific terms when asking his daughter to develop her own beliefs based upon 'the right Standard' and not made of 'Allay (alloys)'. He claimed human 'weights and measures' were inadequate to assess the 'distribution of his Mercy or his Justice'. Women should follow their minds in developing their faith, but should judge belief less critically on the grounds of 'your Sex ... in respect that the Voluminous Enquiries into the Truth, by Reading, are less expected of you'.[32]

Thus, Halifax's daughter was to follow her father's guidelines for pursuing rational Christianity rather than to develop a totally independent path. Such lack of independence would prepare her well for marriage choices: 'young women are seldom permitted to make their own choice; their Friends care and experience are thought safer guides to them, than their own fancies; and their Modesty often forbideth them to refuse when their Parents command'. Although the young of both sexes came under parental guidance as regards marriage, women were given even less independence than their brothers. Thus he advised young women to accept their future husbands even though 'their inward consent may not entirely go along with it'. Unlike More, who in his educational advice to his daughters dealt little with differential power relationships between the sexes, Halifax explicitly discussed the topic:

> You must first lay it down for a foundation in general, That, there is inequality in sexes, and that for the better economy of the world; the Men, who were to be the law givers, had the larger share of reason bestow'ed upon them; by which means your sex is the better prepar'd for the compliance that is necessary for the performance of those duties which seem'd to be most properly assign'd to it.[33]

Of course the duties most associated with women's greater compliance were within the married state. Again, he admitted that the marriage contract is harsh for women and that 'obey is an ungentle word'. Also, an exception should exist for exceptional women that 'nature is so kind as to raise them above the level of their own Sex', and such provisions would mirror women's access to equity courts to overcome their disabilities under common law. Utilising chivalric arguments, Halifax claimed that women's supposed inferiority was mitigated through the power of their gentleness over male reason and strength, their control of the nursery and their lifelong influence on men. Marriage dictated women's lesser status, and 'the institution of marriage is too sacred to admit to a liberty of objection to it'. Women's being 'the weaker sex' has sufficient evidence to accept it, and since the law allows for exceptions in some of the more egregious cases of spousal misconduct, marriage based on inequality between the sexes should stand. To his daughter he stated: 'You are therefore to make the best of what is settled by law, and not vainly imagine, that it will be changed for your sake.'[34]

The remainder of the work offered advice and encouragement on handling difficult husbands, whether they were unreasonable, drunkards or wastrels. Such advice encouraged Halifax's daughter to maintain her modesty and to recognise that 'discretion and silence will be the most prevailing reproof'. While integrating concepts of power, science and toleration, Halifax's picture seems at least as restricted as More's for the adult woman. And he either accepted women's intellectual inferiority or thought his daughter better off if she did so.[35]

Halifax's late seventeenth-century work carried with it many of the admonitions More offered to his daughters and their teachers, but it incorporated the values of the scientific revolution and interposed the arguments between ancients and moderns, a scientific, post-humanist phenomenon. Much concern can be found in both More and Halifax regarding the limited utility of women's learning, and this seems to hold even though they were separated by the scholarship and queenship of Elizabeth I; Reformation arguments for an educated laity; and the expanded democratic views of the 1640–60 civil war, which embraced a more inclusive and practical education, often linked to puritan principles. Men of goodwill, such as More and Halifax, when contemplating female learning seem to have been unwilling or unable to separate it from their understanding of daughters' future lives, and both held quite traditional views in those areas. Each stressed obedience to husband and piety toward God as central goals of their girls' training. This contrasted, especially for More, with pride in their children's capabilities and intellectual interests. More addressed, although not quite straightforwardly, the relative intellectual abilities of the sexes, but did not always apply his views consistently. Halifax held more negative views.

For both men, educational achievement confronted the ultimate goal of domestic modesty for their daughters. Although More's daughter Margaret Roper, who married Thomas Roper – an acquaintance of her father – when in her early twenties, translated works by Erasmus, corrected the Latin of church fathers, wrote original religious treatises in English and later translated them to Latin, Thomas More favoured a limited life for her; one that drew little attention to the scholarship he so encouraged. In a letter to Margaret, he acknowledged that 'men that read your writings would suspect you to have had help of some other man therein', and concluded she would gain little fame from her learning. Still she was content 'to join with [her] virtue the knowledge of most excellent sciences' while never seeking 'vulgar praises', and thus he admired her most since, 'for your singular piety and love towards me, you esteem me and your husband a sufficient and ample theatre for you to content you with'.[36]

The examples of More and Halifax suggest why humanist education did not transform women's lives as it did the lives of apt boys and men exposed to the new learning. Such a pattern did change following 1640, with the growing numbers of women authors who were knowledgeable and skilled in a range of fields encompassing poetry and drama, science, and philosophical defences against attacks on their sex. Some of the earlier views concerning women's inferiority that were common in the sixteenth century would not easily survive an encounter with Margaret Cavendish, Duchess of Newcastle, or Mary Astell, both late seventeenth-century feminists. Yet the Renaissance concept of woman left little opportunity for individual attainment by a member of the female sex and excluded women from the greatest educational and professional advances embedded within humanism and the 'new learning' that emerged from it. Only in later centuries, and beginning with the arguments of women writers of the late seventeenth century, did women come to acquire the characteristics inherent in the qualities of the 'Renaissance gentleman'.

NOTES

Hilda L. Smith acknowledges the support of the Taft Memorial Fund for this project.

1. For discussions of English humanism, see Maria Dowling, *Humanism in the Age of Henry VIII* (London: Croom Helm, 1986), Stephen Greenblatt, *Renaissance Self-Fashioning* (Chicago: University of Chicago Press, 1980) and Arthur Kinney, *Humanist Poetics: Thought, Rhetoric, and Fiction in Sixteenth Century England* (Amherst: University of Massachusetts Press, 1986).

2. Kenneth Charlton's older work, *Education in Renaissance England* (London: Routledge and Kegan Paul, 1965) continues to provide valuable insights into how education was gendered also for men.

3. Lawrence Stone, 'The Educational Revolution in England, 1560–1640', *Past and Present*, 28 (1964), 41–80; David Cressy, *Literacy and the Social Order: Reading and Writing in Tudor and Stuart England* (Cambridge: Cambridge University Press, 1980).

4. The following are the earliest English editions of these important Renaissance texts: Thomas More, *A Fruitful and Pleasant Work ... of the New Isle called Utopia*, trans. R. Roylson and A. Vele, 1551 (the original 1516 Latin edition of *Utopia* was printed abroad as were a number of succeeding editions in Latin); Juan Luis Vives, *A very Fruitful and Pleasant Book called the Instruction of a Christian Woman* (turned out of Latin into English by R[ichard] Hyrde; London 1529?); Thomas Elyot, *The Book named the Governour* (London, 1531), and *Nicholas Machiavel's Prince* (trans. E. D[acres]; 1640); and [Baldassare Castiglione] *The Courtier of Count Baldessary Castilio, Done into English by Sir Thomas Hoby* ([London,] 1561). *The Prince* appeared in England in an Italian edition in 1584, but the first English edition was not available until 1640.

5. The *querelle des femmes* of the sixteenth and seventeenth centuries drew commentaries from philosophers, poets and essayists – a wide range of popular and serious works tackling women's nature. (For further discussion, particularly concerning procreation, see chapter 3 of this volume.)

Although most studies of Renaissance views of women treat the *querelle des femmes*, Joy Wiltenburg's *Disorderly Women and Female Power in the Street Literature of Early Modern England and Germany* (Charlottesville: University Press of Virginia, 1992) probably casts her net the farthest in surveying such attitudes. Boccaccio's *Concerning Famous Women* was translated only in 1963 (New Brunswick, NJ: Rutgers University Press) although it appeared in 1359. The work discusses the lives of 104 women, but within the context that the sex generally was flawed. As the work's translator notes, 'to lavish praise on a woman, Boccaccio can think of no better adjective than "manly", and his greatest condemnation of sluggish and insignificant men is to call them women'.

6. Ruth Kelso, *Doctrine for the Lady of the Renaissance* (Urbana: University of Illinois Press, 1956), p. 36.

7. Heinrich Cornelius Agrippa von Nettesheim, *Female pre-eminence, or, The Dignity and Excellency of that Sex above the Male...*, [trans.] H[enry] C[are] (London: printed by T. R. and M. D., to be sold by Henry Million, 1670). Texts and analysis of the disputes around the writings of Jane Anger, Joseph Swetnam and Esther Sowernam from the late sixteenth and early seventeenth centuries are available in *Half Humankind: Contexts and Texts of the Controversy about Women in England, 1540–1640*, ed. Katherine Usher Henderson and Barbara F. McManus (Urbana: University of Illinois Press, 1985.) I doubt the legitimacy of authors such as 'Jane Anger' and 'Esther Sowernam' because of the proclivity of men to publish on both sides of the issue for financial gain, and internal inconsistencies that make the works seem products of a male, masquerading as a woman, writing for a male audience. For further discussion of this issue see chapter 7 of this volume.

8. Joan Kelly Gadol's 1975 essay was included in *Becoming Visible: Women in European History*, ed. Renate Bridenthal and Claudia Koonz (Boston: Houghton Mifflin, 1977), 137–64. Details of the other books mentioned in this paragraph may be found in the further reading list at the end of this volume.

9. Constance Jordan, *Renaissance Feminism*: Literary Texts and Political Models (Ithaca, NY: Cornell University Press, 1990), pp. 5–7.

10. Ian Maclean, *Renaissance Notions of Woman* (Cambridge: Cambridge University Press, 1980), pp. 82–92.

11. Pamela J. Benson, *The Invention of the Renaissance Woman* (University Park: Pennsylvania State University Press, 1992), pp. 4–5.

12. Kelso, *Doctrine for the Lady*, pp. 278–81.

13. The most accessible, although abbreviated, edition of Vives's educational writings remains Foster Watson's collection of seven treatises written between 1523 and 1538, including three by Vives, entitled *Vives and the Renascence Education of Women* (London: Edward Arnold, 1912). Vives lived from 1492 to 1540 and wrote the brief *Plan of Studies*, intended for the Princess Mary, and his longer *Instruction of a Christian Woman* in 1523.

14. Watson, ed., *Vives and the Renascence Education of Women*, pp. 34, 56 and 19.

15. Thomas Elyot, *The Governour*, introduction by Foster Watson (London: J. M. Dent and Sons, 1937), pp. xv–xvi.
16. Elyot, *The Governour*, pp. 1–8.
17. *Ibid.*, pp. 15–49.
18. Elyot in Watson, ed., *Vives and the Renascence Education of Women*, pp. 217–32.
19. *Ibid.*, pp. 234–9.
20. *Ibid.*, p. 235.
21. *Ibid.*, pp. 235–9.
22. *Richard Mulcaster's Positions*, abridged and edited by Richard L. DeMolen (New York: Teachers College Press, 1971). Richard Mulcaster (1561–86) published his *Positions* in 1581, in which chapter 38 is concerned with the education of girls.
23. Mulcaster, *Positions*, pp. 142–4.
24. *Ibid.*, pp. 133–7.
25. Thomas More (1478–1535), *St Thomas More: Selected Letters*, ed. Elizabeth Frances Rogers (New Haven: Yale University Press, 1961). Elizabeth Frances Rogers also edited his complete correspondence, in 1947. There is no formal discussion by More of women's education. George Savile, Lord Halifax (1633–95), *The Lady's New-Years Gift; or, Advice to a Daughter* (London, 1688).
26. More, *Selected Letters*, pp. 104–5.
27. *Ibid.*, p. 105.
28. *Ibid.*, pp. 150–1.
29. *Ibid.*, pp. 95–100. Although More must have been a supportive father, we have little evidence that he held any substantive views concerning women's education that differed from his friend and contemporary Juan Luis Vives, and we know too little about what Margaret More Roper might have preferred for herself.
30. Halifax, *The Lady's New Year's Gift*, pp. 6–10. In his *Character of a Trimmer*, published in 1688, Halifax advised moderation.
31. *Ibid.*, pp. 16–23.
32. *Ibid.*
33. *Ibid.*, pp. 25–6.
34. *Ibid.*, pp. 26–32.
35. *Ibid.*, pp. 37–76.
36. More, *Selected Letters*, p. 155.

Religion and the construction of femininity

Suzanne Trill

> Why may not I pray with many people in the room, as well as your
> professing woman that prays before men and women, she knowing
> them to be there; but I know not that there is anybody in the room
> when I pray. And if you indict one for praying, why not another?
> Why are you so partial in your doings?[1]

These words are taken from the 1654 description of her own trial given by
Anna Trapnel, a female prophet of the radical Protestant group the Fifth
Monarchists, who lived in expectation of the second coming of Christ in
England in the 1650s. Trapnel's prophecies and pamphlets were perceived as religiously and politically subversive since they anticipated the
rule of Christ on earth with his 'saints' and at the same time expressed
criticism of Cromwell, the army and parliament. The above quotation
from Trapnel's account identifies a number of issues that are pivotal to the
concerns of this chapter on the interrelation of women and religion in
early modern Britain. The ostensible reason for Trapnel's indictment was
the accusation that she was a witch, but her shrewd responses to her
interrogators' questions suggest that their true motivation was a desire to
regulate her expression of her religious beliefs. Denying the justices'
representation of her, Trapnel seeks to persuade her readers that she is, in
fact, as she defines herself, 'the Lord's Handmaid'; she seeks, then, to shift
the terms in which she is represented away from the image of a transgressive woman under the pernicious influence of the devil toward that of
a woman walking in the ways of God. She specifically addresses here the
issue of what constitutes acceptable female expression: '[w]hy may not I
pray ... as well as your professing woman'. Although numerous texts
during this period reiterate the fact that women should be silent, especially
in church and in public on the basis of Pauline injunctions, Trapnel's
argument demonstrates that not *all* women's expression of their faith led
to their arraignment; a conformist, Protestant 'professing woman', after
all, is permitted to pray in public, 'before men and women'.[2]

By such methods, Trapnel indicates that it is not simply her violation of gender-specific conventions of proper feminine behaviour which is at issue here. Indeed, she ingeniously appropriates contemporary cultural norms to her advantage by suggesting that she is behaving in a more feminine, modest manner than her conformist counterpart: she does not consciously transgress the boundaries of private female expression as she does not know 'that there is anybody in the room' when she prays. Conversely, Trapnel implies that the justices, by permitting the 'professing woman' to express her faith publicly, are condoning just such a transgression. In Trapnel's case, it is the *content* of her prayers and the *position* from which she speaks that promotes anxiety. By questioning the justices' 'partial' attitudes to women's public praying, Trapnel exposes some of the contradictions contained within the social and cultural norms governing expectations of women's behaviour.

Although the dominant conventions governing the expectations of proper feminine behaviour during this period can be summed up in the phrase 'Chaste, Silent and Obedient', women's involvement in particular religious groups brings the universal application of that equation into doubt.[3] While many women who participated in contemporary debates about religious doctrine, or their biographers, went to great lengths to establish and affirm their chastity, they were neither silent nor straightforwardly obedient. The fact that they did not wholly conform to the expectations governing proper feminine behaviour problematises the stability of the category 'woman': it highlights the fact that the characteristics associated with that category are socially constructed, rather than naturalised or universal givens.[4] It is my contention that women's involvement with religion in this period brings the instabilities of this category to the fore.

In Britain, the period 1500–1700 witnessed a series of upheavals in religious doctrine and practice that (in)directly affected all inhabitants, whether male or female. But to what extent did these changes affect women in particular? On one level, Christian precepts influenced all aspects of women's lives as they provided a legitimisation of the dominant view of women as constituting the 'weaker sex'; partly as a result of their association with Eve, women were perceived to be inherently unruly and intemperate and were aligned metaphorically with the 'body', which required the guidance of the 'head' (that is, father or husband) in order to be kept in check.[5] Consequently, Christianity provided the ideological basis for a patriarchal system of social order that defined femininity negatively and justified female subjection and subordination. This was true regardless of whether the dominant form of Christianity practised in Britain was Catholic or Protestant, as both viewed women as subordinate to men.

On another level, the minutiae of doctrinal controversies appear to have very little direct relevance to women; the central controversy over the 'real presence' or the 'real absence' of Christ's body during the celebration of the Eucharist, for example, did not have any significant effect upon their position in society. However, such controversies did affect developments in political organisation, which increasingly meant that adherence to a particular doctrinal position correspondingly entailed situating oneself in a precise political position. Insofar as the church and state were related, the continual alterations and reversals in the dominant or legitimate forms of religious practice had a very significant effect upon how anyone's faith was received: to be a Catholic or a puritan in Elizabethan England was to be seen as subversive and potentially treasonable, and being a Quaker or a Fifth Monarchist in the 1650s was to be identified as a potential threat to the authorities. Thus, the historical context in which a woman practised a particular faith was crucial in determining how her expression of it was received. Despite their supposed exclusion from, or ignorance of, doctrinal debates, it was often precisely such subjects that propelled women into the articulation of their faith, and which saw them seeking to persuade others to become involved in their particular form of Christianity.

While it is necessary to recognise that Christianity exerted a predominantly negative influence upon women's social position, it is also important that we do not erase all sense of female agency or assume that they were simply oppressed by religion; as Patricia Crawford has recently argued, it is vital that we appreciate 'how women could both accept beliefs about their inferiority and transcend them'.[6] While women's religious beliefs arguably affected every sphere of their lives, I will focus upon how they determined the value attributed to women's 'speech'; to that end, I will be examining the contexts in which women's speaking was considered to be either 'justified' or unjustifiable, and the extent to which, when a woman expressed her opinion upon religious issues, she was considered to be speaking 'as a woman'.

CHARACTERISING THE EXEMPLARY CHRISTIAN WOMAN

One way of gaining insight into the assumptions that governed expectations of women's behaviour is to examine contemporary texts by male writers that sought to define the character of the ideal Christian woman, such as exemplary biographies and funeral sermons. These texts usually commence with a description of the woman's lineage and stress the godliness of her parents, which the woman inherits and replicates in the ordering of her own life and that of her family. The key aspects of her life and character that are highlighted are her wisdom, piety, humility, meekness, love, constancy, charity, good household government and godly devotion. Above all, these qualities fit the woman for her role as 'wife', 'mother' and 'mistress of the household'. This woman never engages in idle gossiping; instead, great stress is laid upon the wholesomeness of her speech, which is usually comprised of biblical citation. Despite the volume of texts produced in this genre, each one claims that the woman concerned was an exception to her 'sexe'. While this would appear to stress each woman's individuality, it also maintains the illusion that women in general could not achieve such godliness. Corporately, these texts indicate that the delineation of the exemplary Christian women, 1500–1700, did not alter significantly. This suggests that the concept of 'woman' was not particularly affected by religious and political upheavals, and that cultural assumptions about proper feminine behaviour traversed doctrinal boundaries.

In *A Crystall Glasse, for Christian Women*, the Puritan pamphleteer Philip Stubbes depicts his wife Katherine as an example worthy of women's imitation. Yet, the degree to which her femininity is the central concern of the text is problematised by the narrator's assertion that '[w]hilest she lived, [Katherine] was a mirror of womanhood: and now being dead, is a perfect pattern of true Christianity'. In this subtle shift, Katherine's 'womanhood' is eclipsed in death; she becomes a pattern of '*true* Christianity', an apparently ungendered example for others. Her exemplary status is predicated upon her zealous faith: she is commended by those who knew her 'above all, for her fervent zeale which she did beare to the truth'. That this truth is a puritan one is signalled by her extended confession of faith, her explicit denouncement of the 'errors' of Catholic doctrine, her continual meditation upon the Bible and her stout defence of her beliefs against detractors. If she heard 'Papists or Atheists' of whatever social standing 'talk of Religion', Katherine 'would not yield a jot, or give place to them at al, but would most mightilie justifie the Truth of God against blasphemous untruths, and ... confounde them by the testimonies of the word of God'.[7] The obviously favourable manner in which Stubbes is represented for defending her faith suggests that the narrator sees no dichotomy between such bold public discussion and her adherence to proper feminine behaviour; far from exhorting her to keep silent, the narrator commends and authorises her public expression of her beliefs.

In public debate, Stubbes utilises her knowledge of the Bible that has been acquired through continual private reading and meditation, a practice emphasised within Protestantism. Her use of Scripture symbolises her subjection to her husband; 'she would spend her time in conferring, talking, and reasoning with her Husband of the word of God, and religion: asking him what is the sense of this place ... and how expound you that?' In this, the narrator explicitly affirms her obedience to 'the commandement of the Apostle who biddeth women to be silent, and to learn of their husbands at home'. As she does not venture out without her husband, when she engages in the public disputes she is still 'covered' by his authority. Furthermore, she explicitly rejects the possibility of women taking on a full, priestly role in the public church when she affirms 'that it is no more lawfull for a Woman to minister this sacrament [baptism], then it is lawfull for her to preach, or to minister the Sacrament of the Lords Supper'.[8] Consequently, her capacity to defend her faith publicly, while it transgresses the ideal of female silence, is justifiable precisely because she is subject to her husband.

Contemporary texts outlining the principles by which the household ought to be governed at this time stressed the 'priestly' role of the husband, yet women played a significant part in such activities and were encouraged to instruct children and servants. Katherine Stubbes and Mrs Lucy Thornton both fulfil these roles; the latter's diligence in devotional activities and continual meditation on the Bible situate her as one 'that like a teacher ... was capable of great mysteries'.[9] But her talent for teaching complicates her gendered identity as it produces a split between her (female) body and her (masculine) spirit: she was able to move 'beyond the strength of her sex' as 'the new Spirit gave her an understanding of all things, as it is said, "The *natural man* perceiveth not the things of God, but the *spiritual man* discerneth all things"' (p. 337, my emphasis). As the objects of her tuition are servants and children, it would seem that the restrictions upon women's roles as religious instructors are specifically related to a concern that they might seek to exercise authority over adult males.

While Stubbes's and Thornton's knowledge of the Bible and zealous efforts to convert and instruct others reveal their puritan persuasion, John Donne represents Lady Danvers as the epitome of Anglican moderation:

the *rule* of her *Religion*, was the *Scripture*; And, her *rule*, for her particular understanding of the *Scriptures*, was the *Church*. Shee never diverted towards the *Papist*, in undervaluing the *Scripture*; nor towards the *Separatist*, in undervaluing the *Church*. But in the *doctrine*, and *discipline* of the *Church*, . . . she dedicated her soule to *God*.[10]

Lady Danvers is primarily praised for her obedience to church doctrine and her charitable works. While she embodies ideal feminine character- istics, she is not described as 'zealous'; her faith and her femininity are described in rather more moderate terms. Her death, for example, is depicted as follows: she died 'without any change of *countenance*, or *posture*; without any *strugling*, and *disorder*; but her *death-bed* was as quiet, as her *Grave*' (p. 285). In direct contrast to this, Katherine Stubbes's deathbed is marked by an oscillation between two extremes; either she is 'ravished' by joyous visions of Christ or she is tormented by a violent 'combatt with the Devil'. In this context, it is not only permissible but requisite that a woman should be courageous and use forceful language: Stubbes pro- nounced 'her words scornfully and disdainfully' and commands Satan thus, 'Avoid therefore thou dastard, avoid thou cowardly souldier, remove thy seige, & yield the field won, and get thee packing'. Although she threatens Satan with Christ's vengeance, it is her expression of faith that vanquishes him: '[s]he had scarcely pronounced these last words but she fel suddenly into a sweet smiling laughter: saying, now he is gone now he is gone . . . he hath lost the field and I have won the victory'. While it is undoubtedly her faith in Christ that is celebrated, it is Stubbes's own defiant articulation of her belief which confirms her 'victory'.[11]

While Stubbes's deathbed visions are of Christ and the devil, Sister Magdalen Augustine's translation of *The History of the Angellical Virgin, Glorious S. Clare* emphasises St Clare's association with the Virgin Mary, who comforts her on her deathbed and brings her a robe to clothe herself on entry into heaven. As well as indicating the Catholic persuasion of the narrative, this association with the Virgin Mary also invokes a more female-centred community than the texts discussed previously.[12] Al- though her sphere of influence is primarily associated with women, St Clare's gendered identity is not straightforwardly 'feminine'; she is described as a Saint 'of *feminine* sexe, but *masculine* virtue' (A4r, italics as in the original). Her influence, however, is depicted in maternal imagery: 'the holy Church may reioyce to haue produced and nourisshed such a daughter who as a fruitfull mother of virtue hath by her perfect doctrine nourisshed and nursed many disciples in Religion' (pp. 242–3). In ac- cordance with Catholic principles, St Clare's life perfectly combines doctrine with good works, doing with teaching; and, rather than being subject to the authority of an earthly husband, St Clare is instead subject to the Pope and her spiritual guide, St Francis. While the form of her devotions, the context in which they occur, and her institutional position differentiate her from Stubbes, Thornton and Danvers, the qualities for which she is praised are very similar. She was, of course, chaste; she governed her equivalent of a family (the convent) 'with much prudence in the feare and service of God'; and she was diligent, obedient, 'discret in silence graue & aduised in speech'.

The Virgin Mary was not only a role model for Catholic women; Anthony Stafford's *The Femall Glory*, situates her as an exemplar for Protestants, and, to the disdain of contemporary puritans, seeks to reevaluate her position within the English church.[13] The quality for which Mary is most highly praised is her control of her tongue: '[t]he Tongue esteemed the worst part in a woman, was in her the best' (p. 240). In his depiction of the Annunciation, Stafford remarks that 'whereas [m]any of her Sexe' would have continually interrupted the Angel, Mary listens to him patiently. Such virtuous, 'opportune silence', Stafford claims, 'few women obtain'; '[b]ut this wisest of Saints in a seasonable silence, and caution of speech, was alike admirable: Insomuch that through the whole Bible we finde not that she spake above five times' (pp. 53–4). Mary exemplifies the ideal of female expression; on the whole she is silent, and when she does speak it is properly controlled.

Although the central characteristics that define 'femininity' in these texts remain constant, the ways in which they are manifested is mediated by church doctrine. They reveal some contradictory attitudes to the legitimacy of women's expression, but their subjects' exemplary status is not contested. While these women were praised for defending their faith in public, when women's speech concerned doctrinal issues that were directly related to political debates, their 'exemplary' position was rather more controversial.

CONFLICTING IDEALS: ANNE ASKEWE AND MARGARET CLITHEROW

The lives, and deaths, of two sixteenth-century female martyrs illustrate the instability of the category of the 'ideal' woman; whereas for their biographers, John Bale and John Mush, Anne Askewe and Margaret Clitherow are chaste and obedient defenders of their faith, legally they are defined as transgressive, disobedient and obdurate.[14] Both died for their beliefs, Askewe (Protestant) in 1546 and Clitherow (Catholic) in 1586; thus, the contest over their exemplary identification is intricately bound up with the definition of 'true' faith and, correspondingly, 'true' martyrdom. As a Puritan preacher informed Margaret Clitherow: 'Not death, but the cause maketh a martyr. In the time of Queen Mary many were put to death, and now also in this Queen's time, for two several opinions, both these cannot be martyrs.'[15] The timing of one's profession of faith is thus crucial in determining the speaker's identification.

Despite the fact that Henry VIII is popularly known as the monarch whose divorce precipitated the break with Rome, the extent of the changes that occurred in the ecclesiastical and theological organisation of the English church during his reign is debatable. Official doctrine, enshrined in *The Necessary Doctrine and Erudition for Any Christian Man* (1543), endorsed the communion of one kind for the laity; the celibacy of the priesthood; the permanence of vows of chastity; the benefit of private masses; auricular confession; and transubstantiation. It has been suggested, therefore, that the major changes affected by the 'Henrician Schism' were the break away from papal supremacy in political and economic areas, rather than a major shift in actual doctrine.[16] Bale's concern to situate Askewe as one who does not pose a threat to the king, arguing that although she stood 'vp stro[n]glye in the lorde, most gentylle she obeyeth the powers' (36r) and assuring him that she views him as 'the hygh mynyster of God, the father of the lande, and vpholder of the people' (33r), must be understood in this context. It is an attempt to depict her as one whose doctrinal position does not place her in opposition to the king's political authority and is motivated by a desire to distinguish her from contemporary Catholics who were executed as 'traitors for denying the royal supremacy'.[17]

In Bale's narrative, it is for her love of the Word of God that Askewe is executed, and it is this which situates her as a 'true' martyr. Unlike their Catholic counterparts, Askewe and those burnt with her were solely dependent upon Christ for their protection; they had 'non other rel-lyckes aboute the[m], wha[n] they stode at the stake to be brent in Smythfelde, but a bundell of the sacred scriptures enclosed in their hartes, and redye to be uttered agaynst Antichrists ydolatryes' (5v). Askewe dies defending the need for a vernacular translation of the Bible, and her experience testifies to the need to be able to interpret 'the Word' according to individual conscience. By reading the Bible in English, Askewe contravened existing law, which restricted the reading of the Bible to 'male members of the nobility and gentry and to merchant householders'.[18] The central issue for which she is tried is her rejection of transubstantiation. Her arguments align her with Zwingli, who posited the 'real absence' of Christ during the Eucharist; such views did not meet with official sanction until Edward VI's reign, via Cranmer's revision of the Forty-Two Articles; even this was temporary, Cranmer himself being executed as a sacramentary in the reign of Queen Mary.[19] Askewe consistently counters her interrogators' arguments; for example, when faced with 'the verye wordes of Christ. Take, eate. This is my bodye, whych shall be broken for yow', she retorts '[y]e maye not ... take Christ for the materyall thynge that he is sygnyfyed by. For than ye wyll make hym a verye dore, a vyne, a lambe, and a stone, cleane co[n]traye to the holye ghostes meanynge' (20v–21r). In contrast to Askewe's plain speech and biblical arguments, her interrogators are represented as using 'all their power and flatterynge wordes' to try and persuade her to recant (38v). They accuse her of speaking in parables and being a 'paratte', intimating that she does not understand what she is saying and is merely voicing the opinions of others. But Askewe indicates that she is in full control of her expression; she talks in parables for their protection and is conscious that their rebukes occur 'by cause I wolde not expresse my mynde in all thynges as they wolde haue me' (16v–17r).

Askewe's refusal to name her 'associates' leads to her being tortured upon the rack: such punishment of a woman was illegal.[20] Thus, Bale's emphasis upon her sex at this point serves not only as a means to stress God's power working within her, but also as a method of indicting the male authorities:

Ryght farre doth it passe the strength of a yonge, tendre, weake, and sycke woman (as she was at that tyme to your confusion) to abyde so vyolent handelynge, yea, or yet of the strongest man that lyueth. Thnyke not therefore but that Christ hath suffred in her, and so myghtelye shewed his power, that in her weaknesse he hath laughed your madde enterpryses to scorne.[21]

The fact that Askewe is female serves to criticise, and is designed to shame, the male authorities; it also situates her as an exceptional figure not just among women, but also among men. Bale stresses her sex ('[w]hat a constancye was thys of a woma[n], frayle, te[n]dre, yonge and most delycyouslye brought vp' (27v)) in order to exhibit God's glory.[22] In opposition to the authorities' attempts to criminalise her, Bale needs to identify Askewe as exemplary. He defines her as such because she is subject to Christ alone; her obedience to her 'heavenly' husband legitimates her rejection of the earthly law: it is Askewe's defence of doctrinal principles that identifies her as a true Christian woman.

The intersection of doctrinal concerns and 'femininity' is also crucial in the case of Margaret Clitherow, but as a Catholic in the reign of Elizabeth, she was contravening a rather different set of laws. The Acts of Supremacy and Uniformity (1559) established Elizabeth as the 'Supreme Governor of this realm' and authorised only one form of public worship. In response to these acts, the Pope issued Elizabeth with a Bull of Excommunication (1570), denouncing her and calling upon all Catholics to deny her laws or face their own excommunication. Elizabeth reacted by declaring anyone who obeyed the Bull guilty of treason. The Act Against Reconciliation to Rome (1581) made it an offence to say or sing mass, to aid or to maintain priests, and reinforced the fine for those who did not attend public (Protestant) worship. The treasonable nature of the aiding and maintaining of priests was further confirmed by the Act Against Jesuits and Seminary Priests (1585): it was in relation to this last act that Margaret Clitherow was tried.[23] While the narrator leaves us in no doubt that Clitherow did indeed harbour priests, and was therefore 'guilty' according to law, he denies the treasonable nature of her offence and denounces the 'impious and bloody statutes' that condemned her.

Mush goes to great lengths to identify her as an exemplary woman. Clitherow's genealogy establishes her godly background and identifies her as a pattern for others in her virtuous humility, charity, devotion, and in her roles as wife and mother. She is not afraid of defending her faith, nor is she daunted or discouraged by persecution; rather, 'all troubles, persecutions, and cruelty practised against her for Catholic religion and conscience sake daily increased more and more the constancy of her faith' (p. 370). Clitherow is only 'disquieted' when unable to gain access to a priest; apart from this, 'all her actions were tempered with all inward tranquillity and comfort, with discreet and honest mirth, with mild and smiling countenance; ready of tongue, but yet her words most modest, and courteous and lowly' (p. 388–9). Owing to her conversion, she is married to a Protestant, which produces a conflict of loyalties between the obedience she owes to her husband and her duty to the church. For Mush, Clitherow's true submission to male authority is demonstrated in her love of God and her obedience to the priests: '[t]his golden woman did utterly forsake her own judgement and will in all her actions, to submit herself to the judgement, will and direction of her ghostly father' (p. 378), but in the eyes of the law it manifests her guilt.

When on trial, Clitherow annoys her interrogators with 'her smiling cheerful countenance, and the small esteem she made of their cruel threats and railing' (p. 411). When asked to plead, 'she said mildly with a bold and smiling countenance: "I know no offence whereof I should confess myself guilty"' (p. 413). Like Askewe, she denies the framework within which her accusers seek to situate her and argues that 'I never knew or harboured any such persons, or maintained those which are not the Queen's friends' (p. 413). Clitherow refuses to be tried 'on the country'; for Mush, this is an example of her concern for others, but for the justices it positions her as an obdurate woman and legally makes her subject to death *peine forte et dure*.[24] Her actions throughout the trial make those present question her sanity: 'some of them said, seeing her joy, that she was madde, possessed by a smiling spirit' and 'all the people about her condemned her of great obstinacy and folly, that she would not yield' (p. 414). Additionally, her chastity is brought into question; one of her interrogators suggests that 'it is not for religion that thou harboured priests, but for harlotry' (p. 414). Thus, the authorities seek to define her as a 'wanton' woman who is anything but exemplary. Clitherow's sex is significant at her death; the form of her execution, which involves her being stripped and pressed, is represented as an offence to her feminine modesty. And, although there is some possibility that she was pregnant, her refusal to plead is used to preclude a reprieve; in this, the justices' contravene their own laws concerning women, apparently on the basis of religion.

Both during her trial and in the 'privacy' of her cell, Clitherow is questioned about her doctrinal beliefs. She does not deny her Catholicism, but prudently debates general issues rather than specific doctrines. And she uses her sex as a means of defence: 'I am a woman, and am not skilful in the temporal laws. If I have offended, I ask God's mercy ... but in my conscience I have not' (p. 421). The fact that Clitherow is female performs a powerful critique of the justices; by a series of oppositions, the narrator contrasts her heroic constancy, her 'invincible courage', with the cowardice of her male opponents, 'you, men, cowardish in the quarrel'. The gendered division of these oppositions serves to shame her interrogators and undermine their power; '[w]here is now the force of your tyranny and impious law? Hath not the fortitude of one woman shewed the injustice of it? Hath she not weakened both them and your statute?' (p. 435). Here, Mush both relies upon and challenges contemporary assumptions about feminine behaviour. Clitherow's apparent strength contrasts with general assumptions about women's weakness; her 'invincible courage' identifies her as powerful and enables her to emerge 'victorious'. In contrast, the interrogators' masculinity is undermined as 'one woman' is able to demonstrate the 'injustice' of their tyrannical laws.

While they suffer for different doctrines, both Askewe's and Clitherow's experiences call into question the relationship between God's law and earthly law, and between female constancy and male cowardice. The barbarity of the authorities' actions is epitomised by their meting out of physical punishment upon female bodies. For their biographers, Askewe's and Clitherow's speech and actions are justified as a defence of their faith; 'a woman's glory' in such instances is not silence, but the articulate and resolute expression of faith, strengthened by the power of God in the face of adversity.[25] The cases of both women demonstrate the complexities of categorising 'woman'. While Anne Askewe was burnt at the stake as a heretic during Henry VIII's reign, she was later 'canonised' by John Foxe: at different times the same woman's actions produce conflicting meanings.[26] In the case of Margaret Clitherow, the contest over her identification highlights the fact that a woman's 'exemplary' position was to a large extent dependent upon *who* was defining her. Together, their experiences illustrate the historical contingency and material consequences of the 'partiality' of contemporary responses to women's public expression of doctrinal principles.

THY OR MY 'WORD': REWRITING BIBLICAL NARRATIVES

In most of the examples I have discussed so far, the female subject's identity and articulation of faith has been mediated by a male narrator; thus, these texts arguably tell us more about how men desired women to behave than how the women perceived themselves. In this section, and for the rest of the chapter, I will be examining the ways in which women used the Bible and/or church doctrine to define themselves. Despite the fact that biblical discourses have been viewed, particularly by feminist critics, as innately patriarchal and repressive, a significant number of women during the period 1500–1700 appropriated those discourses for their own ends.[27] Not all of them ended up on trial; Mary Sidney Herbert, Countess of Pembroke, and Aemilia Lanyer, for example, demonstrated their ability to utilise such discourses in the apparently non-threatening arena of the production of literary texts. While the reception of these women's texts does not indicate that they were regarded as subversive, neither does their use of biblical narratives represent a simple internalisation of patriarchal prescriptions; in different ways, both women made 'God's' word their 'own'.

The Countess of Pembroke is perhaps now most famous for her translation of the psalms.[28] The fact that Pembroke translated religious poetry could be taken as an indication that she maintained the 'proper' boundaries of female expression. Such an interpretation seems to be supported by a frequently cited quotation from Sir Edward Denny urging Pembroke's niece, Lady Mary Wroth, to follow the 'pious example of your vertuous and learned Aunt, who translated so many godly bookes and especially the holly psalmes of David'.[29] Yet others praise her *Psalmes* as a significant literary achievement, and Aemilia Lanyer cites Pembroke's achievements as an inspiration for other women's writing, including her own.[30] While the majority of sixteenth-century psalm translations were produced by men, Pembroke's contemporaries claim that her versions exceeded them in both form and style. By creating 'skillful songs' of praise, Pembroke produces a version of the psalms that demonstrates her versatility as a poet; in this, God's word becomes her 'own'.[31] This does not, however, make them (auto)biographical. The discourse of the psalms was pivotal to the construction of sixteenth-century Protestant subjectivity; accordingly, Pembroke's *Psalmes* focus more upon the articulation of her faith than on her femininity.[32]

By contrast, Aemilia Lanyer's *Salve Deus Rex Judaeorum* explicitly rewrites Christ's Passion in order to emphasise women's roles in biblical events; written in 1611, this poem can be seen as an intervention in the 'controversy debate' about the nature of 'woman'.[33] Lanyer appears to prioritise her femininity over her faith, and her text has been read as signifying an incipient feminism because she self-consciously constructs an explicitly female persona for her narrator; focuses upon women's actions in biblical narratives; constructs a female audience for her text; and places her own patron (the Countess of Cumberland) at its centre. The poem revises the story of the Fall by exonerating Eve and placing the blame upon Adam; citing Peter's denial of Christ, for example, Lanyer argues that men have inherited Adam's sins and inverts contemporary assumptions by suggesting that it is men not women who are inconstant.[34] While Lanyer does not explicitly engage in current doctrinal debates, the fact that she reinterpreted the story of the Fall implicitly questions the principles upon which doctrinal beliefs about women's inferiority were based.

RADICAL RELIGION AND FEMALE PROPHECY

Although the established church did not simply disappear during the period of the civil wars, 'the single most important aspect of the religious history of the period is the emergence of hundreds of independent and semi-independent congregations, the disintegration of puritanism as well as the Church of England'.[35] Perhaps most famously characterised by Christopher Hill's use of the biblical quotation, 'the world turned upside-down', the civil wars witnessed an increased debate about the controversies that had been raging since the Elizabethan Settlement.[36] While not an entirely new phenomenon, there was also a marked increase in prophetic utterances during this period, with which women were peculiarly, although not uniquely, associated. In contemporary usage, 'prophecy' referred to any 'utterance produced by God through human agency'.[37] The characterisation of the prophet as a conduit for God's voice apparently correlates with contemporary assumptions about female passivity; it was God's spirit, not the woman, who spoke. This would seem to negate the significance of the woman's body; however, in the process of interpreting the message and establishing its veracity, the prophet's physical body became the locus of conflict.

The central issues that concerned the radicals related not only to their concept of God but also to their vision of the political ordering of society. While the most famous political change was the execution of Charles I, it should not be assumed that everyone desired this outcome, nor that it was only Royalists who objected to it. One notable exception was Elizabeth Poole, whose prophecies, delivered before the Rump Parliament and published for public consumption, warned against the execution of the king.[38] Christopher Hill suggests that particular prophets' utterances could be used to further others' political purposes and argues, with David Underdown, that Poole's messages were used in such a way by Cromwell and Ireton.[39] Poole's argument that the king's person should not be touched aligned her with those in the army who did not believe that the execution of the king was necessary and provided a legitimate space in which to give voice to the concerns of Presbyterian ministers whose sermons were openly denouncing the potential regicide. While her prophecies were legitimised by Cromwell, Poole was closely questioned by Ireton about her opinion of the trial itself.[40] A prophet might speak for God, but the meaning of her words and the manner in which they were disseminated was also affected by the authorities' attitudes to her, and how far – or to what ends – they would permit her to express her message.

Poole's pamphlets are not only of interest insofar as they indicate how her words might be used by those around her. Her texts also invoke a complex series of gendered metaphors in order to instruct the army/parliament in their position; Poole identifies them as the 'wife' and

the king as the 'husband', and utilises divorce law and the laws of petty
treason to convince them of their errors.[41] Although their first allegiance
should be to God, she reminds them that 'the King is your Father and
husband' and that their authority to rule is derived from 'his person'.
Consequently, they should not seek to kill him; as she illustrates by the
story of 'Abigall' (p. 5), the king is still their husband, even if a bad one.
Poole tells them that '[y]ou never heard that a wife might put away her
husband, as he is the head of her body, but for the Lord's sake she suffereth
his terror to her flesh, though she be free in the spirit to the Lord' (p. 5);
thus Poole appropriates the civil law that subjugated women to their
earthly husbands in order to persuade the army/parliament of their duty
to their metaphorical husband, the king. In this, Poole invokes the
assumption that the 'male' head is superior, but simultaneously undermines it with the distinction she makes between the spirit and the flesh.
While the wife suffers in the flesh, she is 'free in the spirit to the Lord, and
he being incapable to act as her husband, she acteth in his stead' (p. 5);
thus, when the husband is incapable of fulfilling his role, the wife may act.
While this serves to justify Poole's position as a female prophet, it also
legitimates the army's assumption of power: they can take on this role
because the natural king is 'incapable'.[42] Assuming that *metaphorical* role,
however, does not legitimate the *literal* execution of the king.

Her second pamphlet, published after the execution of the king,
extends this use of gendered metaphors; Poole represents the
army/parliament as an unfaithful wife or 'Strumpet', thereby questioning the naturalisation of gender roles: their failure to trust in God
ultimately undermines their 'masculinity'.[43] As her former advice has
gone unheeded, she is aware that this casts doubt upon her prophetic
powers and her reputation (A2v–A3v). Women's speech or silence was
generally believed to signify their sexual identity, but it was also specifically used to question the veracity of women's prophecies. In *A Message
from God, By a Dumb Woman*, for example, Arise Evans identified one
Elinor Channel as an 'ideal' silent woman: by 'this Dumb woman, God
will put all vain talkers to silence'.[44] Having established Channel's
exemplary character, Evans declares that '[al]though [her text] be but
short, yet you shall find more truth and substance in it, than all Hana
Trampenels [Anna Trapnel's] songs or sayings, whom some account of
as the Diana of the English'.[45] By aligning Trapnel with the story of the
destruction of the worship of Diana, Evans represents her as a blasphemous idolotress who sought to be worshipped as a goddess. His misspelling
of her name as Trampenel implies sexual misconduct (overtones of

'vagrant female') and her excessive speech is contrasted with the brevity of Channel's; for Evans, Elinor is a 'channel' for God's voice, whereas Trapnel is a self-seeking woman whose words were her own.

As a Fifth Monarchist, Anna Trapnel believed in the imminent coming of Christ who would reign on earth with his 'Saints' for 1,000 years,[46] a belief based upon prophecies contained within the Books of Daniel and Revelation, which seemed to be fulfilled in the 1650s.[47] The New Model Army's success in 'purging' parliament in 1648 had led to the establishment of the Rump Parliament in 1649. While this parliament had authorised the dissolution of the monarchy, the execution of the king, and the disestablishment of the episcopacy, it was still perceived by some radicals, including the Fifth Monarchists, to be too moderate. These groups sought to replace it with a church parliament drawn from the congregations; their protests seem to have had some effect for in 1653 Cromwell dissolved the Rump Parliament and established the Barebones Parliament, comprised of a nominated assembly of men ostensibly chosen for their moral and religious virtues.[48] In his inaugural speech, Cromwell drew heavily upon Daniel and Revelation and was hailed as the second Moses. But his inability to deliver his promises led to severe criticism: one of the voices raised against him was that of Anna Trapnel.

Two of her texts, *Strange and Wonderfull Newes from White-Hall* and *The Cry of a Stone*, are comprised of witnesses' reports of her 'Visions, and Revelations touching the Government of the Nation, the Parliament, Army, and Ministry' in which she predicts the downfall of the present government.[49] Trapnel's accounts of her experiences, however, are also crucially concerned with the conflict between her sense of self and the authorities' definitions of her. She blames her transgression of 'feminine' propriety upon the 'Rulers and the Clergy'; it is they whom have made her a public spectacle and an object of curiosity, placing her on 'the worlds stage of reports and Rumours' and making her 'the worlds wonder, and gazing stock' against the wishes of her 'close retired spirit'. Trapnel's desire to remain in the private sphere affirms her 'feminine' modesty; it is, therefore, significant that she always prophesies from an enclosed space, usually her chamber. In order to assert her good character, Trapnel sets up an opposition between the authorities and the people; the latter, invited by the former to view her as 'a monster' or 'ill-shaped Creature', are represented as confirming that she is 'a woman like others, that were modest and civill' (*Report*, p. 49).

Trapnel also consistently distinguishes between her 'own' desires and those of God; she describes herself as having 'a fearful spirit by nature', and explains that it is only because God filled her with 'a spirit of boldness' that she is able to prophesy (*Legacy*, pp. 38–9). She claims that her 'natural' self has been 'put to silence'. This self-abnegation presents peculiar difficulties in ascribing gender to the voice of her texts; at times she represents herself as a disembodied voice: 'Oh, it is for thy sake, and for thy servants sakes, that thy Servant is made a Voyce, a sound, it is a voyce within a voyce, anothers voyce, even thy voyce through her.'[50] She is not a being but a 'voice', and that voice is not her 'own' but God's. Yet it is precisely this 'self-denial' that, for Trapnel, legitimates her expression. It is God's commandment that requires her to break with convention: 'it is for Sions sake that I cannot hold my peace' (*Legacy*, p. 59). However, she is aware that others view her as a woman because of her physical body.[51] The soldiers, for example, 'slight thy handmaid' by defining her trances as 'convulsion fits, and Sickness, and diseases'; they look for physical and rational answers and persist in viewing her as a woman, defining her prophecies as a 'distraction', a sign of 'immodesty', and situating her as an hysteric (*Cry*, p. 67). In contrast to this, Trapnel declares that 'they know not the pouring forth of thy Spirit, for that makes the body to crumble' (*Cry*, p. 29). While the soldiers try to read her body, Trapnel seeks to dissolve it. She justifies her expression on the grounds that God speaks through her and that 'her' discourse is 'purely' religious: 'And may not I speak in my Chamber, and sing in my bed, and pray on my knees? doth the Lord forwarn me, doth Scripture forbid me?' (*Legacy*, p. 59). Such an authorisation of her 'private' expression contradicts the political concerns manifested in its content. Like other radical women's prophecies, Trapnel's directly confronted the political issues of the day. In claiming the authority of God's spirit, these women appear to speak from beyond earthly distinctions of biological sex, even though their audiences evaluate their message by reference to their bodies. While God's spirit authorises their prophecies, these women do not make explicit claims for the legitimacy of women's speaking in or of itself.

QUAKER WOMEN'S WRITING: 'WOMEN'S SPEAKING JUSTIFIED'?

Whereas Trapnel's visions came upon her while she was in an 'insensible' state, Quaker women were not in a trance when they prophesied, 'for the voice of God was also the voice of [their] own conscience or integrity, the light within'.[52] Quaker women adopted the personae of biblical prophets; most notably, as Phyllis Mack explains, they emulated the archetype of 'the agressive, male Old Testament hero'.[53] However, as Nigel Smith points out, 'Quaker writing moves beyond imitation of biblical characters ... to a direct appropriation of biblical voices, which takes place in the absence of a distinctive Quaker *personae*', as the aim of faith and its form of expression required the '*merging* [of] the self with the One light'.[54] Rather than relying upon a form of external authority, this doctrine stressed the woman's own conscience. Sarah Blackborow, for example, criticises the 'Priests' who 'teach the people to neglect the witnesses of God in their consciences, telling them it is of their nature, and persuading them its not sufficient to ... give power over sin', and claims instead that Christ 'is become Teacher himselfe, and his Sheepe heare his voyce; and not one of them can follow a hireling, who are strangers to that Teaching'.[55] Blackborow's statement also reveals an implicit threat within Quakerism to the structure and authority of the institution of the church: refusing the authority of ministers also entailed refusing to pay tithes for their maintenance.[56] In the sense that the Quakers did not articulate explicit political demands, they could be seen as less 'radical' than other sects, but they threatened the social order through their refusal to attend public church services or to swear the Oath of Allegiance.[57] Combined with the notion of the 'merging' of the individual with God, this had profound implications for the Quakers' definition of women.

Judging by congregational records, Quakerism seems to have held a particular appeal for women. Certainly, it provided them with a space to prophesy and proclaim the gospel, both at home and abroad; they were allowed to hold office; there were separate women's meetings; and the number of active female Quakers is demonstrated in the records of those arrested for the disruption of mainstream church services.[58] Quaker writing accounts for a large proportion of texts produced by women during the mid-seventeenth century, which suggests that they encouraged women's expression. However, to seek for a uniquely 'female' voice in these texts runs counter to the Quakers' aspiration to merge the 'self' with God. In Dorothy White and Hester Biddle's writing, for example, the 'I' of the text is God rather than the earthly speaker. Predicated upon the notion of the 'Light' within, these women stress the fact that God speaks in their own language; as Hester Biddle puts it, 'we are not like the World, who must have a Priest to interpret the Scriptures to them ... the Lord doth not speak to us in an unknown Tongue, but in our own Language do we hear him perfectly'.[59] Like the Old Testament prophets, Quaker women such as Biddle and White prophesied the destruction of an unjust nation and chastised their hearers for their sinful lives:

'Drunkenness, Whoredom, and Glutony, and all manner of Ungodliness, Tyranny and Oppresion, is found in thee; Thy Priests preach for hire, and thy People love to have it so ... Stage-Playes, Ballad Singing, Cards, and Dice, and all manner of Folly ... wicked works & actions are not punished by thee.'[60] In these examples, the woman prophet's central concern is the condemnation of the rulers' tolerance of sin, which contrasts with their persecution of the Quakers' godly behaviour. While Quakers produced a variety of texts, their primary concern was the defence of their faith.

The apparent popularity of Quakerism for women may have been skewed by the fact that the 'Friends' preserved the records describing their persecution and deliverance.[61] Quaker doctrine was not straight-forwardly liberating for women; the function of the women's meetings, for example, did not radically challenge contemporary expectations of women's roles; and while in theory women could hold church office, apart from Margaret Fell they were not prominent in church 'hierarchy'. Even the basis upon which women's speaking or prophesying was 'justified' raises as many problems as it solves. While the most famous text discussing this issue is Margaret Fell's *Women's Speaking Justified*, her arguments are not unique to her.[62] Basing their position upon the Scriptures, the Quakers pointed out that God promised to 'pour out my spirit upon all flesh; and your sons and your daughters shall prophesy' and maintained that 'there is neither male nor female: for ye are all one in Christ Jesus'.[63] They ingeniously reinterpreted St Paul's injunctions against women's speaking, arguing that his meaning should be inter-preted metaphorically rather than literally; thus, St Paul's command-ment did not refer specifically to members of the female sex, but was directed at those who were not 'in the Light'. Drawing a distinction between the 'natural' body and the 'spirit', the Quakers argued that *anyone* who was not in the Light should be silent: as Richard Farnworth put it, 'all carnal Wisdom in Male as well as in Female [should] keep silence'.[64] As God's ('spiritual') wisdom runs counter to human ('carnal') wisdom, women were especially suited to the expression of God's word and will.[65] In this, the Quaker justification of women's expression does not challenge contemporary norms: it is precisely because the woman is the 'weaker vessel' that she is an appropriate conduit through which God can speak.

However, it also situates men as subject to the guidance of 'the Light', rather than their 'own' wisdom and questions contemporary assump-tions by metaphorically defining men who were not 'in the Light' as 'women'. Thus, the Quakers' emphasis upon 'spiritual' wisdom also provided the basis of their critique of existing churches. Sarah Blackborow, for example, accuses the priests of speaking without the 'Light', which means that they should be silent. Inverting the dominant reading, she cites St Paul in order to silence them: 'wherever they found either the Male or the Female out of the power, not learned of their Husband the Head, they were forbidden to Prayer or Prophesie'.[66] By invoking the division of authority in which the believer is subject to the 'headship' of Christ, Blackborow insists that a woman who is covered by him does not 'usurp' authority, but is obedient to him; consequently, anyone who tries to prevent her from speaking limits God's power (p. 14).

In *Women's Speaking Justified*, Margaret Fell reinterprets the myths of Creation and the Fall in order to critique the 'naturalised' distinctions between the sexes, and authorise women's speech.[67] But Fell's text is also concerned with specifying which women can speak: she argues that St Paul did not mean that *all* women should be silent and tells her readers 'to make a distinction what sort of women are forbidden to speak' (p. 13). Fell's own characterisation of those forbidden to speak problematically relies upon existing stereotypes of disobedient or transgressive women. She identifies those who are forbidden to speak with 'the Jezebel, ... the false Church, the great Whore, and tatling women and busie-bodies'.[68] Fell is attempting to maintain a distinction between the 'true' and the 'false' church; thus her distinction between legitimate and illegitimate 'female' expression apparently refers equally to men and women: the 'tatlers and the busiebodies' are forbidden to speak 'by the True Woman [of] whom Christ is the Husband, to the Woman as well as the Man, all being comprehended to be the Church', for 'Christ is the head of the Male and Female, who may speak' (p. 16). However, Fell's attempt to define the 'true' church is not simply directed at those outside of the Quaker faith. Her 'justification' of 'women's' speaking was at least partly informed by a desire to control the expression of women *within* the Quaker movement in the 1660s; it is therefore, as Maureen Bell has pointed out, ironic that Fell has been identified as a proto-feminist.[69]

This point illustrates the need to historicise women's writing; seeking to reclaim women's texts to support a specifically 'feminist' history can erase differences between women. Those I have discussed are primarily defined by their adherence to particular religious doctrines: they aimed at different ends and do not form a homogenous group. While their audiences invoke contemporary cultural assumptions in order to try and contain their expression, the very need to do this produces a conflict between the cultural expectations of feminine behaviour and actual female practice. Paradoxically, while Christianity provided an ideological basis for the idealisation of female silence, it also required their speech to defend it; thus, the very discourse that sought to oppress women can also be seen to facilitate a release. During this period, however, this did not necessarily enable them to speak 'as women'; the Quakers' 'justification' of women's speaking defined them metaphorically as men, and other prophets sought to speak from a space which was, theoretically at least, beyond the earthly limitations of sexual identification. However, the struggle to establish the 'truth' of their utterances was integrally connected to their sex; often the women themselves made reference to contemporary assumptions about their supposed 'weakness' in order to legitimise their expression, and the reception of their speech was grounded upon the extent to which they did or did not conform to the culturally delineated ideals. Questioning the 'truth' of the woman's faith, it seems, simultaneously entailed an interrogation of her 'femininity'. The perceived value of woman's speech, or indeed her exemplary status, fluctuated according to the context in which she spoke and whom she was addressing. Such contradictory attitudes to women's articulation of their faith is not simply a matter of historical interest, however. As the recent controversy over the ordination of women priests in the Church of England clearly demonstrates, women's position within the institution of the church and their authority to articulate their faith remains the subject of intense debate.

NOTES

1. Anna Trapnel, *A Report and Plea* (1654), reprinted in Elspeth Graham, Hilary Hinds, Elaine Hobby and Helen Wilcox, eds., *Her Own Life: Autobiographical Writings by Seventeenth-Century Englishwomen* (London: Routledge, 1989), p. 83.

2. The main texts used to justify female silence were I Corinthians 14:34–5 and I Timothy 2:11. See Margaret Olofson Thickstun, *Fictions of the Feminine: Puritan Doctrine and the Representation of Women* (Ithaca, NY, and London: Cornell University Press, 1988).

3. Suzanne Hull, *Chaste, Silent and Obedient: English Books for Women, 1475–1640* (San Marino, CA: Huntington Library, 1982). Diane Willen notes that this ideal 'did not silence the radicals' in her 'Women and Religion in Early Modern England' in Sherrin Marshall, ed., *Women in Reformation and Counter-Reformation Europe: Public and Private Worlds* (Bloomington and Indianapolis: Indiana University Press, 1989), p. 143.

4. Denise Riley, *'Am I that Name?' Feminism and the Category of 'Women' in History* (Basingstoke: Macmillan, 1988) and Toril Moi, 'Feminist Literary Criti-

cism' in Ann Jefferson and David Robey, eds., *Modern Literary Theory: a Comparative Introduction*, 2nd edn (London: Batsford, 1986).

5. The rationale for the connection between the (male) head and the (female) body is not solely attributable to Christian doctrine; see Ian Maclean, *The Renaissance Notion of Woman: a study in the Fortunes of Scholasticism and Medical Science in European Intellectual Life* (Cambridge: Cambridge University Press, 1980).

6. Patricia Crawford, *Women and Religion in England, 1500–1720* (London and New York: Routledge, 1993), p. 1.

7. Philip Stubbes, *A Crystall Glasse, for Christian Women* (London, 1591), A2r, A2v, A2v.

8. *Ibid.*, A2v, A2v, Asv, B4v.

9. John Mayer, *A Pattern for Women* (1619), reprinted in Katherine Usher Henderson and Barbara F. McManus, eds., *Half Humankind: Contexts and Texts of the Controversy about Women in England, 1540–1640* (Urbana: University of Illinois Press, 1985), p. 337. See also Margo Todd, 'Humanists, Puritans and the Spiritualised Household', *Church History*, 49: 1 (1980), 18–34; Willen, 'Women and Religion', pp. 147–8.

10. John Donne, 'A Sermon of Commemoration of the Lady Danvers, 1 July 1627', in Neil Rhodes, ed., *John Donne: Selected Prose* (Harmondsworth: Penguin, 1987), p. 284.

11. Stubbes, *A Crystall Glasse*, C2r, C3r, C3r.

12. Sister Magdalen Augustine, trans., *The History of the Angellical Virgin, Glorious S. Clare* (Douai, 1635), p. 224. The text emphasises St Clare's relationships with her mother, her sister, and her 'daughters', the nuns. Isobel Grundy suggests that 'the life stories of nuns ... [record] a quest for a specifically female community' in 'Women's history? Writings by English nuns', in Isobel Grundy and Susan Wiseman, eds., *Women, Writing, History, 1640–1740* (London: Batsford, 1992), p. 127. See also Marie B. Rowlands, 'Recusant Women, 1560–1640', in Mary Prior, ed., *Women in English Society, 1500–1800* (London and New York: Methuen, 1985), p. 174.

13. Anthony Stafford, *The Femall Glory; or, The Life, and Death of our Blessed Lady, the holy Virgin Mary, Gods owne Mother* (London, 1635). Sidney Lee comments upon the 'scandal' caused by this text in the *DNB* (London, 1898), pp. 44–5. Thickstun, *Fictions of the Feminine*, discusses the role of the Virgin Mary in Protestant texts (pp. 8–9).

14. John Bale, *The Lattre Examinacyon of Anne Askewe* (Wesel, 1547); John Mush, 'A Report of the Life and Martyrdom of Mrs Margaret Clitherow' in John Morris, ed., *The Troubles of our Catholic Forfathers, Related by Themselves* (London: Burns and Oates, 1877), vol. III. For a discussion of the way in which such texts contributed to the debate about the definition of 'woman', see Carole Levin, 'Women in *The Book of Martyrs* as models of behavior in Tudor England', *International Journal of Women's Studies*, 4 (1981), 196–207, and Ellen Macek, 'The Emergence of Feminine Spirituality in *The Book of Martyrs*', *SCJ*, 19:1 (1988), 63–80.

15. Morris, ed., *Troubles*, p. 422.
16. The *Necessary Doctrine* affirmed the *Act for Abolishing Diversities of Opinion* (1539) more popularly known as *'The Six Articles Act'*. See Leo F. Solt, *Church and State in Early Modern England, 1509–1640* (New York & Oxford: Oxford University Press, 1990), p. 37.
17. *Ibid.*, p. 38.
18. *Act for the Advancement of the True Religion* (1543); *ibid.*, p. 36.
19. 'Sacramentary' was a term used to define those who denied the real presence of Christ in the Eucharist; Solt, *Church and State*, p. 55.
20. John Bale, *Lattre Examinacyon* (1547), sigs. 40r–43v. The illegality of such a punishment for women is discussed by Willen, 'Women and Religion', p. 143.
21. Bale, *Lattre Examinacyon*, sig. 46v; John R. Knott also discusses this point in *Discourses of Martyrdom in English Literature, 1563–1694* (Cambridge: Cambridge University Press, 1993), p. 57.
22. In this context 'delycyouslye [deliciously] brought up' implies that Askewe was accustomed to luxury and delicate treatment. The questions of the importance of Askewe's sex, and the role of Bale as narrator, have received much critical attention; see for example, 'Anne Askewe's Dialogue with Authority', in Marie-Rose Logan and Peter L. Rudnytsky, eds., *Contending Kingdoms: Historical, Psychological, and Feminist Approaches to the Literature of Sixteenth-Century England and France* (Detroit: Wayne State University Press, 1991), pp. 313–22; and Leslie P. Fairfield, 'John Bale and the Development of Protestant Hagiography', *JEH*, 24 (1973), 145–60.
23. J. R. Tanner, ed., *Tudor Constitutional Documents, 1485–1603*, (Cambridge: Cambridge University Press, 1948), pp. 130–63.
24. John Morris, ed., *Troubles* (1877), p. 436. Mush explains that Clitherow does not want to be tried by jury ('on' or by her 'countrymen'), in order that the jury will not be guilty of wrongfully convicting her. For details about *peine forte et dure* (literally 'severe and harsh punishment'), see Rowlands, 'Recusant Women', p. 158.
25. Both women provide models for others to emulate during their own trials: Askewe for Joan Bocher and Clitherow for Jane Wiseman; Crawford, *Women and Religion*, p. 33; Philip Caraman, trans., *John Gerard: the Autobiography of an Elizabethan*, 2nd edn (London: Longmans, Green and Co., 1956), pp. 51–4.
26. John Foxe, *The Actes and Monuments* (London, 1583), vol. II, pp. 1246–8.
27. For a clear analysis of the number of texts by women in such genres, see Patricia Crawford, 'Women's Published Writings, 1600–1700', in Prior, ed., *Women in English Society*, pp. 211–82, and listings in Elaine Hobby, *The Virtue of Necessity: English Women's Writings, 1649–1688* (London: Virago, 1988).
28. Historically, Pembroke's achievements have been overshadowed by her brother, Sir Philip Sidney. For a detailed literary biography of the Countess, see Margaret P. Hannay, *Philip's Phoenix, Mary Sidney, Countess of Pembroke* (New York and Oxford: Oxford University Press, 1990).

29. Sir Edward Denny to Lady Mary Wroth, Salisbury, MSS 130/118–19, 26 February 1621/22, cited in Margaret P. Hannay, ed., *Silent But For The Word: Tudor Women as Patrons, Translators, and Writers of Religious Works* (Kent, OH: Kent State University Press, 1985), p. 5.

30. Aemilia Lanyer, *Salve Deus Rex Judaeorum* (1611), reprinted as 'The Authors Dreame' in A. L. Rowse, ed., *The Poems of Shakespeare's Dark Lady: 'Salve Deus Rex Judaeorum' by Emilia Lanyer* (London: Jonathan Cape, 1978), pp. 55–64; John Donne and Samuel Daniel also praise the Countess of Pembroke's *Psalmes*.

31. J. C. A. Rathmell, ed., *The Psalms of Sir Philip Sidney and the Countess of Pembroke* (New York: Anchor Books, 1963), Psalm 47, line 15.

32. The importance of the psalms in the production of Protestant subjectivity is discussed by Alan Sinfield in *Faultlines: Cultural Materialism and the Politics of Dissident Reading* (Oxford: Oxford University Press, 1992), p. 166. See also Barbara K. Lewalski, *Protestant Poetics and the Seventeenth-Century Religious Lyric* (Princeton, NJ: Princeton University Press, 1979) and Rivkah Zim, *English Metrical Psalms: Poetry as Praise and Prayer, 1555–1601* (Cambridge: Cambridge University Press, 1987). Margaret P. Hannay suggests that Pembroke's *Psalmes* do reveal 'feminine' concerns in '"House-confined maids": The Presentation of Woman's Role in the *Psalmes* of the Countess of Pembroke', *ELR*, 24: (1994), 44–71.

33. For examples of texts in the controversy debate, see Usher Henderson and McManus, eds., *Half Humankind*.

34. 'Eve's Apologie' in Rowse, eds., *Shakespeare's Dark Lady*, pp. 103–5.

35. J. F. McGregor and B. Reay, eds., *Radical Religion in the English Revolution* (Oxford: Oxford University Press, 1984), p. 10; John Morrill, 'The Church in England, 1642–1649', in John Morrill, ed., *The Nature of the English Revolution: Essays by John Morrill* (London and New York: Longman, 1993), pp. 148–75.

36. Christopher Hill, *The World Turned Upside Down: Radical Ideas During the English Revolution* (Harmondsworth: Peregrine, 1988). The doctrinal controversies ranged from the clothing of the clergy to the extent of the individual's free will or 'predestination' to salvation.

37. Diane Purkiss, 'Producing the Voice, Consuming the Body: Women Prophets of the Seventeenth Century', in Grundy and Wiseman, eds., *Women, Writing, History*, p. 139. See also Nigel Smith, *Perfection Proclaimed: Language and Literature in the English Radical Revolution, 1640–1660* (Oxford: Clarendon Press, 1989), pp. 26–32.

38. Elizabeth Poole, *A Vision: wherein is manifested the disease and cure of the kingdome* (London, 1648) and *An Alarum of War* (London, 1649).

39. Hill, *The World Turned Upside Down*, p. 279; David Underdown, *Pride's Purge: Politics in the Puritan Revolution* (Oxford: Clarendon Press, 1971), p. 183.

40. Underdown, *Pride's Purge*, p. 183; Elizabeth Poole, 'Bring him to his triall, that he may be convicted in his conscience, but touch not his person', *A Vision* (1648), p. 6.

41. For further information about the legal position of women who killed their husbands, see Frances E. Dolan, 'Home-Rebels and House-Traitors: Murderous Wives in Early Modern England', *Yale Journal of Law and the Humanities*, 4: 1 (1992), 1–31, and 'The Subordinate('s) Plot: Petty Treason and the Forms of Domestic rebellion', *SQ*, 43:3 (1992), 317–40.

42. Diane Purkiss argues that Poole uses such arguments to vindicate her position as a prophet ('Producing the Voice', p. 151).

43. Elizabeth Poole, *An Alarum of War* (1649), pp. 6–7.

44. Arise Evans, *A Message from God, By a Dumb Woman* (London, 1653/4), p. 10. The content of Channel's prophecy reveals Royalist sympathies (p. 4). Evans authorises her speech with reference to I Corinthians 1:27–28.

45. *Ibid.*, p. 7. The story of the destruction of Diana's Temple can be found in Acts 19:34.

46. Toby Barnard, *The English Republic, 1649–1660* (Essex: Longman, 1986), p. 97.

47. Bernard Capp 'The Fifth Monarchists and Popular Millenarianism', in McGregor and Reay, eds., *Radical Religion*, p. 165.

48. *Ibid.*, p. 170.

49. Anna Trapnel, *Strange and Wonderfull Newes from White-Hall* (1654), p. 4. Trapnel does predict the future in her prophecies (for example, her foreseeing of the dissolution of the Rump Parliament in *The Cry of a Stone* (1654), p. 10), but mostly she criticises the present powers (for example *Cry* (1954), pp. 19–20) or the 'priests' (*A Legacy for Saints* (1654), for example, pp. 50 and 59).

50. Anna Trapnel, *Cry* (1654), pp. 41 2. Nigel Smith points out that 'the total negation of the ego in the presence of scripture' is a characteristic of prophetic utterances (*Perfection Proclaimed*, p. 36).

51. The significance of the relationship between prophecy and women's bodies can be read in a number of ways; see Smith, *Perfection Proclaimed*, p. 50; Purkiss, 'Producing the Voice', pp. 139–58; Sue Wiseman, 'Unsilent Instruments and the Devil's Cushions: Authority in Seventeenth-Century Women's Prophetic Discourse', in Isobel Armstrong, ed., *New Feminist Discourses: Critical Essays on Theories and Texts* (London: Routledge, 1992), pp. 176–96; and Roy Porter, 'The Prophetic Body: Lady Eleanor Davies and the meanings of madness', *Women's Writing: the Elizabethan to Victorian Period*, 1 (1994), 51–63.

52. Phyllis Mack, *Visionary Women: Ecstatic Prophecy in Seventeenth-Century England* (Berkeley: University of California Press, 1992), p. 136.

53. *Ibid.*, p. 134.

54. Smith, *Perfection Proclaimed*, pp. 25, 67.

55. Sarah Blackborow, *The Just and Equall Ballance Discovered* (London, 1660), pp. 3–4.

56. This point is emphasised by Margaret Fell in *A Declaration and Information from us the People of God called the Quakers* (London, 1660), p. 2.

57. This is the main issue at stake in *The Examination and tryall of Margaret Fell and George Fox* (London, 1664).

58. The number of women Quakers arrested for disrupting church services was 34 per cent: see Elaine Hobby, '"Oh Oxford. Thou Art Full of Filfth": the Prophetical Writings of Hester Biddle, 1629[?]–1696', in Susan Sellers, ed., *Feminist Criticism: Theory and Practice* (New York and London: Harvester Wheatsheaf, 1991), pp. 160–1.

59. Hester Biddle, *The Trumpet of the Lord Sounded forth unto these Three Nations* (London, 1662), p. 11.

60. *Ibid.*, pp. 5–6. See also Dorothy White, *A Trumpet of the Lord of Hosts, Blown unto the City of London* (1662) and *A Lamentation Unto this Nation* (1660).

61. Maureen Bell, George Parfitt and Simon Shepherd, eds., *A Biographical Dictionary of English Women Writers, 1580–1720* (New York and London: Harvester Wheatsheaf, 1990), p. 250.

62. See also Priscilla Cotton and Mary Cole, *To the Priests and the People of England, we discharge our consciences, and give them warning* (London, 1655); Richard Farnworth, *A Woman forbidden to Speak in the Church* (London, 1655); George Fox, *The woman learning in silence* (1656). Sarah Blackborow also addresses this issue in *The Just and Equall Ballance Discovered* (1660). Elizabeth Bathurst used similar arguments in *The Sayings of Women* (London, 1683).

63. Joel 2:28; Galatians 3:28 (Authorised Version).

64. Farnworth, *A Woman forbidden to Speak in the Church*, p. 4.

65. '[T]he Woman is counted the weaker Vessel, but the Lord filling that Vessel full of his Wisdom, and ruling it by his holy spirit . . . is for the praise of the glory of his grace, that no flesh might glory in his sight' (*ibid.*, p. 4).

66. Blackborow, *The Just and Equall Ballance Discovered*, p. 13.

67. 'God . . . put no such difference between the Male and the Female as men would make' (Margaret Fell, *Womens Speaking Justified* (London, 1666), p. 3).

68. *Ibid.*, p. 15.

69. Maureen Bell *et al.*, eds., *Biographical Dictionary*, p. 259. For further details about the divisions within the Quakers partially caused by James Naylor, see Crawford, *Women and Religion*, pp. 166–80.

CHAPTER 3

Advice for women from mothers and patriarchs

Valerie Wayne

Conduct books were bestsellers during the Renaissance, and those by women were among the most popular books that women wrote between 1500 and 1700. Directing most of their advice to the practice of daily living, they came in the form of manuals, dialogues and commentaries on behaviour, marriage or the household, and their audience included all readers who sought direction in how to lead a godly and proper life. Such works were the counterpart to our modern self-help books in that they offered early modern women advice on how to improve their lives. Most of them were written by men; but between 1604 and 1624 five books by women were published in England that will serve as the focus for this discussion of early modern conduct literature. All of these are mothers' advice books, where the writer's role as mother offers her a position of authority from which to speak. I want first to situate these texts in relation to physiological and religious accounts that displaced women's role in reproduction; then to consider the occasions and contradictions of the mothers' books; and finally to relate them to other conduct literature in terms of the problems they pose for the subjectivity of early modern women.

I

Advice for women, given by their mothers, needs to be understood in the context of the views of motherhood prevailing in the Renaissance. By 1500, the ideological construction of women by men had been occurring for centuries at a prodigious rate, and the importance of women's biological role in reproduction had been displaced through physiological theories and biblical stories. 'The mother of what is called her child is not its parent, but only the nurse of the newly implanted germ ... [F]atherhood there may be, when mother there is none.' These words are spoken by Apollo in Aeschylus' *Eumenides* as a defence for Orestes'

56

murder of his mother on the grounds that she did not engender him, and they articulate the doctrine of 'preformationism' that was one view of conception current in Graeco-Egyptian culture in the fifth century BC.[1] Because that view sees the father as the exclusive source of generation, it has been described as 'the denial of physiological maternity'.[2] When he formulated his account of generation during the next century, Aristotle was reacting against this and other views, including the argument associated with Hippocrates that two seeds or germinal substances, one associated with each parent, contribute to conception.[3] Aristotle's model is called the 'one-seed theory' because it attributes predominant influence to the male seed or semen, which he sees as possessing 'soul'; he literally grants men a seminal role in procreation.[4] Advocates for women during the Renaissance and in the twentieth century have found reason to contest Aristotle's account on these grounds and because he considered woman a mutilated or deformed man.[5] Recent defenders have replied that Aristotle nonetheless improved upon earlier theories such as preformationism and granted women's menstrual fluid an analogous, causative role in generation.[6]

Aristotle had a definite influence over later thinking in this area, but it was the work of Galen, who lived in the second century AD, that was more widely accepted by early modern authorities.[7] Galen adopted a 'two-seed' model that claimed women also produced a generative seed; nonetheless, like other authorities he viewed their seed as weaker than men's because it was colder and less active.[8] So Galen attributed less importance to women's role in procreation than Hippocrates but more importance than Aristotle, because he acknowledged women's capacity to engender a child. Regardless of the relative merits of these theories, all of them evince a problem discussed by Thomas Laqueur:

It is empirically true, and known to be so by almost all cultures, that the male is necessary for conception. It does not of course follow that the male contribution is thereby the more powerful one, and an immense amount of effort and anxiety had to go into 'proving' that this was the case . . . After all, the work of generation available to the senses is wholly the work of the female.[9]

The most immediate evidence about the role of women in the birth of children was supplanted in these physiological accounts by what was thought and made more important – the creation of humankind by men.

The biblical story of the creation of Adam and Eve did not substantially alter this situation because the most well-known account in Genesis presents the first woman as derivative rather than generative since she was made from Adam's rib. That story was endlessly appropriated during the Renaissance for purposes ranging from blatant misogyny to the praise of women. According to *The Scholehouse of Women* (1541), when women gather together they are like bones in a bag, which make a lot of noise, and conspire against the rule of men;[10] for Henry Cornelius Agrippa, on the other hand, writing *Of the Nobilitie and Excellencie of Womankynde*, a bone created by God was far superior stuff to the material of Adam's creation – the 'earth', after which Adam was named – so women are more apt to relate to God than are men.[11] Mary Beth Rose has remarked that 'as myths of Athena popping out of Zeus' head and Eve emerging from Adam's side remind us, Western culture includes a long tradition of reluctance to accept the obvious'.[12] The perceived importance of women's role in procreation was reduced over time by the influence of such myths. St Paul wrote to the Corinthians that 'the man is not of the woman, but the woman of the man', and 'the man was not created for woman's sake: but woman for the man's sake'.[13] John Knox echoed these biblical passages when he argued against the right of women to rule in 1558.[14] In an historical sense, then, both St Paul and Knox were largely correct about who created whom, for the myth of Eve's origin had such a hold on early modern imaginations that it could not be ignored.

But it could be reinterpreted. In the sixteenth century, conduct books frequently retold the creation story as a parable of the companionate relation between the first man and the first woman. Heinrich Bullinger explains in the most popular book on marriage from the sixteenth century, the *Christen State of Matrimonye*, that Eve was not created from the earth least any man 'thinke that he had gotten his wyfe out of the myre', and she was not made from his feet 'as though thou mightest spurne her a way from the[e]'; nor was she made from the head, because 'the husband is the heade and master of the wyfe'. Instead, she was made from Adam's side 'as one that is set next unto man to be his helpe and companyon'.[15] The passage positions itself against an earlier, primarily medieval tradition that denigrated the worth of woman; then it remakes Eve in a more positive image. Yet it also resists any notion of female superiority: Eve is clearly subject to her husband and enjoined against being his master. The retelling is therefore narrated against two alternative constructions of woman. It asserts an affinity between the sexes but denies them equality and refuses either sex extreme superiority over the other. In other words, it offers a careful negotiation between the available positions on marriage in the middle of the sixteenth century, representing a consensus view that was espoused by most humanist, Protestant and puritan writers from 1500 to 1700.[16]

For all Christians, however, Eve had her counterpart in Mary, and the redemption that Mary offered to humankind through giving birth to Christ could become not only a means of cleansing the sins of Eve but of recovering the procreative capacities of women that had been displaced by other accounts. Mary also made it possible for women to claim access to authorship through their maternal role. The mother's book that was most often reprinted during this period, Dorothy Leigh's *The Mothers Blessing*, appeared in at least sixteen editions from 1616 to 1674, which means it was wildly popular in the middle of the seventeenth century.[17] When Leigh discusses the importance of giving children good names associated with virtuous figures from the Bible, she digresses on the topic of Mary:

I presumed, that there was no woman so sencelesse, as not to looke what a blessing God hath sent to us women, through that gracious Virgin, by whom it pleased GOD to take away the shame, which EVE our Grandmother had brought us to... Heere is this great and wofull shame taken from women by GOD, working in a woman: man can claime no part in it: the shame is taken from us, and from our posteritie for ever. *The seede of the woman hath taken downe the Serpents head*: and now, whosoever can take hold of the seed of the Woman by faith, shall surely live for ever. And therefore all generations shall say, that she was blessed, who brought us a Savior, the fruit of obedience, that whosoever feedeth of, shall live for ever: and except they feede of the seed of the Woman, they have no life.[18]

In this passage the meanings of 'seed' as offspring and as a generative substance overlap, and the conjunction becomes a means of justifying Dorothy Leigh's project of offering motherly advice to her children by relating it to Mary's birth of Christ. The phrase 'the seed of the Woman' refers most immediately to Christ as the offspring of Mary, and 'man can claime no part' of this redemptive event because Mary's birth occurred without male participation according to the doctrine of the Virgin birth. Leigh's use of the phrase is adapted from Genesis 3:15, where God says to Satan concerning Eve, 'I will also put enimitie betwene thee and the woman, and betwene thy sede and her sede. He shal breake thine head, and thou shalt bruise his heele.'[19] In *The Institutes of the Christian Religion*, Calvin interprets this passage to mean 'that the posterity of the woman would overcome the devil', so the phrase refers 'not to Christ alone, but to the whole human race'.[20]

However, Calvin also uses 'seed' in its physiological sense to interpret biblical passages contrary to those who 'confidently maintain that the expression as to seed is applicable only to males'. On the basis of genealogies in the Bible, he argues that 'offspring is partly procreated by the seed of the mother', and that Christ has a human nature because 'inasmuch as he was begotten of Mary, [he] was procreated of her seed'.[21] Leigh is therefore on firm doctrinal grounds to imply women's biological contribution to the birth of Christ. The burden of Eve is lifted from women by Mary's motherhood, and 'the seed of the woman', a phrase repeated three times in Leigh's passage, acquires a redemptive role. In the context of ongoing debates about whether one or two seeds had a generative function, the birth of Christ becomes the single, miraculous instance when the woman's seed is the only human contribution to procreation.[22] And in the context of a woman writer attempting to justify her authorship of an advice book to her children, Mary's achievement makes it possible for Dorothy Leigh to write a book with the help of God but not man. If Mary was blessed in bringing to life a saviour as the fruit of obedience, Leigh too may be commended for offering *The Mothers Blessing* as the fruit of her obedient and prayerful exercise of a mother's care. 'The seed of the woman' therefore comes to include not only her body as a generative source, or her progeny, but her book.

II

Even given such a justification, we might still ask what prompted or even permitted the publication of the five mothers' advice books that were first issued from 1604 to 1624 and often reprinted, or the three more that appeared in 1645, 1673 and 1685.[23] The genre itself was not a new one: mothers' advice books had been written as early as the 800s; fathers' advice books also extend as far back in England as 1484, and Lord Burghley, Sir Walter Raleigh and Francis Osborne were among those who wrote them during the Renaissance.[24] Gerda Lerner relates the mothers' books to the larger history of feminism by claiming that they give evidence of women's 'authorization through motherhood'.[25] But the appearance of a cluster of these books early in seventeenth-century England, when they had not been published there in any quantity before, prompts questions about their history.[26] They are related to the long controversy about whether women should nurse their own children or send them out to wet nurses, especially as the dispute is evoked through Erasmus's colloquy, *Puerpera*, or *The New Mother*. The cause for nursing mothers was championed enthusiastically by sixteenth-century humanists in England, and seventeenth-century English puritans firmly endorsed the same position.[27] One of the mothers' books, Elizabeth Clinton's *The Countesse of Lincolnes Nurserie* of 1622, gives most of its attention to this issue. Clinton admits she did not nurse her own eighteen children and writes 'to redeeme my peace' after she has been 'pricked in hart for my undutifullnesse'.[28] (It was common for mothers who did not nurse – primarily upper-class women – to have more children because lactation helped to prevent pregnancy.[29])

Nearly 100 years before Clinton's *Nurserie*, Erasmus had advocated a mother's responsibility for the spiritual as well as physical nurturance of her children in *The New Mother*. The main speaker of this colloquy advises that St Paul assured women they would be saved through childbearing, yet reminds them that their children must 'continue in the faith and love, with holinesse and modestie' in order to be likewise saved, 'so that you have not yet done the part of a mother, unlesse you first frame aright his tender bodie, and then his mind as tender as that with good education'. When the new mother retorts that it is not in her power to assure her child's continuance in faith, her adviser replies, 'It may be so, but for all that, vigilant admonition is of such force, that *Paul* thinkes it to be laide to the mothers charge, if their children degenerate from godly courses.'[30] Erasmus's colloquy recruited mothers in the ideological maintenance of their children through 'vigilant admonition'.

The influence of this humanist account was extensive: Erasmus was probably the most important figure in the reformation in sixteenth-century England. Once his works were banned by the Catholic church in 1559, he became a mentor for Protestants and puritans. His colloquies were used throughout the sixteenth century for instruction in Latin,[31] and the very women who had sufficient education to write advice books could have read them in the original. But those mothers might also have read the three English editions of seven Erasmian dialogues, including *The New Mother*, translated by a puritan minister of Norwich named William Burton and published twice in 1606 and again in 1624.[32] There seems to have been a resurgence of interest in the issue of nursing mothers during these years, which would support Burton's opinion that if readers examine his translation, they 'shalt perceive how little cause the Papists have to boast of Erasmus, as a man their side'.[33] The adaptation of Erasmus's advice in the early seventeenth century was helping to develop a 'new mother' within the culture.

By the second decade of the century, one of those mothers was becoming highly visible. Elizabeth Stuart, daughter to King James I, had married Frederick, the Elector Palatine, in 1613, and she eventually gave birth to thirteen children. Her third pregnancy was very far advanced when she was crowned Queen of Bohemia in November 1619, and in a prayer during the ceremony 'she was proclaimed a nursing mother of the Church' – the Protestant church.[34] But in January 1620, much to the surprise of his English subjects, James I prevented them from celebrating the birth of Elizabeth's third son as was their custom, and James was 'much talked of' as 'a straunge father that will neither fight for his children or pray for them'.[35] He also denied the family refuge in England when the Bohemians were overrun by the Catholic Habsburg armies. Elizabeth remained permanently exiled in The Hague for over forty years. Barbara Lewalski described this popular queen as one who 'became a locus for Protestant resistance and oppositional politics in England for the rest of James's reign',[36] which ended with his death in 1625.

In 1616, Dorothy Leigh dedicated her *Mothers Blessing* to the Princess Elizabeth, 'to make your Grace the Protectresse of this my Booke',[37] and the three remaining mothers' advice books, all Protestant, appeared in 1622, 1623 and 1624, when Elizabeth's plight was worsening and her father refused to offer any support. In 1625, Elizabeth Richardson also completed the first part of her advice book and Lady Anne Southwell finished the first manuscript of her 'Precepts'.[38] So if Erasmus provided the ideological justification for these texts, Elizabeth Stuart may have offered the politico-religious occasion for the Protestant books written in the second and third decades of the seventeenth century. The irony is that she probably did not nurse her thirteen children and that her youngest daughter, Sophie, grandmother to George I, complained in her own memoirs that 'my mother had us brought up far away from the court, because the sight of her monkeys and dogs was more pleasing to her than that of her children.'[39] But the English puritans who aligned themselves with Elizabeth Stuart's cause in the 1620s knew little about her private life. Instead, they were associating themselves with James's popular daughter at a time when his support for Protestants was seriously weakening. Their books assert the importance of a mother's nurturance at a moment of paternal negligence. The positions advocated by those women also received strong support from Protestant men. In 1622 the puritan William Gouge would include six chapters on the importance of nursing in *Of Domesticall Duties*, exhorting mothers that 'what ranke or degree soever they be, that (out of the case of necessitie) they have no warrant to put forth their children to others to nurse'; advice that would have been especially pointed to women of the upper classes. He would also affirm that 'mothers were a maine cause of the piety, or impiety' of their offspring.[40]

This sense of a mother's duty was echoed and enacted by other living mothers. The learned and influential Lady Anne Bacon, also a puritan, is known to have exercised an almost oppressive concern over the spiritual welfare of her sons Anthony and Francis: in her letters she often cautioned them about their behaviour or reminded them to pray with their servants twice a day.[41] When Constantia Munda dedicated her attack on Joseph Swetnam's *Arraignment of Lewd, idle, froward and unconstant women* to her mother in 1617, she alluded to the pains her mother would have borne in childbirth and then described her subsequent labour:

> Seeing you still
> Are a perpetual Labor with me even until
> The second birth of education perfect me,
> You Travail still though Churched oft you be.[42]

A mother's education of her child is seen by this daughter as a 'second birth' requiring a more continuous 'travail' than the comparatively brief pangs associated with a physical birth. While Mary was said to have redeemed humankind, and especially her own sex, through 'the seed of the Woman', early modern mothers were taught that their own salvation depended on nurturing those children with educational and spiritual food. And the one area in which all reformers from 1500 to 1700 granted women parity with men was in their access to salvation through faith: on that basis the sexes were accorded full spiritual equality.[43] Although women might be disqualified from authorship on the grounds of their inadequate education and inferior position, the study of the Bible accompanied by prayers and meditation within the confines of their home was as available to them, and as sufficient for the reform approach to salvation, as anything men could achieve. Leigh advises women that all members of their household, including servants, should be taught how to read the Bible, so a puritan concern for education could sometimes extend to the lower classes.[44]

It was therefore the same motive for the production of conduct books written by men during this period – the encouragement of an ethical and pious life, rather than the general acquisition of knowledge – that prompted women to advise and provide comparable instruction for their children. In the most popular sixteenth-century conduct book for women, *The Instruction of a Christian Woman*, which was first published in Latin in 1523 and then in English around 1529, Juan Luis Vives had said that a woman should learn only for 'her selfe alone and her yonge children or her sisters in our lord';[45] hence the exercise and audience of a woman's knowledge were strictly limited. Although Elizabeth Joceline was an unusually accomplished woman, she shared Vives's opinions. Joceline was raised by her grandfather, a bishop first of Chester and then of Lincoln, who had earlier been Master of Queens' College, Cambridge. She was knowledgeable 'in Languages, Historie, and some Arts' and had such an excellent memory that it enabled her 'upon the first rehearsall to repeate above forty lines in English or Latine: a gift the more happy by her imployment of it in carrying away an entire sermon, so that she could (almost following the steps of the words, or phrase) write it down in her chamber'.[46] Yet in *The Mothers Legacie* of 1624, which appeared in six editions through 1684, she advises restraint in a daughter's instruction:

I desire her bringing up may be learning the Bible, as my sisters do, good houswifery, writing, and good workes: other learning a woman needs not: though I admire it in those whom God hath blest with discretion, yet I desired not much in my owne, having seene that sometimes women have greater portions of learning than wisdome, which is of no better use to them than a maine saile to a fly-boat, which runnes it under water. But where learning and wisedome meet in a vertuous disposed Woman, shee is the fittest closet for all goodnesse. She is like a well-ballanced ship, that may beare all her saile.[47]

This passage uses the conflicting metaphors of 'closet' and 'ship' to describe the educated woman. In the seventeenth century a 'closet' was a small or private room, and like an enclosed space the educated woman was supposed to contain her knowledge and goodness within the society of her immediate family. Joceline claims that the woman who achieved that containment was like a 'well-ballanced ship' that does not capsize because its mainsail is not too large for the size of the boat, but her choice of tropes betrays her own ambivalence toward confinement when she shifts from the closet metaphor, an enclosed space, to a vehicle designed not to stay at home. The very language she uses enacts a transgression of the norms she is supposedly advocating. Although the passage explicitly asserts a concern that even a woman's virtues, especially her learning, might exceed the confines of her domestic space or throw her temperate behaviour off balance, the ship metaphor also reveals Joceline's desire to 'beare all her saile'. Yet there are only two destinations permitted for her voyages – heaven and home.

Joceline seems to speak from her own experience and observation in the passage, as if she knows too well the pain and disorder that can result from too much learning. However, the result of her frustration is to discourage a daughter from aspiring to the very accomplishments that she herself possessed and displayed. The written legacy of learned mothers to their own daughters was therefore not without its contradictions and restraints. Joceline recommends the way of least resistance and less education, rather than disturb the socio-religious order. While her admonitions show little change from those of Vives 100 years earlier, their articulation, like their contradictory figurative language, represents both an advance and a retreat: through the publication of her advice, Joceline is entering the sphere of public discourse generally off limits to women; yet the conservative content of her counsel contradicts the very mode of its utterance. While books like this one were more likely to be published when they encouraged restraint rather than compounding the transgression of women's silence with an argument for their self-assertion, those texts probably reproduced in their audiences the ambivalent reactions from which they arose.

The most eloquent account of why a mother would want to offer advice to her child at all occurs in the earliest seventeenth-century English mother's advice book, *Miscelanea, Meditations, Memoratives*, which was published in 1604 and reprinted three more times until about 1618.[48] Its author, Elizabeth Grymeston, is a Catholic who grounds her right to speak in her duty to love:

My dear sonne, there is nothing so strong as the force of love; there is no love so forcible as the love of an affectionate mother to her naturall childe: there is no mother can either more affectionately shew her nature, or more naturally manifest her affection, than in advising her children out of her owne experience, to eschew evill, and encline them to doe that which is good.[49]

For Grymeston, writing an advice book is the most affectionate and natural manifestation of the strongest form of love that can be said to exist. She claims that her work comes from 'her owne experience', yet her text mixes paraphrases with verbatim and revised quotations from other authors; Elaine Beilin calls her an 'intellectual gatherer who turns all "the fruitfull flowing of hir loftie braine" into "a mothers matchlesse care"'.[50] So that 'experience' was not purely personal; it was as influenced by the ideologies, controversies and texts surrounding her as was Vives's advice. Grymeston contributes to the valorisation of maternal love that was amplified in later centuries when she claims that a mother's affection exceeds all other forms of love. She may be speaking for other women as well as herself when she makes such a claim, and the passage movingly suggests how intensely and differently some women experience love in relation to their own children. But the origins of that advice were mediated by the cultural pressures surrounding their articulation, and the applications of the advice could be far from liberatory. In effect, texts such as this one were important agents in providing still more injunctions on female behaviour, most of which supported the ideological work performed in male-authored texts.

III

The very privilege that allowed early modern mothers to write also depended on and reinforced a sexual division of labour that could work against women and enhance inequalities between the sexes, so the mothers' advice books are not innocent productions: they were fully embedded in the social and economic relations from which they arose and on which they had some effect. Elizabeth Joceline and the Countess of Lincoln came from titled families; Elizabeth Grymeston, Dorothy Leigh, and M. R. (the author of *The Mothers Counsell, or, Live within Compasse* of 1623[51]) appear to have been well-educated gentlewomen. Patricia Crawford suggests in her study of maternity in seventeenth-century England that women in the upper levels of society 'were less likely to be engaged in economic production, and consequently more emphasis was placed on their reproductive labour'.[52] If most of these texts displayed solidarity with the Protestant cause of Elizabeth Stuart, nonetheless their enforcement of women's maternal role could offer still more support for the confinement of women to the domestic sphere that was increasingly advocated for them as the Middle Ages receded.

Women authors were also in general agreement with the male writers of conduct literature on the importance of the duty of chastity, which had traditionally been a primary justification for the restraint of women. Christine de Pisan had described chastity in her fifteenth-century *City of Ladies* as 'the supreme virtue in women'.[53] Dorothy Leigh aligns herself with Christians and 'Heathens' who have written that a chaste woman 'is a great partaker of all other vertues' and then defines a chaste woman against her opposite:

whoso is truely chaste, is free from idlenesse and from all vaine delights, full of humilitie, and all good Christian vertues: whoso is chaste, is not given to pride in apparell, nor any vanity, but is alwayes either reading, meditating, or practising some good thing which shee hath learned in the Scripture. But she which is unchaste, is given to bee idle; or if she doe any thing, it is for a vaine glory, and for the praise of men, more then for any humble, loving and obedient heart that shee beareth unto GOD and his Word.[54]

✗Chastity here becomes a way of invoking a range of Renaissance injunctions on women's behaviour: prescriptions for their apparel, their useful occupation in reading Scripture or doing pious works, their humility and their avoidance of 'vain delights' (which might extend in other authors to dancing, singing or dramatic entertainments). The greatest threat of the unchaste woman is that she 'destroyeth both the body and the soule of him shee seemeth most to love',[55] so the effects of her behaviour on men are given paramount concern. Women's bodies at this time were also constructed by medical discourses to enforce the ideological constraints on their behaviour, since many writers claimed with Leigh that 'God hath given a cold and temperate disposition' to women – cold and moist, as opposed to hot and dry – so that they would incorporate that virtue.[56] The argument attributes a divine purpose to physiological descriptions of the body that were as old as Hippocrates and Aristotle.

Leigh's advice on chastity leads directly to an account of the wife's subjection, which was a logical direction for it:

Thy desire shall be subject to thy husband. As if God, in mercy to women, should say, You of your selves shall have no desires, onely they shall be subject to your husbands.[57]

This passage moves from the duty of wives' subordination, to which they were enjoined by St Paul and most later writers, to a displacement of their desire, on the assumption that their chastity and subjection are most assured if their husbands can determine what they want. It is at this point that definitions of chastity begin to pose a serious threat to women's agency, because subjection is reconfigured as a loss of the desiring self. Leigh sees this occurrence as a 'mercy to women', since they come to want nothing but what they are supposed to want according to their husbands and God.

In *The Flower of Friendship* (1568), Edmund Tilney specifically advises husbands to plan or plot such a displacement:

The wise man maye not be contented onely with his spouses virginitie, but by little and little must gently procure that he maye also steale away hir private will, and appetite, so that of two bodies there may be made one onelye hart, which she will soone doe, if love raigne in hir.[58]

Marital love here is described as the process by which two bodies become one heart, but the effect of love's reign in the wife is an erasure of her desires and will. The husband therefore remains the only subject in the union. The wife loses not only her 'appetite' or sexual desire, but her 'private will', the volition by which she remains a separate person. Tilney is not advising that the wife be brought to submit her volition to God's will as an act of humility and faith; instead he counsels a husband to seduce his wife's will so that it comes to accord entirely with his own. This passage from Tilney's popular humanist dialogue was repeated in the puritan advice book by John Dod and Robert Cleaver, *A Godlie Forme of Householde Government*, first published in 1598: 'The husband ought not to bee satisfied that he hath robd his wife of her virginitie, but in that he hath possession and use of her will'.[59] Dod and Cleaver even echo Tilney's reference to theft. The stealthy pursuit of this goal is supposed to occur alongside the wife's increasing love, so the injunction that wives love their husbands permits and encourages that theft to occur. It is no wonder, in this context, that men from the knight in Chaucer's *Wife of Bath's Tale* to Sigmund Freud have had to enquire what it is that women want: ideologies such as these are so fully directed to the appropriation of a woman that she is not supposed to have any desire of her own.

The redefinition of marriage that evolved during the sixteenth century and has continued into our own day was therefore not without its hazards for women. While the subject position of a wife was given a degree of respectability that it had not previously achieved, wives were defined so that the more they loved, the more they were to subject themselves to their husbands' desires. In theoretical terms, the wife who became a subject through this ideology of marriage was increasingly subjected to a husband who was supposed to appropriate her agency.[60] Perhaps it is understandable, then, that women's maternal role offered them a more enabling subject position, because in relations with their children, subjection and the loss of one's will were inappropriate. It was common in many families at this time for children to kneel down and receive a blessing each day from their parents, and that physical act was a mark of the deference that mothers, too, could claim from their children.[61] Social historians of early modern England have argued that 'in pregnancy and childbirth married women enjoyed their greatest power and autonomy', and although their enthusiasm requires the important qualifications that Gail Paster has given it, motherhood was an area in which women strongly supported and learned from one another.[62] Gouge feels obliged to remind parents that 'women are for the most part prone to pranke up their children above their husbands place and calling, and therefore good reason that therein they should be governed by their husbands'.[63] The preference mothers might have given to their children over their spouses was in part a function of the different effects of their status upon hers: the mother who shaped the behaviour of her child from a superior position was also a wife continually reminded that she was her husband's inferior. So the subject position of a mother was a more empowering place from which women could speak and write than the subject position of a wife.

One form that spousal obedience was supposed to take compared a wife to the looking-glass or mirror. The advice originated in Plutarch's *Moralia* of the first century, which was translated as *The Morals* in 1603. The section called 'Precepts of wedlocke' strongly influenced many Renaissance humanist and puritan writings on marriage:

Like as a mirrour or looking glasse garnished with golde and precious stones, serveth to no purpose, if it doe not represent to the life the face of him or her that looketh into it; no more is a woman worth ought (be she otherwise never so rich) unless she conforme and frame her self, her life, her maners and conditions sutable in all respects to her husband . . . (even so a wife should have no proper passion or peculiar affection of her owne, but be a partaker of the sports, serious affaires, sad countenance, deepe thoughts and smiling looks of her husband.[64])

Plutarch's ideal wife will 'have no proper passion or peculiar affection of her owne' but will mirror the emotional states of her husband. Dod and Cleaver follow Erasmus and Tilney in repeating this advice at the end of the sixteenth century, so it was available in English in many texts.[65] The women who enacted that advice may have felt still another incursion on their affective lives when they tried to mime the emotional responses of their spouses. Once again the very discourse that created wives as subjects also defined them so fully as the object of their husbands' desire that what it created it also destroyed.

Yet Elizabeth Joceline refuses to be fully effaced when she uses the image of the looking-glass in *The Mothers Legacie to her unborne child*. Joceline's book was written when she was pregnant and under 'the apprehension of danger that might prevent mee from executing that care I so exceedingly desired, I meane in religious training' of her child.[66] She feared she would die in childbirth. But she also considered the value of her book if she should live:

Nor shall I thinke this labour lost, though I doe live: for I will make it my owne looking-glasse, wherein to see when I am too secure, when too remisse, and in my childes fault through this glasse to discerne mine owne errors.[67]

By creating her own looking-glass in her text, Joceline has produced a means of self-assessment. Advice to her child therefore provides an alternative mirror, one that finds its source in something other than her husband's emotional state and offers the same possibility to other women. The irony is that the occasion for this advice is Joceline's sense of her imminent death, for if the threat of death is what prompts her to write, it also makes her self-assertion more acceptable because she might not survive to read it – and she didn't. Four of the five mothers' books were written under this threat: Elizabeth Grymeston dedicates her book to her son because she feels herself 'a dead woman among the living' and is 'doubtfull of thy fathers life'; Dorothy Leigh dedicates hers to her three sons because she sees herself 'going out of the world' and has already lost her husband; M. R. offers her *Mothers Counsell* as a last will and testament to her daughter.[68] Elizabeth Joceline writes before the birth of her first child and dies nine days after the birth. The treatise was 'found in her Deske unfinished', accompanied by a letter asking her husband to convey her book to their child.[69] Each of these mothers presents her text as a legacy or will, and Wendy Wall remarks that 'these textual displays fashioned women as writing subjects whose identities were consolidated by a mortality everywhere linked to the tremendous risk of childbirth'.[70] What allows Joceline to create her own looking-glass, given the restrictions placed upon women's right to authorship, is that she may no longer be present to view it.[71] The mother's text therefore became a substitute not for her material but her spiritual presence. It was a sign of her disembodied spirit. And that is a larger reason why its publication was likely to be acceptable – because it marked her absence.

The contradictions associated with this simultaneous constitution and destruction of women's selves also extend beyond the mothers' advice books. Wall remarks on the presentation of those books as wills that 'it is a strangely performative and self-constituting gesture dependent on the erasure of the subject at the very moment of powerful self-assertion',[72] and she finds similar contradictions in other women's texts. While that 'moment' can be construed as the time of authorial composition, it might also apply to the historical moment addressed by the chapters in this book, for the conjunction of the construction of women's selves and their simultaneous erasure appears again and again in the literature of conduct. In many such texts, exemplary wives are those who prove their love for their husbands through death or self-sacrifice.[73] Tilney's Panthea and Porcia both kill themselves when their husbands die; Alcesta kills herself to cure her husband's disease; Paulina slits her wrists when she learns of her husband's imminent death; Julia dies in premature labour on the false inference that her husband has died.[74] These figures achieve the highest status available to married women, yet the proof of love conveyed by them is catastrophic and tragic: the very love that constitutes them also requires their own death. Like Lucrece, who was a paragon of chastity because she killed herself after she had been raped, providing a story that was continuously told and illustrated throughout these centuries,[75] the very best wife in each of these other accounts is one who proves her love through her own annihilation.

IV

The mothers' self-portraits, too, are predicated on their own erasure, and most Renaissance conduct literature constructed a radically contradictory subjectivity for women. When obliged for religious and cultural reasons to identify subject positions that women could take up and speak from, the best that these writings can do is offer positions that are simultaneously self-destructive. Women's subjectivity, as Wall describes it, is discontinuous, unstable, riven, and both absent and present.[76] So at the same historical moment that the (male) humanist subject was being constituted through a variety of early modern discourses, the female subject was being simultaneously asserted and erased.[77] Women's duty to love was the obligation that also required of them the utmost restraint and the ultimate sacrifice.

Yet since these constructions of women were fundamentally contradictory and unstable, they could also be manipulated in various directions. Leigh's emphasis on women's seed and Joceline's alternative looking-glass open up spaces for women to remake themselves in alternative ways, and those who read their texts encountered women authors with some desires, commitments and agency of their own. Even the complicity of these authors in women's subordination was undermined by the mode of publication of the advice and the engagement of those women in a public discussion of their own responsibilities. The contradictory nature of the texts and those who wrote them reminds one that conduct books are sites of social dispute within a culture, where different positions on doctrine and behaviour are tested, negotiated and suppressed. They rarely speak with only one voice on the complicated and intimate issues of daily living. Instead, they pose questions larger than their answers and offer signs of women's resistance and survival as well as their compromise and defeat. These signs make them especially worth returning to – not only as indices of how women consistently lived their lives in the sixteenth and seventeenth centuries, but as evidence of how they were told they should live them and sometimes refused, or just did something else, or appeared to comply with ideological pressures but preserved a private space from which they resisted appropriation.

This last alternative would have been especially relevant to religious women, for whom a meditative relationship with their God was a space into which no man, supposedly, could enter. Certainly, this God was a patriarchal figure who functioned as an ideological agent in constraining women to a domestic role and religious dogma, so a male perspective not only entered but shaped most of those moments of quiet reflection.[78] But their God was also susceptible during private meditation to being reinterpreted in the image of a woman's needs and desires, since there was no censor at those times and He was perhaps felt to be more sympathetic to women's concerns than many of the earthly men around them. Similarly, when God speaks through a woman in a text, His voice is often difficult to distinguish from hers, and if there is the possibility of appropriation on His side, there is the possibility of projection on hers.[79] While the mothers who wrote advice books were useful agents in disseminating the dominant ideology, they also modified received opinion in order to reflect their own interests and concerns. Returning to those texts now, women readers can find there a source of our own release as well as our own restraint. Looking back through our mothers therefore remains an empowering and unnerving experience, since our discovery that we have a history occurs as we learn how equivocal and paradoxical that history could be.

NOTES

This chapter is dedicated to my mother, Eleanor Wayne Westerlund, whose advice throughout my life has been blessedly and sometimes alarmingly free from the dogmas and constraints in the texts examined here. I am grateful to her for the energy and liberty she brings to almost every new encounter. My thanks also go to Margaret W. Ferguson, Suzanne Gossett, Richard Tillotson, Betty Travitsky, and Helen Wilcox for their astute suggestions for revision.

1. *Aeschylus*, trans. Herbert Weir Smyth (London: William Heinemann; Cambridge, MA: Harvard University Press, 1936), vol. II, lines 658–63, p. 335. The long note to this passage in Aeschylus, *Eumenides*, ed. Alan H. Sommer-

stein (Cambridge: Cambridge University Press, 1989) concludes that 'the audience . . . probably saw Apollo's argument as a clever and specious but fallacious piece of forensic pleading', so there was no consensus about preformationism among the earliest audience of the play (p. 208).

2. Joseph Needham, *A History of Embryology*, 2nd edn (New York: Abelard-Schuman, 1959), p. 440.

3. Thomas Laqueur, *Making Sex: Body and Gender from the Greeks to Freud* (Cambridge, MA: Harvard University Press, 1990), p. 39. Also Daryl McGowan Tress, 'The Metaphysical Science of Aristotle's *Generation of Animals* and its Feminist Critics', *Review of Metaphysics*, 46 (1992), 307–41.

4. Laqueur, *Making Sex*, p. 39 and Aristotle, *Generation of Animals*, 2.4.738b (trans. A. L. Peck (London: William Heinemann; Cambridge, MA: Harvard University Press, 1963), p. 185): 'Thus the physical part, the body, comes from the female, and the Soul from the male, since the Soul is the essence of a particular body.'

5. See Ian Maclean, *The Renaissance Notion of Woman* (Cambridge: Cambridge University Press, 1980), 3.1.3 and 3.3.7 (pp. 29, 34) and Maryanne Cline Horowitz, 'Aristotle and Women', *Journal of the History of Biology*, 9 (1976), 183–213.

6. Tress, 'Metaphysical Science of Aristotle's *Generation*', p. 325 *et passim*; Johannes Morsink, 'Was Aristotle's Biology Sexist?', *Journal of the History of Biology*, 12 (1979), 83–112.

7. Maclean, *Renaissance Notion*, pp. 29–38. For an overview of these theories, see also Angus McLaren, *Reproductive Rituals: the Perception of Fertility in England from the Sixteenth to the Nineteenth Century* (London: Methuen, 1984), chapter 1 – a book that Karen Robertson called to my attention.

8. Maclean, *Renaissance Notion*, p. 36.

9. Laqueur, *Making Sex*, pp. 58–9.

10. *The Scholehouse of Women*, excerpted in *Half Humankind: Contexts and Texts of the Controversy about Women in England, 1540–1640* (Urbana: University of Illinois Press, 1985), p. 148. The poem was anonymously published in 1541, 1560 and 1572; it has been attributed to Edward Gosynhyll, but its authorship is still disputed.

11. Henry Cornelius Agrippa, *Of the Nobilitie and Excellencie of Womankynde*, trans. David Clapham (London: 1542; Ann Arbor: University Microfilms, reel no. 71), sigs. Bl$_v$–B2. This work was given as a lecture in 1509 and first published in Latin in 1523. The English edition was dated 1542. For the date of the lecture I am indebted to Albert Rabil, Jr., whose Latin edition of this text is forthcoming from the University of Chicago Press. In quoting from this and all old-spelling texts, I have modernised i/j, u/v, and long s/s.

12. Mary Beth Rose, 'Where Are the Mothers in Shakespeare? Options for Gender Representation in the English Renaissance', *SQ*, 42 (1991), 299.

13. 1 Corinthians 11:8–9. *The Geneva Bible: a Facsimile of the 1560 Edition*, ed. Lloyd E. Berry (Madison: University of Wisconsin Press, 1969).

14. John Knox, *The First Blast of the Trumpet Against the Monstrous Regiment of*

Women, reprinted in *The Political Writings of John Knox* (Washington: Folger Shakespeare Library, 1985), p. 45.

15. Heinrich Bullinger, *The Christen State of Matrimonye*, trans. Miles Coverdale (Antwerp: M. Crom, 1541; reprinted Amsterdam: Theatrum Orbis Terrarum, 1974), sig. A4ᵥ. Bullinger's book was published in thirteen editions from 1541 to 1575. See the *Short-Title Catalogue of Books Printed in England, Scotland, and Ireland and of English Books Printed Abroad, 1475–1640*, 2nd edn, ed. W. A. Jackson, F. S. Ferguson and Katherine F. Pantzer (2 vols., London: Bibliographical Society, 1976 and 1986), vol. II, nos. 4045–53. Hereafter cited as *STC*. A similar moral of Eve's creation from Adam's rib appears in Christine de Pisan's *Boke of the Cyte of Ladyes*, trans. Earl Jeffrey Richards (New York: Persea Books, 1982), p. 23. This work was first written in French in 1405 as *La Cité des Dames* published in Bryan Ansley's English translation in 1521.

16. My use of the word 'puritan' here derives primarily from Margo Todd's *Christian Humanism and the Puritan Social Order* (Cambridge: Cambridge University Press, 1987), an important book for understanding the alignments between humanists and puritans in social theory. Todd's working definition of puritans is that they 'were a self-conscious community of protestant zealots committed to purging the Church of England from within of its remaining "superstitutions", ceremonies, vestments and liturgy, and to establishing a biblical discipline on the larger society, primarily through the preached word' (p. 14). I use the word in this sense throughout this chapter.

17. Dorothy Leigh, *The Mothers Blessing: Or, The godly Counsaile of a Gentle-woman, not long since deceased, left behind her for her Children*, 4th edn, *STC* 15403 (London: John Budge, 1618; Ann Arbor: University Microfilms, Pollard reel no. 1729). There may have been as many as twenty-three editions; those that are extant appeared in 1616, 1617, 1618 (2), 1621, 1627, 1629, 1630, 1633, 1634, 1636, 1640, 1656, 1663, 1667 and 1674. As compared to these reprintings, Vives's *Instruction of a Christian Woman* appeared in nine English editions and Bullinger's *Christen State of Matrimonye* in thirteen, so Leigh's work seems to have been as popular in the seventeenth century as theirs were in the sixteenth. The timing of the reprintings was also very consistent: the only major gap was from 1640 to 1656, and Elizabeth Richardson's text of 1645 was available to fill it. See note 23.

18. Leigh, *The Mothers Blessing*, pp. 34–6.

19. Genesis 3:15, in *The Geneva Bible*.

20. John Calvin, *The Institutes of the Christian Religion*, trans. Henry Beveridge (Grand Rapids, MI: William B. Eerdmans, 1964), vol. I, p. 412. I am very grateful to Elizabeth McCutcheon for suggesting that I consult this section of the *Institutes*.

21. *Ibid.*, p. 413.

22. *Ibid.*, p. 411, does qualify this assertion by saying, 'For although he was not immediately descended of an earthly father, yet he originally sprang from

Adam', but Mary is still the only human means by which Christ's descent is traced.

23. The five mothers' advice books are Elizabeth Grymeston, *Miscelanea, Meditations, Memoratives* (1604); Dorothy Leigh, *The Mothers Blessing* (1616); Elizabeth Clinton, *The Countesse of Lincolne's Nurserie* (1622); M. R., *The Mother's Counsell, or, Live within Compasse* (1623); and Elizabeth Joceline, *The Mothers Legacie* (1624). Information on reprintings of each text will appear at its first full citation. The advice books are discussed as a group in Elaine Beilin's *Redeeming Eve: Women Writers of the English Renaissance* (Princeton, NJ: Princeton University Press, 1987), pp. 266–85. The three later mothers' works are Elizabeth Richardson, *A Ladies Legacie to her Daughters* (1645), Susanna Bell, *The Legacy of a Dying Mother to her Mourning Children* (1673) and anon., *The Mother's Blessing*, cited as nos. 504B, 96B and 612A in Hilda L. Smith and Susan Cardinale, *Women and the Literature of the Seventeenth Century* (New York: Greenwood Press, 1990). Excerpts from Leigh, Clinton, Grymeston and Richardson appear in *English Women's Voices, 1540–1700*, ed. Charlotte F. Otten (Miami: Florida International University Press, 1992).

24. Gerda Lerner, *The Creation of Feminist Consciousness from the Middle Ages to Eighteen-Seventy* (New York: Oxford University Press, 1993), pp. 116–37 discusses the Frankish mother, Dhuoda, who was born in AD 803 and wrote a manual of conduct for her elder son. For a discussion of German mothers' advice books, see Cornelia Niekus Moore, 'Die adelige Mutter als Erzieherin: Erbauungsliteratur adeliger Mütter für ihre Kinder', *Europäische Hofkultur im 16. und 17. Jahrhundert* (Hamburg: Hauswedell, 1981), pp. 505–10. The date of Caxton's translation of Geoffrey de La Tour Landry's *Book whiche the knyght of the toure made* (STC 15296), which was written for La Tour Landry's daughters, was 1484. For the fathers' advice books, see Louis B. Wright, ed., *Advice to a Son: Precepts of Lord Burghley, Sir Walter Raleigh, and Francis Osborne* (Ithaca, NY: Cornell University Press, 1962), and the discussion in Judith Gero John's 'Commands and Whispers: Renaissance Parental Advice Books, their Tradition, and their Value in Literary Studies' (Ph.D. dissertation, Kansas State University, 1992).

25. Lerner, *Creation of Feminist Consciousness*, pp. 116–37.

26. In *The Imprint of Gender: Authorship and Publication in the English Renaissance* (Ithaca, NY: Cornell University Press, 1993), pp. 285–7, Wendy Wall cites Frances Abergavenny's *Praiers ... committed at the houre of hir death to Ladie Marie Fane (hir only daughter)*, which was published in Thomas Bentley's *The Monument of Matrones* of 1582. Betty Travitsky discusses *The Northern Mothers Blessing* (1597), in 'The New Mother of the English Renaissance (1489–1659): a Descriptive Catalogue', *Bulletin of Research in the Humanities*, 82 (1979), 63–89, and Kristen Poole treats Nicholas Breton's *Mothers Blessing*, (1602) in '"The fittest closet for all goodness". Authorial Strategies in Jacobean Mothers' Manuals', *SEL*, 35 (1995), 69–88.

27. Betty Travitsky was the first to observe a connection between the mothers' advice books and the admonitions to mothers about nursing their children,

especially in relation to Erasmus's dialogue. See 'The New Mother' and 'The New Mothers of the English Renaissance: Her Writings on Motherhood', *The Lost Tradition: Mothers and Daughters in Literature*, ed. Cathy N. Davidson and E. M. Broner (New York: Frederick Ungar, 1980), pp. 33–43. A hundred years before the English humanists, Christine de Pisan had advised women to nurse their own children.

28. Elizabeth Clinton, *The Countesse of Lincolnes Nurserie*, STC 5432 (Oxford: 1622; Ann Arbor: University Microfilms, Pollard reel no. 984), p. 17. This is the only edition.

29. Dorothy McLaren observes that 'rich women of the period had an entirely different reproductive pattern, which was mainly due to their having abandoned maternal breastfeeding', in 'Marital Fertility and Lactation, 1570–1720', *Women in English Society, 1500–1800*, ed. Mary Prior (London: Methuen, 1985), pp. 22–53, quote at p. 23. See also Gail Kern Paster, *The Body Embarrassed: Drama and the Disciplines of Shame in Early Modern England* (Ithaca, NY: Cornell University Press, 1993), pp. 198–208 *et passim*.

30. Erasmus, *The New Mother*, trans. William Burton, reprinted in *Seven Dialogues Both Pithie and Profitable*, STC 10457 (London: 1606; Ann Arbor: University Microfilms, Pollard reel no. 833), sig. O.

31. Todd, *Christian Humanism*, pp. 46–8.

32. STC 10455, 10458 and 10458a. On the title page of *Seven Dialogues* (STC 10457), *The New Mother* or *Puerpera* is identified as '5 Is of putting forth Children to Nurse'. At sig. L, where the colloquy begins, it is called 'A Dialogue of a Woman in Childe-bed', which is also the running title.

33. Erasmus, *Seven Dialogues*, trans. Burton, sig. A2.

34. Barbara Kiefer Lewalski, *Writing Women in Jacobean England* (Cambridge, MA: Harvard University Press, 1993), p. 58, citing 'Relation of the Coronation of the King of Bohemia, etc., with the Ceremonies and Prayers', *Mercurius Gallo-Belgicus*, no, 13 (Cologne, 1619), pp. 97–104. The event is also mentioned in Carola Oman's *Elizabeth of Bohemia* (London: Hodder and Stoughton, 1938), p. 196.

35. John Chamberlain, *Letters*, ed. Norman Egbert McClure (Philadelphia: American Philosophical Society, 1939), vol. II, p. 285. Elizabeth's third son was Prince Rupert, who became known as 'Rupert of the Rhine' when he fought for the Cavaliers during the English Civil War. James's prohibition was therefore singularly inappropriate for one who became such a staunch supporter of the Stuarts. See Josephine Ross, *The Winter Queen: the Story of Elizabeth Stuart* (New York: St Martin's Press, 1979).

36. Lewalski, *Writing Women*, p. 61.

37. Leigh, *Mothers Blessing*, sig. A4.

38. Otten, *English Women's Voices*, p. 304. Southwell's 'Precepts' was a commentary on the ten commandments with long passages of advice to her children, which was never published. The first manuscript is British Library Lansdowne MS 740; the second, written in 1627–32, is available as *The Commonplace Book of Lady Anne Southwell*, ed. Sister Jean Kléné (New York:

Medieval and Renaissance Texts and Studies, 1996). My thanks to Donald Foster for this reference.

39. Cornelia Niekus Moore, *The Maiden's Mirror: Reading Material for German Girls in the Sixteenth and Seventeenth Centuries* (Wiesbaden: Otto Harrassowitz, 1987), pp. 43–4. I am grateful to Cornelia Moore for this reference. A slightly different translation of Sophie's remark appears in Ross, *The Winter Queen*, p. 94.

40. William Gouge, *Of Domesticall Duties* (London: William Bladen, 1622; reprinted Amsterdam: Theatrum Orbis Terrarum, 1976), pp. 513 and 546.

41. *The Works of Francis Bacon*, ed. James Spedding (1862; reprinted New York: Garrett Press, 1968), vol. VIII, p. 113. See also M. St Clare Byrne, 'The Mother of Francis Bacon', *Blackwood's Magazine*, 236 (1934), 758–71.

42. Swetnam, *Arraignment of Lewd ... women*, in *Half Humankind*, p. 245.

43. The leading speaker of *The New Mother* remarks that 'membership in Christ' is 'given to all, both men and women by faith' (sig. L2). See also Todd, *Christian Humanism*, pp. 113–17.

44. Leigh, *Mothers Blessing*, pp. 24–6, 58–9.

45. Juan Luis Vives, *The Instruction of a Christian Woman*, trans. Richard Hyrde (London: T. Berthelet, 1529?), facsimile in *Distaves and Dames: Renaissance Treatises For and About Women*, ed. Diane Bornstein (Delmar, NY: Scholars' Facsimiles and Reprints, 1978), sig. E2$_v$. I have discussed the restraints on women's learning in Vives's text at greater length in 'Some Sad Sentence: Vives' *Instruction of a Christian Woman*', *Silent But For The Word*, ed. Margaret P. Hannay (Kent, OH: Kent State University Press, 1985), pp. 15–29.

46. Elizabeth Joceline, *The Mothers Legacie to her unborne Childe*, STC 14625.7 (London: Robert Allot, 1635; Ann Arbor: University Microfilms, Pollard reel no. 1728), sigs. A5$_v$ and A6$_v$, which are from 'The Approbation', an account of Joceline's life signed by Thomas Goad. The work is extant in editions dated 1624 (2), 1625, 1632, 1635 and 1684 (STC 14624–25.7 and Wing J756); the 1635 edition is noted as the seventh impression.

47. *Ibid.*, sigs. B3$_v$–B4.

48. Elizabeth Grymeston, *Miscelanea, Meditations, Memoratives*, STC 12410 (London: Edward Griffin for William Aspley, 1618?), sig. A2. The work was published in four editions, STC 12407–10, which appeared in 1604, 1606?, 1608? and 1618?.

49. *Ibid.*, sig. A2.

50. Beilin, *Redeeming Eve*, p. 269.

51. M. R., *The Mothers Counsell, or, Live within Compasse*, STC 20583 (London: J. Wright, 1630?; Pollard reel no. 1033), title page. This was the only edition. The female authorship of this text has been justifiably questioned, but it does show the author *performing* the role of mother regardless of his or her gender, thereby implying the authority of the mother's voice.

52. Patricia Crawford, 'The Construction and Experience of Maternity in Seventeenth-Century England', in Valerie Fildes, ed., *Women as Mothers in*

Pre-Industrial England (London: Routledge, 1990), p. 14. I am grateful to Betty Travitsky for this reference.

53. Christine de Pisan, *The City of Ladies*, p. 155.

54. Leigh, *Mothers Blessing*, pp. 30–1.

55. *Ibid.*, pp. 33–4.

56. *Ibid.*, p. 38; Paster, *The Body Embarrassed*, pp. 183–5.

57. Leigh, *Mothers Blessing*, p. 38.

58. Edmund Tilney, *The Flower of Friendship: a Renaissance Dialogue Contesting Marriage*, ed. Valerie Wayne (Ithaca, NY: Cornell University Press, 1992), lines 968–71. This text was published in seven editions from 1568 to 1587 (*STC* 24076–7a).

59. John Dod and Robert Cleaver, *A Godlie Forme of Householde Government*, *STC* 5383 (London: Thomas Man, 1598; Ann Arbor: University Microfilms, reel no. 317), p. 168. The text was published in nine editions from 1598 to 1624 (*STC* 5383–8).

60. This formulation uses the simultanous construction and subjection of the subject presented in Louis Althusser's 'Ideology and Ideological State Apparatuses', *Lenin and Philosophy and Other Essays*, trans. Ben Brewster (New York: Monthly Review Press, 1971), pp. 126–86.

61. Lawrence Stone, *The Family, Sex, and Marriage in England, 1500–1800* (New York: Harper and Row, 1977), pp. 512–13.

62. Paster, *The Body Embarrassed*, p. 185. One of the important works that Paster refers to is Adrian Wilson, 'The Ceremony of Childbirth and its Interpretation', in *Women as Mothers in Pre-industrial England*, ed. Fildes, pp. 68–107. At the Shakespeare Association of America meetings in March 1995, Suzanne Gossett gave a paper called 'Resistant Mothers and Hidden Children', in which she called attention to the ways in which women resisted their husbands and patriarchy by exercising control over the placement, religion, finances and marriage of their children. The history of Elizabeth Cary was important for Gossett's persuasive argument.

63. Gouge, *Of Domesticall Duties*, p. 310. 'Pranke up' here means to elevate or show off.

64. Plutarch, 'Precepts of wedlocke', *The Philosophie, commonlie called The Morals*, trans. Philemon Holland (London: Arnold Hatfield, 1603), pp. 317–18. The passage is cited at greater length in Tilney, *Flower*, ed. Wayne, note to lines 1316–20, and discussed in its versions by Erasmus and Tilney in the introduction at pp. 61–3.

65. Dod and Cleaver, *Householde Government*, p. 229. The advice would have been available in nineteen editions: one English edition of Plutarch's *Morals*, two English translations of Erasmus's *Conjugium*, seven editions of *The Flower* and nine editions of *Householde Government*; but this number would be higher if one counted the many important Latin editions of Plutarch and Erasmus.

66. Joceline, *Mothers Legacie*, sig. A8$_v$.

67. *Ibid.*, sigs. B8–B8$_v$.

68. Grymeston, *Miscelanea*, sig. A2$_v$; Leigh, *Mothers Blessing*, sig. A5$_v$; M. R., *Mothers Counsell*, title page.
69. Joceline, *Mothers Legacie*, sig. A7.
70. Wall, *Imprint of Gender*, p. 293.
71. By 1697, Aphra Behn would write *The Lady's Looking Glass, to Dress Herself by, Or, the Whole Art of Charming* (London: S. Briscoe, 1697), a secular work that advised women on the importance of comfortable clothing and showed them how to conquer one's lover with a pen.
72. Wall, *Imprint of Gender*, p. 286.
73. Renaissance texts that recount the lives of exemplary women include Boccaccio's *Concerning Famous Women*, Christine de Pisan's *Book of the City of Ladies*, Erasmus's *Encomium matrimonii*, Vives's *Instruction of a Christen Woman*, Sir Thomas Elyot's *Defence of Good Women*, Agrippa's *Nobilitie and Excellencie of Womankynde*, Tilney's *Flower of Friendship* and its most immediate source, the Spanish text *Coloquious matrimoniales* by Pedro di Luxan.
74. These lives are discussed at greater length and compared to other Renaissance versions in my introduction to Tilney, *Flower*, pp. 63–5 and notes to lines 1020–93.
75. See Stephanie H. Jed, *Chaste Thinking: the Rape of Lucretia and the Birth of Humanism* (Bloomington: Indiana University Press, 1989).
76. Wall, *Imprint of Gender*, pp. 287–96.
77. See the discussion of humanist education in chapter 1 of this volume; also Catherine Belsey, *The Subject of Tragedy* (London: Methuen, 1985) for an excellent account of the juxtaposition between the constitution of the humanist subject and the exclusion of women from subjectivity.
78. In addition to the ways in which the acts of prayer and meditation were constructed by patriarchal religions, language is so much a product of patriarchal cultures that a woman's thinking was also shaped by the conceptual categories made available or excluded by various linguistic forms.
79. See the discussion of women, speech and religion in chapter 2 of this volume.

CHAPTER 4

Women reading, reading women

Jacqueline Pearson

'Who is't can read a woman?'

(Shakespeare, *Cymbeline*, v.v.48)

The ideological controversies of Renaissance, Reformation, Counter-Reformation, civil war and Restoration created a world where reading was a highly politicised, even potentially subversive, act. In addition, there was particular controversy over the scope and significance of women's access to literacy. This has been well mapped in the case of the rise of the woman writer (see chapter 7), but it has been less fully acknowledged that women's reading was almost equally a site for conflict and anxiety. It has been said that the 'act of writing is a projection of the person who writes into the public domain of discourse',[1] and hence risky for a woman confined by traditional ideologies to a private domestic realm. But reading is more ambiguous. Reading at home might keep a woman to an acceptably private and domestic world: the Tudor educationalist Juan Luis Vives identifies reading with domestic handicrafts as ways in which women's thoughts can be prevented from 'walking and wandering out from home'.[2] Yet reading might equally allow the woman access to a dangerously public domain of discourse. As the 'meeting-place of discourses of subjectivity and socialization',[3] the issue of reading disturbed commentators who found threatening both women's command of their subjectivity and their access to an extra-domestic world. In this chapter I shall be less concerned to map the statistical realities of women's reading than to examine the developing stereotypes of women readers, the metaphors of literacy that gendered reading and writing and thus worked to deter women from the world of books, and the ways in which some women opposed these stereotypes or found ways to use them for their own purposes.

Between 1500 and 1700 rates of female literacy seem to have been lower than male in all classes. According to David Cressy, nine-tenths of women were illiterate at the time of the civil war, compared with two-thirds of men.[4] Literacy levels were rising, although this was probably not a steady evolutionary process: the Jacobean backlash against women's education probably inhibited women readers as well as writers. Regional differences were marked, and class was the crucial determinant. These levels of 'illiteracy', however, indicate a less depressing picture of women's exclusion from culture than they might suggest. Literacy has traditionally been tested by the ability to write one's name: but in this period writing was taught separately from, and at a later stage than, reading, so that even the person unable to write her own name might have reasonably fluent reading skills. Moreover, even by 1700 an oral culture had not been entirely replaced by a print culture, and women participated fully in this oral culture as the special guardians of old tales, proverbs, songs, poems and ballads. 'Passive reading' also presented opportunities even to the functionally illiterate in a society where reading aloud was still common entertainment from the great house down to the village.

POLICING WOMEN'S READING

Conduct and educational works throughout the period deal with the issue of women's reading, sometimes in detail, and a central impulse in virtually all such works is to contain its subversive possibilities. Devotional and instructional works are generally permitted and encouraged: history, and especially lives of famous women, are also thought suitable. It seems more important however to ban 'unsuitable' reading, in particular erotic poetry, plays and romance fiction. Vives warned against 'filthy and bawdy rimes', and considered romance fiction as the moral equivalent of 'serpents or snakes': reading such texts teaches 'wanton lust', and encourages women to become 'ungraciously subtle'. The echoes here of the Fall of Eve are not irrelevant. For Vives, a woman cannot be allowed to 'follow her own judgement' in the choice of reading, but must be directed by 'wise and learned men', for she lacks the power to discriminate.[5] Thomas Salter's *The Mirrhor of Modestie* (1574) makes similar points. Romance fiction and 'lascivious' poetry are a 'pestilent infection' and must be avoided, while 'the lives of godly and virtuous ladies' from the Bible and history are recommended.[6] In such cases, women's reading is to be 'an agent of control more than of enlightenment',[7] an important instrument in the construction of traditional femininity as 'chaste, silent and obedient'.[8]

This attempt to contain women's reading continued into the seventeenth, and indeed into the eighteenth century. A few acceptable kinds of reading are added to history and devotional works – travel books and certain kinds of scientific writing become prominent – and novels gradually replace prose romances as the particular enemy of female virtue. After the Restoration women's reading, at least within clearly delineated boundaries, became increasingly acceptable. Even then, however, different social groups had different expectations and taboos. Katherine Philips, writing within a gentry-class, Royalist circle in the 1650s and early 1660s, easily discussed books with friends of both sexes, while Sarah Fyge Egerton, growing up in the late seventeenth century in a narrow professional family, complained of their attempts to limit her reading to 'my Prayer Book' and 'old receipts of Cookery'.[9]

WOMEN'S READING, 1500–1700

Partly because of the rigour with which women's reading was policed, evidence is difficult to acquire and not always fully trustworthy. Few women bother to record their reading, especially light reading. Puritan Lady Margaret Hoby's diary (1599–1605) presents one typical pattern, a great deal of reading almost exclusively religious and devout (the only exceptions being herbals and other medical works).[10] Evidence is ampler in the later periods: as the number of published women writers increases more evidence becomes available about their reading. A good deal of evidence no doubt remains in unpublished manuscripts, letters, diaries, wills and memoirs.

Few women developed libraries of their own,[11] but some catalogued the books they owned, as did Mary Astell's friend Ann, Countess of Coventry. She was wealthy enough to afford any books she wanted and developed a substantial library, which includes the expected texts, Bibles and religious works, history including a 'history of women', geography, conduct works, cookery books and so on, but also a number of books that virtuous women were not supposed to own or read – for instance 'Modern Novells' and a large collection (128 in 1704) of plays. Coventry seems to have been particularly interested in women writers; she owned the poems of Anne Killigrew, and plays by Aphra Behn, Mary Pix, Delarivier Manley and Susanna Centlivre. Coventry's reputation for virtue did not mean prudery, since her play collection includes such notoriously sexually explicit works as Ravenscroft's *The London Cuckolds*. While the conduct books sought to contain and limit women's reading, women whose income allowed were buying and reading according to their own tastes.[12]

Coventry's library catalogues are an unusual survival, though we do have a few additional examples, mostly from the turn of the century. Elizabeth Freke, educated daughter of a Royalist gentry family, itemised all her property, including her books, in diaries from 1671 to 1714. Reading does not seem to have been very important to her, and she rarely refers to it, although she owned nearly 100 books, including Bibles, sermons and other religious works, books on history and geography, poems by Cowley and Quarles, herbals and medical works, a few law books, a translation of the *Iliad*, and two works of fiction, 'Cassandra, a Romance', and Delarivier Manley's *New Atalantis*.[13] This eclectic collection is both typical and individual: the law books emphasise Freke's bitter and litigious later life, while the rest combine amusingly those books women were encouraged to read and the fiction they actually enjoyed.

What is the hardest to find, especially in the earlier periods, is evidence of recreational reading. This is not because women were not reading fiction, plays and love poems: they were certainly doing so. Shakespeare, for instance, was much read by women virtually from the moment of publication: 'A young Gentle Ladie' read his works in about 1635, and so did Ann Merricke in 1639.[14] There are also a number of satirical references to women's voracious reading of his erotic *Venus and Adonis*, which became, according to stereotype, associated with bored, frustrated middle-class wives. On the whole, though, women tended not to record recreational reading because they had absorbed the conservative anxiety about it. Evidence tends to be available only in fragments, often used in penitential and other autobiographies as an emblem of an immature or unregenerate past. Lucy Hutchinson records her childhood enthusiasm for 'wittie songs and amorous sonnetts or poems' (p. 288),[15] and poet An Collins in *Divine Songs and Meditations* (1653) also remembers her early liking for frivolous reading – 'pleasant histories' that she enjoyed although she knew 'they were not true'.[16]

The diary of Anne Clifford (1590–1676), and other evidence about her reading, is especially valuable in this respect. Clifford came from a family where female literacy was encouraged: her mother was also well read and a patron of the arts ('tho she had no language but her own, yet was there few books of worth translated into English but she read them'[17]), and her daughter inherited this love of books. Her diary records much reading, including (unusually) recreational reading. Her portrait also depicts her surrounded by books at all stages of her life, books that were important to her both as 'entertainment and self-definition'.[18] These books, twenty-five volumes in all, include works of the church fathers but also Ovid, Chaucer, Montaigne, *Don Quixote*, Sidney's *Arcadia*, and works of poets patronised by Clifford and her mother like Spenser and Daniel.[19] The Bishop of Carlisle's funeral oration on Anne Clifford predictably praised her 'much reading' of the psalms and Scriptures but less typically also drew attention to her mastery of other 'kinds of learning'.[20]

METAPHORS OF LITERACY

It was not only the instructions of repressive writers and patriarchs that caused anxieties to women readers. It is likely that they were also disturbed by the way in which literacy was routinely described in gendered metaphors, metaphors that can display disturbing contradictions. Literacy could be troped as a feminised realm whose ruler was the goddess Athene, where power was vested in symbolic female figures, and to which access was permitted by female Muses. Some women certainly used this traditional symbolism to argue for their own access to literacy as writers and readers. One woman poet argues that 'There's ten celestial females govern wit, / And but two gods that do pretend to it', and an enthusiastic woman reader of Katherine Philips tropes men's poetry as a violent assault on Daphne, the goddess of the laurel, which symbolised literary achievement, while she offers inspiration freely to female poets.[21] These images were less empowering to actual women, however, than they might seem. Athene was a notoriously male-identified goddess, and the woman writer's relation to the female muse could be a troubling one: a bitter poem of Ben Jonson describes the woman writer as a lustful 'Tribade', a lesbian whose sexual knowledge of the Muse confirmed the unnaturalness of women's writings.[22]

   If women were not encouraged to be active readers or writers, they were urged instead to be muses and inspire male poets, or were defined as passive texts to be read. Sidney's Stella is a 'fair text', which the male poet will write and which a male reader will 'read'; the 'Browes' of Drayton's Matilda are King John's 'Booke'; and Alexander Craig can 'read' Erantina like 'a snowie sheet / Of paper faire'.[23] Shakespeare's poems and plays, too, are filled with women who are read as texts by men:[24] Bianca in *King John* is a 'book of beauty' (II.i.485); Florizel will 'stand and read' Perdita's eyes (*The Winter's Tale* IV.iv.175–6); Lysander reads Helena as 'love's richest book' (*Midsummer Night's Dream* II.ii.121).

However, if women are passive texts to be read, they might also be passively written by men, as Othello fears that Cassio has written 'whore' on the 'most goodly book' that is Desdemona (iv.ii.73–4). Lucrece, herself an incompetent reader unable to 'read' the book that is Tarquin (101), kills herself after her rape because only through suicide can she author herself in such a way that the text of her body will be 'read' accurately (617–18, 1195). For if women are texts, they may easily be misread, as Pericles' reading of Antiochus' daughter as a 'book of praises' (i.i.16) is flawed by his ignorance of her incest with her father. It is hardly surprising that Cymbeline desperately concludes that women are simply unreadable texts: 'who is't can read a woman?' (v.v.48). Both women writers and women readers must have been deterred by these images of femininity as passivity, as absence, as 'Other'.

On the one hand, literacy was a symbolically feminised realm; on the other, it was also figured as a specifically masculine space, the realm of the Father from which (real) women were barred. Either way, women writers or readers were excluded, either by the law of the Father or by the heterosexual erotics of the muse symbolism. If women were to obtain access, it could be only with the assistance of the male, and a common rhetorical pattern was to present males assisting the aspirations of the female reader, while her path is blocked by other women. Lucy Hutchinson's mother sought to limit her daughter's reading, while her father encouraged her, and Elizabeth Tanfield Cary had similar experiences of an even more extreme kind. Her father supported and guided her reading, but her mother tried to limit it, even to the point of forbidding the servants to give her candles (Cary incurred large debts in bribes): in married life this scenario recurred, and her 'despotic mother-in-law' confiscated her books.[25] Margaret Cavendish depicts just such a situation in the relationship between her female polymath Sanspareille and her supportive father and discouraging mother in *Youths Glory and Deaths Banquet* (1662).

Despite the legitimising of certain types of reading for women by commentators like Vives and Salter, women's reading was a site for anxiety. It is not simply that 'bad' reading was banned, 'good' reading permitted: there often seems a dread of all reading. In the metaphors of the period, women's reading was routinely supposed to cause illness, blindness, madness, or simply female rebelliousness, and the lives of real and fictional women often include stories of attempts to restrict their reading. In her fragmentary autobiography, Lucy Hutchinson (1620–after 1675) records her own passion for reading, which kept her from her needlework, that typical act of service to a traditional ideology of femininity ('for my needle, I absolutely hated it'). Her mother, fearing that reading 'prejudic'd [the] health' of her daughter, sought to 'moderate' this passion, and Lucy would rebelliously 'steale into some hole or other to read'.[26]

Women's reading was also troped as insanity. In Ben Jonson's *The Alchemist* (1610), Dol Common's alleged madness is triggered by her reading: even the devotional reading she pretends to might be dangerous for women if it spills over into an insanely self-assertive passion for religious controversy. In 1645 John Winthrop, first governor of Massachusetts Bay, attributed the insanity of the poet Anne Hopkins to her 'reading and writing ... if she had attended her household affairs, and such things as belong to women ... she had kept her wits'. While for Vives reading could be symbolically equivalent to housework, for Winthrop 120 years later the two are incompatible: women's place is the home, and literacy is only 'proper for men, whose minds are stronger, etc.'.[27] Given these associations of female reading with disease, insanity and transgression, it is hardly surprising to find at least one literate mother, Elizabeth Jocelyn in the preface to *The Mothers Legacie* (1624), leaving instructions that her child, if a daughter, was not to be so educated: presumably she wished her daughter to escape the anxieties and ambivalences that she herself must have felt as a literate woman.

Women's reading, then, was troped as – indeed seemed literally identical to – disease, madness, deception, rebellion and transgression of the boundaries of acceptable femininity. Their reading was viewed as problematic because reading and the possession of books figured power: Margaret Cavendish, Duchess of Newcastle, identifies 'books' with 'crown', 'sword' and 'sceptre' as the instruments and symbols of control that men are reluctant to share with women.[28] Reading can be a self-pleasuring, self-assertive act wholly at odds with traditional ideologies of modest, self-denying femininity. Twentieth-century feminist writers have urged women to become 'resisting' readers, reading texts 'against the grain' to expose their politics and use them for our own purposes.[29] This image of the resisting reader would have been understood by seventeenth-century writers. John Marston's paranoid satirist Kinsayder in *The Scourge of Villainie* (1599) is hostile toward his readers, insulting them and criticising them because he fears their power over him and his poem. They are capable in the act of reading of 'quite altering the sense' (p. 3), reading into his poem 'that which I never meant' (p. 6): ultimately the power of creation is theirs as much as it is the poet's.

Kinsayder's envisaged readers are, it seems, exclusively male, as conventional ideologies of gender would consider appropriate to this sexually explicit satire. But female readers might have similar power to reconstruct the poem or use it for their own purposes, a power that sometimes causes anxiety in male poets but is sometimes actively solicited by them. Edmund Spenser seems to have specialised in dedications to female patron/readers. *The Faerie Queene* (1596) is dedicated to Queen Elizabeth, and most of the poems in *Complaints* (1591), *Daphnaida* (1591), the *Fowre Hymnes* (1596) and 'Prothalamion' have female dedicatees, and Spenser was also the author of a number of lost poems 'all dedicated to Ladies'.[30]

'Astrophel' in *Complaints* mourns Sir Philip Sidney, and involves his female survivors, not only being dedicated to his widow, but also incorporating the 'dolefull lay' (p. 549) of Clorinda, apparently a poem by Sidney's sister the Countess of Pembroke. If this is so, the distinction between writer and reader has been renegotiated, and the conventional image of an active male writer and a passive female reader has been paraphrased as a more equal relation between male and female poets who are both readers and writers. A different but almost equally dynamic relationship between male poet and female reader is implied in the dedication of *Fowre Hymnes* (1596) to Margaret Russell Clifford, the mother of Anne Clifford, and her sister Anne Dudley. Spenser records that he had composed 'these former two Hymnes' – presumably 'An Hymne in Honour of Love' and 'An Hymne in Honour of Beautie' – in his youth, but has now been persuaded by his dedicatees that these poems contain more 'poyson' than 'honest delight'. Consequently he has decided to 'reforme' them by adding poems in praise of 'heauenly and celestiall' (p. 586) love and beauty, which the sisters are said to exemplify. Here the power of the female readers is seen to transform the nature of a text. What is for Marston a competitive, even combative, relationship, becomes for Spenser a co-operative one.

Reading did not only figure power: it might be literally a matter of life and death, and might operate in a gendered way that exemplifies the legal disadvantages faced by women in the sixteenth and seventeenth centuries. A literate man like Ben Jonson might save himself from the gallows through the legal loophole of 'benefit of clergy', by which the ability to read identified the (male) reader as a priest and therefore not subject to secular law. This loophole, however, was not available even to literate women. As one female criminal, Mary Carleton, herself to be hanged for theft in 1673, was to write, 'a woman hath no clergy, she is to die by the law if guilty'.[31]

Women's reading was a site of anxiety because reading figured power, but also because of the persistent association drawn between textuality and sexuality. The woman writer was often depicted as a whore because of her intrusion into a public sphere and her control of the pen, a metaphorical penis.[32] But the woman reader was not necessarily safe from similar accusations. In Thomas Cranley's *Amanda, or the Reformed Whore* (1635), the sexual nature of his protagonist is figured in her collection of erotic poetry and fiction, including Shakespeare's *Venus and Adonis*, Marston's *The Metamorphosis of Pigmalions Image*, and Beaumont's *Salmacis and Hermaphroditus*, and in the anonymous *The Yellow Book* (1656) Mrs Wanton owns a play book and a history, which are the moral equivalents of her collection of 'naked Pictures'.[33]

Jacobean city comedy is full of female (mis)readers whose literary tastes warn of their sexual nature. Chapman, Jonson and Marston's *Eastward Ho!* (1605) contrasts the good, dutiful daughter Mildred with her disobedient sister Gertrude: Mildred apparently does no reading whatever (the source of one classical allusion is explained as what she had 'heard a scholar once say' (1.2.42)), while Gertrude has a shameful knowledge of romance fiction that has taught her pride and false expectations, and has encouraged her to marry the flashy gold-digger Sir Petronel Flash. In Thomas Middleton's *A Mad World, My Masters* (1608), the jealous Harebrain fears that his wife's textual pleasures will lead to sexual ones, so he has 'conveyed away all her wanton pamphlets', and in particular the especially dangerous *Hero and Leander* and *Venus and Adonis* (1.2.46ff).

In comedy of the sixteenth and seventeenth century, any special enthusiasm for reading will almost certainly demonstrate the folly of a female character, and probably her sexual immorality. Shakespeare, too, tends to depict acts of reading by women in a range of suggestive and sinister ways. The reading woman may not necessarily advertise transgressive sexuality, but the very act of reading might render her sexually vulnerable. Iachimo, smuggled into Imogen's bedroom, discovers that she 'hath been reading late, / The tale of Tereus' (*Cymbeline* 11.ii.43–4), presumably the story of Philomel from Ovid's *Metamorphoses*. Imogen's reading of this text of rape seems to lay her open to the psychic rape perpetrated by Iachimo as he violates first her personal space and then her reputation.

This combination of circumstances, the story of Philomel from the *Metamorphoses* and a violated woman reader, recurs in the case of Shakespeare's most literate female character, Lavinia in *Titus Andronicus*.

This cultured woman has 'read' to her nephew 'Sweet poetry and Tully's Orator' (IV.i.13–14) and is 'deeper read and better skill'd' than her male relatives (IV.i.33). After her own rape and mutilation she seeks out a copy of 'Ovid's Metamorphosis' (IV.i.42), where the 'tragic tale of Philomel' (IV.i.47) lends her a language to speak the otherwise unspeakable and to reveal the circumstances of her violation. The *Metamorphoses*, an anthology of stories of rape and attempted rape, serves as a parallel for Lavinia's fate. Somehow, women's reading, even if it does not demonstrate their sexual transgressiveness, is fraught with peril. Both Imogen and Lavinia by their reading advertise a sexual knowledge that, despite their personal innocence, renders them vulnerable. Imogen's reading metaphorically, and Lavinia's literally, traps them into an enactment of images from their texts. Like Ovid's Philomel, Lavinia is raped and has her tongue cut out, and like Cicero, author of 'Tully's Orator', she also loses her hands.

DEDICATING TO WOMEN

We can gauge the period's ideology of gendered reading by noting the number, and kinds, of books dedicated to women. Between 1475 and 1640 at least 163 books were 'specifically directed to ... women' in general,[34] and an even greater number, about 1,780 books, were dedicated to individual women. Suzanne Hull divides books directed to women into four major categories: devotional works; books relating to the controversy about women; fiction; and practical guides, which included texts on medicine, midwifery and herbalism, conduct works, cookery books, and works on handicrafts.[35] Devotional texts and practical guides fed directly a conventional ideology of femininity as service: the other two categories were potentially more two-edged. This issue of dedication is an important one, since at least one woman saw this male practice of dedicating texts to women to legitimise the otherwise problematic area of women's reading. Margaret Tyler, translator of *The Mirrour of Princely deedes and Knighthood* (1578), argued that since men dedicated all kinds of books to women, this proved 'then may we women read such of their works as they dedicate to us' (A4).

Anxieties and contradictions about female readers can be seen even in poems and plays dedicated or otherwise addressed to them. Such dedications and addresses are likely to emphasise the purity and also the power of the female addressee: one critic has argued that Stella becomes 'virtual co-author' of Sidney's sonnet sequence.[36] Such addresses, though, are in reality less likely to allow real power or presence to the female reader than at first appears. Mary Sidney Herbert, Countess of Pembroke, was one of the most frequently addressed female patrons of her age, and yet in work dedicated to her by poets like Abraham Fraunce and Nicholas Breton she is fulsomely praised but also 'positioned and controlled', allowed a place within discourse only 'as an object of representation or on condition of her subservience'.[37] Breton especially appears to praise the Countess as woman, patron and poet, but his poems also work to humiliate and silence her by putting his words in her mouth, words that create an image of her as self-abasingly humble, suffering, doubtful about her poetry, and unable to speak.[38]

An ambivalence about the female dedicatees the poems seem to praise, or indeed about the whole prospect of being read by woman, often haunts poetry of the period. William Barksted's *Hiren: or, the Faire Greeke* (1611) dedicates its first book to Henry, Earl of Oxford, its second to Elizabeth, Countess of Derby, 'the Perfection of Perfection, and wise-dome of Womanhood, the intelligent, and worthily admired'. However, this shift of dedicatee comes at exactly that point in the poem where Hiren breaks her vow of chastity. The male is associated with power and with restraint: the Turkish sultan who has become infatuated with his slave Hiren kills her to demonstrate his command over his passions. The poem chronicles the male's growth in self-command, while the female loses it and becomes associated with unchastity and powerlessness; and the female dedicatee/reader is placed so that she too is implicated in these images. Richard Barnfield's 'Cassandra' (1595) invokes Queen Elizabeth as ideal reader, but again not without ambivalence about her power as queen and as reader, which results in a need to control her, 'Queene of my thoughts, but subject of my verse' (p. 73).[39] Barnfield's female protagonist, Cassandra, who has the power of prophecy but whose predictions are never believed, is another powerful woman whose power the poet needs to undercut and control. These contradictions embody Barnfield's ambivalences about powerful women, prophets, queens or readers.

At the same time other narrative poems of the period display less ambivalence and allow their female readers powerful roles, often quite literally so. Samuel Daniel's *The Complaint of Rosamond* (1592), dedicated to the Countess of Pembroke, not only recognises the power and virtue of this female dedicatee/reader but also offers 'Delia', Daniel's usual muse and ideal reader, a crucial role in the poem. Rosamond, mistress of Henry II and murdered by his jealous wife Queen Eleanor, can be saved only if 'Delia' will 'read our story' (line 43)[40] and offer a sympathetic response. The creative power of the poem is fairly evenly divided between the male poet and the ideal female reader: 'Then she must have her praise, thy pen her thanks' (line 903).

READING ROMANCES

The issue of women's recreational reading creates a number of contradictions. Educational and conduct works try to limit it; and yet a growing number of writers were aware of women as a commercially significant audience and targeted them with exactly those kinds of genres that the conduct books banned. Götz Schmitz has argued that the often erotic Ovidian epyllia of the 1590s, and indeed much courtly literature of the time, were aimed at 'a well-situated, well-educated predominantly female public',[41] and Caroline Lucas has pointed out not only how much Elizabethan romance fiction is dedicated to women – works by Sidney, Barnaby Riche, George Pettie and Robert Greene among others – but also how important is the figure of the female reader in these texts.

This conflict between the need to limit women's reading in the interest of conservative ideologies of femininity and the need to expand it in the interests of the market and the growing professionalisation of literature, might well have opened up a liberating space for individual women readers. Much persuasive work has recently been done on romance fiction as a genre that potentially empowers women by placing female experience of love, marriage and the home at the centre of the literary world rather than at its margins,[42] and the same could be said of the women-centred Ovidian epyllia of the 1590s. However, perhaps as a result of an unarticulated anxiety about displays of female self-assertiveness and pleasure, even those writers who dedicated works to women display anxiety and ambivalence about this courted audience. Caroline Lucas has demonstrated how writers of prose romances appealed to a female audience with 'a version of themselves as ... independent, powerful and significant', but then worked to deny the female reader these qualities and indeed to reinforce 'patriarchal prescriptions'.[43] The result is profound contradiction at the heart of apparently woman-centred texts.

The reading of romance fiction tended to be defined as doubly low status, both female and lower class. Although the historical evidence is against this,[44] the stereotypical reader of romance fiction is a maidservant, whose reading is ridiculed for teaching false expectations and a false idea of her own importance.[45] Such reading is foolish or even dangerous for women of all classes: Biddy Tipkin in Steele's *The Tender Husband* (1705) has had her head turned by 'idle romances' (II.31), and in Delarivier Manley's *Secret Memoirs from the New Atalantis* (1709) a young woman makes herself vulnerable to seduction because she has 'read Romances ... and Plays' (I, p. 150) and as a result becomes pregnant, murders her child and is executed. Feminist writers took different views on the reading of romance fiction. Rationalist feminists like Mary Astell, whose agenda depended on demonstrating the intellectual equality of the sexes, wanted women's reading to be more like men's, and argued that women should 'improve' themselves with 'the study of Philosophy' rather than 'reading idle *Novels* and *Romances*'.[46] The anonymous author of *An Essay in Defence of the Female Sex* (1696) puts exactly the opposite argument, that men's reading should be more like women's: women gained 'Command both of Words and Sense', precisely because while boys are laboriously learning Latin and Greek, they learn experience of the world from '*Romances, Novels, Plays* and *Poems*' (pp. 56–7).

Romances certainly had positive uses for their female readers. Dorothy Osborne (1627–95) read poetry, the classics, religious works, history, biography and travel books,[47] but her favourite – or the most strategically useful to her – books are French romances. Osborne's letters, dating from 1652 to 1670, were mostly written during her courtship with William Temple, which was opposed by their families. She sends him books (including La Calprenède's *Cléopâtre* and de Scudéry's *Artamène; ou Le Grand Cyrus* in 1653) and offers critiques of the romances she has read. She accepts that male and female reading practices might be different, if only because it is unlikely that in his busy public life he can find time to 'bee idle enough at London to reade Romances' (p. 57). But romance not only depicts lovers suffering the same opposition as they are, it also in the form of shared reading strengthens their sense of community and so helps that opposition to be withstood.

Most important, Osborne uses romances as a language to refer to their own situation and problems that could not readily be spoken directly. For instance, she asks his opinion of four suffering lovers in *Le Grand Cyrus*, and concurs that the most worthy of 'compass[ion]' (p. 124) is the lover whose mistress is absent: their sharing of romance reading allows them to express the difficulties of their relationship in coded ways, and their favouring of the absent lover allows them to hint at emotions of pain, fear and loss without breaching the protocols of control and restraint that the letter form demands. Osborne also uses allusions to the romances they are reading to warn Temple covertly that she requires his fidelity, that like Doralize in *Le Grand Cyrus* she would not accept a heart 'that had been offerd to any body else' (pp. 145–6). For Osborne, romances are not only pleasurable. They also provide an effective shared language for the emotional troubles undergone by herself and the man she loves, and also perhaps comfortingly predict an eventual happy ending (Osborne and Temple finally married in 1655).

RESISTING READERS

It is, perhaps, not surprising to find real and fictional women as assertive readers of romance, erotic poetry and plays, using such texts to fulfil their own desires. But even reading that the conduct books were certain could only construct chaste, silent and obedient women, could also be used resistingly. Devotional reading was widely recommended, and 'in iconographic convention a solitary woman with a book represented devoutness'.[48] In Aemilia Lanyer's *Salve Deus Rex Judaeorum* (1611) Virtue carries 'in hir hand [a] Booke' (p. 48) and in *The Faerie Queene* Fidelia, the embodiment of faith, also 'did hold / A booke' (I. ix). But women, real or fictional, could use this iconography rebelliously, to their own advantage; or the iconography could be used manipulatively by others. Thus in *Hamlet* the university-student hero takes for granted his own rights to literacy, but Ophelia is shown using books only as an instrument of Polonius' and Claudius' attempt to analyse and control Hamlet. She is told to 'Read on this book' (III.i.44), presumably, given Hamlet's response, a prayer book, which she uses as a stage property to frame convincingly her interview with him. Here women's reading is identified with deception and disorder; the association of the solitary reading woman with devoutness is quite consciously used as a front, and Hamlet recognises it as such, bitterly suggesting to Ophelia that the best place for such (counterfeit) devotion is a nunnery.

In Middleton's *A Mad World, my Masters* the courtesan Frank Gullman passes herself off as a 'sweet virgin' (1.ii.39) largely by reports that she is constantly 'at her book', which observers understand to demonstrate that she is 'religious' (1.i.192–3). Harebrain is taken in and gets her to read devotional books with his wife, but Gullman only hones Mrs Harebrain's arts of deception. Books are to be used as stage properties ('If he chance steal upon you, let him find / Some book lie open 'gainst an unchaste mind'), while she will conceal the 'stirring' book she really reads 'under your skirt, the fittest place to lay it' (1.ii.91–5): again transgressive sexuality and transgressive textuality are inseparable. By surrounding herself with books of 'heavenly meditations', which 'tax pride or adultery' (III.i.80,82), Mrs Harebrain is able to deceive her husband. In Middleton's play male reading of devotional texts may achieve genuine religious enlightenment and amendment: Penitent Brothel is led to repentance by reading just such a text against adultery (IV.i.1–2) as the women use simply for deception. Mrs Harebrain had a number of literary descendants. Lady Wishfort in Congreve's *The Way of the World* (1700) keeps a number of moral and devotional works in her closet to entertain her visitors while she herself is intriguing to win a husband (Congreve mockingly places in this hypocritical library Quarles, author of *Emblems Divine and Moral* (1635), 'Bunyan's works', and puritan critics of the stage like William Prynne and Jeremy Collier).[49]

Real women could also use religious reading as a cover for other textual pursuits: one of Anne Boleyn's ladies in waiting, Mary Shelton, copied 'idle poesies' into the margins of her prayer book.[50] Moreover, even devotional texts could generate 'resisting' readings. A number of women read the Bible gynocentrically, emphasising that Christ was 'borne of a woman, nourished of a woman, obedient to a woman ... healed women, pardoned women, comforted women ... after his resurrection, appeared first to a woman' (p. 78).[51] They also found the Old Testament full of powerful women, like the warrior, poet, and judge Deborah, and women are 'fallen' not as a result of the sin of Eve but because of the 'mistaken rules' of patriarchy.[52] Seventeenth-century women reread key biblical texts, especially on issues of gender, rebelliously, exploding conservative and misogynous readings. Lanyer's *Salve Deus Rex Judaeorum*, Sarah Fyge Egerton's *The Female Advocate* (1687) and Mary Astell's *Reflections upon Marriage* (1700) all offer revisionist readings of Eve, who is seen as 'simply good', sinning only through 'too much love', 'more Noble' and less culpable than Adam: such rereadings authorise rebellious reformulations of traditional gender relations, in which women are given back their 'Libertie' and accepted as men's 'equals, free from tyranny'.[53]

Even religious reading offered seductive kinds of empowerment for female readers. Understandably, levels of female literacy seem to have been especially high in counter-establishment religious groups – among Lollards, early Protestants, recusants, puritans and extreme non-conformist groups like Quakers. Such groups defined and constructed their difference through constant reading of the Bible and other devotional or polemical works, and in such groups women's reading could be a highly subversive and rebellious act. Anne Boleyn is said to have given Henry VIII Protestant texts to read that hardened his own views on the relationship between crown and papacy: in such a case it could be argued that women's reading changed history. Reading is important in the conversion narratives of a number of puritan women (Hannah Allen in *Satan his Methods and Malice Baffled* (1683) has her sense of fear and despair increased or decreased by her reading) and also in the religious careers of recusant women. Catherine Holland, daughter of a Catholic mother and a Protestant father, was drawn to Catholicism out of 'defiance of her father', and one of her 'provocations to revolt' is the harmless and indeed legitimate practice of 'reading Church history'.[54] Another female convert to Catholicism, Elizabeth Tanfield Cary, was also converted by 'illicit reading', which functioned as a 'liberating catalyst' for her.[55] Even the most legitimate reading could be used rebelliously and liberatingly by the resisting female reader.

One final extreme example of a celebration and legitimation of women's reading is provided by Aemilia Lanyer's *Salve Deus Rex Judaeorum*, a remarkably confident and assertive feminocentric poem, which under cover of an account of Christ's passion and resurrection actually works to celebrate female achievement and protest women's oppression. In particular, Lanyer's poem seeks to legitimise women's writing and reading, a task particularly timely in the counter-feminist backlash of the Jacobean age. This is done in a range of ways. The poem carries dedications to 'all vertuous Ladies and Gentlewoman of this kingdome' (p. 77), and also, extraordinarily, to *nine* named noblewomen patrons,[56] who form a group identified both with the nine Muses and with a feminised version of the 'nine Worthies' (p. 49). Books and the acts of reading and writing, especially by women, are symbolically crucial throughout the poem. The Countess of Pembroke, for instance, is encouraged to read this poem, but her literary competence goes further than this since it also enables her to 'reade' the semiotics of salvation in Christ's wounds (p. 45). Moreover, the central tenets of the Christian religion, incarnation, atonement, redemption and judgement, are persistently imaged as acts of reading and writing. Christ is both a reader and a writer, able to 'reade the earthly storie / Of fraile Humanity' (p. 65), and '[w]riting the Covenant with his pretious blood' (p. 69). Christ's example as writer and reader works to authorise and legitimise the roles of the poet and her dedicatees, and to identify female reading not with transgression but with salvation.[57]

Women's reading, like women's writing, was an area of conflict in the sixteenth and seventeenth centuries. While reading was identified by conservative thinkers with deception, disease, madness and outlaw sexuality, women were able to protest against this symbolism and recuperate it as an image of communication and co-operation, legitimate sexuality, rationality, virtue and even salvation. The conflict would continue into the eighteenth century where the works of women like Delarivier Manley, Eliza Haywood, Jane Barker and Mary Wollstonecraft would expose to detailed scrutiny, from a range of viewpoints, the sexualisation of textuality. This chapter provides an overview of some aspects of women's reading in the period: but it is hardly necessary to say that such an overview cannot help but obscure the differences between different classes,[58] different regions, and different parts of the period. Although some stereotypes remain remarkably constant, it is likely that in the fundamental social and religious changes of the period views on women and literacy also altered. What is needed is a more detailed, nuanced examination of the period with more minute concern for these changes. This would be well worth accomplishing, for more understanding of women readers would not only add to the developing understanding of women's history in this period, but would also change the way in which we view some major canonical authors.

NOTES

1. Catherine Sharrock, 'De-Ciphering Women and De-Scribing Authority: the Writings of Mary Astell', in Isobel Grundy and Susan Wiseman, eds., *Women, Writing, History, 1640–1740* (London: Batsford, 1992), p. 109.
2. Juan Luis Vives's *De Institutione Foeminae Christianae* (1523) was translated into English by Richard Hyrde as *The Instruction of a Christian Woman* (?1529). I quote from Foster Watson, ed., *Vives and the Renascence Education of Women* (London: Edward Arnold, 1912), pp. 43–4.
3. Kate Flint, *The Woman Reader, 1837–1914* (Oxford: Clarendon Press, 1993), p. 43.
4. David Cressy, *Literacy and the Social Order: Reading and Writing in Tudor and Stuart England* (Cambridge: Cambridge University Press, 1980), pp. 121, 2.
5. Watson, *Vives*, pp. 34, 60–2.
6. Caroline Lucas, *Writing for Women: the example of Woman as Reader in Elizabethan Romance* (Milton Keynes: Open University Press, 1989), pp. 16–17.
7. Valerie Wayne, 'Some Sad Sentence: Vives' *Instruction of a Christian Woman*', in Margaret P. Hannay, ed., *Silent but for the Word: Tudor Women as Patrons, Translators and Writers of Religious Texts* (Kent, OH: Kent State University Press, 1985), p. 20.

8. Suzanne Hull, *Chaste, Silent and Obedient: English Books for Women, 1475–1640* (San Marino, CA: Huntington Library, 1982).

9. Sarah Fyge Egerton, 'The Liberty', in R. E. Pritchard, ed., *Poetry by English Women: Elizabethan to Victorian* (Manchester: Carcanet Press, 1990), p. 112.

10. Dorothy M. Meads, ed., *The Diary of Lady Margaret Hoby, 1599–1605* (London: Routledge, 1930).

11. Sears Jayne, *Library Catalogues of the English Renaissance* (Berkeley and Los Angeles: University of California Press, 1956); Lucas, *Writing for Women*, p. 138.

12. Ruth Perry, *The Celebrated Mary Astell: an Early English Feminist* (Chicago and London: University of Chicago Press, 1986), pp. 339–54.

13. Mary Carbery, ed., *Mrs Elizabeth Freke, Her Diary, 1671–1714* (Cork: Guy and Co., 1913).

14. Gary Taylor, *Reinventing Shakespeare: a Cultural History from the Restoration to the Present* (London: Hogarth Press, 1990), pp. 91–2.

15. Lucy Hutchinson, 'The Life of Mrs Lucy Hutchinson, by Herself, a Fragment', reprinted in James Sutherland, ed., *Memoirs of the Life of Colonel Hutchinson* (London: Oxford University Press, 1973), p. 288.

16. Elspeth Graham, Hilary Hinds, Elaine Hobby and Helen Wilcox, *Her Own Life: Autobiographical Writings by Seventeenth-Century Englishwomen* (London: Routledge, 1989), p. 60.

17. Anne Clifford, quoted in Meads, *Lady Margaret Hoby*, p. 7.

18. Graham *et al.*, eds., *Her Own Life*, p. 37.

19. G. C. Williamson, *Lady Anne Clifford* (Kendall: Titus Wilson, 1922), pp. 60–1.

20. Meads, *Lady Margaret Hoby*, p. 60.

21. Sarah Fyge Egerton, 'The Emulation', in Pritchard, ed., *Poetry by English Women*, p. 113: 'Philo-Philippa', commendatory verses to Katherine Philips, *Poems by the most deservedly Admired Mrs KP the matchless ORINDA* (1667).

22. Jonson, 'An Epigram on the Court Pucell', *The Under-wood*, 49 (*Ben Jonson: the Complete Poems*, ed. George Parfitt, (1975; Harmondsworth: Penguin, 1988), p. 195).

23. Sidney, *Astrophil and Stella*, sonnets 67, 71 and 3; Drayton, 'King John to Matilda', *Englands Heroicall Epistles*, line 78; Alexander Craig, *Amorous Songes and Sonets* (1606), reprinted in *The Poetical Works of Alexander Craig of Rose-Craig, 1603–1631* (Glasgow: privately printed for the Hunterian Club, 1873), p. 49.

24. In Shakespeare men can read men (see *Cymbeline* III.iii.55–6), and very occasionally women can read men (*Romeo and Juliet* I.iii.82–9), but usually women are the texts and men the readers.

25. Tina Krontiris, *Oppositional Voices: Women as Writers and Translators of Literature in the English Renaissance* (London: Routledge, 1992), pp. 79–80.

26. Hutchinson, 'Life of Mrs Lucy Hutchinson', p. 288.

27. *Winthrop's Journal, 1630–1649*, ed. James Kendall Hosmer (New York: Charles Scribner's Sons, 1908), vol. II, p. 225.

28. Graham, *et al.*, eds., *Her Own Life*, p. 88.

29. Judith Fetterley, *The Resisting Reader: a Feminist Approach to American Fiction* (Bloomington: Indiana University Press, 1978).

30. 'The Printer to the *Gentle Reader*', preface to *Complaints* (1591), p. 470. (All references from Spenser are from J. C. Smith and E. de Selincourt, *Spenser: Poetical Works* (London: Oxford University Press, 1912).)

31. Graham *et al.*, eds., *Her Own Life*, p. 133.

32. See Sandra Gilbert and Susan Gubar, *The Madwoman in the Attic* (New Haven: Yale University Press, 1979), pp. 3–7.

33. Louis B. Wright, 'The Reading of Renaissance English Women', *SP*, 28 (1931), 682–3. See also Louise Schleiner's discussion of women's reading groups in her *Tudor and Stuart Women Writers* (Bloomington: Indiana University Press, 1994), pp. 1–29.

34. Lucas, *Writing for Women*, p. 9. See also Kate Clarke's forthcoming study of the patronage of the Russell women, based on her PhD thesis (Reading, 1990).

35. Hull, *Chaste, Silent and Obedient.*

36. Clark Hulse, 'Stella's Wit: Penelope Rich as Reader of Sidney's Sonnets', in Margaret W. Ferguson, Maureen Quilligan and Nancy J. Vickers, eds., *Rewriting the Renaissance: the Discourses of Sexual Difference in Early Modern Europe* (Chicago: University of Chicago Press, 1986), p. 279.

37. Gary F. Waller, 'The Countess of Pembroke and Gendered Reading', in Anne M. Haselkorn and Betty S. Travitsky, eds., *The Renaissance Englishwoman in Print: Counterbalancing the Canon* (Amherst: University of Massachusetts Press, 1990), p. 331.

38. See Nicholas Breton, 'The Countesse of Pembrookes loue' (1592), 'The Countess of Pembroke's Passion' (ND), and *The Ravisht Soul, and the Blessed Weeper* (1601), reprinted in Alexander Grosart, ed., *The Works in Verse and prose of Nicholas Breton* (Edinburgh, 1879).

39. Richard Barnfield, *Poems, 1594–1598* ed. Edward Arber (London: Archibald Constable and Co., 1896).

40. M. M. Reese, ed., *Elizabethan Verse Romances* (London: Routledge and Kegan Paul, 1968).

41. Götz Schmitz, *The Fall of Women in Early English Narrative Verse* (Cambridge: Cambridge University Press, 1990), p. 129.

42. For example Janice A. Radway, *Reading the Romance: Women, Patriarchy and Popular Culture* (Chapel Hill: University of North Carolina Press, 1984).

43. Lucas, *Writing for Women*, p. 2.

44. Margaret Spufford, *Small Books and Pleasant Histories: Popular Fiction and its Readership in Seventeenth-Century England* (London: Methuen, 1981), pp. 3–7, 75, 72–3.

45. Lucas, *Writing for Women*, pp. 15–16.

46. Mary Astell, *A Serious Proposal to the Ladies* (1694), cited in Vivien Jones, *Women in the Eighteenth Century: Constructions of Femininity* (London: Routledge, 1990), p. 204.

47. References are to Kenneth Parker, ed., *Dorothy Osborne: Letters to Sir William Temple* (Harmondsworth: Penguin, 1987).
48. Harold Jenkins, Arden *Hamlet* (London: Methuen, 1982), p. 276, editor's note.
49. *The Way of the World* III. i. p. 356.
50. Julia Boffey, 'Women Authors and Women's Literacy in Fourteenth- and Fifteenth-century England', in Carol M. Meale, ed., *Women and Literature in Britain, 1150–1500* (Cambridge: Cambridge University Press, 1993), p. 174.
51. Quotations from Lanyer are from A. L. Rowse ed., *The Poems of Shakespeare's Dark Lady: 'Salve Deus Rex Judaeorum' by Emilia Lanyer* (London: Jonathan Cape, 1978).
52. Anne Finch, Countess of Winchilsea (1661–1720), 'The Introduction' (reprinted in *Anne Finch, Countess of Winchilsea: Selected Poems*, ed. Denys Thompson (Manchester: Carcanet Press, 1987), p. 28).
53. Lanyer, *Salve Deus*, p. 103, 104; Fyge, *Female Advocate*, pp. 2–3.
54. Isobel Grundy, 'Women's History? Writing by English Nuns', in Grundy and Wiseman, eds., *Women, Writing, History*, pp. 131, 133.
55. Tina Krontiris, 'Style and Gender in Elizabeth Carey's *Edward II*', in Haselkorn and Travitsky, eds., *Renaissance Englishwoman in Print*, p. 149.
56. Queen Anne of Denmark; her daughter Princess Elizabeth; Arbella Stuart; Susan Grey, Countess of Kent; Mary Sidney Herbert, Countess of Pembroke; Lucy Harington Russell, Countess of Bedford; Margaret Russell Clifford, Countess of Cumberland and her daughter Anne Clifford, Countess of Dorset; and Katherine Howard, Countess of Suffolk.
57. For a fuller treatment see Jacqueline Pearson, 'Women Writers and Women Readers: the Case of Aemilia Lanyer' in Kate Chegdzoy, Melanie Hansen and Suzanne Trill, eds., *Voicing Women: Gender and Sexuality in Early Modern Writing* (Keele: Keele University Press, 1996) pp. 45–54.
58. See the discussion of literacy and class in chapter 7 of this volume.

CHAPTER 5

Women/'women' and the stage

Ann Thompson

'I will wear the breeches, so I will.'

(William Hawkins, *Apollo Shroving* 1.i.194–8)

I

It seems appropriate to begin this chapter on theatrical matters with a prologue – in fact two prologues – the first taken from a relatively obscure play, William Hawkins's *Apollo Shroving*, an example of the academic drama written for scholars at Hadleigh School, Suffolk, and performed by them on Shrove Tuesday, 6 February 1626. In what Hawkins calls the 'Introduction', the male speaker of the prologue is interrupted by a female spectator called Lala (addressed as 'Mistress Lala, Spinster', or 'Dame Lall') who objects to his use of Latin words and classical names, fearing that she will not be able to follow the play if it is in Latin. At the end of the first scene she leaves, somewhat mollified, with this exit speech:

Well, I see now it will be English. It shall go hard but I'll get a part amongst them. I'll into the tiring house, and scamble and wrangle for a man's part. Why should not women act men, as well as boys act women? I will wear the breeches, so I will. (1.i.194–8)[1]

Lala does not reappear as a character later in the play, but we learn from the cast list that the role of Lala was originally performed by Nicholas Coleman, who also enacted the important role of 'Musaeus, Apollo's Priest and Judge' in iv.v and v.vi, so in this sense 'she' succeeds in getting 'a man's part', though like all performers at the time 'she' is a man anyway.

My second prologue is from the better-known Ben Jonson play, *The Staple of News*, first performed in 1625 and constituting Jonson's return to the public theatre after some nine years of writing court entertainments. Here again the male speaker of the prologue is interrupted by female spectators – Mirth, Tattle, Expectation and Censure:

The PROLOGUE *enters. After him, Gossip* MIRTH, *Gossip* TATTLE, *Gossip* EXPECTATION, *and Gossip* CENSURE, *four gentlewomen ladylike attired.*

PROLOGUE. For your own sake, not ours –

MIRTH. Come, gossip, be not ashamed. The play is *The Staple of News*, and you are the mistress and lady of Tattle; let's ha' your opinion of it. Do your hear, gentleman? What are you, gentleman-usher to the play? Pray you, help us to some stools here.

PROLOGUE. Where? O'the stage, ladies?

MIRTH. Yes, o'the stage. We are persons of quality, I assure you, and women of fashion, and come to see and to be seen: my gossip Tattle here, and gossip Expectation, and my gossip Censure; and I am Mirth, the daughter of Christmas and spirit of Shrovetide. They say 'It's merry when gossips meet.' I hope your play will be a merry one.

PROLOGUE. Or you will make it such, ladies. Bring a form here. [*A bench is brought. They sit.*] But what will the noblemen think, or the grave wits here, to see you seated on the bench thus?

MIRTH. Why, what should they think, but that they had mothers, as we had, and those mothers had gossips (if their children were christened) as we are, and such as had a longing to see plays and sit upon them, as we do, and arraign both them and their poets. (Prologue, 1–20)[2]

The women here claim their right to sit on the stage (an area 'reserved for men' according to the editor of the Revels edition), and to watch and judge the play. They reappear at the end of each act and comment according to their characters, providing for Jonson a sort of pre-emptive critical strike as in the induction to his earlier play, *Bartholomew Fair*.

Thus in both these prologues, written and performed by men, women are represented as trying to get on to the stage quite literally, and to challenge men's monopoly both of the right to act and of the right to judge plays as privileged spectators.

Before 1660 there were no women, only 'women' impersonated by men on the English professional stage; after 1662, however, it became obligatory to cast women in female roles; the patent granted to Thomas Killigrew on 25 April 1662 includes the condition:

And for as much as many plays formerly acted do contain several profane, obscene and scurrilous passages, and the women's parts therein have been acted by men in the habit of women, at which some have taken offence, for the preventing of these abuses for the future, we do hereby strictly command and enjoin that from henceforth ... we do ... permit and give leave that all women's parts to be acted in either of the said two companies for the time to come may be performed by women, so long as their recreations, which by reason of these abuses aforesaid were scandalous and offensive, may by such reformation be esteemed not only harmless delight, but useful and instructive representations of human life.[3]

The euphemistic reference to 'some' having 'taken offence' looks back to the puritan attacks on the immorality of the stage that were in part responsible for the closing of the theatres in 1640; hence the casting of women can be represented as a social and moral reform, though, as Elizabeth Howe demonstrates in her important book on *The First English Actresses*,[4] the use of female players had precisely the opposite effect: 'a good deal of the licentiousness of Restoration drama may be blamed on the sexual exploitation of the actresses' (p. 26). Her chapter 'Sex and Violence' traces how the first professional female performers were 'used, above all, as sexual objects, confirming, rather than challenging, the attitudes to gender of their society' (p. 37).

Howe cites the frequent occurrence of 'couch scenes' in which female characters are discovered, to the gaze of male characters and the audience, asleep on a bed or a grassy bank, 'enticingly *deshabillee*', and she compares the treatment of a similar bedroom scene in Shakespeare's *Cymbeline* (*c.* 1610) and Thomas Southerne's *The Fate of Capua* (1700) to demonstrate 'how far the later dramatist converted the device into voyeurism' (pp. 39–42). In addition, she notes how often Restoration plays included scenes in which women are raped and tortured (and how such scenes are added to adaptations of Shakespeare); how dramatists drew attention to the physical charms of the actresses with heightened erotic language; and how 'breeches roles' in which female characters disguised themselves as males were designed to show off the women's bodies and usually came to a climax in a scene in which the character revealed her true sex by displaying her breasts (pp. 43–57).

It is remarkable how quickly female performers were assimilated into the acting companies and even (as Howe argues) came to influence the number and types of roles for women and the development of new sub-genres of both comedy and tragedy. The continuing use of men to play women's parts in the brief period from 1660 to 1662 quickly became the subject of jokes, as in the following from Colley Cibber's *Apology*:

The King [Charles II] coming a little before his usual time to a Tragedy, found the Actors not ready to begin, when his Majesty not chusing to have as much Patience as his good Subjects, sent to them, to know the Meaning of it; upon which the Master of the Company came to the Box, and rightly judging, that the best Excuse for their Default, would be the true one, fairly told his Majesty, that the Queen was not *shav'd* yet: The King, whose good Humour lov'd to laugh at a Jest, as well as to make one, accepted the Excuse, which serv'd to divert him, till the male Queen cou'd be effeminated.[5]

Edward Kynaston, a man who was still acting women's parts at this time, is much praised by his contemporaries for his skill: John Downes for example remarks that '*Mr Kynaston* ... being then very Young, made a Compleat Female Stage Beauty, performing his Parts so well ... that it has since been Disputable among the judicious, whether any Woman that succeeded him so Sensibly touch'd the Audience as he.'[6] Samuel Pepys records that on 18 August 1660 he went with two other men 'to the Cockepitt play [John Fletcher's *The Loyal Subject*] where one Kinaston [*sic*], a boy, acted the Duke's sister but made the loveliest lady that ever I saw in my life – only, her voice not very good' (*Diary*, I, p. 224).[7] And on 7 January 1661 he records seeing Ben Jonson's *Epicoene, or The Silent Woman*:

Among other things here, Kinaston the boy hath the good turn to appear in three shapes: 1, as a poor woman in ordinary clothes to please Morose; then in fine clothes as a gallant, and in them was clearly the prettiest woman in the whole house – and lastly, as a man; and then likewise did appear the handsomest man in the house. (*Diary*, II, p. 7)

But Kynaston was also seen as something of a curiosity, even a freak. Pepys was curious to meet him after seeing him in *The Loyal Subject*: 'After the play done, we three went to drink, and by Captain Ferrers means, Mr Kinaston and another that acted Archas the Generall came to us and drank with us' (*Diary*, I, p. 224), and Colley Cibber notes that '*Kynaston* at that time was so beautiful a Youth that the Ladies of Quality prided themselves in taking him with them in their Coaches to Hyde Park, in his Theatrical Habit, after the Play' (*Apology*, p. 71).

In this chapter I intend to look at some aspects of this transition from 'women' to women – from men performing female roles to real women taking them over – and at the relatively hidden tradition of female performance behind it. I shall also consider the significance of women as patrons and audiences of the drama during this period. And I shall touch more briefly on the debates about the boy actors and the effect of that convention on female roles and the construction of femininity in the theatre, since that topic has been dealt with more thoroughly elsewhere. The role of women as playwrights is discussed in chapter 12 of this volume.

II

When parliament closed the theatres in 1642 all female parts had been played by men. Within two years of the reopening of the theatres in 1660 all female parts had to be played by women, but was there no tradition of

female performance before 1660? In attempting to explore this question
I came across a now neglected essay, 'Women on the Pre-Restoration
Stage', written in 1925 by Thornton Shirley Graves, who argues that
although women were not employed professionally before 1660, 'there is
considerable evidence to suggest that the employment of females in
dramatic entertainments of one form or another was nothing particularly novel in Elizabethan England' (p. 186).[8]

Graves cites the probable participation of women in the medieval
religious drama, in New Year's mummings and disguisings, in pageants
and other entertainments, as well as in tumbling, juggling and rope-
dancing. Foreign women performed in entertainments at court: two
Flemish women piped, danced and played before Henry VIII in 1511 and
some Italian women shocked Thomas Norton with their 'shameless and
unnaturall tumbling' at Elizabeth's court in 1574. French actresses were
included in the companies that visited the court of Charles I in 1629 and
in 1635. Graves also finds accounts of women being displayed as freaks –
the 'hairy wench' and the 'hog-faced woman' – and of women participating in the display of such freaks, usually as wives and business partners of
strolling actors and showmen.

There is much more evidence for this tradition available now, thanks
to the splendid *Records of Early English Drama* series, with its policy of
publishing county-by-county and town-by-town evidence of all records
of dramatic, ceremonial and minstrel activity in Great Britain before
1642. These documents include financial payments made by public bodies and private households to actors, minstrels and other entertainers,
legal records of licences to entertain either being given or refused, legal
records of disputes and prosecutions relating to entertainers or entertainments, and so forth. It is apparent from them that women did indeed
take part in unlawful games and dancing (especially morris dancing on
Sundays); they acted in Christmas shows and in pageants to entertain
royal visitors; they were paid for singing, dancing and playing musical
instruments; they were exhibited as freaks, and they were granted licences to exhibit freaks. Here are some examples of the evidence:

Item in Rewarde given by the said Dukes coimmaundement vnto certain
frenshe men and ii frenshe women playing afore the said Duke the passion of
our lorde by a vise and also to a young maide a Tumbeller by Reaport of Iohn
kyrk being present maister poley. (Gloucestershire, 1521)[9]

Item gyuyn in Rewarde to the Duke of Suffolkes seruant with the daunsyng bere
& the dansyng wyff. (Plymouth, 1528)[10]

Ciprian de Roson with his wife & two assistantes who shewed forth A lycence vnder the seale of the Master of Revelles authorisinge them to shewe [forth] feates of actiuity together with A beast Called an Elke nowe enioyned to depart the Cytty this present day vppon payne of whippynge. (Norwich, 1614)

The same Day in the afternoone Iohn De Rue and Ieronimo Galt ffrenchmen brought before mr Maior in the Counsell Chamber A Lycence dated the 23th of ffebruary in the xiij^th yeare of Quene Elizabeth & in the yeare of our Lord 1616 thereby authorisinge the said Iohn De Rue & Ieronimo Galt ffrenchmen to sett forth & shewe rare feates of Activity with Dancinge on the Ropes performed by a woman & also A Baboone that can do strange feates, And because the lycence semeth not to be sufficient they are forbidden to play. (Norwich, 1616)

Ths day Thomas wyatt & Ioane his wife brought into this Court A lycence dated the xxvj^th of Iune last vnder the hand and seale of George Buck knight maister of the Revelles for the shewynge of one Peter williams a man monstrously deformed And he hath liberty to shew him this present day and no longer. (Norwich, 1618)

This day Adrian Provoe & his wife brought into this Court A lycence vnder the Seale of the Revelles dated the xij^th day of November 1632 whereby she beinge a woman without handes is lycenced to shew diverse workes &c done with her feete, they are lycenced to make their shewes fower dayes. (Norwich, 1633)[11]

In my researches so far, Joan Wyatt is incidentally the only woman whose full name appears; usually the wife is not named. The evidence suggests that women were, often anonymously, performing circus-like physical feats, as suggested by the conjunction of the dancing bear and the dancing wife in Plymouth. The surviving records may of course be selective and arbitrary, but it does look as though the people of Norwich in particular provided a good market for strange beasts, freaks and 'feats of activity', a phrase that seems to have covered various kinds of physical tricks, including gymnastics. Trinculo in Shakespeare's *The Tempest* might almost have been thinking specifically of Norwich when he considers the potential of displaying Caliban as a freak:

Were I in England now (as once I was) and had but this fish painted, not a holiday fool there but would give a piece of silver. There would this monster make a man. When they will not give a doit to relieve a lame beggar, they will lay out ten to see a dead Indian. (II.ii.27–33)[12]

Women also performed regularly on the continental stage and would have been seen there by Royalists in exile during the Commonwealth period. Margaret Cavendish remarks on one such performer, who acted men's parts as well as women's:

She was the best Female Actor that ever I saw; and for acting a Man's Part, she did it so Naturally as if she had been of that Sex, and yet she was of a Neat, Slender Shape; but being in her Dublet and Breeches, and a Sword hanging by her side, one would have believed she had never worn a Petticoat, and she had been more used to Handle a Sword than A Distaff; and when she Danced in a Masculine Habit, she would Caper Higher, and Oftener than any of the Men, although they were great Masters in the Art of Dancing, and when she Danced after the Fashion of her own Sex, she Danced Justly, Evenly, Smoothly, and Gracefully.[13]

In England, women performed at court in masques during the Jacobean and Caroline period, beginning with James I's Queen Anne of Denmark who first performed in Samuel Daniel's *Vision of the Twelve Goddesses* in 1604: she took the role of Pallas Athena and wore a costume that drew Dudley Carleton to comment critically, 'Her clothes were not so much below the knee that we might see a woman had both feet and legs which I never knew before.'[14] The standard edition of Ben Jonson gives a list of forty-five women who appeared in Jonson's masques alone.[15]

These were private rather than public performances, but they aroused controversy over whether women should perform at all, whether they should enact male roles, and whether they should enact 'inappropriate' roles, such as the blackamoors in Jonson's first masque, *The Masque of Blackness* of 1605. Carleton again records his disapproval, both of the ladies' costumes ('too light and Curtizan-like') and of their 'ugly' black-face make-up.[16] As Suzanne Gossett shows, there were tensions in the simultaneous presence in some of the masques of professional performers whose identities were meant to be ignored and amateur masquers whose identities were meant to be recognised. There were also tensions between professional men and amateur women both playing female roles in the same piece, as for example in Jonson's next masque, *The Masque of Queens*, where male actors played the witches in the anti-masque while female courtiers played the queens in the masque itself. Jonson implies that it was Queen Anne herself who initiated this contrast: 'Her majesty ... commanded me to think on some dance or show that might precede hers and have the place of a foil or false masque' (Gossett, p. 99).

There was considerable controversy over Queen Henrietta Maria's first masque in 1626, partly because she herself acted a part and some of her ladies 'were disguised like men with beards' (Gossett, p. 103). The fact that the casting of these entertainments violated class distinctions was also seen as shocking: male courtiers were equally enacting 'inappropriate' roles when they took on lower-class disguises. The Queen's performance in William Montagu's 1632 pastoral *The Shepherd's Paradise* provoked William Prynne's denunciation of female actors in *Histriomastix*, which in turn provoked James Shirley's *The Bird in a Cage* (1633) – a work satirically dedicated to Prynne and containing in its play-within-the-play a comedy called 'New Prison', which was written, directed and performed by women. Kim Walker has argued that this represents an uneasy attempt to authorise the female actor and demonstrates the struggle to legitimate and at the same time contain this threatening phenomenon.[17]

Jonson foregrounds the issue of sex disguise and performance in two plays written shortly after his last masque for Queen Anne. *Epicoene, or The Silent Woman* (1609/10), in which the 'woman' of the title is finally revealed to be a man, has been read as 'a self-referential theatrical statement that it is possible for a boy to pass convincingly as a woman'.[18] Curiously, after Edward Kynaston's triumph in this role, it was regularly played by actresses in the Restoration period. The 1614 play *Bartholomew Fair* comes to a climax with the Puritan Zeal-of-the-Land-Busy's attack on the puppet play and the puppet's response, which is to refute 'the old stale argument against the Players that the Male among you putteth on the apparell of the Female, and the Female of the Male' by saying 'it will not hold against the Puppets, for we have neither Male nor Female amongst us. And that thou may'st see, if thou wilt, like a malicious purblinde Zeale as thou art!' This is followed by the stage direction '*The Puppet takes up his garment*'.

There has, of course, been much recent debate about the role of the boy actor, with many contributions from feminist and gay critics.[19] There is still some disagreement, even amongst feminist critics, as to whether the use of boy actors was a completely neutral convention, invisible to audiences who just accepted the boy actors as the women they impersonated, or whether the convention drew attention to itself, leading to a knowing awareness of the fact of cross-dressing and a focus on performance as such rather than on naturalistic illusion. As Kathleen McLuskie argues in *Renaissance Dramatists*, the heated moral debates invoking biblical authority for the prohibition of cross-dressing must have made this convention less neutral than others – such as the convention that the presence of a lantern signified a scene taking place at night.[20]

There was also a real-life social practice at issue: women were being enjoined to stop wearing men's clothes on the streets at the same time that men were being enjoined to stop wearing women's clothes on the stage. The so-called 'pamphlet war' that had given rise to a number of virulent attacks on women (and a few defences of them) in the late sixteenth century came to focus in the 1620s on the wickedness of women who adopted masculine modes of behaviour and dress.[21] James I himself entered this controversy, ordering the clergy 'to inveigh vehemently in their sermons against the insolence of our women and their wearing of broad-brimmed hats, pointed doublets, their hair cut short or shorn, and some of them stillettos or poniards, and other such trinkets of like moment'.[22]

Not surprisingly, critics have disagreed as to whether the convention of the boy actor was in effect a subversive one, empowering women (or rather female characters) by allowing them to adopt freedoms denied them in a patriarchal culture. This is broadly the line taken by Juliet Dusinberre, Catherine Belsey and Phyllis Rackin, all of whom see at least the potential for disruption of gender norms.[23] Other critics argue that in the end the disguises serve only to reaffirm the sexual hierarchy: all of the witty heroines dwindle into wives by the end of the play. This more negative line is taken by Mary Free and Jean E. Howard.[24]

Another area of debate has been the kind of eroticism involved: did the convention simply incite homosexual desire for the boy actors as the puritans complained and as modern critics like Lisa Jardine have conceded,[25] or did it liberate desire by unfixing it from the simple binary oppositions of male and female, homosexuality and heterosexuality, as Valerie Traub has argued in *Desire and Anxiety*?[26]

Finally, there is debate over the larger issue of 'identification' with character and the extent to which gender is a dominant factor in this process. Generations of female readers and play-goers have happily identified with Shakespeare's heroines and have taken it for granted that one of the author's greatest skills is his ability to create lifelike women. Current literary theory, in discrediting the idea of a coherent, transcendant self, has made character-based readings of texts seem unfashionably naive, but has not really given us an adequate alternative. In her recent book *Reading Shakespeare's Characters: Rhetoric, Ethics, and Identity*, Christy Desmet develops a more sophisticated 'rhetoric of character' that includes the notion of 'cross-gender identification' whereby audiences and readers are invited to put themselves temporarily in the place of the other.[27] It seems arguable that the convention of the boy actor made this a more straightforwardly available move on the part of the original audiences, and indeed the author.

III

While women were not appearing on the professional Renaissance stage, they nevertheless figured as patrons of the drama in two ways: rich women, mainly but not exclusively aristocrats, were the dedicatees of plays, the patrons of dramatists and protectors of the acting companies. They also acted as facilitators and organizers of domestic dramatic entertainments. Then women of all ranks patronised the drama simply as consumers, as members of the audiences for plays and other entertainments, and, increasingly towards the later part of this period, as readers. More work needs to be done in both areas.

David Roberts has discussed the female patrons of drama in the later seventeenth century[28] but there has been little research on the pre-Restoration period. Suzanne R. Westfall's book *Patrons and Performers: Early Tudor Household Revels* has just one reference to an occasion when 'Lady Honor Lisle purchased a text of an interlude called *Rex Diabole* for her household in 1538.'[29] One wonders if this was unusual, or if organizing entertainments of this kind would in fact have been a natural part of a woman's role as hostess to a large household. We do know that the dowager Lady Russell, widow of Francis Russell, second Earl of Bedford, acted in this capacity by sponsoring a show in the style of a pastoral pageant when Queen Elizabeth visited Bisham in August 1592.[30] And women at the courts of James I and Charles I clearly had a hand in organizing masques.

Fourteen women (all of them titled) are known to have been recipients of the dedications of plays between 1583 and 1633. David Bergeron has attempted to investigate the circumstances of each dedication, the relationship of each dramatist to his dedicatee, and their likely motivations and expectations.[31] He concludes that hope of financial reward was the most obvious but not the only motive. In some cases playwrights were appealing for recognition by an influential family, and specifically for recognition by a fellow writer in such a family (there were dedications to Mary Wroth and Elizabeth Cary). New relationships may have been initiated in this way and existing ones furthered. Lady Russell, Countess of Bedford, receives more dedications than any other woman, from writers such as Samuel Daniel, John Davies, Michael Drayton, John Florio, George Chapman and Ben Jonson, stretching over a period of forty-four years from 1583 to 1627. She was clearly an important figure who supported and rewarded writers. She may have been influential in the release of Ben Jonson from prison following his arrest for his part in

Eastward Ho!, and she introduced Daniel to Queen Anne, for whom he wrote his first masque (Bergeron, pp. 283–5).

Mary Herbert (née Sidney), Countess of Pembroke, also patronised writers including Daniel, who emphasised the importance of women as patrons in the revised dedications to his *Cleopatra* in 1611. As Bergeron puts it, these relationships were not just about cash but about 'reputations secured, possibilities gained, doors opened, and the more intangible qualities of guiding and supporting spirits' (p. 290).

Again, there is more information to be gleaned from the invaluable documents collected in the *Records of Early English Drama* series. There are many references to payments made by women (usually aristocratic women) to players, minstrels, bearwards and other entertainers. One woman I would like to single out for attention (and further research) is Joyce Jeffreys of Hereford, an unmarried, untitled, but wealthy woman whose account-book for the period 1638–48 records many payments to various sorts of entertainers including frequent sums to 'the waites of the citty' and one-off payments to 'a man that had ye dawncing hors' and 'a boy that did sing Like a black byrd'.[32] She also hired fiddlers and dancers, including the following instances where female performers seem to be involved:

> [Feb. 1638]   gave Mrs mary wallwin, mary powell & fidlers 18 d.
> [Sept 1639]   given meggc Λ dawnccr j d.
> [April 1640]   gave hoddy: for dauncing: j d. & mr dansies maid 6 d.
> [Jan. 1641]   gave the 2 fidlers 6 d. and Mrs bifords dawghter 6 d.
> [March 1642]   gave megge a dauncer i d.[33]

More is known about women in the audience, based on three kinds of evidence: actual records of individual women known to have attended plays, general references to women as theatre-goers from sources other than the plays themselves, and references in prologues, epilogues and the texts of plays. In his book *Playgoing in Shakespeare's London*, Andrew Gurr lists 15 women amongst his 162 identifiable theatre-goers from 1567 to 1642, which does not seem very many, but he nevertheless assumes a high proportion of women in the audiences and argues that this testifies to the popularity of plays amongst that part of the population who were illiterate (usually supposed to include some 90 per cent of women).[34] Ann Jennalie Cook further assumes that women would have had more leisure to go to the theatre in the afternoon than men.[35] There were, as Alfred Harbage points out, simply more women than men in the population of London at this time by a ratio of thirteen to ten.[36]

Gurr, Cook, Harbage and others draw on a range of references to women in the audiences at the 'public' theatres made by visiting foreigners like Thomas Platter, Philip Julius and Orazio Busino, who regularly marvel at the relative freedom of the English women to attend the theatre. Contemporary attacks on the theatre by preachers and moralists tended to assume that most if not all female theatre-goers were prostitutes or women of easy morals. In her article '"Bargains of Incontinencie": Bawdy Behaviour in the Playhouses', Cook examines this charge in detail and concludes that while it is an exaggeration, it cannot simply be dismissed as groundless:

Playhouses were not simply brothel houses, but neither were they innocent assemblies of spectators solely intent upon the aesthetic satisfactions of the performance. The theaters apparently deserved their reputation as excellent places for men to meet women of all degrees of availability.[37]

The visiting foreigners comment on women going to the theatre unaccompanied by men, but Anne Halkett found this difficult. She writes in her 1644 *Autobiography*:

I loved well to see plays . . . yett I cannot remember 3 times that ever I wentt with any man besides my brothers . . . and I was the first that proposed and practised itt for 3 or 4 of us going together withoutt any man, and every one paying for themselves by giving the mony to the footman who waited on us, and he gave itt to the playhouse, And this I did first upon hearing some gentlemen telling what ladys they had waited on to plays, and how much itt had cost them, upon which I resolved none should say the same of mee.[38]

It is not clear what kind of theatre the independently minded Anne Halkett and her female friends attended, but scholars such as Michael Neill and Keith Sturgess have argued that more women went to the 'private' theatres during the Caroline period, encouraged by the example of Queen Henrietta Maria who attended a number of performances at the Blackfriars and the Phoenix.[39]

It has also been maintained that the presence of 'ladies' had an influence on the development of the drama: James Shirley in his prologues attributes to them a generally civilising effect and a new 'purity of language and action'. In a more negative spirit, some later writers have blamed women for what is seen as a prevailing sentimentalism and lack of vitality in the Caroline drama, though it was by no means just the women in the audience who prided themselves on their refined and sophisticated tastes.

An important source of information about women spectators in the

pre-Restoration drama is, of course, the plays themselves, particularly
the prologues and epilogues to the plays as performed, and prefaces and
commendatory verses in published texts. Richard Levin, having studied
the references to women play-goers in these texts, concludes cautiously
that 'during the Renaissance women were generally regarded as a
significant component of the theater audience, and that their interests
and feelings seem to have been taken into account by at least some of the
playwrights of the period'.[40] A notable example is the epilogue to
Shakespeare's *As You Like It*, in which the actor playing Rosalind addresses the women and the men in the audience in turn as separate
groups. The theatrical evidence used by Levin, however, like that of the
other scholars cited above, comes from the London theatre, and mainly
from the latter part of the period, thanks to the substantial increase in the
relevant prefatory matter. Alan H. Nelson, editor of the Cambridge
volume in the *Records of Early English Drama* series, was prompted by
Levin's essay to collect and publish the evidence for women attending
plays not in London but in Cambridge.[41] He finds examples of women in
the audience at performances put on for royal visits in 1564, 1615 and
1632, and of women attending performances in colleges in 1592, 1600,
1629 and 1632. He argues that the presence of women in the audience,
especially in 1632, increased the pressure for plays to be performed in
English rather than Latin, even in male-dominated Cambridge – a
notable triumph, one would like to suppose, for William Hawkins's
'Dame Lall' referred to at the start of this chapter.

Jonson's Gossips who long 'to see plays and sit upon them, and [to]
arraign both them and their poets' may have been taken equally
seriously – at least as a real threat. In a thoughtful essay that builds on the
accumulated evidence, Jean E. Howard addresses the 'problem' of the
female spectator, who is seen by her contemporary critics like Stephen
Gosson in *The Schoole of Abuse* (1579) as both endangered and dangerous.
Ostensibly her sexual purity and her reputation are potentially harmed
by her presence in the theatre, but she is also worrying to Gosson
because she is difficult to classify: 'in [the public space of the theatre]
women became unanchored from the structures of surveillance and
control "normal" to the culture and useful in securing the boundary
between "good women" and "whores".'[42] A woman in the theatre may,
Howard suggests, become empowered and not simply victimised. She is
'licensed to look' (p. 36), to judge, to exercise autonomy; 'the very
practice of play-going put women in positions potentially unsettling to
patriarchal control' (p. 46). While being careful not to exaggerate the real

power of women in such a situation, Howard argues that their presence in the theatre was 'part of a process of cultural change which could help to unsettle the gender positions and definitions upon which masculine domination rested' (p. 47).

By the time of the Restoration, women were not only in the audience but on the stage and indeed 'behind' it, holding the playwright's pen. Elizabeth Howe makes a strong case for the influence of the first English actresses on the history of the Restoration drama: although they did not, like some of their male colleagues, write their own material, they were more than mere mouthpieces. She cites the development of comedy from 1660 to 1700, with its cynical focus on adultery, inconstancy and conflict between the sexes, which is in part attributable to the provocative view of the actresses and society's attitude to them as whorish, fickle and sexually available.[43] Similarly, she argues for the influence of the actresses on what came to be called 'She-tragedy', with its emphasis on love and pathos. And even further, the particular skills and personalities of the performers inspired the creation of suitable roles, rather as film stars like Bette Davis and Joan Crawford inspired roles in the Hollywood productions of the 1930s and 1940s. Howe specifically analyses the casting of Elizabeth Barry as a sympathetic, even tragic mistress or prostitute, and the pairing of Barry with Anne Bracegirdle in plays contrasting 'the angel and the she-devil'. These are by no means feminist texts, but they are woman-centred in significant ways.

Finally, coming full circle from the prologues with which I began this chapter, it is clear that female performers came to dominate dramatic epilogues during the Restoration period.[44] There were at least 100 epilogues between 1660 and 1710 written to be delivered by specifically named actresses and others written to be delivered by any female speaker. These numbers are far higher than those for epilogues to be spoken by men. If the epilogue determines the mood the audience takes away, then real women did (if only temporarily) get the last word.

NOTES

I would like to acknowledge the help of Sasha Roberts in researching this chapter, and the helpful comments made by friends and colleagues in London, Stratford and Sofia when earlier versions of it were delivered as talks/conference papers. It is dedicated to the memory of Lizzie Howe, whose book partly inspired it, and who was brutally and senselessly murdered when she went to teach at the Open University Summer School in York in 1992.

1. William Hawkins, *Apollo Shroving*, ed. Howard Garrett Rhoads (Philadelphia: University of Pennsylvania Press, 1936).

2. Ben Jonson, *The Staple of News*, ed. Anthony Parr (Manchester: Manchester University Press, 1988).

3. Quoted by Elizabeth Howe in *The First English Actresses: Women and Drama, 1660–1700* (Cambridge: Cambridge University Press, 1992), pp. 25–6.

4. *Ibid.*

5. Colley Cibber, *An Apology for the Life of Colley Cibber* (1740), ed. B. R. S. Fone (Ann Arbor: University of Michigan Press, 1968), p. 71.

6. Montague Summers, ed., *Roscius Anglicanus, or an Historical View of the Stage* (London: Fortune Press, 1947), p. 19.

7. Robert Latham and William Matthews, eds., *The Diary of Samuel Pepys* (11 vols., London: Bell, 1970–83).

8. *SP*, 22 (1925), 184–97.

9. Audrey Douglas and Peter Greenfield, eds., *Records of Early English Drama: Cumberland, Westmoreland, Gloucestershire* (London and Toronto: University of Toronto Press, 1986), p. 359.

10. John M. Wasson, ed., *Records of Early English Drama: Devon* (London and Toronto: Toronto University Press, 1986), p. 223.

11. David Galloway, ed., *Records of Early English Drama: Norwich, 1540–1642* (London and Toronto: Toronto University Press, 1984), pp. 142, 150, 156–7, 211.

12. G. Blakemore Evans, ed., *The Riverside Shakespeare* (Boston: Houghton Mifflin, 1974).

13. Margaret Cavendish, *Sociable Letters* (London, 1664), letter 115, pp. 406–7.

14. Suzanne Gossett, '"Man-maid, begone!": Women in Masques', *ELR*, 18 (1988), 96–113, 98.

15. C. H. Herford, Percy and Evelyn Simpson, eds., *Ben Jonson* (11 vols., Oxford: Clarendon Press, 1925–52), vol. x, pp. 440–5.

16. Gossett, '"Man-maid, begone!"', p. 98. *The Masque of Blackness* has attracted attention from recent critics interested in the issue of race; see for example Yumna Siddiqui's essay in the special issue of *RD* on 'Renaissance Drama in an Age of Colonization' (23, 1992), and Kim F. Hall's essay in Margo Hendricks and Patricia Parker, eds., *Women, 'Race', and Writing in the Early Modern Period* (London and New York: Routledge, 1994).

17. Kim Walker, '"New Prison": Representing the Female Actor in Shirley's *The Bird in a Cage*', *ELR*, 21 (1991), 385–400.

18. Gossett, '"Man-maid begone!"', p. 102.

19. See, for example, Marjorie Garber, *Vested Interests: Cross-Dressing and Cultural Anxiety* (London: Routledge, 1992); Jonathan Dollimore, *Sexual Dissidence: Augustine to Wilde, Freud to Foucault* (Oxford: Oxford University Press, 1991); and Stephen Orgel, *Impersonations: the Performance of Gender in Shakespeare's England* (Cambridge: Cambridge University Press, 1996). I have published a brief survey of relevant work in 'Shakespeare and Sexuality', *SS*, 46 (1994), 1–8.

20. Kathleen McLuskie, *Renaissance Dramatists* (Hemel Hempstead: Harvester, 1989), especially pp. 100–22.

21. For further discussion of the 'pamphlet war' see chapters 1 and 11.

22. Reported in a letter by John Chamberlain dated 25 January 1620, as quoted in Katherine Usher Henderson and Barbara F. McManus, eds., *Half Humankind: Contexts and Texts of the Controversy about Women in England, 1540–1640* (Urbana: University of Illinois Press, 1985), p. 17.

23. See Juliet Dusinberre's section on 'Disguise and the Boy Actor' in *Shakespeare and the Nature of Women* (London: Macmillan, 1975), chapter 4; Catherine Belsey, 'Disrupting Gender Difference: Meaning and Gender in the Comedies', in John Drakakis, ed., *Alternative Shakespeares* (London: Methuen, 1985), pp. 166–90; and Phyllis Rackin, 'Androgyny, Mimesis, and the Marriage of the Boy Heroine on the English Renaissance Stage', *PMLA*, 102 (1987), 29–41.

24. Mary Free, 'Shakespeare's Comedic Heroines: Protofeminists or Conformers to Patriarchy?', *SB*, 4 (1986), 23–5; Jean E. Howard, 'Crossdressing, the Theater, and Gender Struggle in Early Modern England', *SQ*, 39 (1988), 418–40.

25. See Lisa Jardine, *Still Harping on Daughters: Women and Drama in the Age of Shakespeare* (Brighton: Harvester, 1983), pp. 9–36.

26. Valerie Traub, *Desire and Anxiety* (London and New York: Routledge, 1992). See also Susan Zimmerman, ed., *Erotic Politics: Desire on the Renaissance Stage* (London and New York: Routledge, 1992).

27. Christy Desmet, *Reading Shakespeare's Characters: Rhetoric, Ethics, and Identity* (Amherst: University of Massachusetts Press, 1992), especially pp. 134–63.

28. David Roberts, *The Ladies: Female Patrons of Restoration Drama* (Oxford: Oxford University Press, 1988).

29. Suzanne R. Westfall, *Patrons and Performers: Early Tudor Household Revels* (Oxford: Oxford University Press, 1990), p. 110.

30. J. H. Wiffen, *Historical Memoirs of the House of Russell* (1833), quoted by Bergeron (cited in note 31 below), pp. 275–6.

31. David M. Bergeron, 'Women as Patrons of English Renaissance Drama', in Guy Fitch Lytle and Stephen Orgel, eds., *Patronage in the Renaissance* (Princeton, NJ: Princeton University Press, 1981), pp. 274–90.

32. David N. Klausner, ed., *Records of Early English Drama: Herefordshire, Worcestershire* (London and Toronto: Toronto University Press, 1990), pp. 191–2.

33. *Ibid.*, pp. 190–3.

34. Andrew Gurr, *Playgoing in Shakespeare's London* (Cambridge: Cambridge University Press, 1987), pp. 55–9. Literacy rates are difficult to determine in this period. For a brief discussion of the evidence relating to women's literacy, see the introduction to *Her Own Life: Autobiographical Writings by Seventeenth-Century Englishwomen*, ed. Elspeth Graham, Hilary Hinds, Elaine Hobby and Helen Wilcox (London and New York: Routledge, 1989), pp. 10–11. There is further discussion of women's literacy in chapters 4 and 7 of this volume.

35. Ann Jennalie Cook, *The Privileged Playgoers of Shakespeare's London, 1576–1642* (Princeton, NJ: Princeton University Press, 1981).

36. Alfred Harbage, *Shakespeare's Audience* (New York: Columbia University Press, 1949).

37. *SS*, 10 (1977), 271–90, 286.

38. Quoted in Gurr, *Playing in Shakespeare's London*, p. 58. Gurr assumes that this remark refers to play-going in the 1630s.

39. Michael Neill, '"Wit's Most Accomplished Senate": the Audience of the Caroline Private Theatres', *SEL*, 18 (1978), 341–60; Keith Sturgess, *Jacobean Private Theatre* (London: Routledge and Kegan Paul, 1987), pp. 18–25. The older terms 'public' and 'private' theatre were never strictly accurate. Gurr suggests replacing them with, respectively, 'amphitheatre' and 'hall', which would have the advantage of emphasising the outdoor/indoor distinction (as cited in Gurr, *Playgoing in Shakespeare's London*, p. 13).

40. Richard Levin, 'Women in the Renaissance Theatre Audience', *SQ*, 40 (1989), 165–74, 174.

41. Alan H. Nelson, 'Women in the Audience of Cambridge Plays', *SQ*, 41 (1990), 333–6.

42. Jean E. Howard, 'Scripts and/versus Playhouses: Ideological Production and the Renaissance Public Stage', *RD*, 20 (1989), 31–49, 35.

43. Howe, *The First English Actresses*, p. 63.

44. *Ibid.*, pp. 91–8.

CHAPTER 6

Feminine modes of knowing and scientific enquiry: Margaret Cavendish's poetry as case study

Bronwen Price

Ignorance, far more than knowledge, is what can never be taken for granted. If I perceive my ignorance as a gap in knowledge instead of an imperative that changes the very nature of what I think I know, then I do not truly experience my ignorance.[1]

Barbara Johnson's statement not only challenges conventional modes of knowing but demands that we look at the concepts of knowledge and ignorance in a different light. In her view, ignorance does not signal the mere absence and opposite of knowledge. Rather, it is conceived as a means of examining and reconsidering the very terms within which we understand things.

The question of how knowledge is formulated, the cultural practices that inform how it is defined and the uses to which it may be put, have been major preoccupations of a range of feminist writing for some time.[2] Such work unsettles the polarities that have found common currency in the meanings produced by modern Western culture. Johnson, for example, interrogates the conventional opposition between knowledge and ignorance and especially the gender markings inscribed in the cultural meanings of those terms which seek to fix woman (and ignorance) as the supplementary opposite of man (and knowledge). In turn, the effect of this radical questioning is to challenge the way in which we make sense and shape of the world in language: it is to shift, unfix and exceed the boundaries of knowing, and to contest the power relations that underlie gender relations.

In this chapter I consider the work of a leading seventeenth-century woman writer, Margaret Cavendish, Duchess of Newcastle, in the light of this feminist practice. I shall focus on Cavendish's initial work, *Poems, and Fancies*, which appeared for the first time in 1653, exploring, in

117

particular, the relationship between her verse and seventeenth-century ideas about science and the subject. I shall treat Cavendish's work as a case study in revealing how women's writing of the early modern period may problematise boundaries and structures of knowing, and also suggest ways in which it provides alternative modes of knowing.

As is frequently pointed out in this volume (for example, chapters 2, 7 and 10), women's status as writing subjects in the early modern period was ambivalent, informed by a complex set of negotiations concerning the circulation and publication of their work. To speak publicly as a woman meant exceeding prevailing concepts of appropriate feminine behaviour, and this frequently had a bearing on both what and how women wrote: their work often aligns itself with or engineers its way around the values of chastity, modesty and obedience.[3] But in seeking to produce speaking positions, women's writing – sometimes even in spite of itself – often seems to problematise and challenge the limits of discourse and therefore what it is possible to say and know. In common with much other women's writing of the period, Cavendish's work provides an exploration and redefinition of positions from which to speak through its interventions with existing discourses, as well as demonstrating a self-consciousness about the relationship between gender and the processes of writing.

However, while women's writing frequently shares these starting points, it is important to recognise the difference between women's writing and writing contexts. As chapter 9 of this book demonstrates, variations in the conditions of production and reception of women's verse generates a wide range of poetry; there is an extensive array of religious poetry written by women in the early modern period, from the carefully wrought Calvinist psalms of the aristocratic Mary Sidney (1599) to the extemporised prophetic utterances of Anna Trapnel's *The Cry of a Stone* (1654). In each case, though from very different perspectives and contexts, God's word authorises what is spoken. Yet both works participate in the struggle for meanings over religious authority taking place during the period so as to unsettle the submissiveness implied by their speech. While God is located as the source of knowledge underwriting their words, the mediating role that both speakers undertake grants them political agency. The seventeenth century also sees the emergence of a variety of secular verse written by women. Such poetry often interacts with conventions and genres in which women are traditionally located as the objects rather than the subjects of speech. Thus Katherine Philips's poetry employs platonic tropes and the values of feminine virtue, such as chastity and privacy, to construct a world of female friendship unpenetrated by the terms of masculinity, while Aphra Behn's draws upon Ovidian, Petrarchan and pastoral conventions in order to challenge and revise the politics of sexuality and desire inscribed in those codes.[4]

Cavendish's poetry, however, starts from a quite different point of departure from these in taking science and natural philosophy as its chief subjects. While the presentation of philosophical ideas was commonplace in poetry by men and to some extent by women, a series of poems about atomist theory, such as we find in *Poems, and Fancies*, most certainly was not. It is verse such as this that gives Cavendish's work its special character, as well as some of its difficulty. What is perhaps most striking about her poetry is indeed its entry into new areas of investigation, for this enables it to exploit the concept of 'ignorance' and explore other possible knowledges.

Cavendish was writing at a period in which the parameters of modern modes of knowing were being mapped out. Within the epistemological crisis taking place during the seventeenth century, empiricism and rationalism emerged as the dominant methods for gaining access to 'truth' and for attesting certainties, while God was ultimately to be displaced by Man as the origin of knowledge.[5] The foundation of the Royal Society in 1660, the first formal academy of science, signalled the institutionalisation of such concepts of knowledge that were to become so fundamental to modern Western thought.

In broad terms, the Royal Society was built on the ideas of Francis Bacon (1561–1626). Empiricism, observation and experimentation were central to the Baconian paradigm of science, as well as the idea of a 'plain' language in which 'the facts of nature'[6] could be made more readily available. This scientific model was, according to Bacon, for those 'who aspire not to guess and divine, but to discover and know, who propose not to devise mimic and fabulous worlds of their own, but to examine and dissect the nature of this very world itself'.[7] Truth, it appeared, could be obtained if the correct method was employed and if 'proper rejections and exclusions' were made.[8] The authenticity contained in Bacon's paradigm was affirmed through the negation of what were sited as other modes of thought, so that a demarcation was drawn between fantasy and fact, hypothesis and empirical evidence, imagination and observation.

However, while claiming to provide reliable criteria for establishing 'progressive stages of certainty',[9] the language of early modern science had a significant bearing on the construction of gender, power and knowledge. As Keller points out:

the gender markings that have pervaded virtually all of the discourse of modern science ... were especially prominent in early writings. In particular, a series of arguments have been put forth for the central role played by the metaphoric equation, first, between woman and nature, and collaterally, between man and mind, in the social construction of modern science.[10]

In connection with this, Keller stresses the importance of 'the rhetorical shift in the locus of essential secrets from God to Nature... Nature, relieved of God's presence, had itself become transformed – newly available to inquiry precisely because it was newly defined as an object'.[11] Nowhere is this shifting use of language more apparent than in Bacon's writing. His charting of 'a new and certain path for the mind to proceed in' is encoded within metaphors of sexual conquest, appropriation and colonisation, in which the ultimate goal is to enlarge 'the bounds of Human Empire' and to achieve 'the empire of man over things'.[12] Knowledge is thus formulated as conterminous with power, where Man is conceived of afresh – his identity as a thinking, knowing and empowered subject affirmed through his difference from that which is to be known, while the 'female' object/body of nature is cast as lacking intelligence and life. Such boundaries between 'deconstructed nature and reconstructed man'[13] serve, in Baconian discourse, to legitimise the scientific project.

If the seventeenth century marks the inception of such scientific practices, they were also defined, as my examples from Bacon suggest, precisely in reference to resistance and difference – what they excluded or suppressed, what lay outside and beyond the frontiers of knowledge they attempt to establish. In this chapter I shall be concerned with Cavendish's exploration of such areas; modes of knowing that exceeded the boundaries of knowledge being founded during the seventeenth century. The 250 poems that make up *Poems, and Fancies* examine uncharted, speculative areas of science, the earth and universe, and the human body. The volume is divided up into thematic areas, which include the inner workings of the brain, atomist theory, the possible existence of other worlds and battle.

As a woman entering these domains of knowledge, Cavendish disturbed the conventional enclaves of female propriety. The appearance of *Poems, and Fancies* resulted in accusations of plagiarism,[14] and her ideas were largely dismissed on the grounds of her gender. She was excluded from membership of the all-male Royal Society, and on her single notorious visit to a Royal Society meeting she was prevented from participating in any of the proceedings. While her husband, Sir William, was more sympathetic to her interests, she occupied only a peripheral position in his scientific circle, and her work was largely dismissed by her contemporaries as 'eccentric'.[15]

'Eccentric' suggests that Cavendish's work lies outside or off the centre – on the one hand peripheral, but on the other troubling and unsettling received practices of 'central' thought. It is some of the implications of this ex-centricity that we need to consider. In what ways, for example, do her poems make interventions with ideas that have come to be accepted as forming the genesis and basis of modern thought? In what ways does her poetry offer us a different view of concepts of knowledge that have since become predominant? What sort of subject positions can a 'female' speaker take up in approaching bodies of knowledges acquired by patriarchal interests? In the light of these questions I shall examine the way in which Cavendish's poetry troubles the boundaries of epistemological practices being established during the early modern period and destabilises demarcations between knowledge and ignorance in a way which is both interesting and challenging.

I

'The Elyzium', a poem which presents an imaginary journey through the brain, touches on some of these ideas. In particular, it problematises emergent notions of rationalism. If the scientific model of Bacon is associated with the development of empiricism as a central paradigm for examining nature, the philosophy of René Descartes (1596–1650) is linked with the beginnings of modern concepts of rationalism and an interior sense of self, in which the mind is located as the centre and origin of certain knowledge. Cavendish's poem, however, worries such modes of knowing through its investigation of the brain's inner landscape:

> The Elyzium
> The *Brain* is the *Elysian* fields; and here
> All *Ghosts* and *Spirits* in strong dreams appeare.
> In gloomy shades sleepy *Lovers* doe walke,
> Where soules do entertain themselves with talke.
> And *Heroes* their great actions do relate,   5
> Telling their *Fortunes* good, and their sad Fate;
> What chanc'd to them when they awak'd did live,

Their World the light did great *Apollo* give;
And what in life they could a pleasure call,
Here in these *Fields* they passe their time withall.   10
Where *Memory*, the *Ferriman*, doth bring
New company, which through the *Senses* swim.
The *Boat Imagination's* alwayes full,
Which *Charon* roweth in the *Region scull*;
And in that *Region* is that *River Styx*,   15
There some are dipt, then all things soon forgets...[16]

The poem guides us through the cerebral arena in an exploratory journey, where the brain is treated as both the source and the object of knowledge. The brain is not examined from an objectified outer perspective, but rather we are taken inside and wander through it. How does the brain operate? In what ways does one part of the brain act upon another? Are all brains the same? In what sense is the brain an 'elyzium'? It is these questions that we are led to consider. As the brain is opened to our view, so the space of the skull takes on the proportions of mythic tracts, envisaged as a subterranean realm in which 'strong dreams' (line 2) resonate. It is a marginal place that blurs divisions between conscious and unconscious, the terrestrial and the incorporeal, life and death, incorporating the region that leads to heaven and hell (lines 14–15).

It is in this sense that the cerebral terrains of 'The Elyzium' trouble the demarcations being cast by the incipient Cartesian epistemology. In Descartes's writing the brain is located as the site of control and discipline, whose workings are refined to a rational, thinking, knowing subject:

I thereby concluded that I was a substance, of which the whole essence or nature consists in thinking, and which, in order to exist, needs no place and depends on no material thing; so that this 'I', that is to say, the mind, by which I am what I am, is entirely distinct from the body.[17]

For Descartes, this first-person subject is identified with the mind, which must be abstracted as a place of certainty and source of knowledge divided from that which it doubts and knows:

so that if I wish to find anything certain and assured in the sciences, I must from now on check and suspend judgement on these opinions and refrain from giving them more credence than I would do to things which appeared to me manifestly false.[18]

The brain depicted in Cavendish's poem, however, embodies various spectral, half-conscious, unrelated figures who arbitrarily roam through the cerebral sphere and whose 'knowledges' are transcribed within converging, fragmented narratives and half-recorded discontinuous tales. Here there is no solitary, doubting 'I' or concern with an authentic, originary subjectivity. Rather, certainty and doubt are related only to 'Fortunes' and 'Fate' (line 6) – pre-written histories that have no one originary point.

The dualism that Descartes proposes is challenged by other scientific writing of the period. Anne Conway (1631–79), who was among one of the very few other women writing on science during the seventeenth century, also questions Descartes's ideas. Her *The Principles of the Most Ancient and Modern Philosophy* explicitly states that 'The Philosophy here treated on is not Cartesian'[19] and defines 'the Internal Productions of the Mind, *vis.* Thoughts'[20] as a process of vital regeneration. Thoughts are perceived by Conway as living creatures, 'being all our Internal Children, and all of them Male and Female, that is, they have Body and Spirit; for if they had not a Body, they could not be retained, nor could we reflect on our own proper Thoughts'.[21] The mind, then, includes body, which is regarded as crucial in retaining 'the Spirit of the Thing thought on', and provides 'the Seed of our Brain', which enables 'certain Spiritual Generation in us'.[22]

However, although mind, body and spirit are established as inseparable and interdependent, Conway, nevertheless, identifies the body and spirit that make up thoughts in conventional Aristotelian terms: the body is equated with woman and the spirit with man. It is perhaps significant that, even though Conway opposes the dualistic and mechanistic theories of Descartes and Hobbes, her ideas belong more specifically within the received debates of the period and were treated more seriously by the male scientific community than those of Cavendish. Her philosophy particularly coincides with that of Henry More, Van Helmont and Leibniz, and, indeed, her *Principles* was mistaken for the work of Van Helmont after it posthumously appeared in 1690.[23]

Cavendish's poem, however, speaks from outside contemporary scientific discussions and disrupts distinctions between mind, body and spirit more fundamentally than the work of Conway. Indeed, 'The Elyzium' explores the very operations of the brain that Descartes treats as suspect and whose pronunciation is ascribed to 'insane persons'[24] – the mythic, dreams, the unconscious, that state in which discontinuities are displayed, in which fantasies assume a free reign and where resemblances reverberate. The poem itself mirrors the processes it presents, layering resemblance on resemblance, fiction on fiction. It retells old myths in a strange place, so that the brain appears as a dark mysterious continent, full of promise and dread, unpredictable and unknowable.

'The Elyzium' is one of many poems about the brain and its operations. Others include 'Similizing the Braine to a Garden', 'Of the Head', 'The Motion of Thoughts'. While the mind's 'I' is interiorised, autonomous, split off from what is other than itself in Descartes's writing, where 'I admit in myself nothing other than a mind',[25] Cavendish's poems present the brain as an elusive unenclosed arena, within which proportions shift and images flood, as it is linked up with and contains all manner of things. The poems thus seem to trouble the basis and configurations upon which male 'knowledge' is being established in the seventeenth century. Those very separations and oppositions that are identified and classified by the new science are decompartmentalised and reassembled in the cerebral realms of Cavendish's poetry in a way that is ex-centric to what Susan Bordo defines as the 'Masculinization of Thought'[26] inscribed in Cartesian science. Instead, the poems bring into question what constitutes a brain, how it operates, whether it is knowable, whether it is gendered. It is in these ways that Cavendish's poems destabilise the grounds upon which modern concepts of rationalism are founded, and, in turn, the formulation of male identity and knowing to which these concepts are tied. In disrupting the newly constructed cerebral terrains, the poems resist the classifications of identity and difference, subject and object, science and nature, knower and known, so central to gender categorisation.

II

Whereas Cavendish's exploration of the brain eclipses any sense of certainty and mastery of knower over known, the poems dealing with atom theory seem to offer a world established upon fixed knowable principles. While atoms are invisible and infinite, they are presented as working within a comprehensive mechanistic cosmos. The titles of the poems themselves (and there are about fifty in all) indicate the location of the atoms within a process of definition, classification and explanation: 'The joyning of severall Figur'd Atomes make other Figures', 'What Atomes make Change', 'Of Loose Atomes', 'Of Sharpe Atomes'. The nature of matter, it appears, is reduced to a theory of identification, where the practice of measurement is applied as a universalising principle, whereby the invisible is made visible and cognisable. In this way the poems engage in the central considerations of atomist theory and indeed support its basic assumptions: that atoms differ in shape, size and motion; that their shapes are significant to the production of physical qualities; and that a change in nature is a result of changes in the motions of atoms and their configurations as solid bodies.[27]

Cavendish's poems, though, extend the terms of atomist theory beyond the proportions of the received debate, applying it as an explanatory system to a vast array of things, such as illness, psychological change, death, life and creation. It is the implications of the verse concerning the latter topics that indicate the extent to which Cavendish stretches atomist theory, for they suggest, as Lisa Sarasohn argues, an 'atheistic materialism',[28] presenting a non-hierarchical cosmos in which atoms are eternal and infinite and may themselves create a world. The titles of these poems suggest this: 'A World made by Atomes', 'All things are govern'd by Atomes', 'If Infinite Worlds, Infinite Centres'. It is important to note that the political and philosophical theorist Thomas Hobbes (1588–1679), a member of Charles Cavendish's scientific circle and a key advocate of atomism, was himself accused of impiety for his propositions about matter.[29] However, other significant contributors to the atomist debate of the Cavendish circle, such as Descartes and Gassendi, were, according to Sarasohn, 'careful to separate' the concepts of infinity and the eternal 'from their doctrines of matter, because in a Christian cosmology only God can be eternal and infinite'.[30] In this respect Cavendish's poems shift atomism to a degree where it becomes unacceptable within the terms of the central discussion, questioning the authority of the ultimate source and master of knowledge (so far left intact), God the Father.[31]

While Cavendish's atomist theories seem to be secularised, suggesting an early separation between scientific and religious 'knowledge', they are also presented to us in verse. The poems thus unsettle the terms of identification in which they seem to partake, setting into play the demarcations of the discursive practices being established by the emerging epistemology of 'science'. Bacon's advocation of a plain prose style, distinct from rhetoric, was taken up as the appropriate discourse of science. Such a use of language would, it was argued, attend to its 'matter' rather than its use of words, and this would, in turn, provide clearer access to the material matter – the referent – that was being discussed.[32] By placing her classificatory theory of atoms in poetry, though, Cavendish uses a form eccentric to its content. She thus highlights the process of representation and problematises the very methods she employs.

The preface to *Poems and Fancies*, which is addressed 'To Naturall Philosophers', draws attention to this seeming contradictory combination of science and poetry:

I cannot say, I have not heard of *Atomes*, and *Figures*, and *Motion*, and *Matter*; but not throughly *reason'd* on: but if I do erre, it is no great matter; for my *Discourse* of them is not to be accounted *Authentick*: so if there be anything worthy of noting, it is a good Chance; if not, there is no harm done, nor time lost. For I had nothing to do when I wrot it, and I suppose those have nothing, or little else to do, that read it. And the Reason why I write it in *Verse*, is, because I thought *Errours* might better passe there, then in *Prose*; since *Poets* write most *Fiction*, and *Fiction* is not given for *Truth*, but *Pastime*; and I feare my *Atomes* will be as small *Pastime*, as themselves: for nothing can be lesse then an *Atome*.[33]

On the surface it appears that the speaker's reasons for writing in verse are an excuse for 'ignorance' and 'error' and, at this level, science and poetry seem to be compartmentalised.[34] Science is equated with reason, accuracy and authenticity, while poetry is associated with 'Fiction', pursued merely as a 'Pastime', and thus marginalised under the shadows of the serious business of seeking out 'Truth'. This division between serious business and supplementary activity also implies a traditional separation between gender. Thus, as she boldly addresses her male audience in order to justify her participation in atomist theory, the speaker seems to submit to the discrimination and authority of their superior knowledge, presenting her corpus as an object of deficiency. She must confess that she is unqualified to enter the exclusive, censored realm of science, offering only a fake version of this special knowledge, a forgery with no authentic value, pursued merely because she had 'nothing to do'. Similarly, any interest her corpus incites would surely be because the reader had 'nothing, or little else to do', engaging in a passing flirtation with the 'female' text. Her voice is therefore eccentric to the main scientific debate performed in its proper corpus of prose, for her poetic 'Discourse' is probably full of errors, she cannot say for certain, she does not know.

However, the apparent trivialisation of the speaker's theories is double-edged, indicating her deviation from a passive role to one of textual activity. Indeed, her unauthorised entry into and dislocation of the patriarchal domain of scientific debate shifts the boundaries and conditions of this circumscribed area of knowledge to make uncertain the binary oppositions that, on the surface, are accepted. The speaker's 'ignorance' disturbs the knowledge of the paternal think-tank she addresses by not engaging in its terms when discussing atomism, and so questions its sacrosanctity. She makes no claim to 'reason' about atoms, nor is this regarded as important. Authenticity is not part of her project, and is perceived as being of 'no great matter', so that she cannot be in error or show ignorance. The preface thus seems to put into play the premises for producing scientific knowledge. It troubles the paradigm of method and measurement to which the atom poems seem on the surface to contribute by highlighting their representation in verse. The result is that atomist theory is taken out of the proportions of 'rational' thought and the search for 'Truth' and into the realms of fiction. Science is made manifestly textual.

This problematising of the terms of scientific identification comes to the foreground in 'It is hard to beleive, that there are other Worlds in this World', a poem that considers the possible existence of other worlds within the familiar space of the 'known' world. This idea is not unique to Cavendish. Anne Conway, for example, suggests 'that in every Creature, whether the same be a Spirit or a Body, there is an Infinity of Creatures, each whereof contains an Infinity, and again each of these, and so *ad infinitum*'.[35] Conway locates her theory within a notion of divine order, where the infinity of indiscernible life-forms is regarded as signifying the ultimate greatness of God the Infinite, 'for as one Infinite may be greater than another, so God is still Infinitely greater than all his Creatures, and that without any comparison'.[36]

Cavendish, however, provides no such context and instead focuses her attention on the imperceptible worlds-within-worlds for their own sake. But she begins by contemplating and questioning the way in which we make sense of things:

> *It is hard to beleive, that there are other* Worlds *in this* World
> Nothing so hard in *Nature*, as *Faith* is,
> For to beleive *Impossibilities*:
> As doth impossible to us appeare,
> Not 'cause* 'tis not, but to our *Sense* not cleere;
> But that we cannot in our *Reason* finde, *As it seems to us.* 5
> As being against *Natures Course*, and *Kinde*.
> For many things our *Senses dull* may scape,
> For *Sense* is *grosse*, not every thing can *Shape*.
> So in this *World* another *World* may bee,
> That we do neither *touch, tast, smell, heare, see*. 10
> What *Eye* so *cleere* is, yet did ever see
> Those *little Hookes*, that in the *Load-stone* bee,
> Which draw *hard Iron*? or give *Reasons*, why
> The *Needles point* still in the *North* will lye.

As for *Example, Atomes* in the *Aire,*   15
We nere perceive, although the *Light* be *faire.*
And whatsoever can a *Body* claime,
Though nere so *small, Life* may be in the same.
And what has *Life,* may *Understanding* have,
Yet be to us as buried in the Grave...[37]   20

The possibility that there may exist unmapped territory right before
'our' eyes, where there appears to be nothing, suggests the limitations of
'our' capacity to know. 'Impossibilities' are defined only in terms of the
demarcations of 'our' knowledge and belief, for 'Impossibilities' only
seem so because they are to 'our Sense not cleere' (lines 3–4). The
ambivalence of the word 'Sense' implies that sense-perception is inter-
woven with how 'we' make sense of things. The poem, however,
describes the defectiveness of this means of forming understanding,
referring to 'our Senses dull' that 'may scape' 'many things' (line 7) and
impossibilities that only seem so 'But that we cannot in our Reason finde'
(line 5). Indeed, that there may be life unknown to 'us' in other worlds
within this world, suggests also the possibility of other ways of understanding things and other knowledges beyond 'our' comprehension
(lines 19–20).[38]

Nothing, however, seems specifically to signify 'nothing to be seen'. It
is the ocular in particular that is placed in doubt as a key source of
knowledge, for the poem disorientates the clear sense assumed by the
eye, pinpointing its myopia and distortions. The emphasis on, and
questioning of, the visual as the means of achieving knowledge is
especially significant, for, as Emily Martin suggests:

Historically in the West, vision has been a primary route to scientific knowledge.
We speak of 'knowledge as illumination, knowing as seeing, truth as light';
throughout Western thought, the illumination that vision gives has been associated with the highest faculty of mental reasoning... The emphasis on *observation,* on mapping, diagramming and charting, has meant that the 'ability to
"visualise" a culture or society almost becomes synonymous for understanding
it'.[39]

But who are the 'we' whom perceive observation as tantamount to
understanding? In the poem 'we' suggests a corporate eye/I whose
knowledge is authorised by a social agreement – the collaborative eye/I
of a patriarchal scientific body perhaps? However, the voice of the poem
speaks from a non-aligned position from within this 'we' to disrupt the
social bond and to make plural and uncertain the grounds of its knowledge, thus refusing the closure of ocular perception, for even to the most

vigilant onlooker 'nothing' may be 'as buried in the Grave' (line 20) although a source of life.

It is, therefore, perhaps no coincidence that 'nothing' is a term used to describe the female genitalia during the Renaissance, or that nature, whose 'secrets' the scientific eye seeks to unveil and discover, is traditionally regarded as female.[40] The poem, however, puts into play the category 'nothing' by showing that 'nothing' may include many things that are both excluded and hidden from the eye/I of science, for 'buried' implies both non-knowledge and that which is repressed.

In these ways the poem seems, in particular, to work against the incipient Baconian scientific method that, as I suggested above, sought to disclose 'the secrets of nature' by 'entering and penetrating into' its 'holes and corners' through a practice of empiricism, observation and experimentation.[41] In this scientific paradigm the invisible 'inner chambers'[42] of nature are to be made visible and thus 'knowable'. Further, the sexual–political terms Bacon employs are incorporated within a method whose searches claim to hold a mirror up to nature, as if nature were immediately accessible and unmediated by representation:

For I admit nothing but on the faith of eyes, or at least of careful and severe examination, so that nothing is exaggerated for wonder's sake . . .

And all depends on keeping the eye steadily fixed upon the facts of nature and so receiving their images simply as they are.[43]

'It is hard to beleive', however, unsettles these delimitations of science, which form its conclusions 'by proper rejections and exclusions' and through the affirmation of 'a sufficient number of negatives',[44] for the poem admits 'nothing' precisely as a site of 'wonder'. It deflects the transparent observations of the detached knowing eye/I by speculating on the invisible, destabilising the fixture of the scientific gaze to make uncertain 'the facts of nature',[45] so that 'this very world'[46] appears elusive. Solid evidence and hard facts are brought into question by the fluid speculations of the poem, which are allowed to roam unrestrained and release that which lies 'buried' within the Baconian paradigm.

Cavendish's poem, then, disturbs and remaps the boundaries of knowledge and ignorance, foregrounding the problems that are subliminal in the 'atom' poems. 'It is hard to beleive' speaks from an unknowing position, which, at the same time, is one of knowledge; a position that is masterful, but simultaneously one that troubles and destabilises the authority and authorship of the detached, fixed, scientific, presumably male eye/I over 'female' nature, for 'nothing', the poem suggests, cannot be penetrated, deciphered or contained within sight. Knowledge is removed from the visual arena of sense and located within the realms of the visionary – that of non-sense. Ignorance and knowledge are thus put into play, for the means of procuring knowledge is shown to be founded on ignorance, while this challenge to knowledge and its production offers a revaluation of ignorance, which is regarded as providing the source and scope for other possible knowledges in the poem. Once again, Cavendish disrupts the very foundations of the categories of emergent masculine epistemology.

III

'A Description of the Battle in Fight' turns attention from the invisible realms of 'nothing' to the graphic display of the male body at the brink of its potency; from the speculation of unseen life-forms lying within the frame of nature to the spectacle of the battlefield and its scenes of mass destruction; from the non-sense that accompanies the contemplation of other worlds to a meticulous sensuality in the presentation of the theatre of war. It is, indeed, an important poem in the Cavendish corpus precisely because of its analysis of the masculine:

> *A* Description *of the* Battle *in Fight*
> *Some* with *sharpe Swords*, to tell, O most accurst,
> Were above halfe into the bodies thrust:
> From whence fresh streams of *bloud* run all along
> Unto the *Hilts*, and there lay clodded on.
> *Some*, their *Leggs* hang dangling by the *Nervouse* strings,   5
> And *shoulders* cut, hung loose, like flying wings.
> Here heads are cleft in two parts, *braines* lye masht,
> And all their *faces* into slices hasht.
> Braines only in the *Pia Mater* thin,
> Which quivering lyes within that little skin: 10
> Their *Sculls* all broke, and into peeces burst,
> By *Horses hoofes*, and *Chariot wheeles*, to dust.
> *Others*, their owne *heads* lyes on their owne laps,
> And *some* againe, halfe cut, lyes on their *Paps*;
> Whose Tongues out of their mouthes are thrust at length;   15
> For why, the strings are cut that gave them strength.
> *Their eyes* do stare, the *lids* wide open set,
> The *little Nerves* being shrunk, they cannot shut.
> And *some* again, those *glassie bals hangs by*,
> Small slender *strings*, as *Chains* to tye the Eye.   20
> Those *strings*, when broke, *Eyes* fall, which trundling roun,
> Untill the *filme* is broke upon the ground.

In *death*, their *teeth* strong *set*, their *lips* left bare,
Which *grinning* seems, as if they angry were...

Some like *Virgins*, that cast their eyes down low   125
Through shamefastnesse, although no fault they know,
Nor guilty are, but overcome with strength,
Though not consenting, yet is forc'd at length;
As *Chastity*, so *courage* forc'd we finde,
To lay down *Arms* though sore against their minde...   130

All in *death* lay, by *Fortune* they were cast,   153
And *Nature* to new *formes* goes on in hast...

Smoak from their bloods into red *clouds* did rise,   161
Which *flasht* like *lightning* in the living *eyes*,
Their *groans* into the middle *region* went,
Ecchoes in the *Aire* like *Thunder* rent;
Winds rarified, *sighs* such gusts did blow,   165
As if ascended from the *shades* below.
Men strives to dye, to make their names to live,
When *gods*, no certainty to *Fame* will give.[47]

Here we are presented with an improper, eccentric version of 'Man', as
he is literally turned inside out, taking the form of dismembered,
mutilated flesh. The male body appears, not as the property of a single
subject, territorialised, closed and regulated, but as disconnected portions, offering an untotalisable, indefinite sum as 'some' mixed with
'others', thus making non-sense of the thinking, knowing, observing 'I' of
science. The male head is dethroned, lying estranged in the laps of its
owners (line 13). The sphere of the rational centre of man – the mind – is
reduced to pulverised matter, crushed under the hooves of beasts (lines
7–12). The eye is dislocated, gazing blankly and unknowingly, protrud-
ing but unseeing (lines 19–22). The arena of war, indeed, puts into play
the possibility of 'receiving . . . images simply as they are' and of making
discriminations through 'proper rejections and exclusions',[48] as the
visual images of this military crucible merge with the visionary. The
bared teeth of men offer merely a mask of strength and potency, beneath
which lies the death's head (lines 23–4).

The effect of this hybrid site of military intercourse, exchange and
death is to raise questions about male sexuality. The sensual erotic
display of intense and frenetic activity contains a libidinal urgency that
ruptures the solid proportions of the male form, where, at the zenith of its
assertion, it is split open and dismembered; this intense moment of
labour and production points to disempowerment and annihilation. The

'thrust' that links the performance of those emblems of phallic power, the sword and the tongue (lines 1–2 and 15), here indicates debilitation and displacement, the sword striking indiscriminately, the tongue forced out of the mouth.

The military arena provides a spectacle that at once affirms and jeopardises the male subject. It displays a site of homoerotic intercourse in which everywhere man finds himself reflected. But this multi-replication of the male form presents 'him' not as one, but through a hall of mirrors that threatens 'his' own projection, as 'he' becomes the site/sight of a defamiliarised, disproportionate, deficient image of the male I/eye. The phallus is castrated of its emblematic power, dispossessed of its value and potency. Thus 'unmanned', the male subject appears later in the poem like a virgin passively awaiting her defloration. Yet where the blood of the closed virginal body signifies the 'forc'd' inscription of her sexuality by the 'force' of the phallus, the blood of the male marks the declaration of his virility, the proving of his sexuality, where he is both the agent and object of 'force'. In this way the affirmation of masculine identity thus signals its *difference*: the moment of sexual assertion is perceived as the moment in which sexual identity and difference is destabilised.

In the final scene of the poem the effects of the male subject's 'force' are displayed in a theatre of mass death, as the spectacular detail of carnage merges into a vision of hell (lines 161–6). And yet the male form does not remain closed within this final spectacle of death. It re-emerges as a spectre to leave unburied the questions its decomposition has raised about sexuality, for the fruits produced by the self-consuming 'force' of the male are incorporated within the reproductive processes of nature at line 154. The disintegrating proportions of the solid male form signal the non-sense of what the eye sees, dislocating and exceeding visual discrimination, as the male body is decomposed ultimately to re-surface in this poem non-visibly from a subliminal realm. The dissolved visible form of man is submerged within the nether regions – the dark invisible interior body of the earth – to re-emanate chimerically, not in terms of the ocular but of the aural, embodied within the potent voice of nature (lines 163–6).

'A Description of the Battle' problematises the terms of identity and difference established by the emergent male corpus of science. It places in doubt the authority and authorship of the male subject as a source of knowledge by troubling the grounds upon which masculine identity establishes itself. The male subject is put into crisis through its very affirmation as the assertion of its identity is presented as the moment of its difference. The poem, then, provides an unauthorised, eccentric view, which dislocates the boundaries of knowledge and ignorance from a site/sight of difference.

IV

As with most of Cavendish's poems, there is no visible, masterful first-person subject in 'A Description of the Battle', but an unseen eye, which merges interior and exterior, visual and visionary, visible and non-visible. While what is displayed in the poems is rarely presented as the property of a single specific subject, however, the first-person subject is altogether manifest in the ex-centric part of Cavendish's text, the prefaces and epistles. It is this area of Cavendish's corpus – peripheral and yet central – to which I would finally like to turn in my discussion of her interventions into masculine modes of knowing. Prefaces, epistles and apologia are employed as a matter of convention in seventeenth-century texts, but in women's writing they have a particular significance in that they often become the place in which the sexual politics of speaking, writing and knowing is highlighted. Indeed, one might argue that the prefaces to women's writing form a gendered genre. It is here that the questions of how a female voice may negotiate a position from which to speak and what is at stake in speaking is often most acute.

Cavendish's work provides an especially large quantity of prefaces. There are nine that introduce *Poems, and Fancies*, the final one of which is entitled 'An excuse for so much writ upon my Verses'. In addition, there are several epistles interspersed within the poetry. The excessive number of prefaces and epistles in itself indicates their refusal to be given marginal status. Instead, this part of Cavendish's work requires us to take note of the terms within which subject positions are produced and their relation to questions of gender and readership.

Typically, Cavendish's war poems are prefaced by 'An Epistle to Souldiers':

Great Heroicks, *you may justly laugh at me, if I went about to censure, instruct, or advise in the valiant* Art, *and* Disipline *of Warre. But I doe but only take the name, having no knowledge in the* Art, *nor practise in the use; for I never saw an* Army *together, nor any* Incounters *in my life. I have seen a* Troop, *or a* Regiment *march on the Highway by chance, or so; neither have I the courage to looke on the cruell assaults, that* Mankind *(as I have heard) will make at each other; but according to the constitution of my* Sex, *I am fearefull as a* Hare: *for I shall start at the noyse of a* Potgun, *and shut my eyes at the sight of a bloudy Sword, and run away at the least Alarum. Only My courage is, I can heare a sad relation, but not without griefe, and chilnese of spirits: but these* Armies *I mention, were rais'd in my* braine, *fought in my* fancy, *and registred in my* closet.[49]

The latent eye of the poems is apparently manifested in the 'I' of the preface. This first-person subject, however, displays herself only to suggest her tentativeness in taking up this position, presenting herself as the inadequate object of the masterful, knowing eye of 'Great Heroicks'. The 'I' of the epistle exposes the gaps in her knowledge, announcing that she is unlegitimised by the authoritative body of military experts. The speaker confesses that 'I never saw an Army together, nor any Incounters in my life'. This 'I', indeed, refuses to see, 'for I shall . . . shut my eyes at the sight of a bloudy Sword, and run away at the least Alarum'. The speaker therefore presents herself as standing on unstable ground, devoid of strength and authority, lacking the firm base of solid, verifiable knowledge, as she ventures to describe what is acknowledged to be the unauthorised, alien territory of the battlefield.

The unstable ground of 'I', however, also marks a destabilising of the authority that is apparently accepted on the surface to provide a plural view of what is presented. The preface and 'A Description of the Battle' lend ironic readings to each other, for the soldiers of the epistle seem to be afforded a status rendered void and impotent in the poem, and it is this gap between these scenes that releases other meanings not at first visible in the preface. Significantly, the epistle turns on the phallic term 'bloudy Sword', a sight which the speaker cannot stomach here, and yet which is all too visible in the poem. This image, however, has a significance that goes beyond the specific reference to war, symbolising the force of the phallus. The speaking 'I', though, shuts her eyes to this emblem, refusing the authority and inscription of the phallus as master–signifier, excluding from its sight the sign of its professed power, and so looks forward to the unsightly male bodies of the poem, in which the phallic signifier is placed in jeopardy. The 'eyes' of the preface disorientate the primacy of the visible sign as the key defining term of knowledge, relocating the armies in an arena alien from the battlefield – the inner invisible chambers of the brain – a space that is apparently not invaded by the phallus, identified by the speaker as a room of her own: 'these Armies I mention, were rais'd in my braine, fought in my fancy, and registred in my closet'. It is, then, across the corpus of this unstable, unauthorised, unseeing 'I' that a contest of meanings and positions is fought.

In the preface 'To All Noble, and Worthy Ladies' the speaker's corpus is located more explicitly as a place of resistance:

But I imagine I shall be censur'd by my owne *Sex*; and *Men* will cast a *smile* of *scorne* upon my *Book*, because they think therby, *Women* incroach too much upon their *Prerogatives*; for they hold *Books* as their *Crowne*, and the *Sword* as their *Scepter*, by which they rule, and governe.[50]

Here the act of writing is presented expressly as a matter of sexual politics. Books are perceived as a domain of male power, suggesting male sovereignty over language and meaning, and the sword the means through which that power is inscribed and enforced. The speaker thus makes explicit her unauthorised position in seizing these weapons of patriarchy, as 'I' shifts to the plural 'Women'. In writing her own book and claiming the sword as her own metaphor, this plural 'I' of 'Women' thus disrupts the system of differences which holds male 'Prerogatives' in place. The removal of the sword of phallic power points to the militant conclusion of this preface, in which this 'I' of 'Women' requests the solidarity of her sisters in opening up a space for voices that resist the masculine emblems of restraint:

Therefore pray strengthen my *Side*, in defending my *Book*; for I know *Womens Tongus* are as *sharp*, as two-edged *Swords*, and wound as much, when they are anger'd. And in this *Battell* may your *Wit* be *quick*, and your *Speech ready*, and your *Arguments* so *strong*, as to beat them out of the *Feild* of *Dispute*. So shall I get *Honour*, and *Reputation* by your *Favours*; otherwise I may chance to be cast into the *Fire*. But if I burn, I desire to die your *Martyr*; if I live, to be

> *Your humble* Servant,
> M. N.[51]

The speaker calls on women's voices in the form of 'Wit', 'Speech' and 'Arguments' to create a united front with which to defend her corpus and to contest the force of patriarchy. She thus rewrites the symbols of male power. Women's tongues are to replace the phallic sword, to resist the meanings inscribed by it. Being 'sharp' with the capacity to 'wound', they are to open up, enter and remap the arena of writing by deposing male sovereignty, 'to beat them out of the Feild of Dispute'.

This destabilising of the subject positions installed by sexual difference is highlighted in the presentation of 'I', which troubles the demarcations of subject and object. As the first-person subject affirms herself, so she locates herself as flesh/corpus. This 'I'/corpus sites herself as the property of 'Women' to be approved by their 'Favours', and thus confuses the tropes of male poetics as the position she takes up bears the marks of the Petrarchan motif. If her suit is rejected, she must be 'cast into the Fire' to suffer the torments of textual death and so to die women's 'Martyr', but if approved she may 'live, to be Your humble Servant'. Women's swords are, then, significantly regarded by the speaker as 'two-edged'. But this plurality is presented as a mark of the potency of women's tongues to unfix language and shift the terms of sexual difference to which the 'I'/corpus of this preface yields itself as a battleground for meanings.

Cavendish's writing thus challenges the premises that sustain emergent masculine modes of knowing at every turn. It disrupts the grounds of rationalism, dualism and empiricism by calling into question the very terms upon which these epistemological practices are founded. 'A Description of the Battle', indeed, takes apart and de-centres the male identity that makes such practices possible. The poems, however, are located within the frame of the prefaces and epistles, which highlight the relationship between gender, speaking and knowing implied in the poetry. In their disproportionate length and complex self-consciousness, the prefaces refuse marginality. They demand not to be overlooked in providing another plural view of the central text – the poems. While the poems offer an eccentric perspective that discomforts the paradigms being established as central to scientific practice, the prefaces bring to the foreground the positions being contested in the poems – positions that draw attention to the sexual politics inscribed in speaking and knowing which lie buried in the emergent scientific discourses. The tentative, unstable 'I' of the prefaces shifts the grounds of authorised meanings to unsettle the boundaries between knowledge and ignorance, identity and difference, and so from this eccentric, outer textual space opens up a difference of view.

It is this unstable 'I' that links Cavendish's work to other, often quite different texts by women of the seventeenth century. As is shown in chapter 10 of this volume, discursive contradictions and indeterminacy frequently feature, though in varied forms, in early women's writing about the self. In this, Cavendish's work shares with other women's writing in exceeding and unsettling the bounds of discourse through its continual shifts in and fluidity of speaking positions. However, it is also very different from that writing in its particular negotiations with seventeenth-century scientific enquiry. While a number of Cavendish's prefaces claim to enter such areas of investigation from a position of unknowingness, her poems problematise knowledge and signal its contingency. Moreover, the very range of prefaces and epistles that pervade *Poems, and Fancies* draws attention to the significance of the process of reading and the context of reception to what is known and how it might be understood. While the speaker fears the censures of natural philosophers, she suggests the ways in which noble and worthy ladies might read her work otherwise, so as to produce different meanings from her poems. It is through such a difference that Cavendish's work opens up possibilities for radical modes of knowing.

NOTES

1. Barbara Johnson, *A World of Difference* (Baltimore and London: Johns Hopkins University Press, 1987), p. 16.
2. For a variety of recent approaches see, for example, Catherine Belsey, *The Subject of Tragedy: Identity and Difference in Renaissance Drama* (London and New York: Methuen, 1985); Sandra Harding, *Whose Science? Whose Knowledge? Thinking from Women's Lives* (Milton Keynes: Open University Press, 1991); Evelyn Fox Keller, *Secrets of Life, Secrets of Death: Essays on Language, Gender and Science* (New York and London: Routledge, 1992); and Alice Jardine, *Gynesis: Configurations of Woman and Modernity* (Ithaca, NY, and London: Cornell University Press, 1985).
3. Elaine Hobby particularly notes this feature of seventeenth-century women's writing in her outstanding study *Virtue of Necessity: English Women's Writing, 1649–1688* (London: Virago, 1988).
4. For a full discussion of this aspect of Behn's poetry see Bronwen Price, 'Playing the "Masculine Part": Finding a Difference Within Behn's Poetry', in Kate Chedgzoy, Melanie Hansen and Suzanne Trill, eds., *Voicing Women: Gender and Sexuality in Early Modern Writing* (Keele: Keele University Press, 1996).
5. See Belsey, *The Subject of Tragedy*, p. 65.
6. Francis Bacon, *A Selection of his Works*, ed. Sidney Warhaft (Indianapolis: Bobbs-Merrill, 1965), p. 323.
7. *Ibid.*, p. 318.
8. *Ibid.*, p. 364.
9. *Ibid.*, p. 327.
10. Keller, *Secrets of Life*, p. 58.
11. *Ibid.*, pp. 56–8.
12. Bacon, *A Selection*, pp. 327, 447 and 374.
13. Keller, *Secrets of Life*, p. 67.
14. See Sara Heller Mendelson, *The Mental World of Stuart Women: Three Case Studies* (Brighton: Harvester, 1987), p. 38.
15. See Samuel I. Mintz, 'The Duchess of Newcastle's Visit to the Royal Society', *JEGP*, 51 (1952), 168–76, for a detailed account of Cavendish's visit to the Royal Society.
16. Margaret Cavendish, Duchess of Newcastle, *Poems, and Fancies* (1653), reprinted in facsimile with an introduction by George Parfitt (Menston: Scolar Press, 1972), pp. 141–2.
17. René Descartes, *Discourse on Method and the Meditations*, trans. F. E. Sutcliffe (Harmondsworth: Penguin, 1968), p. 54.
18. *Ibid.*, p. 99.

19. Anne Conway, *The Principles of the Most Ancient and Modern Philosophy*, ed. Peter Loptson (The Hague, Boston and London: Martinus Nijhoff, 1982), p. 221. This work was prepared for publication after Conway's death by Van Helmont, and possibly Henry More; see Loptson's introduction, p. 6.

20. *Ibid.*, p. 189.

21. *Ibid.*, pp. 189–90.

22. *Ibid.*, p. 190.

23. See Carolyn Merchant, *The Death of Nature: Women, Ecology and the Scientific Revolution* (San Francisco: Harper and Row; 1980; reprinted with a new introduction, 1990), p. 263.

24. Descartes, *Discourse on Method*, p. 96.

25. *Ibid.*, p. 111.

26. Susan Bordo, 'The Cartesian Masculinization of Thought', in Sandra Harding and Jean F. O'Barr, eds., *Sex and Scientific Inquiry* (Chicago and London: University of Chicago Press, 1987), pp. 247ff.

27. See Robert Kargon, *Atomism in England from Hariot to Newton* (Oxford: Clarendon Press, 1966), p. 72, and Merchant, *Death of Nature*, pp. 206–8.

28. Lisa T. Sarasohn, 'A Science Turned Upside Down: Feminism and the Natural Philosophy of Margaret Cavendish', *HLQ*, 47 (1984), 291.

29. *Ibid.*, p. 291; see also Kargon, *Atomism in England*, p. 62.

30. Sarasohn, 'A Science Turned Upside Down', 291.

31. Kargon, *Atomism in England*, argues that Cavendish's atomism implies 'near heresy' and so 'laid the atomists open to attack on the charge of impiety' (p. 75). However, as Sarasohn points out, Cavendish later abandoned atomism altogether and developed organic vitalistic theories where the natural world was regarded as being composed of 'a hierarchy of matter, integrated into an organic whole' (p. 294). This later work, as Sylvia Bowerbank ('The Spider's Delight: Margaret Cavendish and the "Female" Imagination', *ELR*, 14 (1984), 392–408) shows, attacks More, Hobbes and Descartes for undermining the wisdom of nature (p. 399).

32. See Bacon, *A Selection*, pp. 222–3. Bacon's writing is, nevertheless, full of metaphors that are employed as an integral part of his polemic. Keller, *Secrets of Life*, notes how 'Confidence in the transparency and neutrality of scientific language' (p. 28) and the assumption that nature is directly accessible have prevailed in modern science (pp. 27–31).

33. Cavendish, *Poems, and Fancies*. There are no page numbers in the preface section.

34. I refer to 'the speaker' rather than Cavendish to indicate that there is not a transparent or innocent link between Cavendish the person and the writing positions that are taken up in the preface and the poems.

35. Conway, *Principles*, p. 160.

36. *Ibid.*, p. 160.

37. Cavendish, *Poems, and Fancies*, pp. 43–4.

38. See also Margaret Cavendish, *The Blazing World*, in Paul Salzman, ed., *An Anthology of Seventeenth-Century Fiction* (Oxford and New York: Oxford Uni-

versity Press, 1991), pp. 265–6, in which the attainment of knowledge through sense-perception is treated as suspect.

39. Emily Martin, 'Science and Women's Bodies: Forms of Anthropological Knowledge', in Mary Jacobus, Evelyn Fox Keller and Sally Shuttleworth, eds., *Body/Politics: Women and the Discourses of Science* (New York and London: Routledge, 1990), p. 69. Martin cites from Johannes Fabian, *Time and the Other: How Anthropology Makes its Object* (New York: Columbia University Press, 1983).

40. Evelyn Fox Keller, 'From Secrets of Life to Secrets of Death', in Jacobus *et al.*, eds., *Body/Politics*, p. 178.

41. Bacon, *A Selection*, p. 399. Bowerbank, 'The Spider's Delight', quite rightly suggests that Cavendish's writing in general provides 'an alternative perspective to the prevailing Baconian paradigm' (p. 398).

    The metaphors of sexual mastery that underscore Bacon's writing, as Merchant, *Death of Nature*, shows, were taken up later in the century by the advocates of empirical and experimental science (pp. 188–90). See also Descartes, *Discourse on Method*, which contends that we should 'make ourselves ... masters and possessors of nature' (p. 78).

42. Bacon, *A Selection*, p. 329.

43. *Ibid.*, pp. 320 and 323.

44. *Ibid.*, p. 364.

45. *Ibid.*, p. 323.

46. *Ibid.*, p. 318.

47. Cavendish, *Poems and Fancies*, pp. 173–4, 176–7.

48. Bacon, *A Selection*, pp. 323 and 364.

49. Cavendish, *Poems and Fancies*, p. 167.

50. *Ibid.*: there are no page numbers in the preface section.

51. *Ibid.*

PART II

Writing women in early modern Britain

CHAPTER 7

Renaissance concepts of the 'woman writer'

Margaret W. Ferguson

> S/he who writes, writes. In uncertainty, in necessity. And does not
> ask whether s/he is given the permission to do so or not. Yet, in the
> context of today's market-dependent societies, 'to be a writer' can
> no longer mean purely to perform the act of writing. For a lay-
> wo/man to enter the priesthood – the sacred world of writers – s/he
> must fulfill a number of unwritten conditions.
>
> (Trinh T. Minh-ha, *Woman, Native, Other: Writing,*
> *Postcoloniality, and Feminism*)[1]

Though her words pertain to twentieth-century writers, Trinh T. Minh-
ha provides a useful starting point for this chapter's survey of some
theoretical and practical issues that attend, and complicate, the various
concepts of the 'woman writer' circulating in early modern Britain and
in modern scholarship about that period. The name 'Britain' in this era
signals, we need to remember, a highly contested political and geo-
graphical site: England's formal union with Scotland did not occur until
1707, with Ireland only in 1801, and in this era Scottish and Irish
territories were being forcibly claimed (along with more distant territories across the Atlantic and the English Channel) by a crown that had
annexed Wales only in 1536.[2] In this period of British history many
'unwritten conditions' governed writing as a domain of cultural activity
and also as a domain of (frequently disputed) cultural meanings and
values.

It is important to note at the outset that the Romantic notion of the
writer to which Trinh T. Minh-ha alludes – the writer as an elite
member of a metaphorical priesthood – had not yet gained cultural
currency in early modern Britain. Ironically, in the period prior to the
centuries that concern us here, most writers had literally been priests of
the Catholic church; moreover, throughout the medieval and Renaissance eras notions of human 'authorship' were very unstable and
complex. Many medieval male writers of religious texts adopted the

143

anonymous role of humble transmitter of God's divine authority; sharing the work of producing a manuscript with an illuminator and sometimes another artist, a 'miniaturist', the writer's ideas were often dictated, in large part, by an external figure of religious or secular authority – an abbot, for example, or a king.[3] Even in medieval texts that call attention to the individual writer in prologues or epilogues – the romances of Chrétien de Troyes or the *Lais* of Marie de France, for instance, along with the dual-authored *Romance of the Rose* – the phenomenon that modern critics call 'authorial self-consciousness' needs to be approached with a certain historical scepticism as well as curiosity. We should not assume that we know intuitively what an 'author' is, for as Michel Foucault has argued in 'What is an Author?', 'the link between a proper name and the individual being named and the link between an author's name and that which it names are not isomorphous and do not function in the same way'.[4]

The beginnings, in Britain, of a secular 'profession' of writer or author in the most common modern senses of those terms – persons who write for profit, via print, to an audience the author can neither see nor intimately know – are usually traced to the era of the English Reformation that started in the 1530s, during the reign of Henry VIII.[5] Though writers, like Chaucer, who made their living through court patronage are frequently named as 'auctoritees' and progenitors in certain Renaissance genealogies of male authorship – as are classical writers like Virgil – our modern notions of what it means to 'be' a writer or an author are crucially dependent on the advent of print, an historical event that separates Chaucer from his Renaissance heirs even though many of the latter continued to rely, to varying degrees, on the kind of aristocratic patronage and manuscript circulation that had sustained most secular medieval writers.[6]

The gradual and uneven infiltration of printing into the cultural domain of writing in general, and of 'authorship' in particular, is crucial both for concepts of women writers between 1500 and 1700 and for understanding the continuities, as well as discontinuities, between that era's concepts of writers and medieval as well as modern ones. The latter include ideas of authors as elite 'priests' – as suggested by Trinh T. Minh-ha's passage quoted above – as well as the related but less exalted notions of the writer as individual originator and 'owner' of his or her work, via a system of copyright laws that formally began only in the early eighteenth century though there were important Renaissance precedents for the (culturally new) idea of the author as the person who could sell his or her 'product' and who could be held legally responsible for it.[7] In Foucault's view, liability and punishment are key components of the modern idea of the professional writer or author.[8] Ignored by Foucault but equally important to modern ideas of authorship, as Wendy Wall has recently argued, were socially constructed notions of masculinity; Wall explores the ways in which authorship was redefined 'in the wake of the print industry's collision with manuscript culture' to produce a culturally powerful notion of 'men in print'.[9]

Despite the many changes that have occurred in historical concepts of the author and writer between the Renaissance and the twentieth century, women have consistently had an 'eccentric' relation to dominant social concepts of the writer and the author. Indeed the very phrases 'woman writer' and 'woman author' usually imply that these concepts, when unmodified, are gendered masculine. In some discursive contexts, particularly those that participate in the lively Renaissance debates about 'proper' modes of masculine and feminine behaviour (see chapters 1 and 3 of this volume), the idea of the 'woman writer' is a veritable paradox or oxymoron, one eliciting attitudes of outrage and/or scorn.[10] If women are prescriptively defined as 'chaste, silent and obedient', according to a well-known ideal in Renaissance conduct books, and if both writing and printing are defined, for any number of reasons, as 'masculine' activities and also in opposition to 'silence', then the phrase 'woman writer' will be seen as a contradiction in terms.[11]

Although the idea of a contradiction between the role of 'woman' and that of 'writer' is at the extreme end of an ideological spectrum we shall be examining in this chapter, many conceptual problems, often generating material effects, have shadowed the notion of the woman writer across the centuries from the Renaissance to the present. To understand those problems as they impinged on, and were sometimes countered by, Renaissance English, Irish, Welsh and Scottish women, we need to approach writing first as a component of *literacy* in early modern Britain. Because the types and degrees of literacy at stake here were crucially affected by differences in a subject's social status, religion and place of origin, generalisations are very difficult; they are made even more so by the fact that most research on literacy focuses on England rather than on other areas claimed – in the sixteenth century or the present – by the British monarchy.[12] What follows, then, is a very partial introduction to some of the problems of defining early modern British women's literacy and discerning traces of it in the historical record.

WRITINGS AND LITERACIES

Throughout the European Middle Ages writing as a general activity involving the composition and, far more often, the copying of manuscripts, had been practised predominantly by men trained by and in the institution of the church. Though there were some women, particularly nuns and some well-born ladies, who possessed those skills in alphabetic writing and reading we now associate with basic literacy, and though there were also a number of laymen, especially merchants, who had skills in reading, writing and arithmetic, the word *litteratus* ('literate' or 'lettered') was so closely associated with the social order or estate of the clergy that it was widely understood to mean 'learned in Latin'; and it was hence widely used as a synonym for a male cleric.[13] Neither aristocratic nor common men (with the exception of urban tradesmen) generally considered writing necessary for their mode of living. Noblemen, indeed, often regarded the cleric's or 'clerk's' ability to write as distinctly undesirable for one of noble estate;[14] and commoners too seem often to have regarded the ability to write as a debit – even an ethical blemish – rather than as an asset. Shakespeare, a member of the emerging secular class that wrote for a living though his father signed documents with a mark, ironically depicts a hostile view of writing in his fictionalised portrait of the rebel Jack Cade, who asks a captured clergyman, 'Dost thou use to write thy name, or hast thou a mark to thyself like an honest plain dealing man?'[15]

Though not highly valued by many Englishmen in the early modern period, the ability to write did carry a distinct legal advantage: under the English Common Law, men could escape punishment for a felony by claiming 'benefit of clergy' – a claim they had to substantiate by reading a prescribed verse – in Latin – from the Bible. Many lawyers and tradesmen availed themselves of this benefit, which could be gained through skills in memorisation rather than in reading since the biblical verse, known as the 'hanging verse', was always the same one. Men of various social ranks could thus reap the legal benefit of what counted as clerical literacy; women, however, could not. They could escape hanging only by demonstrating that they were pregnant. The asymmetry of gender dramatised by these legal loopholes points to the significant differences between opportunities for, and theories of, girls' and boys' education in Renaissance Britain. For as long as 'literacy' connoted the knowledge of Latin – as it did well into the eighteenth century – even women who could read and/or write one or more vernacular languages could be socially defined as 'illiterate'. One scholar has even described Latin language learning in the Renaissance as a male puberty rite![16]

No discussion of concepts of the 'woman writer' between 1500 and 1700 can proceed very far without remarking that only a tiny percentage of the population of Britain was educated in either reading or writing during this era. If we define literacy – as many modern historians 'commonsensically' do – as the ability to read and write at some minimal level, we immediately encounter theoretical as well as practical difficulties in estimating the number of British people who were literate in the fifteenth, sixteenth and seventeenth centuries. Nonetheless, it is worth reporting – as a place to start thinking about the issue – the historian David Cressy's estimate that 'more than two-thirds of the men and more than four-fifths of the women in the seventeenth-century [in England] could not write their names'.[17] His estimates for the sixteenth and fifteenth centuries are even smaller; one of the few things historians of literacy agree about is that literacy rates *increased* during the early modern era. By how much, in what parts of the country, and with how much variation according to one's religious leanings, socio-economic status, and native dialect, are questions about which there is less consensus. Though we can take as given the historians' view that fewer women than men were 'literate' throughout the period and in all parts of Britain, we need now to take a brief look at the problems of defining literacy as the ability to read and write, and at the problems of measuring literacy when it is so construed.

Statistics on early modern literacy are notoriously unreliable, partly because the chief method historians have used to measure literacy in this period – the signing of one's name on a document – is biased against both women and lower-class men.[18] These groups had little access to the kinds of property transactions that provide our chief English archive of signed documents before 1642, when the 'Protestation Returns', documents demonstrating allegiance to the Commonwealth government and signed, in principle at least, by all adult males, offer (where they survive) 'the only seventeenth century evidence' about literacy that provides a cross-section from all over England (other parts of the British Isles are not included in this archive).[19] The use of the signature method of measuring literacy is obviously problematic – arguably even useless – for studies focusing on women because social factors other than illiteracy play such a large role in determining the absence of women's signatures from the historical record. Wives were defined by Common Law as 'femes couvertes' (covered women), a phrase that denotes their status as the property of their husbands; 'covered' by the husband's legal being, wives could not own property in their own right, and hence were unlikely to sign a legal document unless they were widowed or were exempted from the law of coverture – as queens were.[20] Signatures of both husband and wife on marriage documents were not legally required until the eighteenth century, and hence marriage documents are not a resource for historians of literacy in this period. The legal definition of the wife as the husband's property crucially colours both the 'facts' and our ability to recover the facts about women's basic abilities to write; this legal definition of the wife also crucially affected early modern women's ability to assume those emergent roles of 'author' that implied one's ownership of a product – a text or an 'opus' – capable of being sold in the markets of early capitalism.

The statistics on literacy rates in general, and women's literacy rates in particular, become even more problematic when one notes that reading was taught separately from – and prior to – writing in the so-called 'petty' schools of Renaissance England, schools which girls attended along with boys although many parents had 'less incentive to keep [girls] there as long as their brothers'.[21] For those children who received any education at all, the first stage of elementary schooling usually involved reading in Latin the Lord's Prayer or Bible verses from a book made of a material designed to be too hard to write on, the 'horn book'.[22] Many children never went beyond this stage, partly because their families needed their manual labour more than their education, and partly – especially in the case of girls – because educational ideologies defined writing as unnecessary, even dangerous, to the child in question.[23] Boys below the level of yeoman, as Margaret Spufford observes, often learned only to read before their parents withdrew them from school around the age of seven; 'writing was commonly taught at an age after the meaningful earning lives of such boys had begun' (p. 27). Spufford further remarks that 'the evidence of many school curricula, like that of the Orwell school, in which boys were taught to read, write and cast accounts, whereas girls were taught to read and sew, knit and spin, shows that girls were not usually taught the skill that is capable of measurement at all.' In her view, we must be extremely sceptical about David Cressy's statistics showing women as a group at the bottom of a social hierarchy of literacy – a hierarchy that shows the literacy rates of groups of *men* to increase in a pattern almost perfectly correlated with a rise in economic status. 'There is', asserts Spufford, 'absolutely no way of knowing how many women below the level of the gentry in England learnt to read' (p. 35). Feminist scholars such as Suzanne Hull and Caroline Lucas, who have inferred literacy rates not from written signatures but from the (less quantifiable) kind of evidence provided by numbers of printed books dedicated to noblewomen and/or explicitly addressed to women, arrive at a considerably higher estimate of the number of English women readers than Cressy does.[24]

For the purposes of this chapter it is equally important to state that we also know little about how many women might have merited the label 'writer' in any of that term's various senses. Despite the modern assumption that if one knows how to read, one can teach oneself to write, the journey from reader to writer – with the latter term understood even in the most material or literal sense – seems to have been full of complex stages (and obstacles) for early modern women; we shall examine shortly some of these stages as they are implied, for instance, by manuals on handwriting instruction. And even when women had some version of the skill of alphabetic writing, the evidentiary difficulties remain for the modern scholar because such women were under considerable social pressure to disguise their possession of such a skill. Significant modes of disguise were writing anonymously or pseudonymously.[25] Even more subtle ways of disguising authorial ambitions may be found in women's choice of certain genres over others (religious poetry, for instance, over epic) and in their decisions to work as translators rather than as 'original' creators. Though 'imitation' of classical and contemporary models was a central element in Renaissance literary theory and practice (and in humanist educational programmes), translation was often devalued and gendered feminine. Some women, however, took advantage of the ambiguities that surrounded the distinction between 'imitation' and 'translation'; women could use the cover of the translator's humble (handmaiden) role to make significant ideological interventions and even to express apparently original ideas through interpolations or loose translations. Women, particularly aristocratic women, could also escape the inhibiting effects of the social ideal of females as silent, 'private' beings by circulating their writings in manuscript rather than submitting them to the press. But the line between manuscript and print 'publication' was often blurred in this era, and some women used that ambiguity to advance their ambitions to reach a public audience with their writings.

To grasp the variety and complexity of concepts of 'the woman writer' in this era, we need to note also that some women who could not write but who could perhaps read or who were literate – in the broad sense of 'knowledgeable' – in non-alphabetic bases of information (medicinal plants, for instance) dictated their words to a male or female scribe. Margery Kempe had done this in the fifteenth century, and scholars are still debating whether the man who recorded Kempe's autobiographical discourse should be regarded as a co-author of the text or simply as a scribe. As Julia Boffey remarks in her valuable study, 'Women Authors and Women's Literacy in Fourteenth- and Fifteenth-Century England', 'it is difficult to assess the amount of first-hand contact' late medieval women may have had with texts either as writers or as readers; intermediaries, generally men, played a crucial role in the production and consumption of writing.[26] Women's mediated relations to texts persisted into the early modern period and beyond. During the English Civil War era, for instance, many radical Protestant women evidently preached but could not write; in his *Gangraena* of 1646, Thomas Edwards scornfully describes one 'Mrs Attaway', a 'she-preacher of Coleman Street', who had read Milton's treatise on divorce and applied its principles to herself in a way that disturbed Edwards greatly (and probably disturbed Milton too, for he later regretted not having published his divorce tracts in Latin, a language very few women could read).[27] Attaway's words are known to us only through the polemical filter of Edwards's treatise; but a version of her words nonetheless exists in the written record and should arguably be studied by feminist scholars concerned with 'women writers'. A number of historical figures from the medieval and early modern eras, men as well as women, enter the historical record only through similarly 'mediated' writing: we know of Mabel Swinnerton, wife of a London bricklayer, for instance, only because her words are recorded as testimony in the trial of one Dr Lamb for the rape of an eleven-year-old named Joan Seager.[28] Such figures challenge modern notions of the (single) authorial 'self' in a way that is important to any student of marginalised social groups. If we are not to see such groups simply as silenced 'victims', we need to learn how to read the evidentiary traces they left us; and we need to include their texts in our anthologies, which are too often ahistorically limited to selections from works by persons who fit into the dominant modern idea of the author.

When we talk about 'authors' or 'writers' in Renaissance Britain, then, and particularly when we talk about 'women authors or writers', we need to remember that we are discussing a very small segment of the population – especially small if we consider the 'population' to include the Irish, Native American and African persons inhabiting (the latter against their will) territories claimed by the English crown. The category of 'women writers' is, moreover, one that potentially complicates, even confounds, commonsensical modern notions about both authorship and literacy. John Guillory has, indeed, usefully suggested that we should define literacy not as a technology or set of self-evident skills but rather as a set of social facts that we cannot perfectly reconstruct and that would correspond to questions such as the following: 'Who reads? What do they read? How do they read? In what social and institutional circumstances? Who writes? In what social and institutional circumstances? For whom?'[29] Building on Guillory's study of 'cultural capital', and also on the work of anthropological literacy theorists such as Brian Street,[30] I would further suggest that the student of women's writing extend that list of questions to include the following, ranging from practical to speculative:

Who teaches handwriting to girls?

How do social status, religion, and region of birth affect opportunities for women's education in an era when girls were generally excluded from the grammar schools and universities of England?

How do texts written in certain hands identified as 'appropriate' for girls get to printers and get published?

If one speaks a dialect or language seen as 'provincial', how does that affect one's ability to get a text published when London is the centre of printing and the royal court sets the standards for 'good' speech?[31]

If a woman dictates her words to a male scribe, is she still to be considered a 'woman writer'?

If one is biologically male but writes, and gets published, under a woman's name, is one a 'woman writer'?

As this list suggests, when the concept of the woman writer is placed within the context of the *problem* of literacy, which necessarily includes the problem of how we know about literacy in a culture different from our own, we can no longer speak with certainty about what counts either as a 'woman' or as a 'writer'.[32]

Keeping these broad theoretical and epistemological problems in mind, we can turn now to some historical considerations that may help us specify some of the particular features of early modern British culture that affected writers who were defined both biologically and socially as 'female'. This group is not – I reiterate – isomorphous with or even representative of the theoretical concept of 'the woman writer' – for that concept needs to encompass 'cross-dressed' male authors and also the existence of anonymous and pseudonymous texts that we must interpret, or learn to interpret, without ever knowing the gender of the historical author. Although some feminist scholars argue, for example, that the rhetorically complex 'defence' of women entitled *Jane Anger, her protection for Women* (1589) was definitely by a woman on the grounds that it would not have been to a man's 'benefit' to use a female pseudonym, I maintain we need to know a good deal more about how a witty and stereotyped name like 'Jane Anger' would have worked to a writer's economic or ideological advantage in Tudor England before we decide on authorship questions such as those presented by the phenomenon of the polemical 'gender-wars' pamphlet.[33] And, perhaps, we should re-examine the desire to *have* certainty on such a question. By increasing our capacity for scepticism, feminist readers and writers can help construct a difficult but important path between complicating and historicising the category of 'woman writer', on the one hand, and, on the other, dissolving that concept altogether before scholars have seriously explored the historical matrices in which persons historically defined as female lived and attempted to articulate their thoughts for particular audiences. Much important work has been done toward that task of historical reconstruction, and what follows surveys, in a necessarily sketchy way, some of the fruits of that labour by considering, first, women's education as writers; and second, their peculiar relations to the new technology of print. Focusing on these topics will allow us to examine some of the typical strategies women adopted – and sometimes overtly described – when they worked as writers with what Aphra Behn called, in 1688, a 'female pen'.

FROM WOMEN'S HANDWRITING TO A CHARACTER NAMED GRAPHINA

In *Writing Matter*, Jonathan Goldberg remarks that Renaissance authors of writing manuals, a genre which burgeoned during the sixteenth and seventeenth centuries throughout Europe, 'scarcely seem aware of the fact that a woman might write'.[34] The silence is not accidental, since the enormous interest in writing, on the part of male humanist intellectuals, frequently went hand in hand with conceptualisations of writing as a fundamentally masculine domain. Pens were repeatedly likened to men's weapons by the international (and multilingual) set of writers who made their living by writing and teaching; and in English, the pun on 'pen' and 'penis' makes the metaphor of the pen as a weapon a particularly gendered concept. An Amazon can shoot an arrow, a martial maid like Spenser's Britomart can wield a sword, but even such 'masculine' women cannot (without risk of ridicule and exposure) claim that women's writing is equivalent to the male's biological power of 'dissemination' or 'penetration'.

New conceptions and practices of writing emerged through the pens of a new Renaissance class of secular male intellectuals, men like Erasmus, Juan Luis Vives and Claudius Désainliens. The humanists' 'writing-weapons', as Désainliens calls them in his dialogue entitled *Scriptio*, were not only used to fashion a 'writing class' but also to awe American Indians: the colonising process was idealised as the product of 'the munificence of our Kings' and the (feminised) American Indians are described as amazed by the Europeans' ability, in Désainliens's words, to 'open up to one another what they think from a long distance by a piece of paper being sent with black stains marked on it'.[35] The 'weapons' of pen or quill here participate in an historical enterprise largely conducted by men and repeatedly described as a 'penetration' of New World lands likened to virginal female bodies.[36] Although a few Renaissance women did write about European colonisation – Marguerite de Navarre, for instance, in a story about Canadian settlers in the *Heptaméron* (1547), or Aphra Behn in *Oroonoko* (1688) – the gendering of the conquest and its key instruments, sword, gun and pen, as masculine, is part of the process of positioning women, like Native Americans and black Africans, in the emerging field of 'literacy' as *receptacles* for European men's words rather than as authoritative wielders of the pen.

The cultural commonplace that women should use needles and distaffs *instead* of pens is clearly part of this ideological complex. A number of Renaissance women ruefully testify to the power of that idea. In the prologue to a book of poems published in 1650, for instance, the English (later American) woman Anne Bradstreet wrote: 'I am obnoxious to each carping tongue, / Who says my hand a needle better fits, / A Poet's Pen all scorne, I should thus wrong...'[37] Paradoxically, given the cultural opposition between pen (masculine) and needle and distaff (feminine), women from the middling and upper classes sometimes used needle and thread as a material substitute for pen and ink: feminist scholars are beginning to study the embroidered 'ABC' samplers done by young girls and women, for instance, and also the more complex, sometimes subversive, messages that skilled embroiderers worked into tapestries and other 'fancy work'.[38] Nonetheless, the idea that needles and distaffs rather than pens were the proper instruments for women's hands clearly troubled many would-be women writers as well as those few humanist educators who did think that women should be taught the 'art' of writing. The Irish author of a dialogue circulated near the end of the seventeenth century, the *Parliament ná mBan* (the parliament of women), has the character Fionuala lament women's relegation to the domestic sphere where we attend 'to our distaffs and spindles, even though many of us are no good about the house'.[39] More than a century earlier in England, the headmaster of the Merchant Taylor's School, Richard Mulcaster, recommended that girls be educated at home so long as their learning of letters did not distract them from their sewing; Mulcaster saw the 'Roman' or 'italic' hand as appropriate for female pupils.[40] In this he was followed by Martin Billingsley, who in *The Pens Excellencie* (1618) opines that an italic hand is suitable for women because it is easy and therefore appropriate for the intellectually weaker sex.

The idea that women should be taught to write, we soon realise, does not necessarily mean that the male educator holds a high opinion of the female's intellectual or moral capacities. On the contrary, writing, like female education more generally, is often construed as 'useful' because it is a means of *controlling* a defective and potentially unruly sex. The concept of the woman writer, for such men, is of a docile user of the pen who follows men's instructions and spends most of her writing time copying men's (or the Bible's) words. Women, Billingsley avers, have limited abilities to concentrate: 'They, having not the patience to take any great paines, besides phantasticall and humorsome, must be taught that which they may instantly learne' (cited in Goldberg, *Writing Matter*, p. 139). Expressing a similarly dim view of women's powers of memory, Juan Luis Vives argues, in his enormously influential *Instruction of a Christian Woman* (written in 1523; first published in English in a translation by Richard Hyrde in 1529, and reprinted eight times before 1600), that both reading and writing should be taught only in ways that contribute directly to a girl's moral education:

When she shall be taught to read, let those books be taken in hand, that may teach good manners. And when she shall learn to write, let not her examples be void verses, nor wanton or trifling songs, but some sad sentences prudent and chaste, taken out of holy Scripture, or the sayings of philosophers, which by often writing she may fasten better in her memory.[41]

Women themselves could exploit the area of ideological ambiguity that male educators sketch out when they recommend that girls discipline their desires and memories by writing. Although the educators attempt to define female literacy as the dutiful *consumption* of men's words

– in contrast to a male literacy limned as the *production* of copious discourse[42] – women did not always respect that ideological division of the field of emerging literacies. A play by Elizabeth Cary entitled *The Tragedie of Mariam, Faire Queene of Jewry* and published in 1613 illustrates some of the ways in which an educated Renaissance woman could try to legitimise her act of writing by dissociating it conceptually from female 'public speech'. The first original drama by a woman to be published in England, *Mariam* offers an extensive meditation on the theme of 'transgressive' female speech and depicts, as an intriguing part of that meditation, a slave girl named Graphina. She is a minor character whose name plays on the Greek word for 'to write', *graphein*; she is repeatedly associated with 'silence', partly because her lover Pheroras prefers her to an 'infant' (from the Latin *infans*, 'speechless') that his brother Herod the king wants him to marry. The wordplay suggests that her name deliberately evokes the classical concept of writing as 'silent' speech. Her status as a handmaiden also evokes 'the traditional presentation of writing as ancillary (literally in the position of a handmaiden) to spoken discourse'.[43] Graphina's style of verbal expression strikingly contrasts with those displayed by the two major female characters in the play, Mariam and Salome, who challenge their husbands' authority through their shockingly 'unbridled' speech. (Salome further challenges masculine authority by boldly pursuing her own sexual desires beyond the bounds of marriage.) Graphina, utterly subservient to the man who wants to marry her, speaks only what he wants her to say. It seems likely that Cary uses Graphina to explore the fundamental paradox of the normative Renaissance ideal of the 'silent' wife who can be educated only if the education promotes chastity, obedience and 'housewifery': the paradox is that the husband does not really want an utterly silent wife; he wants, rather, a woman whose speech answers obediently to his own desires. Graphina, like the docile Kate whom Shakespeare represents at the end of *The Taming of the Shrew*, is in truth not silent but eloquent. Her eloquence, however, is perfectly schooled to express (or perhaps simply to mimic) the patriarchal ideologies held dear by her husband. Such a conception of 'legitimate' female utterance is ironically charged in Cary's play because it does not simply contrast Graphina with Mariam and Salome, but explicitly raises the possibility that 'silence' may be 'a sign of discontent' (II.i.42), an ambiguous or dissimulated sign that hides from the audience the true thoughts of the female writer or the female speaker. By this logic, writing that appears to be obedient, like Graphina's speech, may in fact harbour subversive designs, including – as shown in the next section – designs to go 'public' with and through a medium, writing, that humanist educators sought to mark off as 'private' for women.

'YOU PRESSE THE PRESS WITH LITTLE YOU HAVE MADE': WOMEN AND PRINT

The new technology of print, introduced in England with Caxton's first printed book in 1476, significantly affected the degrees and kinds of literacy distributed among the population of Britain between 1500 and 1700. Printed books played a key role in complicating and proliferating the cultural meanings of the act and product of writing. If a text (including the Bible itself) could be mechanically reproduced and sold for prices much lower than those commanded by laboriously copied medieval manuscripts, then the act and value of writing with a pen (from *penna*, the Latin word for 'wing', denoting the pen's origin in a feather or quill) inevitably changed. So did many ideas pertaining to the concept of 'the author'. The venerable (and of course gendered) medieval notion of God as the author not only of the Bible but also of the 'book of Nature' or the world acquired new meanings, Elizabeth Eisenstein argues, when Renaissance writers like Raleigh, Galileo, Campanella, Bacon and Browne advocated close observation of the 'hieroglyphs' of the 'book of God's work', as Bacon calls it in *The Proficiencie and Advancement of Learning Divine and Humane* (1605).[44] The new emphasis on empirical study of nature as a 'book' no less important than the Bible illustrates the profound 'reorientation' of a sacred textual tradition that occurred during the early modern period. 'New functions performed by print affected [religious] orthodoxy as well as heresy. They changed the very nature of authority and authorship', Eisenstein suggests (p. 454); and Wendy Wall explores the ways in which print publication both fostered and came to symbolise problems of social mobility in Renaissance England; print was therefore often figured as a transgressive act not only for women but also for men – especially those aspiring or born to 'gentle' status (*Imprint of Gender*, pp. 11–13).

Although a few women below the rank of gentry used the new technology of print to earn their living (Isabella Whitney, for instance, discussed below), many well-born women were inhibited from publishing their writing not only by ideologies of gender that defined women as 'private' beings, but also by aristocratic codes that defined the press as 'vulgar'. During the sixteenth and seventeenth centuries the realm of print was widely regarded as 'common' and the writer 'who went to market with his wares' was frequently the butt of satire, as J. W. Saunders has shown in his article 'The Stigma of Print'.[45] My epigraph for this section comes from a poem by Sir John Davies that dramatises the ambiguities that surrounded aristocratic women's relation to the printing press. Dedicating his *The Muses Sacrifice* (1612) to three noblewomen who were both important patrons of poetry and poets themselves, Davies encourages them not to make their creative 'wombs' into 'tombs' by failing to allow their poetic productions to reach a public audience. Even as he is ostensibly urging the noblewomen to publish their works, however, Davies underscores the sexual and social dangers of associating with the 'base' and 'adject Rhymers' who frequent the press. If the noblewomen were to 'presse the Press' with what they have made at home, Davies's metaphors imply that a sexual and social fall might ensue, with 'bastard' verses emerging from the women's entrance into a social space possessed by lower-class men.[46]

One of the noblewomen addressed in Davies's poem was Elizabeth Cary. The daughter of a wealthy lawyer, Cary was married at fifteen to an aristocrat who would become Viscount Falkland. Davies may have served as her handwriting teacher when she was a girl; he refers to her as his 'Pupill' in his dedicatory poem. Whether or not his ambiguous encouragement spurred her decision to allow her *Tragedie of Mariam* to be printed in the year following his poem's publication, her case illustrates a range of positions a woman writer could assume toward publication via printing. Her play appeared with the title-page statement, 'Written by that learned, virtuous, and truly noble Ladie E. C.'; a dedicatory sonnet which might have allowed contemporaries to identify E. C. as Elizabeth Cary was deleted from most of the extant printed copies of the play's one and only pre-twentieth-century edition. The play itself opens with a question about how often the heroine has 'run on with public voice', and the issue of transgressive female speech, as we have seen, is a major thematic concern throughout the play. Equally important, to any reader who knows something about Cary's own life and the mysterious circumstances under which her play was published, is the play's allegorical meditation on the problem of the *audience* of a women's spoken or written words. At one point in the play the chorus suggests that a wife's words should reach the ears of 'none but one'. The 'one' might be construed as the writer's husband (the 'owner' of her mind as well as her body, according to Cary's chorus); but the 'one' might also be construed as a reference to God or even to the writer's own self. The contemporary social practice of manuscript *circulation* is arguably being alluded to here, with the play raising serious questions about whether circulation even within the 'private' domestic sphere is safe for the wife when her husband opposes her most cherished ideas – as Cary's own husband, a Protestant, opposed his wife's leanings toward Roman Catholicism. The distinction between 'private' and 'public' realms became indeed very complex in the context of religious disagreements within the home – disagreements that were discussed in both Catholic and Protestant literature about wifely (and citizenly) behaviour. Cary's play about a husband who unjustly 'silences' or censors his wife's words (by cutting off her head) might well have displeased her own husband had he read it or seen it performed in one of those 'private' dramatic productions that evidently occurred not infrequently in wealthy households. The fact that the play was published in only one small edition, after circulating for some years in manuscript, underscores the difficulties surrounding the practice as well as the theory of 'publishing' by aristocratic Renaissance women.

Later in her life, however, when Cary assumed the role of translator of a religious work rather than the role of 'author' of a play, she not only used her own name but explicitly mentioned her refusal to 'make use of the worne-out forme of saying I printed it against my will, mooved by the importunitie of Friends...'[47] Translation, commonly depicted as a 'female' mode of writing in the Renaissance (for instance by John Florio in the preface to his famous translation of Montaigne's *Essays*) was, as I mentioned above, one of several paths a woman writer could pursue to ensure that her words – and designs – reached an audience even when many members of the potential audience held that women should not be 'authors'. Margaret Tyler, in her fascinating defence of her decision to publish her translation of a Spanish romance in 1578, does make use of the custom Cary mocks; Tyler insists that 'others' encouraged her to undertake the translation. She goes on, however, to argue more boldly that 'it is all one for a woman to pen a story, as for a man to address his story to a woman'; moreover, she hopes that among the 'il willers' in her audience some 'are not so straight that they would enforce me necessarily either not to write or to write of divinitie'.[48] Though Tyler's translation follows fairly closely the Spanish original by Diego Ortuñez de Calahorra, her choice of a text to translate makes an original, and arguably politically subversive, statement to the English audience of the late 1570s; as Deborah Uman has recently shown, *The Mirrour*'s opening narrative about 'contested inheritance, political alliances, disguised identity, illicit marriage and concealed birth' offers an English audience some pointed analogies to contemporary historical events concerning the problem of women's succession – a vexed problem at a time when Elizabeth Tudor was being criticised as a 'bastard' and various factions were seeking to put other women – Lady Jane Gray and Mary Queen of Scots, for instance – on Elizabeth's throne.[49] Behind the humble guise of the translator, women like Elizabeth Cary, Mary Sidney and Margaret Tyler, among others, wrote with strong views and, arguably, more ability to communicate to at least some members of their audience than most modern critics have allowed.

Though translation and other methods of disguising or softening claims to authorial power allowed some Renaissance women to reach an audience – either via manuscript 'circulation' or via print – there is no doubt that the cultural strictures against female self-expression resulted in some works being censored in ways that prevent us from reading them at all. There is a spectrum that ranges from unconscious and conscious self-censorship through unfavourable audience reactions that led certain women to 'recall' their printed works, to explicit, institutionally mandated censorship of the kind suffered by Cary's translation of du Perron. Works by male authors were also affected by various kinds and degrees of censorship, but it is interesting to note that censorship as a cultural phenomenon was often gendered female in the early modern period; a censored text was figured as a 'castrated' one, as Milton vividly suggests in his *Areopagitica* of 1644, a treatise advocating (within certain limits) freedom of the pen and of the press. If, as Foucault argues, modern Western ideas of the 'author' are intricately bound up with ideas about an individual who is responsible – and hence punishable – for transgressive utterance, then ideologies of gender may traverse ideologies of authorship in ways more complicated than critics have generally allowed. The ideological and material complexities of censorship – writing's dark twin – need in any case to be explored if we are to understand a passage like the one in the *Life* of Elizabeth Cary by her daughter that describes one of Cary's early writings (possibly the prefatory sonnet of *Mariam*). This text was designed, the daughter insists, only for her mother's 'private recreation' and later 'stolen out of [her] sister-in-law's (her friend's) chamber and printed, but by her own procurement [it] was called in'.[50] Whatever the historical truth of this story, it dramatises the problems surrounding the act of making one's 'private' works public if one were a noblewoman, or, for that matter, a nobleman: Saunders gives many examples of writers who were born or aspired to 'gentle' status, disavowing, or apologising for, the 'taint' of print.[51] Such disavowals and apologies, and they are legion in the period, suggest that 'self-expression', for women or for men, was hardly the 'good' – much less the 'right' – it is often taken to be today; on the contrary, the desire for 'fame' or 'glory' through one's words was sharply hedged, and sometimes directly countered, by both Christian and aristocratic ideologies that valued self-censorship or self-effacement. Christianity often marked the quest for fame as prideful and pagan; and the emergent ideal of the 'courtier' legitimised self-display only under the paradoxical guise of what Castiglione called *sprezzatura*, a kind of 'scorn' for showing anything like (vulgar) ambition. A certain kind of self-display had, however, been traditional for noblemen, in their roles either as soldiers or as givers of magnificent hospitality. From these traditional paths to 'glory', as well as from newer paths drawn by humanists concerned with literary fame, women were barred.

Margaret Ezell, a feminist scholar who has examined Renaissance women's frequent reliance on manuscript circulation instead of the printing press, urges students to interrogate 'the modern emphasis on publication as the measure of feminine accomplishment' and, correlatively, to distrust bibliographies and books that focus mainly on printed texts by early modern women. 'If all that is known is a list of women who published their works', Ezell argues, 'we do not really know who the women writers of the [sixteenth or] seventeenth century were or how and why they wrote' (*The Patriarch's Wife*, p. 64). Countering many recent feminist constructions of the period that have seen women being silenced by a misogynist culture, Ezell complicates the 'victimisation' picture by looking at some of the ways in which women of various classes regarded the medium of print as politically and theologically dangerous, a medium of 'falasies' (fallacies) in the term of one seventeenth-century Protestant woman, where a writer might well lose control over her (and God's) meanings. Ezell's example is Grace Carrie of Bristol, whose friends encouraged her to publish her treatise of prophecies in the late 1630s. Though she refused to print her treatise, fearing that her 'thoughts might be perverted by "voulgar" readers,' she did not 'remain "silent"'; instead, as Ezell remarks, Carrie 'prepared manuscript copies, two of which are known to have survived' (p. 65).

Ezell describes three forms of manuscript 'exchanges' available to women writers of the early modern era:

They could produce manuscript books, circulate individual items in loose sheets which might also be preserved in commonplace books and manuscript miscellanies, or they could engage in correspondence. Obviously these three modes are related – a poem or essay could begin in a letter, be copied and circulated, and finally end up either in a printed text or in a manuscript volume. (p. 65)

Of these three forms, the manuscript volumes are now the rarest, and they clearly show the interpenetration of print and manuscript cultures during this era: the manuscripts 'have the appearance of a printed book', Ezell remarks, with 'title pages, prefaces or dedications' and sometimes dates and page numbers. Like medieval manuscripts, these manuscript 'books' often have 'intricate border ornaments and designs at the beginnings and ends of sections' (p. 66). Such volumes complicate the modern tendency to draw a clear distinction between public and private realms, and the modern feminist tendency to correlate the former with men, the latter with women. Though there *are* indeed early modern writings that strongly articulate a gendered division between public and private spheres, the existence of manuscript publication, and its use by both men and women, creates an interesting border territory on various ideological maps: manuscript volumes, in Ezell's view, present written texts in a variety of genres, 'in an impressive, substantial form, making their content available and attractive for future generations of readers and perhaps attracting patronage for the author. They were first and foremost presentation pieces ... "private" only in the sense that the author, not the bookseller, had control of the manuscript' (p. 68).

On the issue of 'control', Ezell is perhaps too sanguine; throughout the early modern period writers frequently complain that their work has been 'pirated', whether in manuscript or printed form. An aristocratic author who could afford a 'manuscript volume' might well have had more control over her or his words, during her or his lifetime at least, than an author whose work, once printed, would have been legally owned by the printer or bookseller before the Copyright Act of 1709; but as Saunders remarks, the transcription of manuscripts in the period, or the transcription of transcriptions – 'by friends of friends, by relatives of fortunate possessors of a copy, by literary dilettantes and satellites, by commonplace bookkeepers, and by other unconnected enthusiasts – was a process with which [the author] had nothing to do' (p. 153). An author, whether male or female, could not protect her or his privacy simply by avoiding print – which may be one reason why Elizabeth Cary, meditating in *The Tragedie of Mariam* on precisely the question of 'private' versus 'public' expression, has her chorus imply that a woman who wants truly to keep her thoughts her own should communicate them only to herself or to God.[52] Indeed, as Saunders remarks, the writer of a manuscript could rarely be sure 'how many copies were abroad', nor could the author be sure of their accuracy nor even whether 'during transmission his [or her] own name had been appended' ('The Stigma of Print', p. 153). Though Ezell performs a useful polemical service in exploring a separate realm of 'manuscript circulation' in which women actively participated, we should also appreciate just how complex and permeable the boundaries between manuscript and print publication were during this era. Writers of any social estate had in Saunders's view rather little control 'over the ultimate destinations' of their writings, and there was little they could do 'to prevent an occasional manuscript from falling into the hands of a compiler who might print it'.

Despite the strictures against 'female public utterance' that coloured many women writers' attitudes – or expressed attitudes – toward print, some British women did turn to writing for their living in the sixteenth and seventeenth centuries. As Ann Rosalind Jones remarks, the economic problems that beset the professional male writer in the period were even greater for women; publishers typically paid a writer 'one small fee for a manuscript; no copyright went to the writer and no royalties were paid, however many editions were printed. For a woman writer, negotiations with a publisher were likely to go forward under an even greater power imbalance, given the scarcity of women colleagues in the book trade.'[53] In the 1570s, however, Isabella Whitney – a 'country gentlewoman in London', as Jones calls her – did succeed in publishing two short collections of poems in cheap pamphlet form and aimed at a broad London readership. Whitney presents herself as an 'Author' in her preface to the reader, and though she is modest in an appropriately 'feminine' style (she tells us that she began to read and write only because illness kept her indoors), she writes with 'a constant alertness to a double public: the male readers her publisher invites to buy *A Sweet Nosegay* and an audience of women likely to appreciate her confident self-representation and subversive humour' (Jones, *Currency of Eros*, p. 51).

The example of Whitney and other non-aristocratic women who wrote in a wide variety of discursive genres (many of them 'non-canonical' and even 'non-literary' according to some modern definitions of that term) shows that Virginia Woolf was wrong when she cited Aphra Behn, who wrote after the Restoration, as the first English woman to earn her living by her pen. In *A Room of One's Own* (1928), Woolf imagined the tragic story of 'Judith Shakespeare' to dramatise the paucity of opportunity for would-be women writers in Renaissance England. Modern feminist scholarship has unearthed many sixteenth- and early seventeenth-century women Woolf did not know of, and has thus partially responded to Woolf's eloquent plea for a new history of Britain that would not be so lopsidedly focused on great (and we can add white) men. Nonetheless, as we expand our knowledge of how and what early modern women wrote – in italic hand, in shorthand,[54] in manuscripts that now exist only in printed versions – it is worth remembering that some men wrote under women's names or under initials that we cannot now link to specific historical characters. A 'character', in the sense of an alphabetic letter, is not, in fact, a reliable clue to one's 'personal' character, much less to one's gender. 'Anon.', as Woolf surmised, was often a female; but Anon., in early modern Britain, may also have been a heterosexual or 'sodomitical' male, an 'Indian' educated in a colonial school, or even a black African prince like the one featured in Aphra Behn's novella *Oroonoko*. Behn's narrative plays dizzyingly with different notions of authorship and authority: like Defoe, Behn presents the author both as an 'eyewitness' reporter and as a liar; but she differs from Defoe in presenting the author also as a seductive 'Mistress' to her readers and obliquely, in this particular novella, to the black male hero whose tragic story she relates and whose words she appropriates – or steals – for her own authorial purposes. With Aphra Behn, at the end of our period, we have a writer who expands the concept of the woman writer in both fascinating and disturbing ways. She illustrates how a talented and determined woman unencumbered with a husband or father could make her way as a professional writer and earn the admiration – as well as sometimes the ire – of male contemporaries; but she also illustrates how a literate white Englishwoman could use her 'female pen' to participate in the colonising project, a project that involved enslaving and silencing men and women of colour whose native language was not English.[55] The concept of the 'woman writer' in the early modern period signifies a shifting mix of illusion and empowerment; the consequences of women's emergence as writers were equally complex.

NOTES

1. Trinh T. Minha-ha, *Woman, Native, Other: Writing, Postcoloniality, and Feminism* (Bloomington: Indiana University Press, 1989), p. 8.
2. England's efforts to subdue the population of the 'internal colony' of Ireland intensified after its claim to parts of France was undermined by the decisive loss at the Battle of Calais in 1558; see David Cairns and Shaun Richards, *Writing Ireland: Colonialism, Nationalism, and Culture* (Manchester: Manchester University Press, 1988), pp. 1–2.

3. See Cynthia J. Brown, 'Text, Image, and Authorial Self-Consciousness in Late Medieval Paris', in *Printing the Written Word: the Social History of Books, circa 1450–1520*, ed. Sandra L. Hindmana (Ithaca, NY: Cornell University Press, 1991), pp. 111–12. See also *Discourses of Authority in Medieval and Renaissance Literature*, ed. Kevin Brownlee and Walter Stephens (Hanover: University Press of New England, 1989).

4. Michel Foucault, 'What is an Author?' (1969), reprinted in *Language, Counter-Memory, Practice: Selected Essays and Interviews by Michel Foucault*, trans. Donald F. Bouchard and Sherry Simon (Ithaca, NY: Cornell University Press, 1977), pp. 113–38; the passage quoted is from p. 122.

5. For useful discussions of different aspects of this historical process, see Gerald Eades Bentley, *The Profession of Dramatist in Shakespeare's Time, 1590–1642* (Princeton, NJ: Princeton University Press, 1971); Martin Elsky, *Authorizing Words: Speech, Writing, and Print in the English Renaissance* (Ithaca, NY: Cornell University Press, 1989); and J. W. Saunders, *The Profession of English Letters* (London: Routledge and Kegan Paul, 1964).

6. For a discussion of late medieval modes of (male) authorship in England, see H. S. Bennett, 'The Author and his Public in the Fourteenth and Fifteenth Centuries', *Essays and Studies by Members of the English Association*, 23 (1938), 7–24. The classic study of the 'print revolution' in Europe is Marshall McLuhan, *The Gutenberg Galaxy: the Making of Typographic Man* (Toronto: University of Toronto Press, 1962): see also Elizabeth Eisenstein, *The Printing Press as an Agent of Change* (Cambridge: Cambridge University Press, 1979) and Lucien Febvre and Henri-Jean Martin, *The Coming of the Book: the Impact of Printing, 1450–1800*, translated from the 1958 French edition by David Gerard (London: Verso, 1990).

7. See Lyman Ray Patterson, *Copyright in Historical Perspective* (Nashville: University of Tennessee Press, 1968), and Joseph Loewenstein, 'The Script in the Marketplace', *Representations*, 12 (Autumn, 1985), 101–14.

8. See Foucault, 'What is an Author', p. 124, and also Loewenstein, who argues persuasively that though 'Foucault's nearly exclusive concentration on the effect of the censoriousness of Church and State on the development of modern authorship has been salutary', it has also slighted 'the effect of the *market* in books on that development' ('The Script in the Marketplace', p. 111n7).

9. Wendy Wall, *The Imprint of Gender: Authorship and Publication in the English Renaissance* (Ithaca, NY: Cornell University Press, 1993), p. xi.

10. For useful discussions of the paradoxes in English Renaissance women's modes of authorship, see Elaine Beilin, *Redeeming Eve: Women Writers of the English Renaissance* (Princeton, NJ: Princeton University Press, 1987), and Mary Ellen Lamb, *Gender and Authorship in the Sidney Circle* (Madison: University of Wisconsin Press, 1990), both with further bibliographies.

11. See Suzanne Hull, *Chaste, Silent, and Obedient: English Books for Women, 1475–1640* (San Marino, CA: Huntington Library, 1982), and chapter 3 of this volume.

12. Irish women, for instance, emerged as writers later than Scottish and English women did; see B. Cunningham, 'Women and Gaelic Literature', in Margaret MacCurtain and Mary O'Dowd, eds., *Women in Early Modern Ireland* (Edinburgh: Edinburgh University Press, 1993), pp. 152–8. For a discussion of the seventeenth-century Scottish poet Mary MacLeod, see Derick Thomson, *An Introduction to Gaelic Poetry* (London: 1974; 2nd edn, Edinburgh: Edinburgh University Press, 1989), pp. 132–7.

13. See H. Grundmann, 'Litteratus-illiteratus: der Wandl einer Bildungsnorm vom Altertum zum Mittelalter', *Archiv für Külturgeschichte*, 40 (1958), 1–66; and also his 'Die Frauen und die litteratur im Mittelalter', *Archiv für Külturgeschichte*, 26 (1936), 129–61. See also Rosamond McKitterick's introduction to *The Uses of Literacy in Early Medieval Europe* (Cambridge: Cambridge University Press, 1992).

14. For a discussion of aristocratic views of clerkly skills as a 'derogation' of nobility, see Margaret Ferguson, *Trials of Desires: Renaissance Defenses of Poetry* (New Haven: Yale University Press, 1983), chapter 2; and also M. T. Clanchy, *From Memory to Written Record, England, 1066–1307* (Cambridge, MA: Harvard University Press, 1979), p. 23.

15. Quoted from *Henry VI Part 2*, IV.ii.103 (The Riverside Shakespeare edition; Boston: Houghton Mifflin, 1974).

16. See Walter Ong, S. J., 'Latin Language Study as a Renaissance Puberty Rite' *SP* 56 (1959), 103–24. See also the discussion of literacy in chapter 4 of this volume.

17. David Cressy, *Literacy and the Social Order: Reading and Writing in Tudor England* (Cambridge: Cambridge University Press, 1980), p. 59.

18. For a useful discussion of the problems of measuring literacy, see Keith Thomas, 'The Meaning of Literacy in Early Modern England', in Gerd Baumann, ed., *The Written Word: Literacy in Transition* (Oxford: Clarendon Press, 1986).

19. See Margaret Spufford, *Small Books and Pleasant Histories: Popular Fiction and its Readership in Seventeenth-Century England* (London: Methuen, 1981), p. 22.

20. 'By marriage, the husband and wife became one person in law – and that person was the husband', writes Lawrence Stone in *The Family, Sex and Marriage in England, 1500–1800* (1977; abridged edn Harmondsworth: Penguin, 1979), p. 136.

21. Quoted from John Lawson and Harold Silver, *A Social History of Education in England* (London: Methuen, 1973), p. 121. The so-called 'petty' schools, founded by charitable organizations or local governments to replace the Catholic schools that had existed before the English Reformation, were sometimes taught by a woman and hence known as 'dame schools'; they paid their teachers poorly and usually charged students 3 or 4d a week per pupil – a sum 'far more than the really poor could pay', as Josephine Kamm observes in *Hope Deferred: Girls' Education in English History* (London: Butler and Tanner, 1965), p. 65. For a discussion of these schools and the teaching of reading prior to writing, see Margaret Spufford, 'Elementary Education

and the Acquisition of Reading Skills', *Small Books and Pleasant Histories*, pp. 19–44.

22. The horn book, as Josephine Kamm explains, 'acquired its name from the thin sheet of transparent horn which was laid over a strip of parchment and mounted on an oblong piece of wood. It usually contained the *paternoster*, the alphabet, a set of syllables, and sometimes Roman numerals' (*Hope Deferred*, p. 34).

23. For further discussion of women's education, see chapter 1 in this volume.

24. See chapter 4 in this volume; also Caroline Lucas, *Writing for Women: the Example of Woman as Reader in Elizabethan Romance* (Milton Keynes: Open University Press, 1989), especially chapter 1.

25. In her *Reflections Upon Marriage* of 1706, Mary Astell writes that the 'Celebrated Name of *Author*' should be rejected by women because 'Bold Truths may pass while the Speaker is *Incognito*'; cited and discussed in Catherine Sharrock, 'De-ciphering Women and De-Scribing Authority: the Writings of Mary Astell', in Isobel Grundy and Susan Wiseman, eds., *Women, Writing, History: 1640–1740* (London: Batsford, 1992), pp. 111–12.

26. Julia Boffey in Carol M. Meale, ed., *Women and Literature in Britain, 1150–1500* (Cambridge: Cambridge University Press, 1993), p. 161. On Kempe, see, for example, Janel M. Mueller, 'Autobiography of a New "Creatur": Female Spirituality, Selfhood, and Authorship in *The Book of Margery Kempe*', in *Women in the Middle Ages and the Renaissance: Literary and Historical Perspectives*, ed. Mary Beth Rose (Syracuse: Syracuse University Press, 1986), pp. 155–71.

27. For discussions of Mrs Attaway, see Mary Nyquist and Margaret Ferguson, *Re-membering Milton: Essays on the Texts and the Traditions* (New York: Methuen, 1987), p. xiii, and Keith Thomas, 'Women and the Civil War Sects', *Past and Present*, 13 (1958), 42–62.

28. For Swinnerton's testimony, printed in London in 1628 under the title *A Brief Description of the Notorious Life of J. Lamb*, see Charlotte F. Otten, ed., *English Women's Voices, 1540–1700* (Miami: Florida International University Press, 1992), pp. 29–32.

29. John Guillory, *Cultural Capital: the Problem of Literary Canon Formation* (Chicago: University of Chicago Press, 1993), p. 18.

30. See Brian Street, *Literacy in Theory and Practice* (Cambridge: Cambridge University Press, 1984).

31. See George Puttenham's advice that the writer take as his (or her?) model the 'usuall speach of the Court, and that of London and the shires lying about London with lx. myles, and not much above' (*The Arte of English Poesie* (1589); facsimile reprint, Kent, OH: Kent State University Press, 1970), p. 157.

32. Compare Guillory's call for a reconsideration of the concept of 'woman writer' in the context of the modern debate on 'expanding the canon', *Cultural Capital*, p. 16; and also on this issue, Denise Riley, *'Am I that Name'? Feminism and the Category of 'Women' in History* (Minneapolis: University of Minnesota Press, 1988).

33. Katherine Usher Henderson and Barbara F. McManus are among those who take 'Jane Anger' as the name of a historical woman; see their *Half Humankind: Contexts and Texts of the Controversy about Women in England, 1540–1640* (Urbana: University of Illinois Press, 1985), p. 21, and, for a text of the pamphlet, pp. 173–88.

34. Jonathan Goldberg, *Writing Matter: From the Hands of the English Renaissance* (Stanford: Stanford University Press, 1990), p. 138.

35. Goldberg, *Writing Matter*, pp. 60–1. Desainliens's *Campo di Fior* (London, 1583) was a version in English, Latin, Italian and French of Vives's 1538 dialogues for schoolboys, *Linguae Latinae Exercitatio*.

36. On the significance of this metaphor, see Louis Montrose, 'The Work of Gender in the Discourse of Discovery', *Representations*, 33 (Winter 1991), 1–41.

37. Anne Bradstreet, *The Tenth Muse Lately Spring Up in America* (London, 1650), cited from *The Complete Works of Anne Bradstreet*, ed. Joseph R. McElrath, Jr. and Allen P. Rabb (Boston: Twayne, 1981), p. 7. See also M. Ferguson, 'A Room Not Their Own: Renaissance Women as Readers and Writers', in Clayton Koelb and Susan Noakes, eds., *The Comparative Perspective on Literature* (Ithaca, NY: Cornell University Press, 1988), pp. 93–116.

38. See Rozsika Parker, *The Subversive Stitch: Embroidery in Women's Lives, 1300–1900* (London: Woman's Press, 1984); also, on the associations between writing and spinning, Tilde Sankovitch, 'Inventing Authority of Origin: *The Difficult Enterprise*', in Mary Beth Rose, ed., *Women in the Middle Ages and the Renaissance: Literary and Historical Perspectives* (Syracuse: Syracuse University Press, 1986), pp. 23–42; and Betty Travitsky and Adele Seef, eds., *Attending to Women in Early Modern England* (Delaware: University of Delaware Press, 1994), pp. 200–3.

39. Cited in M. MacCurtain, 'Women, Education and Learning', in MacCurtain and O'Dowd, eds., *Women in Early Modern Ireland*, p. 174.

40. See Mulcaster's chapter, 'The Education of Girls', in *Positions* (London 1581; facsimile in Richard Mulcaster, *The Training up of Children* (New York: da Capo, 1971)).

41. Juan Luis Vives, *De Institutione Foeminae Christianae*, trans. Richard Hyrde (1529), reprinted in *Vives and the Renascence Education of Women*, ed. Foster Watson (New York: Longmans, Green and Co., 1912), p. 55.

42. On humanist theories and practices of writing as the production of *copia*, see Richard Halpern, *The Poetics of Primitive Accumulation* (Ithaca, NY: Cornell University Press, 1991), pp. 48–9 *et passim*.

43. Unnamed in Cary's source text, Graphina appears in act 2 scene 1 of *The Tragedie of Mariam*; the quoted phrase is from the endnote to line 18 of that scene in the edition of the play by Barry Weller and Margaret Ferguson (Berkeley: University of California Press, 1994), p. 120. All citations are from this edition.

44. See Eisenstein, *The Printing Press*, p. 455 and n5.

45. See J. W. Saunders, 'The Stigma of Print: a Note on the Social Bases of

Tudor Poetry', *Essays in Criticism*, 1–2 (1951/52), 139–64. On the social implications of print versus manuscript publication, see also Margaret Ezell, *The Patriarch's Wife: Literary Evidence and the History of the Family* (Chapel Hill: University of North Carolina Press, 1987); Wall, *The Imprint of Gender*; and Harold Love, *Scribal Publication in Seventeenth-Century England* (Oxford: Oxford University Press, 1993).

46. Quoted from Alexander B. Grosart, ed., *The Complete Works of Sir John Davies of Hereford* (2 vols.; London: Chatto and Windus, 1876), vol. II, p. 5.

47. Quoted from Cary's preface to her translation of a French treatise published in 1620 by Jacques Davy du Perron; the translation, which was dedicated to Queen Henrietta Maria and which was suppressed by Archbishop Abbot, with only a few copies escaping burning, is entitled *The Reply of the Most Illustrious Cardinall of Perron, to the Answeare of the Most Excellent King of Great Britaine* (Douay, 1630).

48. 'M. T. to the Reader', the preface to *The Mirrour of Princely Deedes and Knighthood* (London, 1578), quoted from Betty Travitsky, ed., *The Paradise of Women: Writings by Englishwomen of the Renaissance* (1981; reprinted New York: Columbia University Press, 1989), pp. 145–6.

49. Deborah Uman, 'Mirrors of Succession: Women and the Quest for the Crown in Elizabethan England and Margaret Tyler's Translation of *The Mirrour of Princely Deedes and Knighthood*', (unpublished conference paper).

50. *Life*, in *The Tragedie of Mariam*, p. 190.

51. See, for example, Alexander Bradshaw's letter prefacing the printed edition of the *Shepherds Starre* by his brother Thomas: 'I have made bolde to publish the booke which you left me for my private use. I was moved thereunto by your friends, and my favorets heere in England.' Cited in Saunders, 'The Stigma of Print', p. 145.

52. Catherine Belsey discusses this ambiguity about the implied audience of a wife's words in Cary's chorus in her important discussion of 'Speech and Silence' in *The Subject of Tragedy: Identity and Difference in Renaissance Drama* (London: Methuen, 1985), p. 181.

53. See Ann Rosalind Jones's aptly titled chapter 'Writing to Live', in *The Currency of Eros: Women's Love Lyric in Europe, 1540–1620* (Bloomington: Indiana University Press, 1990), pp. 36–52; the citation is from p. 36.

54. On the fascinating issue of women's use of shorthand, see the remark made in 1652 by Sir Ralph Verney, warning a friend, 'let not your young girl learn Latin, nor shorthand: the difficulty of the first may keep her from vice ... but the easiness of the other may be a prejudice to her, the pride of taking sermons notes hath made multitudes of women unfortunate'. Quoted in R. Valerie Lucas, 'Puritan Preaching and the Politics of the Family', in Haselkorn and Travitsky, *The Renaissance Englishwoman in Print*, p. 235n10.

55. See Margaret Ferguson, 'News from the New World: Miscegenous Romance in Aphra Behn's *Oroonoko* and *The Widow Ranter*', in David Lee Miller, Harold Weber and Sharon O'Dair, eds., *The Production of English Renaissance Culture* (Ithaca, NY: Cornell University Press, 1994), pp. 151–89.

CHAPTER 8

Courtly writing by women

Helen Hackett

In this strang[e] labourinth how shall I turne?

Mary Wroth, 'A Crowne of Sonetts dedicated to Love'

I

'Courtly writing' is a phrase with literary–generic as well as social connotations. The modern phrase 'courtly love'[1] refers to mediaeval and Renaissance literature in which a male lover laments his desire for an unyielding mistress; a tradition which was influenced by the fourteenth-century Italian poet Petrarch, whose lyrics expressed his love for the chaste Laura, and by neo-Platonic philosophy, which regarded uncon-summated passion for a beautiful woman as spiritually elevating. Other genres also are distinctively courtly: panegyric, for instance, the poetry of praise that sought the favour of a potential patron or of the monarch, was obviously intrinsic to court life. Chivalric romance, a genre of rambling fantastic narrative concerning the adventures of knights and ladies, was set in fictional pseudo-mediaeval courts, but often reflected the culture of the real contemporary court. 'Closet' drama (discussed briefly at the end of this chapter and in chapter 12 of this volume) was also associated with court circles.

Several influential accounts of courtly writing might suggest that it was entirely practised by men. J. W. Saunders describes how courtier poets preferred manuscript circulation among an exclusive coterie over the ungentlemanly exposure of print publication; all his examples are male.[2] Daniel Javitch argues that the conduct and poetry alike of male courtiers consisted in elegant dissimulation.[3] Arthur Marotti regards the courtly poetry of unfulfilled heterosexual male desire as the metaphorical ex-pression of frustrated political ambitions.[4] All three are interested in the self-fashioning of the male courtier; women appear in their accounts, at most, as inspiring, requesting, or providing an 'admiring circle' for poems.[5] They might leave us thinking not only that courtly writing was not practised by women, but that it offered no subject position for women to occupy.

However, courtly literature itself provides many fictional models for female self-expression. For instance, an important source for Elizabethan concepts of courtliness, *The Book of the Courtier* by Castiglione, gave prominence to women.[6] It is a fictional dialogue among prominent figures of the court of Urbino, of both sexes, who debate what accomplishments combine to make the ideal courtier. The dialogue takes place in the chambers of the Duchess of Urbino, it is presided over by her vivacious lady-in-waiting Emilia Pia, and the third volume (of four) concerns the definition of the ideal courtly lady. Such participation by ladies in courtly pursuits is often replicated in Elizabethan fiction. In George Gascoigne's romance 'The Adventures of Master F. J.', the ladies Elinor, Pergo and Frances preside over and participate in games of *questioni d'amore*, where a circle of wits of both sexes tell and judge stories of the vicissitudes of love.[7]

Heroines in courtly fiction also wrote poetry: in Sir Philip Sidney's *Arcadia*, for example, poems are composed and recited not only by male suitors, including Pyrocles in the feminine guise of an Amazon, but also by Pamela, Philoclea, Gynecia and a shepherdess.[8] Moreover, courtly poetry by men sometimes gave fictional voice to women: in Sidney's *Astrophil and Stella*, Stella is given both reported speech (sonnets 60, 61, 62, 68 and 81) and direct speech (sonnet 63, songs 4 and 8);[9] Spenser's mistress, in *Amoretti* 75, mocks him as a 'Vayne man' for his romantic yet futile gesture of writing her name upon the strand.[10] At such points, although the sonnet mistress is a fictional construct of the male author and a foil to his subjectivity, she does in a sense answer back, and provides a model for female poetic utterance. Female retort was popular with readers, to judge by the success of the genre of 'female complaint', influenced by Ovid's *Heroides*, in which abandoned female lovers from mythology or history lamented their fates. Examples included Samuel Daniel's *Complaint of Rosamond* (1592), Michael Drayton's *England's Heroical Epistles* (1597), and Shakespeare's *A Lover's Complaint* (1609).[11]

In fact, Penelope Rich, upon whom Sidney's Stella was based, was herself the subject of such a fictional complaint: a pair of Jacobean verse epistles imagine Sidney bitterly upbraiding her for her marriage to Lord Rich, and her reply. She begins abjectly, describing herself as a martyr to shame, but becomes increasingly eloquent on her own miseries in her enforced marriage, and even strident as she reminds Sidney that he (according to this version of events) took her virginity: 'were I a mayde againe thou shouldst not leaue mee / Yet fayth and if I were thou wouldst deceaue mee' (lines 65–6).[12] If, as seems likely, the epistles are by a man,[13] then such words from the fictional Penelope might demonstrate that even a male ventriloquist's use of a 'female' voice could express women's grievances sympathetically. Yet it may be that readers were intended not to sympathise so much as to condemn and/or relish Penelope's sexual forwardness: a few lines on, she boldly proposes to Sidney the continuation of their affair despite her marriage (lines 69–70).

Thus courtly writing did offer fictional models for female articulacy; yet, as this last poem illustrates, it was also bound by the widespread cultural tendency to equate women's public self-display and verbal freedom with sexual promiscuity. Courtly writing might seem to offer immunity from such defamation in its emphasis on exclusivity and privacy. Its characteristic setting is the refined circle of intimates, as represented by Castiglione and his imitators, and as described by Saunders; even more secludedly, romance heroines usually compose their verses in solitude, as a private outlet for their passions. However, they are almost always overheard reciting their poetry, or else their writing is discovered by a reader. Such revelation of hidden feelings serves a narrative purpose in moving the plot forward, but it also highlights the fact that courtly poetry was rarely absolutely private; indeed, the survival of poems for us to read today depends on some form of transmission. Once disclosed, however exclusively, a poem was labile; even limited exposure unleashed it from the author's control and could result in wider circulation, possibly reaching as far as print.[14] In fact, the privacy of courtly writings can consist largely in their textual assertions of their own privacy.

Even coterie circulation could therefore endanger female authors' reputations. Sir John Harington expressed his own disdain of print by sexualising his muse and her relations with her readers: she 'never sought to set to sale her wryting', but preferred to 'sport' with select friends.[15] If the muse's relations even with her select readers were sexual, then a female poet could easily stand accused of immodest intercourse. Courtly ladies' over-exercise of their tongues was criticised with palpable sexual innuendo by Richard Brathwaite in 1631, who said that 'in no way detract they more from their honour, than by giving too much free scope to that glibbery member'.[16] If speech was morally vulnerable, then writing, with its potential to pass from hand to hand, must have been much more so.

Yet we know that courtly writing by women did exist, because it was the object of both praise and blame. Ben Jonson, in his 'Epigram on the Court Pucell [slut]', satirised the female authorship of Cecelia Bulstrode as sexual deviance: 'with tribade [lesbian] lust she force[s] a muse'.[17] On the other hand, one of the principal themes of *The Arte of English Poesie* by George Puttenham, an Elizabethan work devoted to the definition of courtly poetry, was praise of Queen Elizabeth as 'being alreadie, of any that I know in our time, the most excellent Poet'.[18] The writings of Lady Mary Wroth were praised by a number of well-known poets, including Jonson, who in her case wrote flatteringly that 'I . . . / Since I exscribe your sonnets, am become / A better lover, and much better poet'.[19] Arguably such compliments can be dismissed as exercises in panegyric. Nevertheless, both the criticisms and the commendations show, in contradiction of the impressions given by some modern accounts, that courtly poetry was written by women, and that it was known and recognised on the contemporary literary scene.

However, attempts to identify courtly writing by women can be frustrated by the very processes of coterie circulation, wherein much writing was unsigned and unattributed, or else attribution was attached by someone other than the author. It is therefore often unclear whether we are reading a man using a female voice, as in the examples above, or a woman's own composition. The problem of authenticity is a complex one, since of course even autobiographical writing by a woman entails the construction of a literary self; however, if we think of authenticity as a scale, it can be hard to establish whereabouts upon it to place many courtly texts. The uses of female voices by male authors are also diverse, and may include exploitative voyeurism into a female figure's private thoughts and feelings, without precluding a Renaissance or modern reader's sympathy for or identification with that figure.

John Soowthern's *Pandora* (1584), a collection of poems, includes 'Foure Epytaphes, made by the Countes of *Oxenford* after the death of her young Sonne, *the Lord Bulbecke*', and an 'Epitaph, made by the Queenes Maiestie, at the death of the Princesse of *Espinoye*'.[20] The former can be read as moving laments by a bereaved mother: the Countess grieves that 'a womans last chylde, is the most beloued', and that '*Destins*, and Gods, you might rather haue tanne, / My twentie yeeres: then the two daies of my sonne' (first epitaph, line 14; second epitaph, lines 9–10). But the problem with these poems, as with the epitaph attributed to the Queen, is that they use exactly the same idiosyncratic versification and style as the other poems in the volume, which are presented as Soowthern's own. It seems likely that they are his compositions, in dramatic voices.

Some manuscript collections of poems by Edward de Vere, the Earl of Oxford, include a poem subscribed 'Vavaser', meaning Anne Vavasour, one of Queen Elizabeth's Gentlewomen of the Bedchamber, who had an affair with Oxford in 1580–8 that produced an illegitimate son. The poem is a female complaint: it opens with a presumably male speaker 'Sittinge alone upon my thought in melancholye moode', who then overhears 'a fayre yonge ladye come her secreate teares to wayle'. A ten-line section of the 22-line poem consists of the lady's direct speech, and is also an echo-poem: as she exclaims, 'O heavenes ... who was the firste that bred in me this fevere?' the echo replies 'vere', and so on, line by line.[21] It may be that the whole poem is by Oxford and the label 'Vavaser' denotes its subject rather than its author. It is also possible that it was a joint composition, with Vavasour's lines inset within Oxford's frame, although if this were so, she chose to write lines that present herself abjectly while flattering Oxford's birth, youth and beauty.

There is a more appealing version of female desire in another poem, subscribed 'Vavaser' in one version, 'Thoughe I seeme straunge sweete freende'. This poem is spoken by a woman who reassures a lover of her devotion, though she has to conceal it from the curiosity of others. Such concern with the disjunction between outward behaviour and inward feeling, and with self-defence against intrusive interpreters, is by no means unusual in courtly poetry; sonnets 23 and 27 of *Astrophil and Stella* are other examples. However, the speaker's sex renders her especially vulnerable:

> We seely dames that falles suspecte, do feare [hapless; false]
>   And liue within the moughte of enuyes lake [moat; envy's]
> Muste in our heartes a secrete meaning beare
>   Far from the reste whiche outwardlye we make.[22]

Some poems associated with another notable female lover, Mary Queen of Scots, also involve the poetic exposure of private love, and raise problems of attribution. The casket produced in evidence at her first trial contained not only letters implicating her in the murder of Darnley, but also sonnets in French expressing her love for Bothwell. The question, again, is whether Mary Stuart composed these poems, or was used as a persona by someone else; and, if the latter, whether the poems were written supportively, or as part of a smear campaign, which is how they came to be used. There are twelve sonnets, again using the tradition of the female complaint to voice the Queen's constancy, powerlessness and jealousy. Bothwell is absent, provoking a tormenting yearning like that of the Petrarchan poet: 'Toute la nuit ou ie languis icy' ('all night long I lie and languish here'). Again as for the Petrarchan poet, it is this unquenched desire that produces writing:

> Ne vous voyant selon qu'aues promise
> iay mis la main au papier pour escrire.
> (Not seeing you, despite your word to me,
> I take up pen and paper, and indite.)[23]

Other poems more certainly attributable to Mary Stuart include a sonnet in praise of Pierre de Ronsard, the French courtly poet who had written sonnets to Mary during her youth as wife of the Dauphin;[24] and a sonnet to Elizabeth I written in 1568, the year of Mary's flight to England and subsequent imprisonment. Her desire to see her sister-queen is strikingly like the erotic yearnings of a Petrarchan poet or an Ovidian heroine:

> Une seul penser qui me profficte et nuit
> Amer et doulx, change en mon coeur sans cesse.
> (A longing haunts my spirit, day and night,
> Bitter and sweet, torments my aching heart.)

Mary even uses the characteristically Petrarchan image of the poet as a ship at sea, seeking guidance and safety from the one s/he woos.[25]

Elizabeth may have had this poem in mind when she wrote 'The dowbt off future foes', a poem which is probably a meditation on the 1569 Northern Rebellion in support of Mary. Mary seems to be referred to as 'the dawghter off debatte', and Elizabeth sternly rebuffs the ship image: 'no Forrene banished wight shall ancore in this port'. The poem is in poulter's measure, a metre regarded as unsophisticated in later decades, but it creates an effective sense of unease through its riddling language, its imagery of tides, webs, clouds and cloaks, and its forceful alliteration and rhythm. Insecurity is both defied and expressed:

> The dowbt off future foes exiles my present joye
>   and wytte me warnes to shunne suche snares as threaten mine anoye
> For falshode nowe dothe flowe and subjects faithe dothe ebbe
>   which shuld not be yf reason rulde or wisdome weaved the webbe.[26]

The circulation of this poem looks like a calculated exercise in apparently unwilling publication. Lady Willoughby allegedly copied it 'covertly' from the Queen's writing tablet, at which the Queen was supposedly much offended.[27] However, its circulation would have done her no harm, announcing a resolution to defend the nation and resist the Queen of Scots which was secret and personal, and therefore heartfelt and sincere. Not merely was a private artefact brought to public light, but its very privacy was strategically publicised in the process.

Another poem by Elizabeth, 'On Monsieur's Departure', may have served a similar purpose. It probably refers to the final departure from England in 1582 of Elizabeth's last serious suitor, the Duke of Anjou. It consists of a series of conventional Petrarchan 'contraries of love':

> I grieve and dare not show my discontent,
> I love and yet am forced to seem to hate...
>   I am and not, I freeze and yet am burned,
>   Since from myself another self I turned.   (*Poems*, p. 5)

However, their marriage had effectively ceased to be a realistic prospect in November 1579, when widespread popular objection was joined by the decision of the Privy Council not to oppose the match but not to support it either.[28] The negotiations had been sustained until 1582 for reasons connected with the Netherlands conflict, and the poem probably served an equally political purpose, soothing any feelings on the French side that they had been toyed with, and announcing to England's enemies in Spain that France was still regarded as England's ally. Perhaps, though, the poem also voices Elizabeth's knowledge that now, at forty-eight, she would never have a child; a husband was not the only potential 'other self' that she had renounced.

While in 'On Monsieur's Departure' Elizabeth speaks as a Petrarchan lover, in other poems she speaks as the self-conscious object of reams of courtly love poetry. In 'When I was fair and young', she describes her Laura-like immovability when 'Of many was I sought their mistress for to be' (*Poems*, p. 7). A Latin poem in reply to Paul Melissus's profession of devotion to her tells him 'vatum es princeps; ego vati subdita, dum me / Materium celsi carminis ipse legis' ('you are a prince of poets, I a subject to a poet when you choose me as the theme of your lofty verse'), wittily acknowledging the two-way currents of power and dependence that run between a queen and her panegyrists.[29]

Elizabeth engaged in poetic exchanges with her courtiers, which formed part of the ritual pursuit and dispensation of royal favour. Some lines in which she complained 'A haples kynde of lyfe, is this I weare' were answered in consolatory verse by Sir Thomas Heneage (May,

Courtier Poets, pp. 342–3); and a lament by Sir Walter Ralegh on the loss of her favour, 'Fortune hath taken thee away, my Love', provoked her response 'Ah silly pugg, wert thou so sore afrayd?' (May, *Courtier Poets*, pp. 318–19). Ralegh bemoans his fate with reference to lofty abstractions such as Fortune, Sorrow, and Joy, and proudly concludes, 'But Love farewell, though fortune conquer thee, / No fortune base shall ever alter me.' Ralegh himself was base-born, of non-aristocratic lineage, with no claims to rank or title except those bestowed by Elizabeth; he thus at once alludes to and defiantly repudiates his dependence on her. Her reply opens with intimacies that are both affectionate and diminishing: she exhorts her 'silly pug', her lapdog, 'Mourne not my Wat, nor be thou so dismaid'. She goes on discreetly to register the fact that, in implying that she is subject to blind fortune while he is not, he has committed an affront to hierarchy: 'No fortune base, thou saist, shall alter thee; / And may so blind a wretch then conquer me?' She asserts her supremacy over both fortune and him: 'never thinke that fortune can beare sway, / If vertue watche and will her not obay.' The whole exchange is, on the surface, an affectionately playful dialogue, but is underwritten by a contest for power in which the Queen's political subject and social creation seeks to convert her into his poetical subject and creation, but by Elizabeth's assertion of her own poetic subjectivity is firmly put back into his place.

One of Elizabeth's ladies-in-waiting, Lady Mary Cheke, also had the last word in a verse exchange, in a witty riposte to a misogynistic epigram by Sir John Harington (May, *Courtier Poets*, pp. 245–6). Meanwhile another female courtier poetically addressed the Queen herself: Mary Sidney, Countess of Pembroke, not only famously translated the psalms, but also composed panegyric, demonstrating that its purposes extended beyond the careerist self-promotion of male courtiers. The Countess's 'Dialogve between two shepheards, Thenot and Piers, in praise of *Astrea*', was published in 1602, having apparently been composed for an aborted visit by Elizabeth to the Countess's seat of Wilton in 1599.[30] Astraea, goddess of justice, was a conventional fictional persona for the Queen.[31] The dialogue consists of Thenot's attempts to find sufficiently lofty comparisons for her – he tries all the bounties of the earth, Wisdom, Virtue, the Spring, the sun, and so on – each of which is cuttingly dismissed by Piers. Piers castigates Thenot as a liar, since any attempt to represent Elizabeth's perfection is inevitably a distortion: 'Compare may thinke where likenesse holds, / Nought like to her the earth enfoldes' (lines 17–18).

In his insistence that 'Thou needst the truth but plainely tell' (line 4), Piers represents a dogmatic Protestant point of view, from which panegyric is problematic in its potential for idolatrousness. His solution is neo-Platonic: Elizabeth's perfection is such that it lies beyond representation. Other Protestant panegyrists also praised the Queen by asserting the inadequacy of praise: examples include Lyly, Spenser and Barnfield.[32] Mary Sidney's use of this topos of unrepresentability, plus her use of the dialogue form as a kind of *occupatio* whereby Thenot's extravagant compliments are copiously delivered even as they are debated, forms a solution to the Protestant panegyrist's dilemma that is both elegant and self-conscious – Margaret Hannay has called it 'metapanegyric'.[33] The dialogue's combination of wit with philosophical depth is summed up in its final paradox, where words state the incapacity of words:

> PIERS. Words from conceit do only rise, [conception or imagination]
> Aboue conceit her honour flies;
> But silence, nought can praise her. (lines 58–60)

The poem comes to an end, neatly and emphatically, because an end to poetry in silence is the logical conclusion of its argument.

Mary Sidney also prepared a copy of the translation of the psalms by herself and her brother for presentation to the Queen, including a dedicatory poem, 'Even now that Care'.[34] She employs the gender-inflected paradoxes conventional in panegyric of Elizabeth: her rule is a miracle, 'Men drawne by worth a woman to obay / one moving all, herselfe unmov'd the while' (lines 83–4). She professes humility and service, presenting the psalm volume as a gift betokening allegiance: it is a cloth woven by the Sidneys to be re-bestowed by the Queen as a livery robe (lines 33–4). Yet some have detected in these professions, as in the whole sequence of Sideian psalms, implied admonitions that Elizabeth must do more to show herself a true Protestant monarch.[35] The use of praise to instruct – celebrating an epitome of perfection which was less a present image of the person praised than an ideal for them to aspire to – was another solution to the problem of Protestant panegyric.[36] Moreover, the Countess's brother Philip had advocated a more interventionist foreign policy in support of Protestantism, and had been killed defending the Reformed faith in The Netherlands before he could complete the translation of the psalms. Thus, when the Countess's dedication opens with a courteous apology for claiming the attention of one 'On whom in chiefe dependenth to dispose / what Europe acts in theise most active times' (lines 7–8), this is also a political injunction to Elizabeth. It has often been recognised that panegyric by male poets could express dissent through strategic ambiguity;[37] Mary Sidney's poem can be viewed as an equally dextrous deployment of courteous compliment for veiled political critique.

III

The Countess herself established 'a kinde of little Court', as Nicholas Breton termed it, at her estate of Wilton, where she gathered a circle of writers. Breton drew on Castiglione for comparison: 'who hath redde of the Duchesse of Urbina, maie saie, the Italians wrote wel: but who knowe the Countesse of Penbrooke [sic], I think hath cause to write better'.[38] Yet in some ways Wilton was less a court than an anti-court, both as an alternative court to Elizabeth's, and as a pastoral retreat from her court, a place for restorative escape from politics and ambition. It was at Wilton, in a self-imposed exile from court after incurring royal disfavour, that Philip Sidney began writing his pastoral fiction, *The Countess of Pembroke's Arcadia*, which he told his sister was 'done only for you, only to you' (*New Arcadia*, p. 57). One of her own works, a translation of Philippe de Mornay's *Discourse of life and death*, rejected the pursuit of 'court fortune' and 'courte ambition', and recommended escape 'out of the corruption of the world, into some countrie place from the infected townes, there quietlie employing the tyme in some knowledge and serious contemplation'.[39]

While her literary activities both did and did not emulate Castiglione's model, the Countess engaged with another courtly authority, Petrarch, whose *Triumph of Death* she translated. In this work the elusive Laura descends from heaven after her death and finally speaks her mind. It is thus another case where a female voice is the invention of a male poet; yet in translating it the Countess to some degree reappropriates Laura and her voice for the expression of female subjectivity. The eulogising of Laura's inflexible chastity is tinged with hypocrisy in Petrarch and his imitators since, despite their neo-Platonism, the end for which they yearn is the satisfaction of their desires. However, when a woman writer performs the praise of Laura's 'chaste heart, faire visage, upright thought, / wise speache, which did with honor linked goe' (lines 8–9), she lays claim to Laura as a heroic figure of female resolution and autonomy, even if a female heroism based on chastity and stoicism can seem disappointingly restrictive to the modern reader.[40]

Laura reveals that she returned Petrarch's love, but in order to train him to overcome shallow carnality she purposefully alternated between concealment and discreet disclosure of her feelings. When he was 'woe-vanquisht' she would look at him sweetly,

> But if thy passion did from reason swarue,
>> Feare in my words, and sorrowe in my face
>> Did then to thee for salutation serue.　　　(lines 106–8)

She claims – or he claims by giving her these words – that she was always the one in control. She says that this description of their relationship can hardly surprise him, since 'Thow know'st, and hast it sung in manie a place' (line 111). In fact, throughout there is an ironic self-awareness that Petrarchan poetry is an expression of male desire generated by, and dependent on, the distance and silence of the mistress. Laura contrasts Petrarch's poetic volubility with her own demeanour:

> Thow didst for mercie calle with wearie throte
>> In feare and shame, I did in silence goe,
>> So much desire became of little note.
> But not the lesse becoms concealed woe,
>> Nor greater growes it utteréd, then before.　　　(lines 142–6)

In speaking of an existence constrained by silence, Laura describes the conditions of early modern female subjectivity; while her assertion of silence as a token of true and deep feeling suggests the appeal of this poem to a female translator. Meanwhile, just as Mary Sidney might be felt to speak through Laura, and therefore through Petrarch, so Laura describes how she herself was able to speak only in the disguising medium of Petrarch's own words: she suggests that she discreetly revealed her love when she sang his verses.

> But clear'd I not the darkest mists of yore?
>> when I thy words alone did entretaine
>> Singing for thee? my loue dares speake no more. (lines 148–50)

A complication of voices also occurs in 'The Dolefull Lay of Clorinda', one of the *Astrophel* anthology, compiled by Spenser, of memorial verses by various poets for Philip Sidney. Spenser's own contribution, 'Astrophel', ends by introducing the 'Lay':

> first his sister that *Clorinda* hight,
> . . . began this dolefull lay.
> Which least I marre the sweetnesse of the vearse,
> In sort as she it sung, I will rehearse.　　　(lines 211, 214–16)[41]

It remains unclear whether the 'Lay' is by the Countess or Spenser; it presents a similar problem to the elegies attributed to women in Soowthern's *Pandora*, since it has exactly the same versification as the male poet's frame.[42] Some collaboration between Spenser and the Countess is not inconceivable; but even if it is the Countess's own composition, its seamless incorporation in the larger structure of 'Astrophel', and what Spenser styles his 'rehearsal' of it, effectively constitutes the performing of one poet's words by another. Its function is the voicing of both passionate grief and resignation to Astrophel's death, which the Countess, or Spenser's version of her, is able to speak from a position of privileged intimacy: 'Great losse to all, but greatest losse to me' (line 36).[43]

Most of the Countess's works are about death, especially that of her brother; she is not known to have written anything before his death in 1586, and she repeatedly claims it as justification for her writing. Her poem dedicating the psalms to Elizabeth refers at length to Philip's death, and is followed by a dedicatory poem to his memory, 'To the Angell spirit of the most excellent Sir Philip Sidney', in which she attributes her writing to 'zealous love, Love which hath neuer done, / Nor can enough in world of words unfold' (lines 27–8).[44] For Petrarch, Laura's chastity and death generated desire and hence poetry; for Mary Sidney, her brother's death is a loss that both produces a passionate voicing of desire and renders it immune from charges of immodest self-exposure (although some have suspected her of incestuous feelings).[45] She also acted as literary executor to Philip, supervising publication of the 1593 edition of the *Arcadia*, 'Certaine Sonnets', the *Defence of Poesy*, *Astrophil and Stella* and *The Lady of May*.[46]

The Countess's contributions to courtly writing further included translating and patronising classical 'closet' drama. However, despite the range of her literary activities she remains chiefly known as the translator of the psalms. She has been seen as working on 'the margins of discourse',[47] confining herself to decorous genres like religious translation, though often using them for the discreet expression of controversial views.

IV

Such careful negotiation of cultural boundaries was not observed by Mary Sidney's niece, Lady Mary Wroth, a prolific writer who chose to work in the secular, erotic genres of prose romance (*The Countess of*

Montgomery's Urania, 1621), sonnet sequence ('Pamphilia to Amphilan-thus', 1621), and pastoral 'closet' drama (*Love's Victory*). Her family heritage probably gave her confidence in these genres, in which she emulated not only her uncle Philip, but also her father Robert, who was a sonneteer. However, the female side of her literary lineage was used against her by one of the critics of her *Urania*, Sir Edward Denny, who urged her to write 'as large a volume of heavenly layes and holy love as you have of lascivious tales and amorous toyes that at the last you may followe the rare, and pious example of your vertuous and learned Aunt'.[48]

Denny particularly objected to the *Urania* because he thought that one of its many stories-within-a-story recounted a recent scandal in his family. Wroth vigorously denied this, but offered to try to recall copies of the book.[49] It seems that it caused a furore for two reasons. First, it breached the decorum of gender and genre: although Margaret Tyler had translated a Spanish romance, *The Mirror of Knighthood*, in 1578, with great success, she had felt the need to include a defensive preface,[50] and the *Urania* was the first published English romance with a female author. Secondly, Wroth apparently put too much recognisable fact into it, not only from the private lives of courtiers whom she knew, but also from her own life. Her heroine, Pamphilia, is a writer, and is in love with her cousin, Amphilanthus; Wroth herself had an affair with her cousin William Herbert, Mary Sidney's son. Other characters, such as Bella-mira and Lindamira, have life stories that uncannily resemble Wroth's own, including unhappiness in love and a fall from grace at court. Wroth enjoyed the friendship of Queen Anne in the early years of James I's reign, and participated in court masques, but the death of her husband in 1614, and her motherhood of two illegitimate children by Herbert, were followed by a fall from favour. It may be that she hoped to use courtly fiction for the veiled expression of personal grievances; if so, she failed by making private knowledge and feelings too public. A contemporary reported the feeling at court that she 'takes great libertie or rather licence to traduce whom she please, and thincks she daunces in a net'.[51]

Despite this, within the text privacy and secrecy are dominant themes. While Amphilanthus is a chivalric hero, repeatedly sallying forth on quests and into romantic dalliances, Pamphilia remains in her palace, relishing solitude and retiring to her chamber or secluded groves. For some time she does not even reveal her love to Amphilanthus, preferring to guard and tend it as her own private treasure. Her topographical withdrawal is accompanied by withdrawal into the mind, and emotional release in verse. As she walks alone in the garden,

> so stilly did she mooue, as if the motion had not been in her, but that the earth did goe her course, and stirre, or as trees grow without sence of increase. But while this quiet outwardly appear'd, her inward thoughts more busie were, and wrought, while this Song came into her mind.[52]

The *Urania* has two parts, the published volume of 1621, which contains four books, and an unpublished two-book manuscript sequel. The poems that punctuate the narrative, by other characters as well as Pamphilia, often reappropriate the genres of sonnet and complaint from their ventriloquistic use by male poets to dramatise female desire and grief.[53] The published volume also ends with a sonnet sequence, 'Pamphilia to Amphilanthus', which honours the Petrarchan tradition and the Sidneian tradition of *Astrophil and Stella*, but innovates in that the lyric voice is female. Whereas Mary Sidney's poetry was generated by death, Wroth's is generated by the absence of the beloved – 'I seek for some smale ease by lines';[54] and while for Mary Sidney her brother's death was protection against the immodesty of authorship, the lover's absence secures Wroth/Pamphilia from charges of unchastity.[55]

Pamphilia disdains wits who prize and flaunt their own poetry, since 'wher most feeling is, words are more scant'; instead, 'silently I beare my greatest loss' (P45). Obviously these assertions have a degree of ironic Astrophil-like disingenuousness, since they are themselves written and published. Their point is to distinguish between outward show and true, deep feeling: 'know more passion in my hart doth move / Then in a million that make show of love' (P41; compare P46). Concealment equates with exclusiveness, superiority and purity. Many of the sonnets turn inwards, or avoid direct address even to Amphilanthus, instead apostrophising abstract entities like Love, Grief, Time, Sorrow and Night. One sonnet is addressed to 'You blessed shades':

> How oft in you I have laine heere oprest,
>   And have my miseries in woefull cries
>   Deliver'd forth, mounting up to the skies
> Yett helples back returnd to wound my brest.   (P34)

The speaker represents herself as at once speaking into a void, and speaking only to herself, such that we might need to remind ourselves that these are published poems, and that what we are witnessing again is the purposeful publication of privacy. The claim of privacy operates to offset the moral dubiousness of publication, especially when the published matter treats of female desire.[56]

Fourteen sonnets within the larger sequence form a corona, 'A crowne of Sonetts dedicated to Love' (P77–90). Each of these sonnets begins by repeating the last line of the previous one, until the final line loops back to the first line of all. Their subject is a further abstracted and self-scrutinising meditation upon love. Their opening/closing line, 'In this strang labourinth how shall I turne?' describes both the corona's own intricate, inescapable form, and the speaker's self-absorbed, bewildered psychological predicament. At the same time, her enclosure in a labyrinth both guarantees and symbolises the unpenetrated, enclosed purity of her body.

If the love poems of male courtiers can be seen as metaphorical expressions of the frustrations of a courtly career, Wroth's verses, too, can be seen as laments not only for erotic disappointments but also for exile from royal favour and courtly success. They are infused with the imagery of courtly life and its opposite, pastoral retreat.[57] At one point Pamphilia complains of her debasement to a spectacle in terms that draw on her experience as a participant in court masques: 'I should nott have bin made this stage of woe / Wher sad disasters have theyr open showe' (P48).[58] Her introversion is enacted as withdrawal from specifically courtly pastimes:

> When every one to pleasing pastime hies
> Some hunt, some hauke, some play, while some delight
> In sweet discourse, and musique shows joys might
> Yett I my thoughts doe farr above thes prise.   (P26)

Gender makes a difference to the role of courtly lover, in that Pamphilia's grief is created by Amphilanthus's very masculine freedom to go out and be active while she remains fixed in one place. Wroth's attachment of the sonnet sequence to a chivalric romance intensifies the contrast between the male adventurer and the princess in her chamber in her palace; Pamphilia's topographical fixity is both dictated by her gender, and representative of the virtues of chastity and constancy demanded of her gender. This is illustrated by the contrast between a song by 'Pamphilia' and one by her 'Amphilanthus'. Pamphilia beseeches:

> Sweetest love returne againe
> Make nott too long stay...
> Lett us not thus parted bee
> Love, and absence ne're agree.   (P28)

The poem could easily serve as a companion piece to William Herbert's own 'Song', 'Soules joy, now I am gone' (the poem used by George Herbert as the basis for 'A Parodie').[59] Both Wroth's and Herbert's poems resemble Donne's 'Valedictions', but with the difference that, where Herbert and Donne describe themselves as roving travellers leaving the woman fixed at home, for Wroth 'you must needs depart, / And mee haples leave'. Herbert soothingly asserts that they will not be parted in spirit, 'Since I must leave my selfe with thee, / And carry thee with me'. Wroth attempts a similar confidence: her heart will go with him, 'Soe in part, wee shall nott part / Though wee absent bee'. However, she remains unconvinced, and, rejecting such facile consolation, can arrive only at a stoical but somewhat resentful resolution:

> Butt can I live having lost
> Chiefest part of mee
> Hart is fled, and sight is crost
> These my fortunes bee
> Yett deere hart goe, soone returne
> As good there, as heere to burne.

In the *Urania*, Pamphilia does show poems to Amphilanthus at crucial moments, granting disclosure as a token of their intimacy (*Urania* 1.2.217), and she does reveal her feelings, sometimes in fictional guise, when she and her friends entertain one another with stories of love (*Urania* 1.2.188; 3.399–400); in short, she is a member of a coterie. Wroth's drama *Love's Victory* also concerns a coterie of friends and lovers who engage in pursuits like *questioni d'amore*. Musella and Dalina object when such games are proposed in a mixed company, because they will dangerously reveal 'the secretts of the mind'.[60] However, when Dalina is later alone with three other ladies, she considers it safe to enjoy the risky pleasure of sharing confidences:

> Now w'are alone lett euery one confess
> truly to other what our lucks haue bin
> how often lik'd, and lou'd, and soe express
> our passions past: shall wee this sport begin?
> non can accuse vs, non can vs betray
> vnles owr selues, owr owne selues will bewray.
>
> (p. 112, f. 20v)

At some points characters stress the need for women's reticence: Lissius chastises Climeana, 'fy I doe blush for you, a woman woo? / the most vnfittingst, shamfull'st thing to doe' (p. 127, f. 24r). However, a central plot concerns Philisses and Musella, who, through fear of confession, discover their mutual passion too late, when Musella's mother has betrothed her to another. They go to the Temple of Love to stab themselves in a love pact, but Silvesta intervenes and offers a potion, like that taken by Juliet, which will simulate death. The spectacle of their 'corpses' prompts Simeana to deplore the tragedy of hidden love:

> Now heere of mee the mournfull'st end of loue
> that hart for hart could finde, and hartless proue:
> Philisses, and Musella had lou'd long,
> and long vnknowne w*hi*ch bred ther only wrong.
>
> (p. 203, f. 43r)

When they rise from the 'dead', Musella's suitor releases her and their marriage provides a happy ending, but not without the forceful moral that adherence to codes of modesty can lead to misunderstanding and potential tragedy. Perhaps such radical advocacy of confession could only comfortably be expressed in the private genre of 'closet' drama.[61]

As we have seen, much courtly writing took place in the ambiguous territory where the public and private overlap and mingle, demonstrating that they are relative, not absolute, categories. For female writers, courtly writing offered opportunities in its claim to be private, but the tremulousness of the boundaries of privacy necessitated their constant reinforcement. Hence the courtly writing of women is characterised by written professions of reluctance to write, eloquent disclaimers of eloquence, and the publicising of its own privacy.

NOTES

I am grateful to Jennifer Summit for showing me her work in progress on the writings of Elizabeth I.

1. The term '*amour courtois*' was coined by Gaston Paris in 1883 to describe mediaeval troubadour poetry in southern France (J. A. Cuddon, *A Dictionary of Literary Terms* (1977; revised edn, Harmondsworth: Penguin, 1982), pp. 163–4).
2. J. W. Saunders, 'The Stigma of Print: a Note on the Social Bases of Tudor Poetry', *EC*, 1:2 (1951), 139–64.
3. Daniel Javitch, *Poetry and Courtliness in Renaissance England* (Princeton, NJ: Princeton University Press, 1978).
4. Arthur Marotti, '"Love is not Love": Elizabethan Sonnet Sequences and the Social Order', *ELH*, 49 (1982), 396–428.
5. J. W. Saunders, 'From Manuscript to Print: a Note on the Circulation of Poetic Manuscripts in the Sixteenth Century', *Proceedings of the Leeds Philo-*

sophical and Literary Society (*Literary and Historical Section*), 6:8 (1951), 507–28, especially 511; Arthur Marotti, 'Manuscript, Print, and the Social History of the Lyric', *The Cambridge Companion to English Poetry, Donne to Marvell*, ed. Thomas N. Corns (Cambridge: Cambridge University Press, 1993), pp. 52–79.

6. Baldassare Castiglione, *Il libro del cortegiano* (1528), trans. Sir Thomas Hoby, *The Courtyer* (1561).

7. George Gascoigne, 'The Adventures of Master F. J.' (1573), reprinted in Paul Salzman, ed., *An Anthology of Elizabethan Prose Fiction* (World's Classics Series; Oxford: Oxford University Press, 1987), pp. 16–18, 53–8, 67–73.

8. Sir Philip Sidney, *The Countess of Pembroke's Arcadia [The New Arcadia]*, ed. Maurice Evans (Harmondsworth: Penguin, 1977), pp. 241–2, 378, 634–5, 643, 650–1, 659–60, 662–3, 681–4.

9. *The Oxford Authors: Sir Philip Sidney*, ed. Katherine Duncan-Jones (Oxford: Oxford University Press, 1989).

10. Edmund Spenser, *The Shorter Poems of Edmund Spenser*, eds. William A. Oram, Einar Bjorvand, Ronald Bond, Thomas H. Cain, Alexander Dunlop and Richard Snell (New Haven and London: Yale University Press, 1989), p. 645.

11. See John Kerrigan, ed., *Motives of Woe: Shakespeare and 'Female Complaint': a Critical Anthology* (Oxford: Clarendon Press, 1991).

12. Josephine A. Roberts, 'The Imaginary Epistles of Sir Philip Sidney and Lady Penelope Rich', *ELR*, 15 (1985), 75. The date of the poems is *circa* 1607–23.

13. *Ibid.*, 61–2.

14. Saunders, 'From Manuscript to Print', 521–8. See also Margaret Ferguson's discussion of women's publication in chapter 7 of this volume.

15. Sir John Harington, 'Epigram 424', reprinted in Norman E. McClure, ed., *Letters and Epigrams of Sir John Harington* (Philadelphia: University of Pennsylvania Press, 1930), p. 320.

16. Richard Brathwaite, *The English Gentlewoman* (1631), quoted in Ann Rosalind Jones, *The Currency of Eros: Women's Love Lyric in Europe, 1540–1620* (Bloomington and Indianapolis: Indiana University Press, 1990), p. 25.

17. Ben Jonson, *The Complete Poems*, ed. George Parfitt (1975; Harmondsworth: Penguin, 1988), p. 195.

18. George Puttenham, *The Arte of English Poesie* (1589), ed. Gladys Doidge Willcock and Alice Walker (Cambridge: Cambridge University Press, 1936), p. 4; see also pp. 63, 236 and 247–8.

19. Jonson, 'A Sonnet, to the Noble Lady, the Lady Mary Wroth', *The Under-wood*, 28, *Complete Poems*, pp. 165–6; see also Mary Wroth, *The Poems of Lady Mary Wroth*, ed. Josephine A. Roberts (Baton Rouge and London: Louisiana State University Press, 1983), pp. 16–19.

20. John Soowthern, *Pandora, The Musyque of the beautie, of his Mistresse Diana* (1584), facsimile with introduction by George B. Parks (Facsimile Text Society; New York: Columbia University Press, 1938), sigs. Ciii.v–Di.r.

21. Steven W. May, 'The Poems of Edward DeVere, Seventeenth Earl of Oxford and of Robert Devereux, Second Earl of Essex', *SP*, Texts and Studies (1980), 38–9, 79–81. See also Steven W. May, *The Elizabethan Courtier Poets: the Poems and Their Contexts* (Columbia, Missouri and London: University of Missouri Press, 1991), pp. 282–3; and E. K. Chambers, *Sir Henry Lee: an Elizabethan Portrait* (Oxford: Clarendon Press, 1936), pp. 152–3.

22. Chambers, *Sir Henry Lee*, pp. 153–4. See also May, 'Poems of Oxford and Essex', 79; Emrys Jones, ed., *The New Oxford Book of Sixteenth-Century Verse* (Oxford: Oxford University Press, 1991), pp. 160–1, no. 93.

23. Sonnets 11 and 12, in Betty Travitsky, ed., *The Paradise of Women: Writings by Englishwomen of the Renaissance* (Westport, CT: Greenwood Press, 1981), pp. 197, 259. I use the same translations as Travitsky.

24. *Ibid.*, pp. 204, 260–1.

25. *Ibid.*, pp. 198, 259–60.

26. David Norbrook, selected and introduced, and H. R. Woudhuysen, ed., *The Penguin Book of Renaissance Verse, 1509–1659* (Harmondsworth: Allen Lane/Penguin, 1992), p. 95, no. 13.

27. Elizabeth I, *The Poems of Queen Elizabeth I*, ed. Leicester Bradner (Providence, RI: Brown University Press, 1964), p. 72; May, *Courtier Poets*, pp. 47–8.

28. J. E. Neale, *Queen Elizabeth I* (1934; Harmondsworth: Penguin, 1960), pp. 246–7; Christopher Haigh, *Elizabeth I* (Harlow: Longman, 1988), pp. 76–7.

29. Elizabeth I, *Poems*, pp. 10, 77–8, trans. James E. Phillips. As in the case of 'On Monsieur's Departure', Bradner doubts the Queen's authorship but May (*Courtier Poets*, p. 317) does not.

30. Mary Sidney, Countess of Pembroke, *The Triumph of Death and Other Unpublished and Uncollected Poems*, ed. G. F. Waller (Salzburg: Institut für Englische Sprache und Literatur, Universität Salzburg, 1977), pp. 181–3.

31. See Frances A. Yates, *Astraea: the Imperial Theme in the Sixteenth Century* (London: Routledge, 1975).

32. See Helen Hackett, *Virgin Mother, Maiden Queen: Elizabeth I and the Cult of the Virgin Mary* (London: Macmillan, 1994), pp. 112–13, 187–8.

33. Margaret P. Hannay, *Philip's Phoenix: Mary Sidney, Countess of Pembroke* (New York and Oxford: Oxford University Press, 1990), p. 166. *Occupatio* is the rhetorical technique of refusing to describe something while actually giving a description of it.

34. Norbrook and Woudhuysen, *Penguin Book of Renaissance Verse*, pp. 131–4.

35. Hannay, *Philip's Phoenix*, pp. 88–91.

36. See Hackett, *Virgin Mother, Maiden Queen*, pp. 43–5, 125–6.

37. See Annabel Patterson, *Censorship and Interpretation: the Conditions of Writing and Reading in Early Modern England* (Madison: University of Wisconsin Press, 1967).

38. Nicholas Breton, *Wits Trenchmour* (London, 1597), pp. 18–20; dedication to

the Countess of Pembroke, in *A Pilgrimage to Paradise* (Oxford, 1592); both quoted in Mary Sidney, *Triumph of Death*, p. 7.

39. Philippe de Mornay, *A discourse of life and death*, trans. Mary Sidney (London, 1592), sigs. C1r, B2r and C2v, quoted in G. F. Waller, *Mary Sidney, Countess of Pembroke: a Critical Study of her Writings and Literary Milieu* (Salzburg: University of Salzburg Institut für Anglistik und Amerikanistik, 1979), pp. 137–8.

40. See Mary Ellen Lamb, *Gender and Authorship in the Sidney Circle* (Madison: University of Wisconsin Press, 1990), chapter 3, 'The Countess of Pembroke and the Art of Dying'.

41. Spenser, *Shorter Poems*, p. 577.

42. For the arguments, see Hannay, *Philip's Phoenix*, pp. 63–7; Spenser, *Shorter Poems*, pp. 563–8; Mary Sidney, *Triumph of Death*, pp. 53–9; and Waller, *Mary Sidney . . . A Critical Study*, pp. 89–93.

43. Spenser, *Shorter Poems*, p. 579.

44. Mary Sidney, *Triumph of Death*, pp. 92–5; see also p. 5, and Waller, *Mary Sidney . . . A Critical Study*, p. 89.

45. See Mary Sidney, *Triumph of Death*, p. 53; Waller, *Mary Sidney . . . A Critical Study*, pp. 76, 100; Hannay, *Philip's Phoenix*, p. 149.

46. Hannay, *Philip's Phoenix*, pp. 69–76.

47. *Ibid., passim.*

48. Wroth, *Poems*, p. 239.

49. *Ibid.*, pp. 31–5, 236–41.

50. See Travitsky, ed., *Paradise*, pp. 144–6; and Tina Krontiris, *Oppositional Voices: Women as Writers and Translators of Literature in the English Renaissance* (London and New York: Routledge, 1992).

51. Wroth, *Poems*, pp. 12–14, 22–6, 30–1, 36.

52. Lady Mary Wroth, *The Countesse of Mountgomeries Urania* (London, 1621), book 2, p. 177. Compare book 1, p. 121. This volume is henceforth referred to as *Urania* I. *Urania* I, book 1 is available in Salzman, ed., *Elizabethan Prose Fiction*.

53. For example, 'Lindamira's Complaint' (*Urania* 1.3.423–9; Wroth, *Poems*, U37–43), and Wroth, *Poems*, U35, U52, N15.

54. Wroth, *Poems*, p. 90, P9. All further references to 'Pamphilia to Amphilanthus' are to this edition.

55. See Jones, *Currency of Eros*, pp. 34–5.

56. See Jeff Masten, '"Shall I turne blabb?": Circulation, Gender and Subjectivity in Mary Wroth's Sonnets', in *Reading Mary Wroth: Representing Alternatives in Early Modern England*, eds. Naomi J. Miller and Gary Waller (Knoxville: University of Tennessee Press, 1991), pp. 67–87.

57. See Jones, *Currency of Eros*, pp. 123–5, 141–54.

58. Compare P100, and P25, which may allude to Jonson's *Masque of Blackness*, in which Wroth participated.

59. George Herbert, *English Poems*, ed. C. A. Patrides (London: J. M. Dent, 1974), p. 211.

60. Lady Mary Wroth, *Love's Victory: the Penshurst Manuscript*, ed. Michael G.

Brennan (London: Roxburghe Club, 1988), p. 59, f. 7r. All further references are to this edition.

61. See Wroth, *Love's Victory*, pp. 13–14, for discussion of whether the play was performed. For additional discussion of Wroth's works, see Maureen Quilligan, 'Lady Mary Wroth: Female Authority and the Family Romance', in George M. Logan and Gordon Teskey, eds., *Unfolded Tales: Essays on Renaissance Romance* (Ithaca, NY: Cornell University Press, 1989), pp. 257–80, and Helen Hackett, '"Yet tell me some such fiction": Lady Mary Wroth's *Urania* and the "Femininity" of Romance', in Clare Brant and Diane Purkiss, eds., *Women, Texts and Histories, 1575–1760* (London: Routledge, 1992), pp. 39–68.

CHAPTER 9

Women's poetry in early modern Britain

Elizabeth H. Hageman

I

This chapter takes as its starting point the inspirational work of two brilliant twentieth-century women. In *A Room of One's Own* (1929), Virginia Woolf writes the story of Judith Shakespeare, William's imaginary sister. Judith's story demonstrates the social and economic forces that prevented early modern women, even women of genius such as the imaginary Judith, from writing plays for London's public stage. Recent scholarship confirms Woolf's assertion that 'it would have been impossible, completely and entirely, for any woman to have written the plays of Shakespeare in the age of Shakespeare', but we now know that even though literacy rates were considerably lower for early modern British women than for men, there were in Shakespeare's England enough women who did read (or who heard books read aloud to them) to create a market for books addressed specifically to them (see chapter 4 of this volume). And in Shakespeare's England there were also women who wrote, if not Shakespeare's plays, then other literary works: closet dramas, autobiographies and biographies, journals and diaries, mothers' advice books, tracts defending women's virtue, almanacks, prose fiction – and poetry. Woolf, we now know, was not correct when she wrote of the Elizabethan period, 'it is a perennial puzzle why no woman wrote a word of that extraordinary literature when every other man, it seemed, was capable of song or sonnet'.[1]

In *The Resources of Kind: Genre-Theory in the Renaissance*, Rosalie L. Colie writes about literary kinds (genres, forms) in the period she calls 'the long Renaissance' – 'a period that, for purposes of discussion, I take to begin with Petrarca and to end with Swift'. Professor Colie quotes Claudio Guillén's definition of genre as 'a challenge to match an imaginative structure to reality', and she discusses 'the social importance of generic systems'. She says she 'would like to present genre-theory as a means of accounting for connections between topic and treatment within the literary system, but also to see the connection of literary kinds with *kinds* of knowledge and experience; to present the kinds as a major part of that *genus universum* which is part of all literary students' heritage'.[2] When I read *Resources of Kind* in 1973, I did not notice that Professor Colie had not included any examples from women's writing, but now – twenty-three years later – I want to use Professor Colie's ideas about genres and genre-systems to suggest the range and variety of writings by women poets of the early modern period. I want, also, to stress the wit and ingenuity with which women writers of the sixteenth and seventeenth centuries used the resources of kind to assert their own experiences of two other sorts of 'kind': birth, origin, descent (*OED*, definition 1) and also gender (definition 7).

Many of the poems I shall discuss were printed soon after they were written, some in pirated editions and others in books issued by their authors. Other poems circulated in other forms: as songs set to contemporary music; as epitaphs engraved on funeral monuments; and in manuscript copies – single sheets on which individual poems were transcribed and also more extensive collections of poems copied out by the poets themselves, by friends or by professional scribes. Both women and men of this period created poetical miscellanies of poems and excerpts from poems, sometimes rewriting them to fit their own tastes. Thus a manuscript book, now Folger Library MS V.b. 198, kept by Lady Anne Southwell (1573–1636) includes a version of Sir Walter Ralegh's 'The Lie' with twelve lines not present in any other seventeenth-century copy, those twelve lines perhaps composed by Lady Southwell herself.[3] And now in the Princeton University library is a manuscript book in which Robert Overton (*c.* 1609–*c.* 1672) adapted poems by Francis Quarles, John Donne, Katherine Philips and others to write verses in memory of his wife Ann.[4]

Manuscript poetry is often quite different from poetry written to be printed. Intending to send verses back and forth to one another, manuscript poets often use what Margaret Ezell has called 'interactive genres', including answer poems such as Katherine Philips's response to Vavasor Powell (to be discussed below) and also more friendly answer poems in which, for example, lovers write back and forth to one another. Manuscript poets often write different versions of a poem for different occasions, never envisioning one version or another as their 'final intention'.[5]

In the sixteenth and seventeenth centuries print was a relatively new medium. Since printed books were so much cheaper than manuscripts, print technology was useful to people seeking a large readership for their ideas and for stationers eager to make money by selling multiple copies of books. Printed circulation was, however, shunned by poets (both male and female) who wished to avoid the appearance of commercialism and sometimes shunned by women reluctant to appear immodest in an age when they were taught that chastity, silence and obedience were one and the same (essential) virtue.[6] Even among poets who chose not to print their verse, we must distinguish between those who kept their writing entirely (or almost) private and those who chose manuscript publication rather than print because manuscript copies were more prestigious than printed books. That owners of books might prefer manuscripts over printed exemplars is verified by Folger Library MS V.b. 231, a complete manuscript copy of the 1669 edition of Katherine Philips's poems. And some printed books, Isabella Whitney's *The Copy of a Letter* of 1567 and *A sweet Nosegay* of 1573, for instance, and various multi-authored collections such as *Poems, by Several Persons* (Dublin, 1663) are formatted as imitations of manuscript miscellanies, offering perhaps prestige to a potential owner who was not a member of a poetic coterie but who could afford to purchase a book that looked like a manuscript.[7]

That early modern Britain was simultaneously a manuscript and a print culture is especially significant for a study of women's poetry. First, it serves as a reminder that if we want to know what women wrote in this period, we must look beyond lists of printed books and search for manuscript poems as well. Second, we must be careful to avoid the modern assumption that poetry that was never printed is (or was thought by its age or its author to be) inferior to printed poetry. Third, as our studies of women writers move back and forth between various modes of production, we must remember that issues raised by Rosalie Colie of 'connections between topic and treatment within the literary system' include connections between words and the medium – voiced song, carved tombstone, written or printed page – in which they are conveyed.

II

In 1985 Margaret Hannay and others argued in a collection of essays entitled *Silent But For The Word* that a large proportion of writing by sixteenth-century women was religious in nature, largely because religious writing was one of a very few socially acceptable outlets for women's scholarly and literary skills. Although I shall note below that early modern England saw women writing many secular poems, I want first to note the impressive vitality of Christian poetry of the period. As the authors of *Silent But For The Word* also observe, writing in the service of religion is not a passive activity, especially not in the sixteenth and seventeenth centuries, when England was permeated by so many religious controversies.[8] When Anne Askewe, for example, wrote the song John Bale printed in 1547 as 'The Balade whych Anne Askewe made and sange whan she was in Newgate [prison]', she was indeed struggling for god 'Lyke as the armed knyght / Appoynted in the field' (lines 1–2). Twice examined by government officials about her religious beliefs and ultimately burned at the stake for heresy, Askewe lived and died with such courage that the Protestant martyrologist John Foxe wrote that when she, John Lascelles, John Adams and Nicolas Belenian died at Smithfield, Askewe's example gave courage to those 'strong and stout menne' and 'they did set apart all kynde of feare'.[9]

Among other sixteenth-century Reformers were Ann Lok, who in 1560 appended a cycle of sonnets inspired by Psalm 51 to her translation (from French) of *Sermons of John Calvin, upon the song that Ezechias made after he had been sicke, and afflicted by the hand of God, conteyned in the 38. Chapter of Esay* [Isaiah], and Anne Dowriche, who in 1589 printed a militantly political poem on the recent French civil wars: *The French Historie, That is, A Lamentable Discourse of three of the chiefe, and most famous bloodie broiles that have happened in France for the Gospell of Jesus Christ.* In 1599 Mary Sidney, Countess of Pembroke, presented to Queen Elizabeth a manuscript book comprising paraphrases of the 150 biblical Psalms of David – 47 by her late brother, Sir Philip Sidney, and 103 by the Countess herself. As Margaret Hannay has demonstrated, the Countess's gift urges the Queen to renewed dedication to the international Protestant cause for which Sir Philip had died in 1586. The book is prefaced by a poem to Elizabeth, beginning 'Even now that care which on thy Crown attends', and by 'To the Angel Spirit', in which the Countess images Philip Sidney as a Protestant martyr. As she paraphrases the psalms, Mary Sidney stresses ideas of particular force to Calvinists. Her Psalms 82 and 83, for example, warn against the destruction with which God strikes his enemies, and Psalm 101 treats the responsibilities of a godly monarch.[10]

Like other Calvinist poets, Mary Sidney applies the psalms 'to her own condition'. An aristocratic woman, she amplifies, recasts and even adds references to such topics as marriage, pregnancy, childbirth, child rearing and gender restrictions. The Countess omits passages that are, in Hannay's words, 'untrue to female experience', and she writes in a voice 'carefully non-masculine and occasionally even feminine'.[11] The poetic skill with which Sidney makes her political and religious argument is extraordinary. Gary Waller notes that she uses 164 different stanza forms and ninety-four metrical patterns – her goal, he suggests, is 'to extend the formal range of English lyric and to demonstrate the capacity of Elizabethan poetry to match the variety and flexibility of the French'.[12] She writes sonnets – both Spenserian (Psalm 100) and Petrarchan (Psalm 150); an acrostic on the phrase 'Praise the Lord' (Psalm 117); and a 22-part meditation, each part in a different verse form, and each part beginning with a different letter of the alphabet (Psalm 119). Her verse rhythms and diction vary from those of homely conversation to exalted celebration. Widely circulated in manuscript copies, at least seventeen of which are still extant, Mary Sidney's psalms had a wide influence on subsequent English poetics.[13]

If one thinks about Askewe's ballad, Lok's sonnets, Sidney's psalms, and also her magnificent translation (in *terza rima*) of Petrarch's *Triumph of Death*, one begins to see how various was early modern women's religious writing. Even among English Calvinists, one sees women writers of different social classes writing in a variety of modes. Early in the seventeenth century Elizabeth Melville, Lady Culross, presented a vision of hell in *Ane Godlie Dreame*, first printed in Scottish dialect (1603) and then in English (apparently in 1606). And in 1621 Rachel Speght, a woman from the new middle class, printed *Moralities Memorandum, with a Dreame Prefixed*. In its way, Speght's dream is also a vision of hell: it images her wandering in search of knowledge until she finally comes upon Death, 'a fierce insatiable foe' (line 267), who is killing her mother with a 'pearcing dart' (line 280). The loss 'cut my feeble heart, / So deepe, that daily I indure the smart' (lines 293–4), and Speght responds with the assertion that she will 'blaze [proclaim, make known] the nature of this mortall foe, / And shew how it to tyranize begun' (lines 297–8). The poem that follows, however, is not as energetic as that promise might suggest. As its title, *Moralities Memorandum*, hints, it is a businesslike record of death's place in God's world. Speght first narrates the introduction of death into Eden as a result of 'Jehovahs just decree' (line 25). She then lists three kinds of death, three reasons to think on death, and seven benefits from such meditation, closing with a rather literal reminder that one should follow Isaiah's caution to 'Put thou thy house in order' before being taken 'Unto that place prepar'd for Gods elect' where 'We may with Christ in glory ever raigne' (lines 742, 751 and 756). As Barbara Lewalski notes, in this poem Speght reveals a 'bourgeois concern with wills and the disposition of property,

pointing to such arrangements as one major benefit of regular meditation on death'. Even the epigraphs of the companion poems are different in tone, the *Dream's* epigraph a Latin phrase – 'Esto Memor Mortis'
(Thou shalt be mindful of death) – the *Memorandum's* an English tag:
'Lord Jesus come quickly'.[14]

In the generation after Speght, Anne Bradstreet in 1630 emigrated
from Northumberland to America, where her father and husband each
served as Governor of Massachusetts. Apparently without her knowledge, a volume of Bradstreet's poems was printed in London as *The Tenth
Muse Lately Sprung Up in America* (1650), a book Bradstreet revised and
enlarged for a 1678 Boston edition entitled *Several poems compiled with great
variety, Wit, and Learning, full of Delight*. Many of her poems speak of the
experience particular to a woman in a land that was first unfamiliar and
then her home. In a poem 'In honour of that High and Mighty Princess,
Queen Elizabeth, of most happy memory' she looks back in both time
and geography to a queen who 'will vindicate our wrong. / Let such, as
say our sex is void of reason, / Know 'tis a slander now, but once was
treason'. She expresses old-world Calvinism in elegies on the deaths of
family members and in 'Upon the Burning of Our House July 10th,
1666', and she writes 'A Dialogue between Old England and New,
concerning their present troubles. Anno 1642', which concludes with
New England advising Old England to eschew its past and accept a new
parliamentarian government: 'Farewell dear Mother, Parliament, pre-
vail, / And in a while, you'l tell another tale'.[15]

An Collins was also concerned about England's 'Present Troubles',
but she saw the civil war years from a different perspective than
Bradstreet. In 1653, the year Oliver Cromwell appointed the Nominated
Parliament and became Lord Protector of England, she published *Divine
Songs and Meditations*. Her book is a spiritual autobiography, its theology
described by the editors of a recent anthology, *Kissing the Rod*, as 'if not
actually ... Catholic, ... devoutly anti-Calvinist'.[16] In a prefatory note
'To the Reader', she addresses 'Christians who are of disconsolate
spirits', and she includes in her volume 'A Song composed in time of the
Civil Warr, when the wicked did much insult over the godly'. If Collins is
a Roman Catholic poet, or if she is an Anglican who sees the new
government as a disastrous turn in British history, her book may be
much more radical than at first appears. What is on the surface an
'innocuous' spiritual autobiography may in fact be a book offering
political inspiration to those who share her religious beliefs.

From the second half of the century come poems by women in several radical sects. For example, the Fifth Monarchist Anna Trapnel included poetry in several prophetic books printed between 1654 and 1658; the Baptist Anne Wentworth printed a 'Song of Triumph' in her *Vindication of Anne Wentworth* (1677); and the Quaker Mary Mollineux wrote poetic *Fruits of Retirement, or Miscellaneous Poems, Moral and Divine*, which circulated in manuscript during her lifetime and was printed posthumously in 1702. And although England was officially a Protestant country during most of the sixteenth and seventeenth centuries, a collection of early modern women's religious verse would certainly include poetry by Roman Catholic women. For instance, in the late sixteenth century Anne Howard, Countess of Arundel, wrote a verse prayer that gains additional interest to historians of women's poetry because it incorporates a prayer perhaps by her husband's great-great grandmother, the Duchess of Buckingham. At the turn of the century neo-Latin verse by Elizabeth Jane Weston was printed in a book entitled *Parthenicon* (1607),[17] and in the late seventeenth century Jane Barker, who converted to Roman Catholicism, wrote poems such as 'Fidelia arguing with her self on the difficulty of finding the true Religion'.[18]

Early modern English literature includes as well a book of Christian poetry by a woman possibly of Italian–Jewish descent: *Salve Deus Rex Judaeorum* (1611) by Aemilia Lanyer.[19] In a concluding note 'To the doubtfull Reader', Lanyer asserts that the phrase *Salve Deus Rex Judaeorum* (Hail god, King of the Jews) came to her in a dream 'many yeares before I had any intent to write in this maner' and is 'a significant token, that I was appointed to performe this Worke'. The title page announces the fourfold topic of *Salve Deus*: The Passion of Christ, Eves Apologie in defence of Women, The Teares of the Daughters of Jerusalem, and The Salutation and Sorrow of the Virgine Marie. As *Salve Deus* follows the account in the gospel of Matthew of the last days of Christ, much of Lanyer's attention is on the women who are influenced by his death. Most striking is an extensive 'apology' – defence – of Eve, a double-voiced passage in which the poem's narrator and Pontius Pilate's wife together warn the Roman king that condemning Christ to death will exceed even the sin for which womankind has been (falsely) blamed. One in a long history of writers who argued against the Augustinian idea that woman is to blame for the fall of humanity,[20] Lanyer is a wonderfully effective defender of Eve. With sly wit, for example, she puns on the word 'simply' (completely, honestly, like a simpleton) as she says that Eve was 'simply good, and had no powre to see, / The after-comming harme did not appeare' (lines 765–6). Ringing change after change on the biblical story of the fall of humanity and the subsequent Christian theology of that event as, ultimately, a fortunate fall, Lanyer ironically holds that in the future 'Men will boast of Knowledge, which he tooke / From Eves faire hand, as from a learned Booke' (lines 807–8).

In the introduction to her edition of Lanyer, Susanne Woods presents *Salve Deus Rex Judaeorum* as an 'unapologetic creation of a community of good women for whom another woman is the spokesperson and commentator'.[21] The community of women with whom Lanyer aligns herself are the biblical women treated in her title poem and also British women to whom she addresses prefatory poems and prose letters: Queen Anne, Princess Elizabeth, and aristocrats such as Lady Susan, Countess Dowager of Kent, whom the poet identifies as 'the Mistris of my youth' ('To the Ladie Susan', line 1). In 'The Authors Dreame to the Ladie Marie, the Countesse Dowager of Pembroke', Lanyer celebrates Mary Sidney for her 'holy Sonnets' (line 121). When she awakens, she determines to present to that lady her own 'fruits of idle houres', for 'there is hony in the meanest flowres' (lines 194 and 196).

Issues of social class run throughout *Salve Deus*, beginning on the title page when Lanyer is identified as 'Wife to Captaine Alfonso Lanyer Servant to the Kings Majestie', and extending to the final poem, 'The Description of Cooke-ham', printed immediately after Lanyer's poem on the Passion. Lanyer's country-house poem celebrates Margaret Clifford, Countess of Cumberland, and her daughter Anne. As the wife of a court musician, Lanyer is a member of the middle sort, and though she can use her poetic skill to gain aristocratic patronage, the language of supplication with which she praises her 'betters' is a constant reminder of the class distinctions that separate women from one another. At the very centre of the poem on Cooke-ham, she inserts a complaint against Fortune: Fortune the goddess whose turning wheel brings the loss of friendship, and also Fortune as a determiner of social class. At the moment she notes the Earl of Dorset's taking Anne Clifford away from Cooke-ham, Lanyer interrupts her narrative to cry,

> Unconstant Fortune, thou art most too blame,
> Who casts us downe into so lowe a frame:
> Where our great friends we cannot dayly see,
> So great a diffrence is there in degree.   (lines 103–6)

With a deft use of the humility topos – 'My Wit too weake to conster [construe] of the great' (line 112) – Lanyer pulls back from complaint to praise. Her concluding lines are then typical of the poem in their simultaneous expression of humility and their validation of Lanyer's poetic voice as she says that the Countess's virtues now 'lodge in my unworthy breast, / And ever shall, so long as life remaines, / Tying my heart to her by those rich chaines' (lines 208–10).

The recent rediscovery of Lanyer's book forces the revision of literary histories that have credited Ben Jonson with writing the first (and best) English country-house poem. Although the composition of neither Lanyer's 'The Description of Cooke-ham' nor Jonson's 'To Penshurst' can be dated precisely, Lanyer's publication date of 1611 precedes Jonson's by five years. Jonson's 'To Penshurst' images a country house whose mistress is 'noble, fruitful, chaste withal' (line 90); her 'huswifery' is so efficient that Penshurst is always ready for guests, even guests as important as King James and Prince Henry (the husband and brother of the two royals to whom Lanyer addresses *Salve Deus*). Penshurst's master, Robert Sidney, welcomes the poet at his table, a table replete with the classical pleasures of good food and good conversation. By contrast, Lanyer images not a house, but the country landscape that the Countess of Cumberland infused with life. Lanyer remembers Cooke-ham as a female paradise interrupted and destroyed by Dorset. When the Countess then left Cooke-ham,

> Each brier, each bramble, when you went away,
> Caught fast your clothes, thinking to make you stay:
> Delightfull Eccho wonted to reply
> To our last words, did now for sorrow die.   (lines 197–200)

Both nature and nature's God, Lanyer appears to argue, prefer qualities traditionally associated with femininity.

III

Celebrated today for her poems about female friendship, Katherine Philips (1631/2–64) also wrote some poems ('The faire Weather at the Coronation [of Charles II]', for example, and philosophical poems such as 'Happyness', 'Death', 'The World' and 'The Soule') that use no images or speech patterns which her culture associated specifically with women. More often, however, Philips is explicit about her position as a female poet writing in what we would now call a masculinist culture. In 'Upon the double murther of K[ing] Charles', Philips uses gendered language as she confronts the Welsh clergyman Vavasor Powell, who had written a poem claiming that Charles I had broken the Ten

Commandments.[22] She presents herself as an outraged defender of justice, forced to break nature's law that woman be silent on public matters and to speak as did Croesus's mute son when he cried out to warn his father that he was about to be killed:

> I thinke not on the state, nor am concernd
> Which way soever that great Helme is turnd,
> But as that sonne whose fathers danger nigh
> Did force his native dumbnesse, and untye
> The fettered organs, so here is a cause
> That will excuse the breach of natures lawes.
> Silence were now a Sin: nay passion now
> Wise men themselves for merit would allow. (lines 1–8)

In 'Wiston-Vault' Philips (using her *nom de plume*, Orinda) laments the 'poore weak man' who is 'in his very epitaphs accus'd' (lines 9 and 12) by friends who did not trust his name to live without a monument. By contrast, she says, her own life is inscribed on Lucasia's heart:

> I quit this pomp of death, and am content
> Having her heart to be my monument.
> Though ne're stone to me, 'twill stone for me prove
> By the peculiar miracle of Love.
> There Ile' inscription have, which no Tomb give's
> Not here Orinda Lyes, but here she live's. (lines 17–22)[23]

The only word that Philips underlines in her manuscript book of poems (now to be found in the National Library of Wales – MS 775B) is the word 'men', in line 19 of 'A Friend', highlighting who it is who would claim that women are not capable of true friendship:

> If soules no sexes have for *men* t'exclude
> Women from friendships vast capacity
> Is a design injurious and rude
> Onely maintain'd by partiall tyranny
> Love is allow'd to us and Innocence
> And noblest friendship does proceed from thence.
> ('A Friend', lines 19–24)

Philips often crosses gender lines to use language familiar to readers of heterosexual love poetry, such as John Donne's, and also male friendship poetry such as George Turberville's and William Cartwright's. In 'Friendships Mysteries', for instance, she echoes Donne's 'Canonization' when she bids Lucasia,

> since we see
> That Miracles Mens faith do move
> By wonder, and by Prodigy
> To the dull angry world let's prove
> There's a religion in our Love.   (lines 1–5)

In 1653, the same year that An Collins printed her *Divine Poems*, Philips wrote 'To my deare Sister Mrs C: P. on her nuptialls', a lovely epithalamion wishing her sister-in-law Cicily Philips joy in her marriage to John Lloyd. In twenty-four lines, one for each hour of the wedding day, Orinda presents 'my great solemnitys', the word 'my' perhaps contrasting the poet's ceremonial role with that of her husband James Philips, who as a justice of the peace performed the actual marriage. Cicily's marriage was the first to be solemnised in Cardigan after the Nominated Parliament, of which James Philips was a member, decreed marriage a civil ceremony, legal only if performed by a justice of the peace. Unlike poets who focus on the groom's joy, Orinda mentions John Lloyd only with a pronoun and only in the context of hope for Cicily's happiness:

> May his, and her pleasure and Love be so
> Involv'd and growing that we may not know
> Who most affection or most peace engrossd
> Whose love is strongest, or whose bliss is most.
>
> (lines 15–18)

The secular ceremony established by the 1653 law was considerably shorter than the solemnity outlined in England's traditional *Book of Common Prayer* or even in the 1644 *Directory for the Public Worship of God*, which was in effect in 1648 when Philips herself was married. Line 13 of Philips's epithalamion ('May her content and duty be the same') may allude to the fact that the new ceremony retains the old stricture that a wife is to obey her husband. And perhaps the word 'duty' in the last line of the poem in Philips's own manuscript copy (though not in seventeenth-century printed editions) suggests that the groom, too, should be dutiful: 'While every day like this may sacred prove / To Friendship duty, gratitude and love' (lines 23–4).

Of Philips's poems, the one that survives in the most contemporary manuscript copies (thirteen) is 'The Virgin', an imitation of Martial's epigram 10.47, a poem often translated and imitated by sixteenth- and seventeenth-century poets.[24] Beginning (in Ben Jonson's translation) 'The things that make the happier life, are these', and ending, 'Will to be, what thou art; and nothing more: / Nor fear thy latest day, nor wish therefore' (lines 12–13), epigram 10.47 recommends the kind of classical moderation figured by Renaissance male writers in poems such as 'To Penshurst' and 'To Sir Robert Wroth' (also by Jonson). In his translation, Jonson praises a life of 'wise simplicity' (line 13); Philips, in her imitation, one of 'wise lowliness' (line 15). In her first line, Philips reverses Martial's grammar: in listing 'The things that make a Virgin please', she will treat not what will please the virgin, but what will make the virgin pleasing to others. Playing against poems such as Robert Herrick's epigrammatic verses on his dishevelled mistresses, his 'Delight in Disorder', for example, celebrating 'sweet disorder' and 'wild civility' (lines 1 and 12), Philips seems to advise a flirtatious manner as she lists among the wise virgin's attributes 'An Eye, wherein at once do meet, / The beams of kindness, and of wit' (lines 5–6). It may seem to a twentieth-century reader that suggesting 'A Conversation, at once, free / From Passion, and from Subtlety' (lines 9–10) is patronising. But in Philips's other poems 'Passion' often means the kind of strong feeling that prohibits thought (perhaps here, the passionate language of radical Protestants); and in the seventeenth century 'Subtlety' can mean craft, or slyness – an attribute associated by Anglicans such as Philips with 'papists'. When Philips closes her 22-line poem (twenty-two, a number associated in classical and Renaissance numerology with moderation), by recommending a religion 'strong and plain, / Not superstitious, nor profane' (lines 21–2), it becomes clear that she is listing qualities that will make a virgin pleasing to a sensible, honourable man.

Almost every woman poet treated in this chapter uses a female variant of the humility topos – generally 'acknowledging' in a comic or defiant way that she is 'only a woman'. Aemelia Lanyer, for example, writes that it 'is seldome seene, / A Womans writing of divinest things' ('To the Queenes most Excellent Majestie', lines 3–4); and Anne Bradstreet says

> Let Greeks be Greeks, and Women what they are,
> Men have precedency, and still excell,
> It is but vaine, unjustly to wage war,
> Men can doe best, and Women know it well;
> Preheminence in each and all is yours,
> Yet grant some small acknowledgement of ours.
>
> (Prologue to *Quarternions*, lines 37–42)

Even the most ironic use of the woman's humility topos is a sign of an anxiety that might be best explained by an episode in the career of Mary Wroth, niece of Mary Sidney. When in 1621 Wroth printed her *Urania*,

Sir Edward Denny objected in the letter quoted by Helen Hackett in her chapter on courtly literature (see p. 181 of this volume). Denny also wrote thirteen doggerel couplets attacking Wroth in grossly sexual terms:

> Hermaphrodite in show, in deed a monster
>   As by thy words and works all men may conster
> Thy wrathfull spite conceived an Idell book
>   Brought forth a foole which like the damme doth look.

(lines 1–4)

Wroth responded with twenty-six equally angry lines, hers beginning

> Hirmophradite in sense in Art a monster
>   As by your railing rimes the world may conster
> Your spitefull words against a harmless booke
>   Shows that an ass much like the sire doth looke.

Denny ended his poem with the couplet 'Work o th' Workes leave idle bookes alone / For wise and worthyer women have writte none'; Wroth concluded hers, 'Take this then now lett railing rimes alone / For wise and worthier men have written none'.[25]

The force of Denny's attack and its interest to his contemporaries is registered in the fact that his poem survives until the present day in at least three seventeenth-century copies and also that it was quoted more than thirty years later by Margaret Cavendish, Duchess of Newcastle. In a prefatory letter 'To all Noble, and Worthy Ladies' in her *Poems, and Fancies* (1653), Cavendish anticipates that she 'shall be censur'd by my owne Sex; and Men will cast a smile of scorne upon my Book, because they think thereby, Women incroach too much upon their Prerogatives; for they hold Books as their Crowne, and the Sword as their Scepter, by which they rule, and governe. And very like they will say to me, as to the Lady that wrote the Romancy,

> Work Lady, work, let writing Books alone,
> For surely wiser Women nere wrote one.

Cavendish here turns Denny's words to her own comic purpose, her letter a carnivalesque assertion of the natural skill of women in writing poetry. Poetry, she says, is woman's work. It 'is built upon Fancy' and women's 'Braines work usually in a Fantasticall motion'. Rejecting the commonplace that women should sew rather than write, Cavendish claims that sewing and poetry are essentially the same: 'For Fancy goeth not so much by Rule, & Method, as by Choice: and if I have chosen my Silke with fresh colours, and matcht them in good shadows, although the stitches be not very true, yet it will please the Eye; so if my Writing please the Readers, though not the Learned, it wil satisfie me; for I had rather be praised in this, by the most, although not the best'. At the close of her dizzying display of playful logic, Cavendish urges women to join in her defence, 'for I know Womens Tongus are as sharp, as two-edged Swords, and wound as much, when they are anger'd'. Women, in short, can claim the traditional powers of both the sword and the pen. True 'Renaissance men', perhaps, are not men at all – but women.[26]

In *Poems, and Fancies*, as in several of her prose works, Cavendish queries modern science. The first woman to be invited to visit, but never to join, the Royal Society, Cavendish treats questions of mechanical atomism discussed within the circle of scientists – including René Descartes, Pierre Gassandi and Thomas Hobbes – of which she and her husband were members when, during the Interregnum, they lived in France.[27] Perhaps most attractive to modern readers are the poems in which Cavendish interrogates the scientific enterprise itself. In 'A Discourse of Beasts' she uses an innocent voice to ask,

> Who knowes; but Beasts, as they do lye,
> In Meadowes low, or else on Mountaines high?
> But that they do contemplate on the Sun,
> And how his daily, yearely Circles run.
> Whether the Sun about the Earth doth rove,
> Or else the Earth upon its own Poles move.
> . . . .
> 'Gainst their Astrology no Man can prove
> For they may know the Stars, and their Aspects,
> What Influence they cast, and their Effects.
>
> (lines 1–6 and 12–14)

In 'Of Fishes', she writes, 'Who knows, but Fishes which swim in the Sea, / Can give a Reason, why so Salt it be?' (lines 1–2); and 'Of Birds',

> Who knowes; but Birds which in the Aire flyes,
> Do know from whence the Blustring Winds do rise?
> May know what Thunder is, which no Man knowes,
> And what's a blazing Star, or where it goes.   (lines 1–4)

Cavendish was quite correct in supposing that her book would cause comment. On 14 April 1653 Dorothy Osborne wrote to William Temple, 'And first let mee aske you if you have seen a book of Poems newly come out, made by my Lady New Castle. for God sake if you meet with it send it mee, they say tis ten times more Extravagant then her dresse. Sure the poore woman is a litel distracted, she could never bee soe rediculous else as to venture at writeing a book's and in verse too, If I should not sleep this fortnight I should not come to that.' Three weeks later Osborne writes, 'You need not send mee my Lady Newcastles book at all for I have seen it, and am sattisfyed that there are many soberer People in Bedlam, i'le swear her friends are much to blame to let her goe abroade.'[28] Osborne's letter is a useful document in the history of early modern women's poetry. But it must be read in the context of other evidence of women's confidence in their role as poet – with, for example, Katherine Philips's pleasure at the success of her verse translation of *Pompey*, or Lady Anne Southwell's letter defending poetry over prose. As Jean Klene says of the latter, 'the voice in the letter differs radically from male voices. Her analogy for poetry, for example, describes it as the "silke thredd that stringes your chayne of pearle; which being broken, your jewells fall into the rushes; and the more you seeke for it, the more it falls into the dust of oblivion".'[29] In fact, we know that not even Dorothy Osborne was hostile to every woman writer, for she was the friend to whom Katherine Philips in January 1663/4 wrote a letter that both claims that Philips had nothing to do with the printing of her poems and also records pleasure that her friend preferred her translation of Corneille's *Pompey* to a rival translation by five (male) court wits.[30]

In 1673, in *An Essay to Revive the Antient Education of Gentlewomen*, Bathsua Makin insisted that women have long excelled at poetry. 'Their excellency in this, tends as much to their vindiction as any thing yet spoke to... A good Poet, must know things Divine, things Natural, things moral, things Historical, and things Artificial, together with the several terms belonging to all Faculties, to which they must allude. Good Poets must be universal Scholars, able to use a pleasing Phrase, and to express themselves with moving Eloquence.' When she turns to poets who wrote in English, Makin lists Anne Bradstreet, Katherine Philips (whose 'Works in print speak for her'), the four daughters of Sir Anthony Cook, Lady Russell (the Countess of Bedford), Lady Bacon, Lady Killigrew, Mary Sidney (Countess of Pembroke), Lady Jane Grey, Lady Arbella Stuart, Queen Elizabeth and the three daughters of Lord Burghley.[31]

Working from sources such as Pollard and Redgrave's and Wing's short-title catalogues of printed books, indices of manuscripts in European and American libraries, and sale catalogues of auction houses such as Sotheby's and Christies, twentieth-century scholars have compiled much longer lists of early women poets, including many, such as Lucy Hutchinson and Aphra Behn, whose work it has not been possible to discuss in this chapter. In recent years many of the women's poems have been reprinted or, in the case of manuscript poets, printed for the first time. Considerably more archival research and analysis of early modern women's poetry, however, remains to be done. We need to continue the tasks of relocating women's poetry and solving questions of attribution of poems (or parts of poems) possibly by women. We need to understand more fully the relationships among poets who thought in terms of a female literary tradition, and also the manifold ways that women poets influenced their male counterparts. Knowing, as we now do, how attuned early modern British women were to literary, political, religious and social issues of their time, we will continue to discover more about their uses of poetry to further causes of particular interest to them – and also about their uses of poetry within private, exclusively female, conversations.

NOTES

1. *A Room of One's Own* (San Diego, New York and London: Harcourt Brace Jovanovich, 1929; reprinted with a foreword by Mary Gordon, 1981), chapter 3, especially pp. 41–50. The two most extensive anthologies of poetry by women of this period are Betty Travitsky, ed., *The Paradise of Women: Writings by Englishwomen of the Renaissance* (Westport, CT: Greenwood Press, 1981), and Germaine Greer, Susan Hastings, Jeslyn Medoff and Melinda Sansone, eds., *Kissing the Rod: an Anthology of Seventeenth-Century Women's Verse* (London: Virago, 1988; New York: Farrar, Straus and Giroux, 1989).

2. Barbara K. Lewalski, ed., *The Resources of Kind: Genre-Theory in the Renaissance* (Berkeley, Los Angeles and London: University of California Press, 1973), especially chapter 1, 'Genre-Systems and the Functions of Literature'. In an aside, Professor Colie makes one telling comment on women's literature when she writes 'in an era of women's lib, [about] a category apparently inconceivable to Roda-Roda, *eine Frau allein*' who might write 'in the high style, a volume of confessional poetry; in the middle-style, a cookbook; in the low style, a narrative of successful call-girling. Which is to say: though there are generic conventions all right, they are also metastable' (p. 30).

3. See also Jean Klénè, C.S.C., ed., The Commonplace Book of Lady Anne Southwell (New York: Renaissance English Text Society, 1996).

4. David Norbrook, '"This blushinge tribute of a borrowed muse": Robert Overton and his Overturning of the Poetic Canon', *EMS*, 4 (1993), 220–66.

5. See the discussion of manuscript culture in chapter 7 of this volume. On manuscript poetry in general, see Peter Beal, *Index of English Literary Manuscripts, 1500–1700* (2 vols.; London: Mansell, 1980–93); Harold Love, *Scribal Publication in Seventeenth-Century England* (Oxford: Clarendon Press, 1993);

and Arthur F. Marotti, *Manuscript, Print, and the English Renaissance Lyric* (Ithaca, NY, and London: Cornell University Press, 1995). For women's manuscripts in particular, see Love, *Scribal Publication*, pp. 54–8; Marotti, *Manuscript, Print*, pp. 48–61; and Margaret J. M. Ezell, *The Patriarch's Wife: Literary Evidence and the History of the Family* (Chapel Hill: University of North Carolina Press, 1987), *passim*. For the phrase 'interactive genres' see also Ezell, 'The *Gentleman's Journal* and the Commercialization of Restoration Coterie Literary Practices', *MP*, 89 (1992), 328.

6. One of the most recent, and most sophisticated, treatments of this issue is Wendy Wall, *The Imprint of Gender: Authorship and Publication in the English Renaissance* (Ithaca, NY: Cornell University Press, 1993).

7. Wall, *Imprint of Gender*, stresses 'Whitney's anxieties about publication tak[ing] the form of tropes of contagion in the *Nosegay*' (p. 298). For the Dublin volume, which includes poems by Katherine Philips attributed to 'A Lady', see Elizabeth H. Hageman, 'Making a Good Impression: Early Texts of Poems and Letters by Katherine Philips, the "Matchless Orinda"', *SCR*, 11 (1994), 48–9.

8. *Silent But For The Word: Tudor Women as Patrons, Translators, and Writers of Religious Works*, ed. Margaret P. Hannay (Kent, OH: Kent State University Press, 1985).

9. See the fuller discussion of Anne Askewe in chapter 2 of this volume. For Askewe's writing as it was edited by the two sixteenth-century polemicists, John Bale and John Foxe, see Elaine V. Beilin, ed., *The Examinations of Anne Askew* (New York and Oxford: Oxford University Press, 1996).

10. Margaret P. Hannay, '"Princes you as men must dy": Genevan Advice to Monarchs in the *Psalmes* of Mary Sidney', *ELR*, 19 (1989), 22–41.

11. Margaret P. Hannay, '"House-confined maids": The Presentation of Woman's Role in the *Psalmes* of the Countess of Pembroke', *ELR*, 24 (1994), 44–71.

12. G. F. Waller, *Mary Sidney, Countess of Pembroke: A Critical Study of her Writings and Literary Milieu* (Salzburg, Austria: Institut für Anglistik und Amerikanistik, 1979), pp. 190–2. Like most other readers of the Sidneian Psalms, Waller presents Mary Sidney as building on Sir Philip Sidney's earlier work, but he sees her as 'much more ambitiously experimental than her brother' (p. 191).

13. For Mary Sidney's versification and its influence, see Susanne Woods, *Natural Emphasis: English Versification from Chaucer to Dryden* (San Marino, CA: Huntington Library, 1984), pp. 169–82 and 290–302. Woods argues that the Countess's 'contribution to English verse [is] among the least acknowledged major achievements in the history of English poetry' (p. 169). See also Barbara Kiefer Lewalski, *Protestant Poetics and the Seventeenth-Century Religious Lyric* (Princeton, NJ: Princeton University Press, 1979), pp. 241–4.

14. For Speght's writing, see Barbara Keifer Lewalski, ed., *The Polemics and Poems of Rachel Speght* (New York and Oxford: Oxford University Press, 1996). For another verse memorandum by a woman poet, see 'The Memorandum of Martha Moulsworth, Widdowe' (1632), in Robert C.

Evans and Barbara Wiedemann, eds., *'My Name was Martha': A Renaissance Woman's Autobiographical Poem by Martha Moulsworth* (West Cornwall, CT: Locust Hill Press, 1993).

15. On Bradstreet's changing relationship with England and America, see especially Patricia Caldwell, 'Why Our First Poet Was a Woman: Bradstreet and the Birth of an American Poetic Voice', *Prospects*, 13 (1989), 1–35. My quotations from Bradstreet are from *The Complete Works of Anne Bradstreet*, ed. Joseph R. McElrath, Jr, and Allan P. Robb (Boston, MA: Twayne, 1981). (McElrath and Robb do not lineate the poems.)

16. Greer *et al.*, eds., *Kissing the Rod*, p. 148; see, however, Elspeth Graham, Hilary Hinds, Elaine Hobby and Helen Wilcox, eds., *Her Own Life: Autobiographical Writings by Seventeenth-Century Englishwomen* (London: Routledge, 1989), p. 55, for the opposing view that Collins's use of words such as 'saints' for ordinary Christians suggests she is a Calvinist. An edition of Collins's poems prepared by Sidney Gottlieb is forthcoming from the Renaissance English Text Society.

17. For the Countess of Arundel and Elizabeth Jane Weston, see Louise Schleiner, *Tudor and Stuart Women Writers* (Bloomington: Indiana University Press, 1994), pp. 93–106.

18. Greer *et al.*, eds., *Kissing the Rod*, pp. 355–7.

19. For the possibility that the family of Aemilia Lanyer's father, Baptist Bassano, was Jewish, see Roger Prior, 'More (Moor? Moro?) Light on the Dark Lady', *Financial Times*, London, 10 October 1987, p. 17, and 'Jewish Musicians at the Tudor Court', *MQ*, 69 (1983), 253–65, both of which are cited by Barbara Kiefer Lewalski in *Writing Women in Jacobean England* (Cambridge, MA and London: Harvard University Press, 1993), p. 395.

20. Elaine V. Beilin, *Redeeming Eve: Women Writers of the English Renaissance* (Princeton, NJ: Princeton University Press, 1987), argues that defending womankind against the charge that we are responsible for all of the world's evils was the central project of English women writers in the period 1520–1640, from Margaret More to Mary Wroth. See the opening section of chapter 3 in this volume.

21. *The Poems of Aemilia Lanyer: 'Salve Deus Rex Judaeorum'*, ed. Susanne Woods (New York and Oxford: Oxford University Press, 1993), page xxxi. My quotations from Lanyer's poetry are from this edition.

22. For a photographic facsimile of Powell's poem in National Library of Wales, Powis Castle (1959 deposit; Herbert of Cherbury MSS and papers, parcel 14/7a (ii)) see Elizabeth H. Hageman and Andrea Sununu, '"More Copies of it abroad than I could have imagin'd": Further Manuscript Texts of Katherine Philips, "the Matchless Orinda"' *EMS*, 5 (1994), plate 1. My quotations from Philips's poetry are from the transcripts for a forthcoming edition that Andrea Sununu and I are preparing for the series Women Writers in English, printed by Oxford University Press.

23. I am grateful to Kira Narlee, a student at the University of New Hampshire, for calling this contrast to my attention. Ms. Narlee also notes that in

'Wiston-Vault' Philips critiques her century's class structure in her assertion that 'alike we must / Put off distinctions, and put on our dust' (lines
1–2).

24. Other English translators of Martial's epigram 10.47 include Henry Howard, Earl of Surrey, Thomas Randolph and Sir Robert Southwell (the
son-in-law of Philips's friend Sir Edward Dering); for imitations, see, for
example, Sir Henry Wotton's 'The Character of a Happy Life', written in
six four-line stanzas, and an anonymous Latin poem transcribed beside an
English translation beginning 'The things that make a Bishops life more
fair' in Folger Library MS V.a. 125. I am grateful to Peter Beal, who called
my attention to the fact that Philips's poem is an imitation of Martial and
who noted that it is transcribed immediately before another imitation of
epigram 10.47 (the other headed 'A Happy Life, out of Martiall' and
beginning 'They swell with love that are with valour fild') in the commonplace book of Elizabeth Lyttelton, now Cambridge University Library,
Add. MS 8460: see Geoffrey Keynes, *The Commonplace Book of Elizabeth
Lyttelton, Daughter of Sir Thomas Browne* (Cambridge: Cambridge University
Press, 1919).

25. Printed in *The Poems of Lady Mary Wroth*, ed. Josephine A. Roberts (Baton
Rouge: Louisiana State University Press, 1983; rpt. 1992), pp. 32–5.

26. Margaret Cavendish, *Poems, and Fancies* (1653; Menston: Scolar Press, 1972),
sig. A3r–v. Cavendish also quotes Denny's poem in her *Sociable Letters* (1664;
Menston: Scolar Press, 1969), sig. b. See also the discussion of the symbolism of pens, swords and needles in chapter 7 of this volume.

27. For a full discussion of Cavendish's attitudes to scientific knowledge, see
chapter 6 of this volume. See also Carolyn Merchant, *The Death of Nature:
Women, Ecology and the Scientific Revolution* (San Francisco: Harper and Row,
1980), pp. 270–2.

28. *The Letters of Dorothy Osborne to William Temple*, ed. G. C. Moore Smith
(Oxford: Clarendon Press, 1928), pp. 37 and 41.

29. Jean Klene, 'Recreating the Letters of Lady Anne Southwell', in *New Ways
of Looking at Old Texts: Papers of the Renaissance English Text Society, 1985–1991*,
ed. W. Speed Hill (Binghamton, NY: Medieval and Renaissance Texts and
Studies, 1993), p. 249.

30. For a photographic facsimile and discussion of Philips's letter to Dorothy
Temple, now in the Theatre Collection, Harvard Library (uncatalogued),
see Hageman, 'Making a Good Impression', 50–3.

31. Bathsua Makin, *An Essay to Revive the Antient Education of Gentlewomen*, intro.
Paula L. Barbour (1673; reprinted Los Angeles: Augustan Reprint Society,
William Andrews Clark Memorial Library, 1980), pp. 16–20. For Makin's
own poetry, see Greer *et al.*, eds., *Kissing the Rod*, pp. 224–9. For further work
on Makin's life, see J. R. Brink, 'Bathsua Reginald Makin: "Most Learned
Matron"', *HLQ*, 54 (1991), 313–27, and Frances Teague, 'The Identity of
Bathsua Makin', *Biography*, 16 (1993), 1–17.

CHAPTER 10

Women's writing and the self

Elspeth Graham

Academic interest in what is variously referred to as 'autobiography', 'self-writing', 'life-history narrative', 'life-story writing' and 'auto/biography' has grown enormously over the last twenty years. The variety of terms used to designate this form of writing and the debates over the implications of these terms point to the cluster of fascinations and anxieties that are focused on it. Since any fundamental definition of autobiography identifies it as the life or life-history of the self who is writing, the form brings into conjunction precisely those terms and concepts that have most preoccupied philosophers, social scientists, historians and literary critics in the past few decades. The notion of the self is a troubled one. What constitutes identity or selfhood, or (more recently) subjectivity is, as Liz Stanley puts it, one of 'the major epistemological issues of our time'.[1] What constitutes a 'life' or 'life-history' and how selfhood is related to 'life-history' and to writing or, more generally, language, are equally contentious matters. The study of autobiography has come to be associated not only with autobiographies themselves, with the nature of the genre and the difficult and puzzling issues inherent in identification of it as a genre, but serves, too, as a place where the assumptions underlying disciplinary divisions and concerns can be explored or questioned or affirmed. There is a curious circularity in discussion of autobiography: we have sought most urgently to identify it as a genre at precisely the historical moment when those terms that we identify as definitive of it are under question.

SELF AND WRITING, 1500–1700

When we come to look at women's self-writings of the period 1500–1700 we encounter in a particularly direct way many of the theoretical and critical issues that surround twentieth-century discussion of the form. Three immediate recognitions are forced upon us: the clear lack of any stable form of self-writing, which relates to a wider unfixity of genres in the period; women's ambiguous status as subjects; and our own incomplete recovery of early modern women's writings. The last of these has obvious implications. While we now have access to a much greater body of writings from the period than we did fifteen or twenty years ago, there are still large gaps in our knowledge of what women actually did write. *The Book of Margery Kempe*, written and partially transcribed in 1436 and fully transcribed in 1438 for its illiterate author, was discovered in manuscript in 1934, and has since then been hailed as the first autobiography written in English – the autobiography of a woman. But between this and the early seventeenth century there is no coherent body of autobiographical writings by women: there are no known prose narratives of the self, although there are some existent diaries and journals of aristocratic women from the late sixteenth century. It is hard to assess precisely the extent to which this indicates an absence of what we might call an autobiographical impulse in the sixteenth century, although it is generally accepted that the appearance of a significant number of published self-writings occurs in the seventeenth century, rather than earlier.

There are historical issues to be considered about the emergence of self-narratives generally, and about the particular conditions of women's lives. But we need to be aware, too, that publication histories may inform our understanding of what was written. In the mid and late seventeenth century spiritual confession became an established genre, and exemplary women's writings in this form often found their way into print and thus proved durable and recoverable. Manuscript writings have clearly had a less secure chance of survival. Issues of contemporary value affect a work's chance of preservation, and the values of succeeding periods influence what is catalogued or republished. We are beginning to be aware of the existence of a much greater variety of women's writings from the early modern period than was once dreamed of,[2] but there is much material that has not been fully researched. For instance, two manuscripts containing one of the earliest prose narratives of the self by a woman, Dionys Fitzherbert's fascinating account of her personal history and period of mental or spiritual crisis, written in the early seventeenth century, have only recently been 'discovered' in the Bodleian Library by Kate Hodgkin.[3] Obviously analysis and interpretation of women's self-writing in the early modern period can only be based on what is available, and this itself is shaped by criteria guiding preservation of writings and recovery.

The status of manuscript writings raises further issues concerning the genre of autobiographical confession, and the relation of public to private texts. A variety of factors determine whether a text had a manuscript or printed circulation. In the case of Dionys Fitzherbert, for example, it seems likely that she had no access to print, since there was not at this point a print culture of spiritual writings by 'ordinary' people. Her writing seems to have been motivated by her sense of personal need to voice her own version of her sufferings, which was at odds with the interpretation made by those who surrounded her. However, since she had her manuscript transcribed, it is clear that she intended it to be circulated. It is in this sense a published and public text. But in the case of other manuscript self-narratives, this may not be so clear. Alice Thornton's self-writing from the later seventeenth century, one of the best-known early modern English women's life-histories, is known largely through its publication as *The Autobiography of Mrs Alice Thornton of East Newton, Co. York* in 1873 by the Surtees Society. Evidence suggests, however, that Alice Thornton wrote at least three manuscript versions of her life and that these were conflated by the Surtees Society editor, producing an artificial text that conformed to nineteenth-century notions of autobiographical concerns and structure.[4] Insofar as we can disentangle the versions produced by Thornton herself, we might now seek to designate one as more authoritative than the others, either because it is an earlier version and therefore perhaps more directly derived from the lived actuality of her life, or conversely we might see a later version as more consciously formed and having a greater structural and aesthetic coherence. Or we might refuse to choose between versions, seeing the writing of multiple versions of the self as a crucial part of the autobiographical impulse.[5] Then, since the texts were originally manuscript documents, presumably intended for circulation amongst members of Thornton's family (and retained by the family until at least the 1930s), there are issues of designation of them as public or private. Family circulation constitutes a sort of limited public status, especially since aristocratic and gentry families in the seventeenth century cannot be simply viewed as private domains, and distinctions between the private and public need to be made cautiously in relation to this period.[6]

In brief, then, when we examine self-writing from the early modern period we are forced to consider a variety of issues beyond simple matters of women's place within a generic tradition. Publication histories shape our sense of what was written and may determine our evaluations of texts. Issues of self-writings are shown to be tied up quite

directly with issues of social class or rank, with groups and group cultures
as well as individual motivations and personalities. Even before we begin
to examine actual texts, we find that our understanding of women's
written articulations of the self is enmeshed with our understanding of
the wider discourses of the period and the literary and historical processes that have shaped even our most basic knowledge of what was
written.

Beyond these fundamental matters, there are then issues relating to
form and definitions of selfhood more generally. In the sixteenth and
seventeenth centuries concepts of both genre and selfhood are more
clearly unstable than they may appear to be in later centuries. Recent
discussion of the origins of the novel (so closely linked to self-writing)
provides instances of our troubled attempts to identify generic demarcations in the period. There are increasingly plausible critical arguments
suggesting a move of the date of the rise of the novel back from its
conventional eighteenth-century location to the seventeenth century.
But as Roger Pooley points out, 'there is no one clear line of filiation
between seventeenth- and eighteenth-century fiction' and no 'generi-
cally secure code' for the early novel. Referring to Bakhtin's influential
analysis of genre where it is asserted that 'in its earliest stage, the novel
and its preparatory genres had relied upon various extra-literary forms
of personal and social reality, and especially those of rhetoric', Pooley
points to a range of 'forms within the form' of prose-fiction: 'rhetoric,
certainly, and letters, poems, trial narratives and gallows confessions,
sermons, political speeches, travellers' tales, allegory.'[7] The boundaries
between fiction and autobiography, always uncertain, were thus especially unfixed in the early modern period.

Although anxiety and complex argument exists about the nature of
the relationship between truth and the imaginative, and this relates to
written forms, what is most notable in the period is the indeterminacy of
forms. Rather than attempting to 'sort out' forms by considering what
they later become, we should perhaps focus on the significances of
fluidity itself. Self-writing is situated in this context: where narrative
structures are fluid, where 'truth' is variously defined, and where clear
fiction/non-fiction boundaries, later clustering around the establishment of drama, poetry and the novel as identifiably 'literary' forms of
writing, are not pre-existing or dominant determinants. It is not surprising, then, in this context of general generic instability, that self-narratives
are enormously variable in structure and focus. Even to use the term
'autobiography', if this is seen to presume a specific set of generic

features, becomes misleading. 'Self-writing' perhaps more clearly represents the variety of strategies and forms that are used by writers seeking to articulate and assert themselves through that very writing of the self. As with fictional prose of the period, self-writing cannot be easily or clearly defined through reference to a coherent set of core characteristics. Many narratives of the self include within them letters, diary entries, poems, extracts from journals; many take the form of spiritual confessions. It is hard to distinguish a specific form of self-writing from a more generally collective group of forms of self-articulation including the diary, journals and trial records. The exploration and exploitation of a variety of forms, rather than adherence to a recognised format for articulating the self, is the crucial characteristic of self-writing, and in particular of women's self-writing, of the period.

Any notion of self-writing, no matter how widely defined or described, must necessarily depend on some notion of the self, however. But this, too, is a shifting and uncertain concept in relation to the sixteenth and seventeenth centuries, particularly with reference to women. The period has long been recognised as a crucial moment in the development of individualism in England, and the relatively sudden proliferation of writings displaying a preoccupation with the self, including those by women and men from non-aristocratic backgrounds, commonly linked with processes of emergent individualism.[8] But to link self-writing in the period with the development of any general, commonly shared notion of selfhood would be misleading. Although an individualist society and culture clearly does emerge from the period, and emphasis on the self in general grows, a *coherent* notion of self does not emerge uniformly. Notions of 'self' and the social primacy of the individual self are formulated within divergent discourses and are variously inflected. The period, seen from a long view, is marked by a shift away from the political structures of patriarchalism, where identity is rank-based, located by place in a series of family/state analogies, to a social-contract structure where the individual is presumed to have inherent qualities and rights. This process of change is not smooth, however, and the dominance of one or other system of political thought and organisation is not accepted by all at any given moment in the period. Consequently, very different versions of the politically defined self co-exist in the period.

Similarly, in other discourses defining the self we find widely variant notions of identity jostling together. Religion is crucial to almost all systems of thought and is at the centre of the conflicts and changes of the period.[9] A variety of religious positions provide differing versions of selfhood. Calvinism, the orthodox doctrine of the Church of England throughout the period, as well that of many dissenting sects of the 1640s and following decades, provides one particularly influential version.[10] It takes the notions derived from Luther, and central to Protestant thought in general, of the individual's own responsibility for his or her own relationship to God and of justification by faith alone (rather than good works), and adds to these the doctrine of predestination. Protestant doctrine is usually seen to emphasise the interiority of the self – real selfhood is perceived as lying in the conscience, or in the 'inner man', rather than in behaviour or outward manifestations of virtue. Predestination, the belief that before the Creation God had selected the ultimate destination of each individual among ranks of the elect or reprobate, especially contributes to this splitting of inner and outer manifestations of selfhood. For Calvinists, behaviour is at best an indicator of the inner state of a man or woman. But it may, much more dangerously, mask an inner state, beguiling others into erroneously perceiving an individual as godly, or worse, misleading the individual himself or herself into a false sense of assurance of his or her own godliness. Hypocrisy, the technical term for a mismatch between an apparently righteous 'outer man' but a sinful 'inner man', was a constantly feared condition. The tendency of Calvinists is, then, towards particularly intense introspection as the believer attempts to monitor the rightness of an inner core of self. Calvinist writing is characterised by the presentation of a deeply interiorised, spiritual notion of self, constructed in complex relation to a watchful, interpreting self. It is a selfhood riven by paradox: constructed as singular (alone and often lonely and isolated) but relational, since it is established in relation to God, God's word and other individuals who mark positions of greater or lesser spirituality; unchangeable (since predetermined) yet responsible for responding to God's calling and thus for its own salvation; passively dependent on God's will, but always actively self-scrutinising and self-creating through the advised practices of journal-keeping and self-confession.

For some sectaries and non-conformists, however, different versions of the self were available. To Quakers, as one instance, who valued the promptings of the Inner Light above any doctrinal law or the Bible itself, self was often experienced ecstatically. The boundaries of individual selfhood could be blurred. Conflation of self with others, individual and personal utterance with biblical text, external event and biblical history with spiritual vision is characteristic. Comprising one of the most individualistic of sects, Quakers also displayed a capacity for collective

selfhood. Delineation of personal identity was characteristically subor-dinated to presentation of the identity of Quakerism itself.

Among other discourses offering versions of the self, medical dis-courses provide a quite different construction of identity. The period sees the gradual replacement of humoural accounts of being by anatomical versions of the human body. These differing accounts of the make-up of the human, again, exist side by side throughout much of the period, the one offering an integrated mind–body model, based on a system of analogy and correspondence, and classifying individuals and maladies through typologies; the other providing a mapping of physical being based on empirical scientific principles.[11] Legal definitions of the self, and the effects of legislation and the appeal to court procedures in the period, provide further versions of identity. Interpersonal disputes deriv-ing from notions of the integrity of the individual demonstrate how legal proceedings were sought as a means of arbitrating between individuals in order to establish boundaries to the self through the rightful protection of property, whether this was economically defined or was concerned with more abstract notions of property, such as the important possession of reputation.[12] Issues of 'propriety', signifying self-ownership, feature strongly in legal and political writings of the period. The actual econ-omic shifts of the period and related changes in social structure have long been associated with changing formulations of selfhood.[13] These, too, were enacted unevenly, and through intense and, at times, violent conflict.

Even a cursory glance at some of the variety of discourses offering versions of selfhood reveals not just a lack of broad consensus over notions of identity in the period, but suggests that discourses governing self-articulation are not only in contradiction with one another but are internally conflictual. This, of course, is commonly recognised as being true of all periods: conflict and contradiction are inherent in all ideologi-cal structures. What is strikingly apparent in relation to the sixteenth and seventeenth centuries is, however, the particular ideological turbulence of the period, marked both by the major social and political conflicts of the civil war, and at the level of individual lives throughout the period.

For women, issues of the indeterminacy of constructions of selfhood are especially pronounced. The words of T. E., the author of *The Lawes Resolutions of Womens Rights* (1632), have been much quoted in analyses of women's writing and historical role in the period, since they summarise the position of women so succinctly. Women, T. E. states, have no role or identity in law:

women have no voice in Parliament, they...have nothing to do in constituting laws, or consenting to them, or interpreting of laws or in hearing them interpreted at lectures, leets or charges, and yet they stand strictly tied to men's establishments, little or nothing excused by ignorance.[14]

Historical evidence suggests that T. E. somewhat exaggerates women's non-participation in legal transactions, and fails to give a sense of how women might exploit their subordination to men. Rather than 'being little or nothing excused by ignorance', it seems that women sometimes were able to take advantage of their lack of legal responsibility, since culpability for a woman's illegal actions could be attached to her husband if he could be shown to have known of or have been present at the criminal act.[15] But formally, as Kermode and Walker put it:

Women's status in legal, institutional and conventional terms was indeed derivative, defined in terms of their subordinate relationship to men and the status and occupation of their menfolk. Their social identity was also bound up with the life cycle. Women were described in formal discourses as daughter, wife or widow of 'X'.[16]

T. E., again, eloquently describes how women were subordinate to, first, their fathers and then their husbands:

in this consolidation which we call wedlock is a locking together. It is true, that a man and wife are one person, but understand in what manner.

When a small brook or little river incorporateth with Rhodanus, Humber or the Thames, the poor rivulet loseth her name; it is carried and recarried with the new associate; it beareth no sway; it possesseth nothing during coverture. A woman as soon as she is married is called 'covert'; in Latin 'nupta', that is, 'veiled'; as it were clouded and overshadowed; she hath lost her stream. I may more truly, far away, say to a married woman, her new self is her superior, her companion, her master.[17]

This does not imply, however, that women have identities that they lose on marriage. All women, T. E. adds, 'are understood either married, or to be married, and their desires are subject to their husbands'.[18] Women, then, have no identities of their own: they are always identified as subordinate and through relation to men. Social convention, likewise, offers an ambiguous identity. As Catherine Belsey has pointed out, patriarchal formulations offer a series of analogous roles to men: (king), father, master. For women, roles are discontinuous. A woman may be a mistress to servants, but she is subordinate to her husband and the comparability of the roles of father and mother in relation to children is uneasily maintained.[19] Similarly in theological, biological and philo-sophical discourses women are predominantly defined relationally and negatively. The period inherits Aristotelian notions of women being botched or incomplete men.[20] Galenic medicine, based on the doctrine of humours, depicts women as characteristically made up of cold and moist humours, rendering them volatile, slippery in nature and prone to all forms of excess and uncontainability.

Recent work on gender and sexuality in the early modern period presents two clusters of ideas. One suggests that women are negatively defined and lack positive identity. The other emphasises the fluidity of constructions of gender between discourses and, setting sixteenth- and seventeenth-century notions of the sexual make-up of women and men against later codifications of difference between the sexes, demonstrates the arbitrariness and historical variability of all constructions of gendered and sexual difference.[21] What is clear, however, is that women in the sixteenth and seventeenth centuries were generally under constraint to be silent, not to speak publicly or to publish. Writing the self for such women is a matter of negotiating, exploiting or denying a whole range of social and discursive determinants.

Amongst late sixteenth- and seventeenth-century self-writings we find a wide range of styles, preoccupations and forms. In the discussion of a series of self-writings that follows, I have concentrated on the most obviously autobiographical forms – prose narratives of the self, and the diary. And, with the exception of Dionys Fitzherbert's account, which raises especially interesting issues about form, identity and discursive context, the texts chosen for exploration are all among those that are easily available in modern editions. My aim is to consider texts that are representative and to raise issues relevant to a wider range of women's self-writings.

BODY, WORLD AND SOUL: THE SELF-WRITINGS OF HANNAH ALLEN AND DIONYS FITZHERBERT

Suffering and discursive contradiction feature strongly as aspects of the comparable self-writings of Dionys Fitzherbert and Hannah Allen, although there are formal differences between the texts, and the dates of their writings are separated by three-quarters of a century. Both accounts deal with personal crisis. Each text is troubled in different ways by the writer's attempt to name, outline and, through this, possess her suffering. The later text, Hannah Allen's *Satan his Methods and Malice Baffled*, published in 1683, conforms to the structure of conventional spiritual confession that became an established mode from the 1650s onwards. It is a retrospective, linear narrative that begins with childhood, providing the customary statement of social, family and religious identity at its beginning:

> I, Hannah Allen, the late wife of Hannibal Allen, merchant, was born of religious parents. My father was Mr John Archer of Snelston in Derbyshire, who took to wife the daughter of Mr William Hart of Uttoxeter Woodland in Staffordshire, who brought me up in the fear of God from my childhood.[22]

This factual summary of the key markers of her identity (establishing the social rank of her first husband, family lineage and geographic origins, and asserting her pious background) immediately moves, again quite conventionally, to her first intense experience of religious feeling. For Allen, initial apprehensions of faith are both implicitly and explicitly linked with suffering and pain. She relates how, aged twelve, she was sent to stay with her paternal aunt in London for her 'better education'. But,

> after some time spent there and at school, I being not well in health, had a desire to go down for a time to my mother, being a widow (my father dying when I was very young) where I stayed almost two years. In which time, it pleased God to work in me earnest breathings after the ways of God. But the enemy of my soul, striving to crush such hopeful beginnings in the bud, cast in horrible, blasphemous thoughts and injections into my mind, insomuch that I was seldom free, day or night, unless when dead sleep was upon me. But I used to argue with myself to this purpose. (p. 200)

A series of tensions, which comes to characterise the narrative as a whole, is first noticeable here. Allen is working from a doctrinal position which holds that God works in the world, through its events, and 'calls' the individual directly. Satan likewise has a real presence in the world and battles against God, through his influence on the soul of the individual. Although ultimately the account of the inner struggle to resist Satan's promptings and to respond to God's is of prime significance and corresponds to an established spiritual pattern (calling, repeated crises of faith and despair, then final arrival at some degree of security in faith), and the structure and focus of the narrative must highlight this, there are simultaneous pressures to locate this inner strife within the context of the actuality of a life lived in the world. In correspondence with these demands, this passage reads as if Allen is struggling to condense factual details, necessary for the chronological and situational coherence of her narrative. She becomes more expansive as she describes the nature of her spiritual conflicts. But it is in the condensed contextual detail that we find traces of the problems and inconsistencies underlying the text, which the narrative attempts to regulate. A number of surrounding painful experiences, such as a series of losses and separations experienced by Allen, are mentioned incidentally and parenthetically. Her father's death is referred to in brackets. Similarly, a little later, when she has described her return to London and the resumption of her stay with her uncle and aunt after her marriage, she moves swiftly, in the space of half a sentence and without comment, from her uncle's death to her admission to the sacrament. More arrestingly still, her husband's death is mentioned almost casually, and its circumstances are, again, provided parenthetically: '(for he died beyond sea)'. Although the narrative subordinates reference of such emotional sufferings to her spiritual malaise, they are established in conjunction with the spiritual. In her brief description of her married life, she writes:

And in the time of his [her husband's] life, I was frequently exercised with variety of temptations, wherein the Devil had the more advantage, I being much inclined to melancholy, occasioned by the oft absence of my dear and affectionate husband, with whom I live, present and absent, about eight years. (p. 201)

Here she refers both to spiritual temptation and to the medically defined condition of melancholy, which she connects quite directly with her husband's absences. Affective relationships, illness and spiritual suffering are established in a hierarchy of causes of suffering: separation from her husband occasions melancholy which makes her vulnerable to Satan's malign promptings. Such a classification of causes of her suffering is reinforced by her editor's full descriptive title to the narrative:

Satan his Methods and Malice Baffled. A narrative of God's gracious dealings with that choice Christian, Mrs Hannah Allen (afterwards married to Mr Hatt) reciting the great advantages the Devil made of her deep melancholy, and the triumphant victories, rich and sovereign graces, God gave her over all his stratagems and devices. (p. 197)

Here again it is suggested that spiritual suffering and the medical condition of melancholy co-exist but are separable. Emphasis, nevertheless, is on the spiritual import of the narrative: its significance is in demonstrating God's victory over Satan in the struggles of her soul.

The final sections of Allen's narrative, however, suggest a more complex set of alignments between the discourses – medical, spiritual and gendered – informing the text. Here Allen describes how a cousin, Mr Shorthose, who is a minister, and who also 'had some skill in physic himself and consulted with physicians about me' is instrumental in restoring her to well-being.[23] In the person of Mr Shorthose the medical, the familial, spiritual authority and masculine trustworthiness are brought together. Allen's despair, under Mr Shorthose's ministrations, is alleviated. Her recovery is then described, not in terms of spiritual assurance, but social conformability:

I passed that winter much better than formerly, and was pretty conformable and orderly in the family. And the next summer was much after the same manner, but grew still something better, and the next winter likewise still mending, though but slowly, till the spring began and then I changed much from my retiredness and delighted to walk with friends abroad.

And this spring it pleased God to provide a very suitable match for me, one Mr Charles Hatt, a widower living in Warwickshire, with whom I live very comfortable both as to my inward and outward man, my husband being one that truly fears God. (pp. 298-9)

Her experience of intense despair (which has included long periods of extreme religious doubt; fear that she was damned, had committed the 'unpardonable sin' or was a hypocrite; identification with biblical sinners; and several suicide attempts) is not now presented as characterised by purely spiritual symptoms, but by forms of social disruptiveness. Likewise, the closure to her narrative is not provided by a statement of spiritual ease or confidence, but by the reporting of her remarriage. Although Allen's narrative appears on the surface to conform to conventional spiritual patterns of cause and effect, it is ultimately significant in that it moves between differing explanations for her affliction and recovery: spiritual, medical, affective and conformity to accepted gender roles.

Hannah Allen was a Presbyterian. To any member of such a religious group, whose beliefs were predicated on Calvinist doctrine, in the decades following the civil war there is an established form for self-representation. Allen's narrative was published as an exemplary spiritual life and conforms, on the surface at least, to the accepted model. Issues of gender distinguish Allen's text, however, from those of male counterparts.[24] Not only are crises triggered by deaths of men close to her, but her recovery is described in terms of feminine conformability. It is possible to speculate, too, that the inclusion of medical explanations for her suffering proceeds from an emphasis, in the period, of the particular susceptibility of women to melancholic illness, linked with their proneness to excess and their unstable humoural make-up.

Distinguishing between spiritual despair and melancholy was often, in the earlier part of the period especially, a problematic matter. Kate Hodgkin has summarised how 'The distinction between the organic illness of melancholy and the spiritual suffering of religious despair is unstable and shifting, and the ability to distinguish between the two a matter at once of grave importance and of insuperable difficulty.[25] And she has shown Dionys Fitzherbert, an early seventeenth-century woman from a gentry family, wrote her account of the 'mental crisis of some kind' she suffered in her early twenties in order to contest the diagnosis of her crisis.[26] Others surrounding her had identified her affliction as melancholy. She sought to challenge this by detailing her experience and narratively configuring her suffering as a form of religious punishment for falling from grace after her calling by God. Fitzherbert's narrative is, then, directly located in the awareness of the implications of competing discursive constructions of experience. Although Hannah Allen's and Dionys Fitzherbert's narratives are similarly based on negotiation of rival discourses of pain, they are differently motivated and the conflicts that inform them have different effects.

Fitzherbert's account of what she terms her 'fall' reads almost as a negative of Allen's narrative. *Satan's Methods and Malice Baffled* involves descriptions of involuntary losses and Allen's ultimate restoration within a community; Fitzherbert's narrative similarly deals with separations and dislocations, but its impulse is to insist on these. Her story is one of anguished separations and distancings, which she initiates, but which then rebound on her. Not only is her motivation to write compelled by her need to identify her affliction as spiritual rather than melancholic, separating rather than aligning the available explanatory discourses, but her account of her fall, and the large body of material prefatory to the account itself – letters from authoritative figures supporting her account; an interpretation of a miraculous sign she has witnessed; and a sort of open letter 'To the glorious and renounced Church of England our deare Mother"[27] – mark her attempt to relocate herself within a quite different social, religious and gendered framework from that she was brought up in.

Her calling itself is both defiantly and anxiously described as extraordinary. She writes:

a word concerning my first calling the which I sayd was by a grieveous siknes speking of it as it was the first introduction of mene where by god wrought by unspekable way in my hart a fervent & ardent desire of serching and reading the holy scriptures whereby I was converted & so borne a new of the word of god and so continued with out any other help[.] (4r)

She persists alone in her reading and spiritual self-education until she feels convinced in her religious understanding, when she is 'confermed both by the ministry of the word and use of the sacraments'. She adds: 'the which thing I have writen lest any objection might aris through the extraordinarynes of my calling' (viii). She is anxious to assert her own responsibility for her spiritual education, but needs to legitimate it through reference to her formal reception into the Church of England. Her calling detaches her from her non-religious family; she is alienated by and from their life of worldly pleasure and concerns.

She then further distances herself from her father by refusing to marry the suitor he proposes to her. Her father arranges for her to leave the family home and to join the household of a kinswoman. This does not prove a sympathetic environment and she takes up a series of positions in the households of various aristocratic ladies over the following few years. Even where she is treated with kindness, however, she is impelled to move on, driven by a restless 'gad[d]ing humer to be gone' (8r). Her ultimate collapse is apparently triggered by her father not sending her money at one New Year. As she becomes obviously ill, she attempts to disguise her malady, claiming she is suffering from 'the wind colike in [her] stomach' (9v). But she catches herself failing to maintain this pretence of commonplace illness when she unthinkingly eats an apple offered to her (which she would have refused had she been suffering from a genuine colic.) A description of extraordinary physical and mental collapse ensues. The apple core appears to stick in her throat, she believes it has become irretrievably jammed or fused into a part of her mouth and she vomits violently. In an apparently delusory state she identifies her vomit with the fire of hell burning inside her, and she imagines being laid in the yard of the Charterhouse in London 'for all people to wonder at and all the yeard shuld flow with the mater that came out of my mouth & [I] did ashuredly think all the bed cloths were as wet it as myght be' (10v).

In the months that follow she remains 'distracted', a term she herself uses and which usually signifies insanity. During this period her family, especially her brothers whom she later states she loved dearly, appear as enemies to her; she lays her head on their swords in order for them to kill her. She believes that her favourite brother is not, in fact, her brother; she thinks she has stolen the clothes she is wearing from the lady whose household she was living in when she became 'distracted'; she is tormented by a sense of her sinfulness; she perceived herself as a criminal (and understands that this is why she is bound to her bed during her most violent 'distraction'); she suffers physical symptoms which suggest to her that she is near to death: 'allso the pallet of my mouth was quit broken away and the gall [was] within my body' (10r). At one moment she writes that her thoughts

did so confound my understanding that I did not belive the most sencible thinges that be[,] no not that I was child to my owne parents but sister to on Mistress H whom I had loved derly and bene much be holding to[,] but now accounted her as on of my greates enmmys as well becaus I was some what indeted to her and that allso by her procurment I came to doctor C and now did verely think I was her owne sister and that my name was mary which was the name of a sister of hers that I had heard her often say was ded and she did much resemble me which words I did remember and thought I was the same and that she sayd she was dead becaus her meaning was I should be burnt which was all the deaths I could conceve of. (12r)

A series of confusions and sliding identifications is apparent throughout this passage and the longer description of what she can remember of her condition at this time. Her ambivalent feelings towards members of her family, whom she both loves but has sought to differentiate herself from, are now, in modern terms, projected, so that family members appear threatening to her, or else figure as strangers. Her spiritual difference from her family and period of living apart from the family household comes to be mentally constructed as a sundering from blood relationship with them. Her identification with Mary, the dead sister of her friend, presents complex possibilities of interpretation. She takes the likeness that has been remarked between her and Mary, not as likeness but as absolute identity, suggesting her own slippery lack of self-identity. Her fear of her own death conflates with her knowledge of Mary's actual death, blurring her sense of boundary between life and death. This is particularly strongly associated with her fear of fire and burning. She feels she is consumed by internal fire: the burning of her gall and the apparent disintegration of her mouth suggest a literal, physical corrosion, but she understands this metaphorically, too, as a precursor to the burning of hell-fire which will consume her after death. Slippage between life and death, the literal and the metaphoric, burning as divine punishment and burning within a domestic environment, are evident in her fear that she will burn to death. She *is* burning, she *will* burn in hell, but she also expects and is terrified of death *by* burning:

allso to avoid the torment of the fier that above all things I fered for I never rose out of my bed that I thought I shuld have gone into it againe but that they would set me up in the chimny and make a small fier under my fete & ther shuld burn for ever and never dy beliveng most ashuredly none did dy other wis but by death was ment to be burnt so as I shuld be[.] (11v)

Several possible meanings of burning to her can be speculated upon. There is the possibility of fear of fire as a domestic hazard, a real fear in an age when fire, especially in cities, presented a permanent danger. But it is possible, too, that Fitzherbert identifies with Marian martyrs, accounts of whose deaths by burning had been made well known by Foxe's *Acts and Monuments* (popularly known of as *The Book of Martyrs*). The association of her own identity with the dead Mary might be enough to trigger a loose association with the reign of Mary. Or, her terrors may arise from her spiritual waverings. At one stage in her illness she is 'tempted' to convert to Roman Catholicism and throughout her account there are hints of her attraction to Catholic doctrine and the possibility of life within a closed order. We might speculate on a strand of ambivalent and guilt-ridden identification with Catholicism (again, given her capacity to condense and displace meanings, perhaps loosely associated with her 'Mary' identity).

Then, issues of sexuality might be raised. As with her other close relationships, her friendship with Mrs H. is ambivalent. She has dearly loved her; now she perceives her as an enemy. Fitzherbert's explanation for this shift in feeling is unclear. She first labels Mrs H. an enemy because she 'was some what indeted to her'. Dependence on or indebtedness to others appears to offer a threat to Fitzherbert's fragile selfhood. Just as she guiltily inverts her gratitude to the mistress of the household in which she has been living, for giving her a cloak and other items of clothing, by coming to believe she has stolen these, so she inverts other potential feelings of gratitude, turning objects of such initially benevolent feelings into objects of hate. Dependence and independence are variously and dangerously linked issues for her. This is related to her sexual history. Having refused the husband proposed by her father, incurring his anger, she remains single – it appears by choice – throughout her life. Her defence of her single state is vehement, and in her letter to the Church of England, prefixed to her account in the 1630s, she politicises her position, reproving the church for its neglectful attitude to single women who have chosen to dedicate themselves to God rather than marrying, and to widows who devote themselves to the church once their family commitments have ended. Her conscious refusal to marry is articulated through her statement of total commitment to God. This bears traces of Catholic notions of feminine spirituality (the devout woman as bride of Christ) but may – and any interpretation here can only be entirely speculative – imply a resistance to the notion of sexuality in marriage.[28] An uneasy and unconscious erotic, or intensely emotional, attachment to Mrs H. could be hypothesised.

While her indebtedness to Mrs H. is given as a first reason for her turnabout in feelings towards her, the second reason given concerns Mrs H.'s having procured a certain doctor for Fitzherbert. Throughout the text her attitude towards medical doctors is, once more, ambivalent. Although as Kate Hodgkin has brilliantly shown, the whole impulse of the narrative is towards proving her affliction is spiritual and not organic, and is fascinating both for its attempt, in Foucauldian terms, to speak the silence of the mad, and for its struggles to find a language and mode of writing that appropriately separates the medical and spiritual (when the discursive context in which she is writing regularly blurs the distinction), Fitzherbert herself does not make clear demarcations.[29] This is not simply because of her lack of an appropriately distinguishing vocabulary. She recognises that some physicians helped her as much as ministers and preachers did. Fitzherbert's identification of Mrs H. as an enemy may proceed from her sense that her friend was in collusion with those who opposed her by treating her medically. It may, however, arise from an extension of her fear of being indebted.

More generally, the opposition of the spiritual and the organic in the text is vehemently but uncertainly maintained. Hodgkin suggests that Fitzherbert is aiming to make mind/body separations through her rejection of one framework of explanation and her endorsement of another. However, what is at stake is not an abstract identification of the causes and proper treatment of her condition, but the legitimacy of her rejection of familial and social norms of behaviour and of accepted gender and sexual roles. Fitzherbert presents herself as someone at odds with her times, which she sees as frivolous and vainglorious. The validity of her position depends on recognition that her sufferings are spiritually determined and her behaviour is spiritually sanctioned.

Although she does have supporters among influential puritan ministers and members of the puritan aristocracy, her narrative testifies to the implications for a woman of her class, at this time, who attempts to reject the social and discursive frameworks that govern her identity. Her self-wrenching from her social anchors comes to be enacted as bodily or mental wrenchings. In her vomitings, delusions, fantasies of imprisonment, burning and bodily 'overflow' she lives out not only the pain occasioned by separations and rejections in her own life-history, but the most frightening aspects of the spiritual, medical and familial discourses offering identity to women such as her in the early seventeenth century. Unlike Hannah Allen, she does not inherit a ready-made confessional form in which to articulate her experience and situate it within an acceptable narrative framework. In her shifts between detailed reminiscence of her troubled state and spiritual assertion or biblical referencing to others similarly troubled, she is not following a given pattern. Her writing is more vehement and more defensive than Allen's. The narrative shifts, like the shifts in subject position pronouns used in the text to refer variously to her present self in relation to her past self, herself in relation to others who sought to help her, or herself in relation to others whom she would help, are abrupt and ambiguous. Formally, ontologically and ideologically this is a high indeterminate text. It represents a woman striving to forge and claim her own identity through an almost self-invented form and through its depiction of a self looking back on its own near dissolution.

LADY MARGARET HOBY, ALICE THORNTON AND KATHARINE EVANS AND SARAH CHEEVERS

Matters of the bodily, the worldly and the spiritual are configured in quite different formations in the final three self-writings I shall briefly look at. The *Diary of Lady Margaret Hoby, 1599–1605* has been referred to as 'the earliest known diary by a British woman'.[30] Lady Hoby's ostensible purpose in keeping her diary was to record her religious exercise. Although references to spiritual activity dominate the diary, a strong sense of the variousness of her life also emerges: she is concerned with her domestic activities and her relationship with her husband, family and dependants as well as with noting down every occasion of religious observance. Juxtaposition of references to her religious duties with the details of secular aspects of her life implies an integration of the spiritual into a daily routine. The diary represents and is shaped by notions of an exemplary woman's life. Such a life should be directed by the spiritual, but there is no absolute division between spiritual and social aspects of virtuous femininity. The important distinctions are between the frivolous and the virtuous, although at some moments guilt at her failure to observe properly her religious obligations emerges. In her entry for Tuesday, 21 August 1599 she records, for instance:

After I was ready I prayed, and then I went a while about the house and so to breakfast and then to work ... then I went to private prayer. After, I walked a little, and so to supper; after which I went to prayers, and not long after, according to my wonted use, to bed, save only I did not so diligently think of that I had heard, which I beseech the Lord to pardon for Christ's sake. Amen. Amen.[31]

This picks up on concerns expressed in the preceding days. On 19 August she wrote:

After I came home I prayed and so to dinner, at which, and after, both myself did talk and hear of more worldly matters than, by God's assistance, I will hereafter willingly do. Till 3 a clock I was with Mr Hoby, not so careful, the Lord forgive it me, as I ought, to meditate of what I had heard, speaking and thinking of many idle matters; then we went to church and, after the sermon, I walked till 6 a clock, about which time I prayed and examined myself, craving pardon for these my infirmities. (p. 56)

At such moments there is a clear tension between her enjoyment of worldly pleasure and her sense of religious propriety, which should inform all aspects of her life and relationships. Throughout the diary reference is made to her accomplishment of the expected duties of members of an aristocratic household – she bakes and preserves fruit, she spins wool; she manages the estate, distributing corn, dealing with land and property transactions and receiving rents; she cares for injured and sick servants, estate workers and the poor; she visits neighbours. But the entries in the diary draw back from the comment on these. No opinion is offered except in spiritual matters, when she confines herself to monitoring the fulfilment of her duties. References to what were presumably important and complex matters in her life are sandwiched between notations of religious observance. On 19 July 1660, for instance, she writes: 'after private prayer I writ an answer to a demand Mr Hoby had given me overnight; after I went about and writ in my sermon book' (p. 60). Houlbrooke, following Meads, suggests that this possibly concerns 'a demand that she make over her lands to him in her life-time'.[32] The spiritual purpose of her diary-keeping makes selections for her. The rhythm of reference to the spiritual replicates the place of religion in a life – it serves to punctuate the events of a day and a life, providing through its repeated observances a way of interpreting and patterning what is significant, and of guiding response to non-spiritual matters. What we see in the *Diary of Margaret Hoby* is how, for an aristocratic woman, private and public roles are intermeshed.[33] Hoby's participation in 'public prayer', and in the religious education of her dependants, is as much a part of her role and identity as her private 'self-fashioning' through personal prayer, meditation and spiritual exercise. Hers is not a diary characterised by inner ruminations. Rather, it demonstrates, through its purpose and its form, a conscious attempt to shape the self according to prescriptions for virtuous, aristocratic, femininity. The writing of the diary and the living-out of principles are interrelated.

In the later writings of Alice Thornton we see how similar impulses are differently managed. Alice Thornton was born into a family belonging to the minor aristocracy, but married a man beneath her in social rank and lived the life of a gentry woman. The earliest version of her self-writing, on which I shall mainly focus here, is entitled

A book of Rembrances of all the remarkable deliverances of myself, husband and children with their births, and other remarks as concerning myself and family, beginning from the year 1626.[34]

This title presents her account as a family memoir, but hints at its actual major concerns. The phrase 'all the remarkable deliverances' is a conventional one in the period, referring to difficulties overcome or illnesses survived, and implies thankfulness to God for rescue from difficulties and danger, rather than claiming personal resolution or strength as a preserving force. However it makes implicit reference, as well, to the churching service for women after childbirth and the period of childbed, contained in *The Book of Common Prayer*, and foreshadows, perhaps, one of the major concerns of Thornton's narrative: the description of the births of her nine children (six of whom died perinatally or in infancy and all but one of whom predeceased her). This version of her self-writing is set up, then, as a pious exercise to express thankfulness to God for allowing her survival of loss and suffering and for leading her to salvation through such suffering. Predicated on such an impulse, it comes to read as a catalogue of instances of misery and pain. The text, which seems to have been written in 1666 following the death of her husband, is constructed from brief, note-form records (perhaps taken from earlier journals or diaries) and longer passages, describing in detail the most intensely felt sufferings and losses of her life. Particularly difficult pregnancies and births and, most especially, the deaths of her mother and husband – and the events surrounding these – are eloquently and fully described, detailing bodily suffering and emotional response.

The correspondence of passages of emotional articulacy and verbal fluency to moments of great loss and physical and emotional collapse may suggest that, for a woman such as Thornton, the negations of death and severe suffering provide, paradoxically, the place from which the self can most strongly be asserted. It is precisely at moments when the self seems to be threatened by disintegration, where any stable 'I' as a fixed point or source of meaning seems to be absent, that subjectivity is declared. Death – and its shadows, illness and collapse, or, in another of her words, 'overthrow' – figures not as completion, nor as a moment of transition between life and afterlife, but almost as a beginning. It is not simply that Alice Thornton spends a whole life mourning in order that she might live after death. Rather, her struggles for spiritual acceptance of loss and pain merge with her articulation of the experience of an enormous variety of sufferings in order to provide a starting point from which to assert herself and the nature of her life in the world. That this might have been the case in a quite literal sense is suggested by the existence of variant versions of her life. If, as I suspect, her *Book of Rembrances* is the first of her autobiographies (preceding other versions that tell us much more of her wider life, beyond her illnesses and losses, relating them to political events and social changes in England during her long lifetime), it served initially to stimulate her into textually creating and recreating herself from a variety of perspectives.

The texts I have considered so far all deal with personal negotiations of a cluster of dominant concerns in the lives of early modern women. My final brief discussion serves to introduce a different formulation of selfhood – where the personal is meshed with the collective. While *A Short Relation of Cruel Sufferings*, like the other texts I have discussed, brings together life in the world, the spiritual and the bodily, it does so in a distinct manner. Katharine Evans and Sarah Cheevers were Quakers. In *A Short Relation of Cruel Sufferings* they tell us how they set out for Alexandria in late 1658 or early 1659 to follow the footsteps of the apostle Paul. When their ship stopped for supplies at Malta they disembarked and began to distribute Quaker writings. They were imprisoned in the Maltese Inquisition for three and a half years. Their account of imprisonment was written during their incarceration and sent to fellow Quakers in England. Their construction of themselves is entirely bound up with their Quaker faith. At the centre of this was their belief in the Inner Light or the Spirit. Quakers were guided by this Light or Spirit or Christ (interchangeable terms) within to find salvation, which, in divergence from the Calvinist doctrine of predestination, was available to all, not just an Elect. It was the prime guide to Quakers, more important than the Scriptures. God worked through the Living Word: the operation of the Spirit and the persons of Quakers themselves who had a tendency to identify themselves as the incarnation of the Word, as living texts. For Quakers, therefore, the possibility of a series of mergings, between individuals, between the Word of God and human voices, between biblical history and the lives of seventeenth-century believers is commonplace, marks the ecstatic nature of their belief and experience, and directly emerges from their specific spiritual stance.

Evans and Cheevers write, near the beginning of their description of their imprisonment:

They said it was impossible we could live long in that hot room. So, the next weekday they sat in council. But oh, How the swelling sea did rage and the proud waves did foam even unto the clouds of heaven and proclamation was made at the prison-gate. We did not know the words, but the fire of the Lord flamed against it. (Katharine): my life was smitten and I was in very great agony, so that my sweat was as drops of blood, and the righteous one was laid into a sepulchre, and a great stone was rolled to the door, but the prophecy was that he should rise again the third day, which was fulfilled. But the next day they came to sit upon judgment again . . . And they brought many propositions written in a paper, but the friar would suffer the magistrate to propound but few to us, for fear the Light would break forth.[35]

Here we see an impulse to reproduce precisely the source of particular moments of utterance, in the attribution to Katharine of her particular words. Simultaneously however, we see the verbal and temporal blurrings characteristic of ecstatic Quaker writing. The passage moves backwards and forwards, without any form of distinction, between the biblical account of Christ's life, crucifixion and entombment and the immediate circumstances of the women's imprisonment. The description of bodily suffering brings together, or hovers between, the literal and the figurative in the phrase 'my sweat was as drops of blood', where the reference to blood has both bodily and scriptural meanings and echoes. The women present themselves simultaneously as actual historical persons in a very real physical environment, and as Christ figures embodying a much larger historical truth. They come to represent themselves as individuals and as representatives of Quakerism generally, and to represent Quakerism, in turn, as embodying oppressed Christianity through worldly and divine history.

The self-writings I have discussed here represent only a few of the forms used by women in the period. And the cluster of discourses – worldly, bodily, spiritual and medical – that I have attempted to track through them represent only some of the concerns of women writing themselves and their lives. What emerges from this selection, however, is how manipulations of autobiographical form are deeply enmeshed with other discourses governing the self. In writing the self, these women were attempting to bring into alignment round the concept of self a variety of possibilities for establishing identity. In their need to speak the truth – however defined – they wrestle with structures of articulation. Where an autobiographical mode is most clearly established, we see discontinuities between overt and accepted structures of the self and disclosure of underlying issues, as in the case of middle-class, late seventeenth-century writing of Hannah Allen. By the end of the period spiritual constructions of the self had acquired an established form and this form provides an influential model for later spiritual and secular autobiographical writing. But for women such as Dionys Fitzherbert, Margaret Hoby, Alice Thornton, Katharine Evans and Sarah Cheevers (and many others not discussed here), for whom such a mode was inappropriate or unavailable, we find that the instability of the form is enmeshed with the fluid interaction of discourses defining the identities of women.

NOTES

Thanks to Kate Hodgkin for giving me the reference to Dionys Fitzherbert's manuscripts and to Julia Atherton for helping to transcribe them. Thanks, as well, to Timothy Ashplant, Lesley Ling and Phillip Lloyd for bibliographic help.

1. Liz Stanley, *The Auto/Biographical I. The Theory and Practice of Feminist Auto/Biography* (Manchester: Manchester University Press, 1992) p. 5.

2. It was, for example, widely held until recently that there were no women dramatists in the period before 1660. That this was not the case, and that women participated in the theatrical in a variety of ways, is demonstrated in chapters 5 and 12 of this volume, and by S. P. Cerasano and Marion Wynne-Davies, *Renaissance Drama by Women: Texts and Documents* (London and New York: Routledge, 1996).

3. MS E. Mus. 169, Dionys Fitzherbert's original text, and its transcription in a fair hand, MS Bodley 154. See Kate Hodgkin, 'Dionys Fitzherbert and the Anatomy of Madness', in Kate Chedgzoy, Melanie Hansen and Suzanne Trill, eds., *Voicing Women: Gender and Sexuality in Early Modern Writing* (Keele: Keele University Press, 1996) for an excellent interpretation of Fitzherbert's writings.

4. See Elspeth Graham, Hilary Hinds, Elaine Hobby and Helen Wilcox, eds., *Her Own Life: Autobiographical Writings by Seventeenth-Century Englishwomen* (London: Routledge, 1989), pp. 147–64 for comments on the various manuscripts and extracts from the presumed first version of Thornton's autobiography.

5. Compare Felicity A. Nussbaum, *The Autobiographical Subject. Gender and Ideology in Eighteenth-Century England* (Baltimore: Johns Hopkins University Press, 1989), pp. 18–23.

6. For discussion of this issue with relation to women's writing, see S. P. Cerasano and Marion Wynne-Davies, eds., *Gloriana's Face: Women, Public*

and Private, in the English Renaissance (Hemel Hempstead: Harvester Wheat-sheaf, 1992).

7. Roger Pooley, *English Prose of the Seventeenth Century, 1590–1700*, (Longman Literature in English Series; London: Longman, 1992), pp. 17 and 18.

8. Ian Watt, *The Rise of the Novel. Studies in Defoe, Richardson and Fielding* (London: Chatto and Windus, 1957); Michael McKeown, *The Origins of the English Novel, 1660–1740* (Baltimore: Johns Hopkins University Press, 1987). For definitions of individualism and a survey of basic elements of individualist thought, see Steven Lukes, *Individualism* (Key Concepts in the Social Sciences Series; Oxford: Blackwell, 1973).

9. See, for example, chapter 2 of this volume.

10. See Hinds *et al.*, eds., *Her Own Life*, pp. 12–16 for a summary of the beliefs of other sects.

11. See Jonathan Sawday, *The Body Emblazoned: Dissection and the Human Body in Renaissance Culture* (London: Routledge, 1995), and Thomas Laqueur, *Making Sex: Body and Gender from the Greeks to Freud* (Cambridge, MA, and London: Harvard University Press, 1990).

12. See Jenny Kermode and Garthine Walker, eds., *Women, Crime and the Courts in Early Modern England* (London: University College London Press, 1994).

13. Max Weber, *The Protestant Ethic and the Spirit of Capitalism* (1904–5), inaugurates a tradition of association of Protestantism, economic change and the development of a middle-class selfhood. He is followed by R. H. Tawney and Christopher Hill, among many others.

14. T. E., *The Lawes Resolutions of Womens Rights* (London, 1632), pp. 6, 2; compare Graham *et al.*, eds., *Her Own Life*, p. 9.

15. Graham *et al.*, eds., *Her Own Life*, p. 9.

16. Kermode and Walker, eds., *Women, Crime and the Courts*, p. 9.

17. T. E., *The Lawes Resolutions of Womens Rights*, pp. 124–5.

18. *Ibid.*, p. 6.

19. Catherine Belsey, *The Subject of Tragedy: Identity and Difference in Renaissance Drama* (London and New York: Methuen, 1985), pp. 152–60.

20. See discussions in chapters 1 and 3 of this volume; see also Ian Maclean, *The Renaissance Notion of Woman: a Study of the Fortunes of Scholasticism and Medical Science in European Intellectual Life* (Oxford: Oxford University Press, 1980).

21. Laqueur points to the variability and instability of constructions of sexual difference through history; the instability of categories of gender informs much recent post-structural feminist writing and criticism arising out of Queer Theory. See, for instance, Judith Butler, *Gender Trouble: Feminism and the Subversion of Identity* (New York and London: Routledge, 1990).

22. Graham *et al.*, eds., *Her Own Life*, p. 200. Reference throughout is to this edition of *Satan his Methods and Malice Baffled*.

23. Graham *et al.*, eds., *Her Own Life*, p. 208.

24. See Elspeth Graham, 'Authority, Resistance and Loss: Gendered Difference in the Writings of John Bunyan and Hannah Allen', in Anne Laurence, W. R. Owens and Stuart Sim, eds., *John Bunyan and his England,*

1628–88 (London and Ronceverte, Hambledon Press, 1990), for a sustained examination of issues of gender in *Satan's Methods.*

25. Hodgkin, 'Dionys Fitzherbert and the Anatomy of Madness'; see note 3, above.

26. Fitzherbert's narrative and the surrounding documents were written over a period of time. The main body of her narrative was written in the first decade of the seventeenth century, but insertions, prefatory letters and documents were added in 1634–5, when she states she was near to death.

27. MS E. Mus. 169, viii. I have retained Fitzherbert's own spelling in this and other quotations from her manuscript, except for my substitution of the modern full form 'that' for the conventional early modern abbreviation Y^t, expanded forms for her abbreviations of titles such as 'mistress' and 'doctor', and 'v' for her use of 'u' when it signifies 'v'.

28. As is argued in chapter 2 of this volume, this version of feminine spirituality is imported from Catholicism into some strands of Anglican thought. It is opposed, however, by puritans within the Church of England. Fitzherbert's belief system overtly corresponds with puritan thought. But instances such as this suggest her doubt about her precise location within strands of Protestant (and Catholic) thinking.

29. Hodgkin, 'Dionys Fitzherbert and the Anatomy of Madness'.

30. Maureen Bell, George Parfitt and Simon Shepherd, *A Biographical Dictionary of English Women Writers, 1590–1720* (New York and London: Harvester Wheatsheaf, 1990), p. 107.

31. Ralph Houlbrooke, ed., *English Family Life, 1576–1716: an Anthology from Diaries* (Oxford: Basil Blackwell, 1988), p. 56. Reference throughout is to extracts from the *Diary* in this edition. For the full text, see D. M. Meads, ed., *Diary of Lady Margaret Hoby, 1599–1605* (London: Routledge, 1930).

32. Houlbrooke, ed., *English Family Life*, p. 60n 11.

33. See Helen Wilcox, 'Private Writing and Public Function: Autobiographical Texts by Renaissance Englishwomen', in Cerasano and Wynne-Davies, eds., *Gloriana's Face*, pp. 47–62.

34. Extracts from this version of her autobiography are in Graham, *et al.*, eds., *Her Own Life*, pp. 147–64.

35. *Ibid.*, p. 120.

The possibilities of prose

Betty S. Travitsky

In 1500 the printed prose writings in English by women consisted at most of one work;[1] but by 1700 women in Britain were prolifically represented in printed prose and had assumed what Catherine Belsey and others have termed a 'subject' position.[2] The number of printed English prose works written by women up to 1700 (and recovered in this century through gendered textual archaeology and restoration) is so large that they cannot all be named in this chapter. Instead, representative writings are examined here in a chronological survey, with particular attention given to those from the dense final quarter of the period.[3]

The following comments by Gerda Lerner help to explain this shift in female subjectivity:

Writing women, working prior to the recognition that women might be capable of participating as autonomous thinkers in the public discourse . . . had to remove three obstacles before their voices could be heard at all: (1) that indeed they were the authors of their own work; (2) that they had a right to their own thought; (3) that their thought might be rooted in a different experience and a different knowledge from that of their patriarchal mentors and predecessors.[4]

Yet another of Lerner's core insights is particularly pertinent to the notion of the 'possibilities' of prose: 'Women, ignorant of their own history, did not know what women before them had thought and taught. So, generation after generation, they struggled for insights others had already had before them . . . [causing] the endless repetition of effort, the constant reinventing of the wheel' (p. 19).

Despite the deep learning of a few exceptional women translators, chiefly in the earliest part of the period, most of the printed prose writings by Englishwomen between 1500 and 1700 seem analogous to primitive art since they are not rooted in any written tradition. Most of the women writers considered in this chapter were predictable products of a mindset that had nurtured female silence and compliance and that had viewed outspoken women with distrust.[5] In their somewhat anomalous prose writings one can trace the development of a sense of subjectivity and the beginnings of a consciousness that sometimes deepened into anger. These materials also form a continuum of interrelated, even merging forms. Life writing evolved into semi-fictional and fictional narratives, into skills books and manuals based on life experience, and into speeches and polemic that were, of course, anchored in lived experience; the translation of works by approved authorities broadened to the creation of original prose treatises on secular and religious subjects.

Given the well-known difficulties experienced by early modern women attempting to express themselves in print, it would be hard to invent a more fitting beginning to the history of women's prose writings in English than the fact – surely stranger than any fictional construct – that the first printed English prose known to have been fully composed by an English woman was literally *written* by a series of male amanuenses to whom the mystic spiritual autobiographer Margery Kempe (*c.* 1373–*c.* 1439) dictated (*c.* 1436–38) the record commonly regarded as the first autobiography extant in English. Kempe's *Boke* (printed in 1501 as the *Short Treatyse of Contemplacyon*) is recorded in the third person and recounts the yearnings and experiences of an extraordinary 'creatur' from the middling ranks of fifteenth-century English society: a mother of fourteen, visited by God, who travelled on pilgrimage, dressed in white, and repeatedly experienced an uncontrollable, disruptive gift of 'terys of compunccyon, deuocyon, & compassyon' that caused her intense grief at home and in public until, after more than twenty years, she convinced her husband to live in a celibate marriage.[6]

Before moving into the survey of two centuries of women's prose, we might note here the significance of the fact that the title page of the first of the translations from Latin by a female Tudor prodigy, of Erasmus's *A Devout Treatise upon the Pater Noster* (1524), translated by Margaret More Roper (1505–44), does not name Roper, but merely describes her as 'a yong, vertuous and well lerned gentylwoman of .xix. yere of age'. Nor does Richard Hyrde name Roper in his preface to the work, but he comments instead on the joy occasioned the translator and her husband by her erudition – the 'especiall comforte, pleasure and pastyme, as were nat well possyble for one unlerned couple, eyther to take togyther, or to conceyve in their myndes, what pleasure is therin'. This comment, unallayed by any suggestion that Roper sought a public use for her erudition, suggests that this very learned woman was an instance of what Lerner terms 'women's historical "complicity" in upholding the patriarchal system'.[7] We might note that Hyrde also refers to 'the laboure I have had with it about the printing'. By the seventeenth century many English women were running printing establishments. Does Hyrde's comment suggest that he had acted on Margaret Roper's behalf because an early sixteenth-century woman could not appropriately have entered a printer's shop and attended to the ordinary authorial tasks connected with the printing process?[8]

Eighty years later, approximately 100 years after Kempe's *Boke* reached print, another Catholic woman and one who has been called the 'first woman essayist' in English, addressed a sophisticated outpouring of experience – in the form of a new sub-genre, the mother's advice book – to her son Bernye, the only survivor among the nine children she had borne. To create her *Miscelanea. Meditations. Memoratives* (1604), Elizabeth Grymeston (before 1563–before 1604), skilfully borrowed from a range of writers, stating, 'neither could I euer brooke to set downe that haltingly in my broken stile, which I found better expressed by a grauer authour'. Paradoxically, she created in her knowledgeable weaving what she herself terms 'the true portrature of thy mothers minde'; the volume has been compared to Robert Burton's *Anatomy* on a smaller scale.[9]

The changes in the prose about to be considered in this chapter can hardly be better demonstrated than by the distinction in tone and content between Kempe's loosely organised autobiographical account of her quest for an unusual form of saintliness, and the semi-fictitious rogue autobiographies attributed in 1663 to two actual persons, Moll Frith and Mary Carleton (though actually penned in part by other persons). These accounts are precursors of the rogue novels that Defoe narrated in a female voice early in the next century. Nor could a more fitting antithesis be imagined to Kempe's prolonged, circumstantial and agonised effort to reach an accord on marital chastity with her husband, in the text which begins the period under discussion here, than the conclusion to the period provided by *Some Reflections upon Marriage* (1700), an acerbic, finely argued critique of 'Arbitrary Dominion' in marriage by the Anglican Mary Astell (1666–1731).[10] Astell's essay also provides a fine contrast to Hyrde's complacent comments on marriage in his preface to Margaret Roper's translation of 1524. Indeed, the sixteenth and seventeenth centuries represent an enormous shift in female consciousness and norms, as well as in women's exploitations of the possibilities of prose.

1501–1569

Kempe's *Short Treatyse of Contemplacyon*, the brief excerpt from her dictated account that was printed by Wynkyn de Worde from the much longer manuscript of her *Boke* first discovered in this century, blends into the tones of other religious and confessional writings by women, including the translated religious materials which comprise the majority of their printed prose writings during the first seventy years covered by this survey. Earliest, if not most prodigious, among the translators was the Lady Margaret Beaufort, Countess of Richmond and Derby (1443–1509), mother of Henry VII, a pious, bookish and energetic woman who translated two works into English from French in the first decade of the century. The first of these was Book 4 of a work that repeatedly attracted the attention of women writers of the early modern period, Thomas à Kempis's *The Imitation of Christ* (1504); the second, *The Mirroure of Golde for the Synfull Soule*, a Carthusian treatise ascribed to Jacobus Gruitroede, first appeared in about 1506. Beaufort's two translations are the first acknowledged writings by an Englishwoman to appear in print during the lifetime of the translator.[11]

The careful translations by English women that followed these pioneering efforts are predominantly the work of a small number of 'Tudor prodigies' associated with elite circles in sixteenth-century England. Women of the early modern period in England were profoundly affected – indeed it can be argued that the writers among them were enabled to write – by the efforts of a series of religious and educational reformers: Christian humanists seeking reform within the Catholic community; Protestant reformers calling for instruction for religious purposes; and educational reformers seeking to increase access to education for girls as well as for boys. These reformers effected an increase in female literacy – first among a select group of privileged women and later among less privileged women, as well. Translations by early modern women are significant, therefore, as testimony to the novel ability of some women to engage in a relatively learned activity.[12]

We might note a harbinger of the future in the translation into English in 1521, by Brian Anslay, of *The Boke of the Cyte of Ladyes*, an utopia written from a consciously feminist perspective by Christine de Pisan (1365–1429), an early participant in the *querelle des femmes*.[13] While several of de Pisan's works were translated and printed in English in the early Tudor Period, there is surely a hint of interest in the 'question' of women in the fact that her *Cyte of Ladyes* was translated into English by a man at this time. But it would be more than 100 years until an Englishwoman, Margaret Cavendish, would create a 'new blazing world', and English utopias by men did not remake patriarchy. It was almost a century later, in 1617, that the battle waged by Christine de Pisan, if not her conscious effort to create a work of art, was definitely taken up by an English woman.

Following the translation of the *Cyte of Ladyes* and almost twenty years after Beaufort's translations had appeared, another work by an English-woman was printed, the translation of Erasmus by Margaret More Roper. Hyrde's remarkable preface, which has been called 'the first reasoned claim of the Renascence [*sic*] period, written in English, for the higher education of women', points to the exemplary motives of the translator.[14] Yet, it is symptomatic of the hurly-burly of the time that even an exact translation of religious material could not be considered apart from contemporary, political events. Roper's *Devout Treatise* was connected to the circle of Sir Thomas More and his programme of humanist reform; as such, it was brought to the attention of the authori-ties, along with several other works connected to the More circle, when the humanist printer Thomas Berthelet neglected to exhibit it to the ecclesiastical authorities.[15]

Stirring events were affecting women, as women, in the early sixteenth century. The prominent marital difficulties of Henry VIII – his mistreat-ment of Catherine of Aragon (1485–1536) and of their daughter Mary Tudor (1516–58), and his repeated changes of queens – as well as the religious upheaval connected to Henry's marital problems and the vehement polemic on both sides associated with it, resulted in some extraordinary writings by Tudor prodigies in the forties, fifties, and sixties. Several of Henry's queens were learned, but his last queen, Katherine Parr, is most central to this account. Parr is commonly credited with having introduced a spirit of sobriety to the court where she surrounded herself with a coterie of pious women. She inspired one young stepdaughter, Elizabeth Tudor (1533–1603), to undertake the translation of a work by Marguerite de Navarre, edited by John Bale for publication as *A godly medytacyon of the christen sowle* (1548).[16] Parr also induced her other stepdaughter, Mary Tudor, to participate in the translation of the *Paraphrase of Erasmus upon the newe testamente* (1548).[17] Parr's impact on the larger events of her time is probably underrated today, but a widely circulated tale of an attempt to entrap her suggests the perception of her importance by her contemporaries.[18]

Parr compiled a collection of prayers entitled *Prayers or Meditacions*

(1545), abstracted largely from Book 3 of the 1530 translation by Richard Whytford of that seminal work, Thomas à Kempis's *Imitation of Christ*. Parr's moving *Lamentacion of a sinner . . . bewayling the ignoraunce of her blind life* (1547), the account of a reformed spiritual odyssey far more learned than Margery Kempe's if no more agonised, is the earliest original book written by an Englishwoman to be printed within her lifetime. Of many stunning passages, Parr's references to Henry perhaps seem the most charged today, but the indications in the text that she had accepted the doctrine of justification by faith are probably the reason why this work, which had circulated in manuscript for some time, was not printed until several months after Henry's death. The book is the first put in print by an Englishwoman with the explicit intention of influencing the public.[19]

Katherine Parr is also connected with the events surrounding what are arguably the most stirring life writings by a woman in the first half of the century, the *First examinacyon* and *Lattre examinacyon* of Anne Askewe (1521–46).[20] Like Kempe's *Boke*, but for more sombre reasons, Askewe's examinations were put in print through the efforts of a male contemporary, in Askewe's case the energetic John Bale (who also edited Elizabeth Tudor's translation of Marguerite de Navarre). For Askewe's daring to read resulted in dire consequences; her incarceration, torture and execution rendered her incapable of propagating her work herself. Askewe, who apparently joined Parr's circle, was outspoken and angry, wilfully subverting the expectations that she be silent and obedient. The records of her courage under interrogation are often stunning, perhaps particularly when they relate to the silencing of women: 'Then he asked me, whye I had so fewe wordes? And I answered God hath geven me the gyfte of knowlege, but not of utteraunce'.[21]

Within two years of Askewe's execution, another very young and very learned Tudor prodigy, Anne Cooke Bacon (1528–1610), better known as daughter of Anthony Cooke, wife of Nicholas Bacon, and mother of Francis Bacon, had translated (five) *Sermons of Bernardine Ochine of Sena* (1548), a work reprinted in several enlarged editions later in the century. In a prefatory letter addressed to her mother, Bacon justified her study of Italian on the basis of the serious uses to which she had now put her knowledge of that tongue: 'Since it hath pleased you, often, to reprove my vaine studye in the Italyan tongue . . . I have taken in hande to dedicate unto youre Ladyship this smale number of Sermons . . . as yeldyng some parte of the fruite of your Motherly admonicions'.[22]

Given this proselytising impulse and the intertwining of the religious and the political in the period, one might pause to note that the prefatory letters penned by many women writers – even to translations of religious works – often connect clearly to polemic and functions like manifestos; in the writings of Margaret Tyler and Aemelia Lanyer, as we will see, the thrust is more political and social than religious, but the religious and the political are difficult to disentangle in this period.

Askewe's fate apparently resulted from her connection in the last days of Henry's life with the circle surrounding Katherine Parr, and it seems to have effectively silenced them. A twentieth-century reader might nonetheless marvel, perhaps anachronistically, whether women could not have been *expected* to react in print to such ensuing events as the ill-fated claim of the Lady Jane Grey (1538–54) to the crown. To such speculation one might adduce a translation by yet another Tudor prodigy, the partial rendition into English by Jane Lumley (1537?–76/7) of Euripides' *Iphigenia in Aulis* (*c.* 1550; British Library MS Reg. 15A). In the story of the sacrifice of 'Iphigeneya' by her father, the play recounts a parallel to the sacrifice in 1554 of the Lady Jane, the nine-days' queen, to the ambitions of her father and father-in-law. (See chapter 12 of this volume for a fuller discussion of *Iphigenia* as drama.) The tale possibly held particular interest to a young noblewoman capable of translating from the Greek and related to some of the principal actors in the contemporary debacle.[23]

Jane Grey's execution was associated by the actual ascent to the throne within a single decade – and for the first time in English history – of not one but two queens, surely further grist to female imagination and self-authorisation. While Mary Tudor's rule was largely a disaster, Elizabeth gave her name to one of the most glorious periods in English history. The prominence of these female rulers in life, and the celebration (and criticism) of their reigns in print resonated throughout the early modern period – in male denunciations of the 'monstrous regiment of women', in celebrations of the 'Faerie Queene', in plays and even in recorded dreams relating to the sexuality of the Virgin Queen.[24]

Proclamations and public speeches, though associated at this time only with a few eminent women at the very top of the social pyramid – Katherine Parr, Jane Grey, Mary and Elizabeth Tudor – also resonated. Elizabeth's references to herself as a female prince and assurances of her personal courage assuredly raised the consciousnesses of all her subjects and have been the subject of considerable scholarly attention. Later in the period women (often of considerably lower rank) – Quaker women and women prophets from other sects, as well as women political petitioners – delivered themselves of public addresses and petitions descended from these speeches and proclamations.[25]

In the second half of the century new types of prose writings by women continued to appear in print, although it was verse, not prose, that broke new ground in the 1550s. Two important prose translations should be noted. The translation by Mary Bassett (*c.* 1522–72), daughter of Margaret More Roper, of her grandfather's 'Exposition' was included in the 1557 edition of More's English *Workes*, prefaced by the printer with the comment that 'the gentlewoman which translated it seemed nothing willing to have it goe abrode'.[26] A translation by Ann Lok (*c.* 1530–*c.* 1590), *Sermons of John Calvin upon the songe that Ezechias made* (1560), testifies to Lok's friendship with John Knox, the fiery preacher who had earned Elizabeth's ire through his mistimed denunciation of female rule, *First Blast of the Trumpet* (1558), as well as to Lok's convictions. Her appended 'Meditation of a Penitent Sinner' (discussed in chapter 9 of this volume) contains the earliest printed sonnet sequence in English by the 'mother of English sonneteering', who was literally the mother of the very early sonneteer, Henry Lok.[27]

In 1563 John Foxe brought considerable attention to the martyrdom of Anne Askewe and contributed significantly to the shaping of a perception of the Lady Jane Grey as one of the most poignant of the privileged, learned women of the century. Including Askewe's records and portions of Lady Jane's manuscript writings and public statements at the time of her execution in his *Book of Martyrs*, Foxe captured both women's unswerving commitment to their faith.[28] Another substantial contribution to the Protestant cause in this decade was Anna Bacon's acclaimed translation of Jewel's Latin *Apologie or answeare in defence of the Churche of Englande* (1564), said by Mathew Parker to have 'passed judgement without reproach' and praised for 'making his good work more publicly beneficial'.[29]

1570–1605

In the 1570s, with Elizabeth on the throne for over a dozen years, prose writings of a new type were added to the canvas by two women of lower rank. The verses of Isabella Whitney (flourished 1566–73), who had first appeared on the literary scene with an anthology of sprightly poems the decade before, are more significant than her prose, but Whitney's *Sweet Nosegay* (1573) mingles prose and verse innovatively in an autobiographical narrative detailing her hard lot. The spirit of the entire work demonstrates that some intrepid women were fitting themselves into literary print culture.[30] *The Mirrour of Princely deedes and Knighthood*, a translation by Margaret Tyler (flourished 1578) of the romance by Diego

Ortuñez de Calahorra, is the earliest production by a woman of the prose fiction denounced by the theologians who had originally promoted the education of women for pious purposes. Tyler was apparently an elderly retainer of the Howard family, though nothing more is as yet known of her. She survives to our day in a stirring preface to the *Mirrour* defending her translation:

If men may & doe bestow such of their travailes upon gentlewomen ... why not deale by translation in such arguments ... my perswasion hath bene thus, that it is all one for a woman to pen a story, as for a man to addresse his story to a woman. But amongst al my il willers, some I hope are not so straight that they would enforce me necessarily either not to write or to write of divinitie.[31]

To note the extraordinary productions and statements by Whitney and Tyler, however, is not to suggest that women's writings were undergoing a revolution. Traditional materials continued to appear, including manuscripts of a religious nature (later printed by Thomas Bentley) by Elizabeth Tyrwhit (died 1578), a member of Parr's circle, and by Frances Abergavenny (died 1576). Mary Stuart (1542–87) composed her unfinished 'Essay on Adversity' in this decade, and Grace Sherrington Mildmay (*c.* 1552–1620) began recording the earliest known mother's advice book, a genre (more fully discussed in chapter 3 of this volume) that would appear in print in the next century.[32]

The fusion of old and new continued in the 1580s. Thomas Bentley, 'of Graies Inne Student', compiled seven books or 'Lamps of Virginitie'. Having 'taken no small comfort ... by the reading and perusing of divers verie godlie, learned, and divine treatises, of meditations and praier, made by sundrie right famous Queenes, noble Ladies, vertuous Virgins, and godlie Gentlewomen of al ages', he had thought 'what great profit, and singular pleasure might thereby come also to other of like mind to my selfe, if ... [they] were by some painefull hand collected togither, and revived ... either for the renowne of such heroicall authors and woorthie women, or for the universall commoditie of all good christians'. Significantly, Bentley had decided 'to make the same an absolute and perfect booke for the simpler sort of women', who, one infers, could read the work.

Such was the genesis of *The Monument of Matrones* (1582), the most important, and surely the longest, anthology of printed and manuscript writings by women on religion in the period, including writings by a number of women whose work would otherwise have been lost. Most of the writers are familiar and of high rank: Elizabeth Tudor, Katherine

Parr and Jane Grey, for example. Some writings are by high-ranking but less well-known women: *Precious perles of perfecte godlines* by Frances Abergavenny (died 1576); *Morning and Evening Prayers* (1574) by Elizabeth Tyrwhit. Some writers are women of lower rank: 'a right vertuous and godlie Matrone and Gentlewoman named Mistresse Dorcas Martin' who translated 'An Instruction for Christians', and 'maister Bradfords mother', who composed a 'Praier . . . a little before his martyrdome'. *The Monument* also includes sections of often unattributed prayers particularly for women, a catechism for mother and child, and lists of godly women; it is therefore a monumental male construct of ideal womanhood, and a valuable gauge for our understanding of this ideal.[33]

Other printed religious writings of the decade include the forty-nine unpretentious prayers in *A Handfull of holesome (though homelie) hearbs* by Anne Wheathill (flourished 1584): 'Lord call me, plucke me Lord from mine ungodliness, that I may knowe thee, loue thee, & put my hope wholie in thee. O glorious God, my maker, sauiour, & sanctifier, dwell in me and giue me grace to dwell in thee, Amen' (1584).[34] Ann Lok's often reprinted translation of John Taffin's *Of the Markes of the children of God* appeared in 1590. In both cases the prefaces are memorable. Wheathill claims her work 'a testimoniall to all the world, how I have and doo (I praise God) bestowe the pretious treasure of time, even now in the state of my virginitie or maidenhood', while Lok more rousingly declares, 'because great things by reason of my sex I may not doo, and that which I may, I ought to doo, I have according to my duetie, brought my poore basket of stones to the strengthening of the walls of that Jerusalem, whereof (by grace) wee are all both Citizens and members'.[35]

Conventional or traditional these women may have been, yet they were expressing a sense of self (an issue considered in chapter 10 of this volume). We might, therefore, note again that the possibility or potentiality most realised in the prose writings by women in early modern England was the expression of subjectivity, of the sense that they, to recall Gerda Lerner's words with which I began, as 'writing women . . . might be capable of participating as autonomous thinkers in the public discourse . . . that indeed they were the authors of their own work; that they had a right to their own thought; that their thought might be rooted in a different experience and a different knowledge from that of their patriarchal mentors and predecessors'. This consciousness, expressed in conventional writings like Wheathill's and translations like Lok's, matches the new literary strain sounded by Margaret Tyler and Isabella Whitney. It continues to sound at the turn of the century, most notably in the prose preface to a polemical verse history by Anne Dowriche, *The French Historie* (1589), in which Dowriche (inconsistently) claims to have composed the work 'onlie . . . to edifie' and to have 'described' the events 'in verse' in part 'for mine owne exercise', in part 'to restore againe some credit if I can unto Poetrie, having beene defaced of late so many waies by wanton vanities'.[36]

Significantly in terms of this continuum, the decade witnessed the publication of the first original polemic attributed to an Englishwoman. *Jane Anger, her protection for women* (1589), is the first defence of women to appear in English under the name of a woman. There *were* several Jane Angers alive in England in 1588/9, although it may always remain impossible to show whether the author of the *Protection* merely employed a female pseudonym. (See chapter 7 of this book for further consideration of this point.) The work is notable for its bold, catchy arguments: 'The greatest fault that doth remaine in us women is, that we are too credulous, for could we flatter as they can dissemble, and use our wittes well, as they can their tongues ill, then never would any of them complaine of surfeiting.'[37]

Mary Sidney Herbert (1561–1621), 'Philip's Phoenix',[38] demonstrated materially the strong interconnection for early modern women between religious and secular writing in 1592, in a volume containing two translations from the French – a prose rendering of Philippe de Mornay's *Discourse of Life and Death* and the verse *Antonius* (a translation of Robert Garnier's *Marc Antoine* which was to be reprinted as *The Tragedie of Antonie* in 1595). *Antonie* is discussed in chapter 12 of this book, but we might note that this major woman writer chose to translate a drama with an unusually favourable construction of a faithful and motherly Cleopatra. Translated, as Diane Bornstein has shown, in a 'concise' but 'eloquent' style, the *Discourse* would have appealed to Mary Sidney on several levels: it expanded her brother's programme of 'introducing his friend's writings to a larger English public' (p. 127), dealt with death, a subject with deep resonance to her at that time of her life, and partook of the tradition of classical Stoicism.

In the same year, Philip Stubbes constructed in his *Christall Glasse for Christian Women* a dramatic memorial to his pious young wife Katherine Stubbes (1571?–90). Attributing a deathbed statement, 'A most heavenly confession of the Christian faith', to his wife, Stubbes also recounted her spirited combat with Satan on her deathbed, 'A most wonderfull conflict betwixt Sathan and her soule'. Such assertive but pious behaviour enabled some women to subvert restrictions on public speech in approved ways.[39] Similarly, subversion was effected in writings on approved domestic concerns for which women could claim some authority. The tendency is particularly pronounced in the popular, seventeenth-century sub-genre of the mother's advice book, exemplified in the first decade of the century by the *Miscelanea* (1604) of Elizabeth Grymeston.

A preface addressed in 1605 by the long-lived Elizabeth Cooke Russell (1528–1609), another of the daughters of Anthony Cooke, to her 'entierly beloved and onely daughter, the Lady Anne Herbert', as 'a last Legacie... A most precious Jewell to the comfort of your Soule', also validated public speech. Affixed to Russell's polemically inspired translation of *A Way of Reconciliation*, a treatise on the Eucharist (from the French of John Poynet), the preface also demonstrates the merging of prose types characteristic of many works by early modern women. The work is the last of the polemical religious translations by the Tudor prodigies.[40]

1606–1649

Elizabeth Tudor's learning and her very presence on the throne have traditionally been associated with the appearance of writings by women in the sixteenth century, yet women in the seventeenth century produced more writing in general, more original – as opposed to translated – writings, and more outspoken writings than sixteenth-century women had. The movement toward subjectivity gradually strengthened; indeed, the far less supportive attitude of James I toward women apparently bred a contentious climate in which some empowered women, when attacked, were ready to wield verbal cudgels in their own defence.

The continuum was substantially advanced by the prose preface to *Salve Deus Rex Judaeorum* (1611), an original poem of considerable power by another woman of the middle ranks, Aemelia Lanyer (1570?–1645), whose retelling of the traditional account of the Fall of Man, minimising female culpability, appeared in the very year in which the King James Bible was issued (see chapters 2 and 9 of this book). In that preface, preserved in only some copies of the text, Lanyer advanced the pro-woman polemicist position: 'some forgetting they are women themselves, and in danger to be condemned by the words of their owne mouthes, fall into so great an errour, as to speake unadvisedly against the rest of their sexe; which if it be true, I am perswaded they can shew their owne imperfection in nothing more.'[41]

Lanyer's preface was to find several important echoes within this decade, including the next work by a woman to appear in print, the posthumous *Mothers Blessing* (1616) by Dorothy Leigh. For Widow Leigh was quite intrepid, explaining to her sons that she was fulfilling their father's injunction that she educate them:

> when I had written these things unto you, and had (as I thought) something fulfilled your Fathers request, yet I could not see to what purpose it should tend, unlesse it were sent abroad to you: for should it bee left with the eldest, it is likely the yongest should have but little part in it. Wherfore, setting aside all feare, I have adventured to shew my imperfections to the view of the world, not regarding what censure for this shall bee laid upon me, so that herein I may shew myselfe a loving Mother and a dutifull wife.[42]

If the prose writings of this decade are all redolent of feminist consciousness, a crescendo was reached in three responses in 1617 to Joseph Swetnam's *Arraignment of Lewd, idle, froward and unconstant women* (1615). Here the evolving female sense 'that women might be capable of participating as autonomous thinkers in the public discourse', which can be teased from comments in some earlier texts, evolves into explicit mention by women writers of earlier female authorship, building a tradition of female authority without a 'reinventing of the wheel'. The first of these pamphlets, *A Mouzell for Melastomus* by Rachel Speght (*c*. 1598–after 1630), was disparaged in the responses that followed it and has been underrated in our own century, but the work, in fact, is eloquently argued: 'the resplendent love of God toward man appeared, in taking care to provide him an helper before hee saw his owne want'; '[m]arriage is a merri-age, and this worlds Paradise, where there is mutuall love'. The assertive tone of the 'Mouzell', a refutation of Swetnam on biblical grounds, is followed by 'Certaine Quaeries', hard-hitting jibes that attack foolish points in *The Arraignment*: 'you count it *Wonderfull to see the mad feates of women, for shee will not bee merry, then sad*: but me thinkes it is farre more wonder-foole to haue one, that aduentures to make his Writings as publique as an In-keepers Signe, which hangs to the view of all passengers, to want Grammaticall Concordance in his said Writing.'[43]

Yet the responses that followed Speght were even bolder. *Ester hath hang'd Haman* by Ester Sowernam, pseudonym (flourished 1617), was written because Sowernam was disappointed with Speght's rebuttal: 'whereas I expected to be eased of what I began, I do now finde my selfe double charged, as well to make reply to the one, as to adde supply to the other'. Perhaps most notably, Sowernam brings Swetnam to trial: 'as he had arraigned women at the barre of fame and report; wee resolued at the same barre where he did vs the wrong to arraigne him ... wee brought him before two Judgesses, *Reason*, and *Experience*, who being both in place, no man can suspect them with any indirect proceedings'.[44]

The Worming of a Mad Dogge by Constantia Munda, pseudonym (flourished 1617), the third of the responses of 1617, has been more frequently ascribed to a male author than the others; it is more venomous and more casually learned than the first two pamphlets. Yet the tone is wonderfully in tune with a consciously feminist perception of life. To doubt that this caustic work could have emerged from a woman's pen is to disparage female ability unnecessarily, even though we are unaccustomed to the level of invective engaged in by Munda: 'private abuse of your owne familiar doxies should not breake into open slanders of the religious matron together with the prostitute strumpet; of the nobly-descended Ladies, as the obscure base vermine that have bitten you; of the chaste and modest virgins, as well as the dissolute and impudent harlot.'[45]

Controversial writings by women, as well as controversy about women's writings, continued over the next ten years with the emergence of several important literary figures. Of these, Mary Wroth (1586–1640), niece of Mary Sidney Herbert and Sir Philip Sidney is easily the most significant. Her writings, including her huge prose romance *The Countesse of Mountgomeries Urania* (1621), are discussed at length in chapter 8 of this volume, but the *Urania* cannot be passed over here. An imitation of *The Countesse of Pembrokes Arcadia*, Wroth's romance has great inherent and historical importance. It is the earliest original contribution by a woman to the genre of prose fiction, a genre that has been shaped overwhelmingly by women, and it revises Sidneian romance, emphasising female consciousness, particularly by focusing on the theme of male inconstancy and by celebrating female heroism and self-definition. The printed *Urania*, together with a manuscript sequel, is now available in print for the first time since Wroth was forced to halt the sale of the work after she was attacked by noblemen who read unflattering allusions to themselves in the romance.[46]

More placid works were also brought to light in the 1620s. *The Countesse of Lincolnes Nurserie* (1622) by Elizabeth Clinton, Countess Dowager of Lincoln (1574–1630?), is a cross between the mother's advice book and a manual on breastfeeding, an activity endorsed by the male theorists whose efforts to enhance female piety had inadvertently done so much to enhance female consciousness (see chapter 3 of this volume). Clinton's pamphlet touchingly joins biblical exegesis and practical experience: 'Think alwaies that having the child at your breast, and having it in your armes, you have *Gods blessing* there. For children are Gods blessings'. Ironically, Clinton laments her own negligence in not having breastfed her own children.[47]

A posthumous advice book by Elizabeth Joceline (c. 1595–1622), *The Mothers Legacie* (1624), put in print by her grieving husband, was reprinted in many languages during the century. Perhaps the basis for its great popularity was the pitiful forecast by Joceline of her death in childbed, her rationale for penning a legacy: 'I may perhaps bee wondred at for writing in this kinde, considering there are so many excellent bookes, whose least note is worth all my meditations. I confesse it, and thus excuse my selfe. I write not to the world, but to mine owne childe; who it may be, will more profit by a few weake instructions coming from a dead mother (who cannot every day praise or reprieve it as it deserves) than by farre better from much more learned'.[48] (The advice books of both mothers, Clinton and Joceline, are fully discussed in chapter 3 of this volume.) Meanwhile, a similarly blameless, though polemical, exemplary life was recorded by Helen Livingston, Countess of Linlithgow (flourished 1629), in her *Confession and Conversion*, providing a refutation of the Catholic doctrines she had renounced.[49]

But the remaining prose writers of this decade, Lady Eleanor Davies Douglas (1590–1652) and Elizabeth Cary, Lady Falkland (1586–1639), are major figures whose lives were engulfed in controversy. Cary's outrageous attitudes and actions included her insistence on private study and enquiry, her conversion and commitment to Catholicism despite her husband's mistreatment, and her spectacular success in abducting some of her children and converting most of them to her way of thinking. Many of Cary's writings seem to be lost; her verse drama *Mariam* (1613) is dealt with in chapters 7 and 12 of this book. Of interest here are several prose works by Cary from the 1620s: a translation and two accounts of Edward II, blending dialogue and prose narrative in an innovative way and dealing relatively compassionately with the dilemma of Isabella, his wife, and rather critically with Edward and his favourites. These texts were first printed late in the century, and the attribution to Elizabeth Cary has been questioned. The unusually sympathetic treatment of Isabella as well as comments in one of the prefaces, however, lend weight to the attribution to Lady Falkland.[50]

At the end of the decade it was definitely Cary who translated from French a long polemical work, *Reply of the Cardinall of Perron* (1630), addressed by Davy du Perron to James I. The translation is distinguished particularly for the subjectivity Cary expressed in her prefaces. The first, to Henrietta Maria, wife of the king to whom du Perron had addressed the work, reads in part: 'you are fittest to receive it for him, who are such a parte of him, as none can make you two, other then one. And for the honour of my Sexe, let me saie it, you are a woeman, though farr above other woemen, therefore fittest to protect a woman's worke... And last (to crowne your other additions) you are a Catholicke and a zealous one, and therefore fittest to receive the dedication of a Catholicke worke.' The preface to the general reader abjures the usual writer's disclaimers in a most audacious way: 'it were a great follie in me, if I would expose to the view of the world, a work of this kinde, except I judged it to want nothing fitt, for a Translation. Therefore, I will confesse, I thinke it well done, and so had I confest Sufficientlie in printing it... I will not make use of that worne-out forme of saying I printed it against my will, mooved by the importunitie of Friends.'[51]

Cary's strong individualism, however, pales beside the extreme eccentricity of Eleanor Davies Douglas, an eccentricity that led to her being given the mocking title 'Never Soe Mad a Ladie', and, more sombrely, to a year's incarceration in Bedlam, London's lunatic asylum. The most prolific of the many female prophets of the civil war years and interregnum, Lady Eleanor was not a member of a sect. Her extremely high rank, her attacks on the king, Archbishop Laud, and her two husbands, the notoriety attached to the public burning of her works, her confinements in Bedlam and the Tower, and her repeated public denunciations of the dramatic proceedings that led to the execution of her brother Mervyn, Baron Touchet, for the sensational crimes of rape and homosexuality, combined to mark Lady Eleanor and her writings for special attention. Her complex and often obscure writings continued – indeed increased in frequency – till the very end of her life, eventually numbering over sixty tracts; they began in this decade with *A Warning to the Dragon* (1626), written immediately after Lady Eleanor experienced a first revelation by the prophet Daniel. In 1633 Douglas published several tracts: *All the Kings of the Earth*; *Given to the Elector*; *Woe to the House*.

A Warning signals the advent in mid-seventeenth-century England of a large number of women who viewed themselves as prophets, who peopled the public arena and who wrote large numbers of polemical pieces; Elaine Hobby estimates that '[w]ell over half the texts published by women between 1649 and 1688 were prophecies'.[52] Though these writings are also considered in chapter 10 of this book, it is important here to note their significance among women's prose writings. Unlike the majority of these women prophets, Eleanor Davies Douglas was not a Quaker, but like many of them she believed the millenium had come, she believed herself to be moved by the spirit of God, and she was fearless in communicating her beliefs. From the beginning, she attempted to influence persons in high office – including the king – with her visions; the doom she prophesied was, of course, viewed in political terms by her contemporaries.

More conventional writers continued to write, among them Bessie Clerksone (died 1625), a latter-day Margery Kempe, 'a deare Christian' of 'the parish of Lanerk', whose prolonged and painful *Conflict in Conscience* (1631) was recorded by her minister William Livingstone. Alexia Grey (1606–40), a Catholic woman of considerably higher status than Clerksone, underwent a somewhat mystical experience that led her to take vows; she later undertook the publication of an English translation, *Rule of the Most Blessed Father Saint Benedict Patriarke of all Munkes* in 1632, dedicating her labour to her abbess, Lady Eugenia Poulton. Alice Sutcliffe (flourished 1624–33), a Protestant woman writer connected to the court, composed a long tract, *Meditations of Man's Mortalitie* (1633), with a preface dedicated to Katherine, Countess of Buckingham, and Susanna, Countess of Denbeigh, requesting that they 'passe a favourable *Censure* of my proceedings, it beeing, I know not usuall for a *Woman* to doe such things'. It would seem, however, that it *was* somewhat usual for a woman to have 'chosen a subject not altogether *Pleasing*'. The same subject interested a recusant, Jane Owen (died before 1634), who addressed the part-original, part-translated *Antidote against Purgatory* (1634) to her fellow Catholics, with the aim of 'the advancing of the spiritual good of your soules ... to inculcate, & make deep impressions in your minds, of the horrour, and most dreadfull torments of Purgatory ... to set before your eyes, the best meanes to prevent, at least to asswage, and mitigate them'.[53]

Two livelier and more unconventional works complete women's prose writings in English up to 1640. The first is a translation of Jean Camus's *Admirable Events* (1639) by Susanne DuVergerre, who, in the tradition of her Protestant forerunner Anne Dowriche, but with infinitely more grace, and in contrast to Margaret Tyler, attempted 'to wrastle, or rather to encounter with those frivolous books, which may all be comprized under the name of Romants ... by diversion, setting relations true and beneficiall, in the place of those that are prophane'.[54] The second is *The Women's Sharp Revenge*, a polemic on gender widely believed to have been written by John Taylor, though appearing in 1640 under the names Mary Tattlewell and Joan Hit-him-home (pseudonym). In sometimes moving language, the tract maintains the persona of a woman successfully throughout. Sounding a complaint later expressed by Anna Maria van Schurman, the authors lament that women

have not that generous and liberall Educations, lest we should bee made able to vindicate our owne injuries... If wee be taught to read, they then confine us within the compasse of our Mothers tongue, and that limit wee are not suffered to passe... if we be weake by Nature, they strive to makes us more weake by our Nurture. And if in degree of place low, they strive by their policy to keepe us more under.[55]

The turbulent 1640s are chiefly characterised by an outpouring of public petitions and tracts by women (allied to the earlier proclamations and speeches of noblewomen), a strong departure from the ideal of silence and obedience. Early in the decade two petitions, *To the Right Honourable, the High Court of Parliament* and *To the Supreme Authority*, were delivered to parliament by hundreds of women. Dozens of petitions, sometimes from smaller groups and for individual causes, were delivered over the decade.[56] Among tracts by women preachers and prophets, the close-to-fifty works written by Lady Eleanor Douglas in this decade easily predominate. Rich in biblical references, particularly to Daniel and Revelation, and written both in prose and in verse, her pamphlets are characterised by elusive syntax and elliptical phrasing, as in this brief excerpt from *The Lady Eleanor Her Appeal* (1646): 'And thus not only providing for that aforesaid admired Guest, but adored him almost; how it afterward came to pass, like that least of all seeds, how it sprang up, as follows.'[57]

Another important religious polemicist in this decade was the Independent Katherine Chidley (flourished 1626–45), the wife of a tailor. Author of several vigorous attacks on Thomas Edwards and, more generally, on the established church, Chidley is also believed to have been associated with the activities of Leveller women petitioners in the 1650s. Her *Justification of the Independent Churches of Christ* (1641), *A New-Yeares Gift* (1645) and *Good Counsel to the Petitioners* (1645) call for independent church government in a clear, robust style. Chidley strikingly overturns her subordination, telling Edwards, 'if you overcome me, your conquest will not be great, for I am but a poore worme, and unmeete to deal with you'. These writings point the way to the torrent of polemical writing by women that would characterise the coming years.[58]

Tradition is represented during the decade by the appearance of Elizabeth Richardson's *A Ladies Legacie to her Daughters* (1645), a series of forty-eight prayers addressed to Richardson's daughters and daughters-in-law, but preceded by the following familiar disclaimer: 'I had no purpose at all when I wrote these books, for the use of myself and my children, to make them public, but have been lately overpersuaded by some that much desired to have them that I would suffer them to be printed.'[59]

1650–1700

The interregnum is the decade in which a flood of works by women participants in the sects begins, instancing the sufferance of women's participation in public affairs in times of turmoil.[60] This decade is marked by several important firsts, each demonstrating yet another of the possibilities of prose: an English woman writer figures an imaginary world in which women are militarily and politically active and in which they ensure their independence after marriage; another begins to publish a series of works by which she incontrovertibly earns her living; a serious, original treatise on women's education written by yet another woman is translated into English.

Between 1650 and her death in 1652, over a dozen more extraordinary tracts by Eleanor Davies Douglas appeared, and there was also a huge outpouring of radical tracts and prophecies by Quaker and Baptist women, and by women from other sects, during the decade. There is not the space here for even a brief listing of the women prophets. One of the most outstanding was Anna Trapnel (flourished 1654–80), a Fifth Monarchist and author (sometimes by proxy) of several works in lyrical prose: *Strange and Wonderful Newes from White-hall*, *Report and Plea*, *Legacy for Saints* and *The Cry of a Stone* (all 1654). Some of these works were composed while Trapnel was in a trance-like state, and recorded by an amanuensis; some while she was travelling, by divine command, to Cornwall; some while she was imprisoned for her outspokenness.[61]

Two of the more outstanding non-Quaker women writers of this decade are Mary Cary (flourished 1647–53) and Elinor Channel (flourished 1654). Cary, a Fifth Monarchist millenarian, figured herself in a series of works as a passive instrument of God while making strong claims for women's right to prophesy (along with outspoken criticisms of parliament). Her *New and More Exact Mappe* (1651) is remarkably assertive. Channel, like Margery Kempe, was apparently unable to write; like

Kempe, again, she undertook a process of conjugal negotiation until she persuaded her husband to allow her to travel to London to deliver a message to Cromwell; although she did not speak directly to Cromwell, she did find an amanuensis (*Message from God* [1654]). As extraordinary as these women seem, however, Cary and Channel stem from the somewhat softer 'Southern' group of female prophets described by Phyllis Mack, whose 'lives ... were conducted within a more complex, urbanized culture. Southern prophets were married to tradesmen, artisans, or publishers; they were relatively well educated, with access to mystical literature imported from the Continent and published by their own families.' In distinction, according to Mack, the women prophets from the North 'were more physically and verbally aggressive; they made more hazardous and repeated missionary journeys, and they wrote with greater anger and a more militant class consciousness.'[62]

Because the Quakers decided in 1672 to preserve two copies of every text their members had produced from the beginning of the movement, we have a fortunate survival of a mass of prophecies by Quaker women, indeed, 'the largest body of early women's printed texts [created] in the Restoration', although these writings have since been excluded from evaluations both of the Quaker canon and of early modern women's writings.[63] Only one women writer can be cited here, Margaret Fell Foxe (1614–1702), undoubtedly the most influential of all the women Quakers of the seventeenth century. Her first work, *False Prophets, Antichrists, Deceivers, which are in the World* (1655), like Eleanor Davies Douglas's, centres on Revelations; her second, *A Loving Salutation* (1656), is an attempt – which she was to repeat – to convert the Jews. Her most important work was still ahead of her at this time.

The decade is distinguished as well by the appearance of several non-polemical publications by women. The earliest of these is Anne Weamys' *A Continuation of Sir Philip Sidney's 'Arcadia'* (1651), the second original prose romance in English by an Englishwoman which, in fact, continues various strands in Sidney's *Arcadia*. Far shorter than Wroth's *Urania*, the work is an important landmark in the history of women's writings and has recently become available in print.[64]

In 1653, Margaret Lucas Cavendish, Duchess of Newcastle (1623–73), began her publication history with two works, her (verse) *Poems, and Fancies* and her *Philosophicall Fancies*, containing a number of brief essays. Two other prose works of this decade, *Philosophical and Physical Opinions* and *The World's Olio* (both 1655) are significant for their blend of serious purpose and naive, not to say primitive, method and manner. Her

Natures Pictures (1656), a collection of short tales in both verse and prose, includes extraordinary accounts of militaristic women as well as an account of her own life; both consciously and in ways that a twentieth-century reader can find amazingly unaware, Cavendish attempts to assert a sense of autonomy and betrays her dependence on her husband.[65]

Given the autonomy exercised by so many women during this decade, it is not really surprising that the interregnum gave rise to *An Almanack or Prognostication for Women* (1658) by Sarah Jinner (flourished 1658–64), an early example of professional (i.e. paid) women's writings, and one that would be followed by several other women by the end of the century. Aimed primarily at female readers, the prognostications contained in Jinner's *Almanack* seem to have provoked a rejoinder in the *Womans Almanac* (1659), apparently written by a male writer using the pseudonym Ginnor; Jinner's own almanacks continued to appear till 1664.[66]

Most of the remaining printed prose of the 1650s consists of more conventional writings on religion. The popular *Whole Duty of Man* (1659) was – as claimed by her daughter – probably written by Dorothy Pakington (died 1679). The spiritual and meditative *Confessiones Amantis* and *Spiritual Exercises* (1658) by Gertrude More (1606?–33), member of the Benedictine convent at Cambrai and great-great-granddaughter of Sir Thomas More, were collected and printed by More's confessor Dom Augustine Baker; they include some account of convent life. The attribution of *A Choice Manuall of Rare and Select Secrets in Physick and Chyrurgery* (1653) a compilation of medicinal and culinary recipes credited on the title page to Elizabeth Grey, Countess of Kent, is disputed.[67]

The extraordinary prose writings of this decade are capped by the translation into English in 1659 of an important, original and learned treatise in Latin, *De ingenii muliebris*. Written in 1641 by a Dutch woman, Anna Maria van Schurman (1607–78), this work introduced the English reading public to a serious disputation by a woman on the education of women. We have come a long way from the reforming notions of men that women should be adequately educated to run well-ordered homes and raise children to piety, and even a long way from Hyrde's impassioned plea for women's education. In *The Learned Maid: or, Whether a Maid may be a Scholar?*, we have also transcended the first results of those reform ideas: a Latin study on the education of women, written by a serious and important woman scholar in a format that would have distinguished any male theoretician, has been translated into English.[68]

After the Restoration the sects were persecuted increasingly, and women sectaries – like the male members of the sects – were reduced to relative silence. Quakers themselves rechannelled the activities of Quaker women in the 1670s. But if polemical writings by women were reduced in number, other writings by women throve. Margaret Cavendish was undoubtedly the dominant figure of the decade; her *Playes* (1662) and *Playes, never before Printed* (1668), discussed in chapter 12 of this volume, are a sort of hybrid of closet drama and narrative, notable for the repeated exploration of the issue of women's oppression. This theme continues to be sounded in Cavendish's *Orations* (1662) and *CCXI Sociable Letters* (1664). The unconventional form of Cavendish's writings is alluded to in her *Philosophical Letters* (1664), in which her lack of systematic education is explicitly noted by the author; her original approach to modes of knowing is fully discussed in chapter 6 of this volume. In *Observations upon Experimental Philosophy* (1666), she joined her extraordinary description of an imaginary *New Blazing World* to an untutored discussion of such issues as the nature of matter and motion. The text for which she was hitherto best known, her *Life of the thrice Noble . . . William Cavendishe* (1667) is another unconventionally structured, even disjointed, work; yet it succeeds in conveying a sense of the complexity of this woman and the strength of her feelings for her husband.[69]

Along with a dozen other works in prose, Margaret Fell Fox's most famous tract, *Womens Speaking Justified* (1666), first appeared in this decade. A less radical work than it is often depicted as being, the work is thoroughly grounded in biblical exegesis; it brands some women (not to be included among those whose public speech is justified) 'whoring women', 'tatling women', and women who 'usurp authority over the man'. Nevertheless, the work is extremely important (see also chapter 2 of this volume) for its careful argument in defence of women's public voice: 'the Church of Christ is a Woman, and those that speak against the Womans speaking, speak against the Church of Christ, and the Seed of the Woman, which Seed is Christ'.[70]

Two less conventional figures to whom writings are attributed are Mary Frith (or Mal Cutpurse) and Mary Carleton (1634–73), or the German Princess; both these extraordinary and colourful women *were* historical persons. There are extant legal records of the public correction of Frith, a somewhat disreputable, cross-dressing character celebrated in Dekker and Middleton's *Roaring Girl*, for appearing on stage during the production of that play; Frith's supposed 'Diary' is incorporated into *The Life and Death of Mrs. Mary Frith, Commonly Called Mal Cutpurse* (1662). Mary Carleton – a confidence woman whose life is known to have ended on the gallows – may not have written all of *Vindication of a Distressed Lady* (1663) and *Historicall Narrative* (1663), though this work does definitely include some material by her, but it is important to note the printing in this one decade of rogue histories attributed to two women. The pietist life record with which this chapter began has now evolved into amoral adventure stories; its further evolution into rogue fiction and the novel is already begun.[71] *The Forc'd Marriage*, the earliest of the eighteen plays of Aphra Behn (*c.* 1640–89), appeared in 1670 and should be mentioned in this context, although it is considered as drama in chapter 12 of this volume.

More sedate are the conduct and cookery books that appeared in the 1660s, including *The Ladies Directory* (1661), *Cook's Guide* (1664), and *Queen-like Closet* (1670), of a prolific, middle-class schoolmistress, Hannah Wolley (1621?–76?), who, like Sarah Jinner, wrote as a means of making a living.[72] Along with *The Gentlewomans Companion* (1675), a disputed work often attributed to Hannah Wolley, several well-informed trade manuals were published by women in the 1670s. *The Midwives Book* (1671) by Jane Sharp is one of the most interesting monuments to the doomed battle of the midwives to retain control of their traditional work despite encroachments by male physicians: 'Man in the act of procreation is the agent and tiller and sower of the ground, woman is the Patient or Ground to be tilled; who brings Seed also as well as the Man to sow the ground with'. Written in a colloquial English and using English terms for the anatomy, a radical departure from earlier practice, the text was very popular, going through four editions by 1725.

Another strong tract was the *Essay to Revive the Antient Education of Gentlewomen* (1673) by Bathsua Makin (*c.* 1610–82), earlier the tutor to Princess Elizabeth. Makin, a very highly educated woman who knew and corresponded with Anna Maria van Schurman, insisted, like van Schurman and the earlier male reformers, that a good education for women would enhance, not disrupt existing social order. Her carefully and eloquently argued treatise, which also served as a prospectus for her school at Tottenham High Cross near London, follows van Schurman's, but also echoes some of the complaints of Mary Tattlewell:

The Barbarous custom to breed Women low, is grown general amongst us, and hath prevailed so far, that it is verily believed (especially amongst a sort of debauched Sots) that Women are not endued with such Reason, as Men; nor capable of improvement by education, as they are... Were a competent number of Schools erected to Educate Ladyes ingenuously, methinks I see how asham'd Men would be of their Ignorance, and how industrious the next Generation would be to wipe off their Reproach.[73]

Life writings by Ann Fanshawe (1625–80) and Anne Wentworth (flourished 1676–9) appeared late in the century. Fanshawe's *Memoirs*, which she addressed to her son in 1676, recall her life abroad in service to the Royalist cause with his diplomat–father (who died when their son was an infant). If Fanshawe's account is pleasant, almost idyllic, the life writings of Anne Wentworth read more like a horror story. Yet the fact that Wentworth recorded a history of marital abuse demonstrates her sense of herself as a subject; indeed she took her writing so seriously that one condition she made for a reconciliation with her husband was that she be allowed to continue to write. Her *True Account* (1676) combines, in the spirit of Eleanor Davies Douglas, an account of her personal sufferings with predictions of the punishment of her enemies, including her husband. *A Vindication of Anne Wentworth . . . preparing . . . all people for Larger Testimony* (1677) employs many of the biblical allusions found in the writings of earlier prophets like Douglas to refer to her personal experience. Her *Revelation of Jesus Christ* (1679) details long-term abuse by her husband and defends Wentworth against accusations of loose living levelled against her after her husband expelled her from their home, accusations reminiscent of those made against Anne Askewe.[74]

Jane Lead (1624–1704), the middle-aged founder and leader of the Philadelphian society (an outgrowth of the theosophism of Jacob Boehme), was a charismatic mystic. Her many complex visions, often centreing about the mystical 'Sophia', reinterpret knowledge and experience in feminine terms, as in the description of the 'Wonder Woman': 'the Mother of the Virgin-Birth will be more dignified and honoured then the foregoing Ministration in the Birth of Jesus was. Therefore an oriental bright flaming garment is allotted her, with a Crown beset with Stars.' Among Lead's works in this decade are *Heavenly Cloud New Breaking* (1681) and *Revelation of Revelations* (1683).[75]

A further instance of more familiar exhortations and descriptions of persecution are the life writings and prophecies of a Quaker, Dorcas Dole (flourished 1682–5), which do not concern political affairs. Her *Salutation and Seasonable Exhortation to Children* (1682), exhorting the young to think upon their end, is written from Newgate; *Once More a Warning* (1683) and *Salutation of my Endeared Love* (1685) are also written from prisons.[76]

Early in her life, the recusant Elizabeth Cellier (flourished 1678–88) was accused of involvement in the Meal-Tub Plot (an alleged Catholic plot to assassinate Charles II), though she was acquitted on trial. Cellier later served as midwife to the royal family and won the support of a grateful James II to establish a 'colledg' for the training of midwives and a 'cradle-hospital', for foundlings. In *To Dr.—An Answer to his Queries* (1688), she argues against the physicians who were attempting to control obstetrical work. The pamphlet follows a familiar pattern of argument, combining biblical 'proofs' and a series of practical observations and proposals. The core of Cellier's argument is that midwives, actually experienced in obstetrical procedures, are more fit to practise obstetrics than physicians who

> have not yet studied it, but will when occasion serves ... I doubt it will not satisfy the women of this age, who are so sensible and impatient of their pain, that few of them will be prevailed with to bear it, in compliment to the doctor, while he fetches his book, studies the case, and teaches the midwife to perform her work, which she hopes may be done before he comes.[77]

Aphra Behn (*c.* 1640–89), whose works feature prominently in chapter 12 of this book, also made over a dozen important contributions to the developing genre of prose fiction. Behn is extraordinary in her time for her perception and presentation of the political, racial and sexual structures that underlie human relationships, perhaps most particularly for her forthright presentations of men tyrannising over women and of women's efforts to control their lives. Particularly significant are her *Adventures of the Black Lady, The Fair Jilt, History of the Nun, Love-Letters between a Nobleman and his Sister* (especially interesting for the Richardsonian use of letters to forward the narrative), *Oroonoko*, and *The Lucky Mistake*.[78]

Life writings continue through the end of the century in such records as the *Account of the Travels, Sufferings, and Persecutions of Barbara Blaugdone* (1691) by Quaker Barbara Blaugdone (*c.* 1609–1705). Repeatedly imprisoned, threatened and set upon by those she preached to, Blaugdone was always delivered from great hurt: 'they sent forth a great wolf-dog upon me, which came fiercely at me to devour me, and just as he came unto me, the Power of the Lord smote the dog, so that he whined and ran in crying, and very lame'.[79]

An Essay in Defence of the Female Sex (1696), apparently by a female medical practitioner named Judith Drake, is noteworthy as a rigorous protest against the double standard, the inferior education of women and the non-recognition of women's writings. In addition, it is noteworthy for the inclusion of a number of '*Characters of Pedant, a Squire, a Beau, a Vertuoso, a Poetaster, a City-Critick, etc.*' Drake asserts that her 'Characters ... were not written out of any Wanton Humour ... but to illustrate what I have said upon the several Heads, under which they are rang'd, and represent not single Men, but so many Clans, or Divisions of

Men, that play the Fool seriously in the World'.[80]

The last prose writer to be noted here is Mary Astell (1666–1731). Astell's *Serious Proposal to the Ladies* (1694) is a carefully thought out proposal for the establishment of a college for women, in the tradition of such earlier writers as Bathsua Makin, Hannah Wooley and (although limited to a particular calling) Elizabeth Cellier:

Now as to the Proposal, it is to erect a *Monastery*, or if you will (to avoid giving offence to the scrupulous and injudicious, by names which tho' innocent in themselves, have been abus'd by superstitious Practices,) we will call it a *Religious Retirement*, and such as shall have a double aspect, being not only a Retreat from the World for those who desire that advantage, but likewise, an Institution and previous discipline, to fit us to do the greatest good in it.

An exchange with John Norris on such subjects as the nature of evil and pain was published in 1695 as *Letters Concerning the Love of God*. As noted earlier, Astell's *Some Reflections upon Marriage* (1700) neatly brings the period to a close with a tautly argued prose protest of the position of women in marriage.[81]

As the seventeenth century drew to a close many of the possibilities of prose writing for women had been realised. Women were asserting their right to their own thoughts, their own arguments (and their difference from traditional thoughts and arguments), and finding their place in the literary marketplace. They were creating imaginative drama and narratives of sometimes great power, handbooks on practical subjects, life stories, essays, rigorous treatises, mystical and sometimes learned tracts. The opportunities offered by prose rhetoric, often in translated form, had enabled the Tudor female prodigies to find modes of expression; later, the potential of prose as polemic and as the medium of practical advice was richly fulfilled by female petitioners and prophets, housewives and midwives. Women were participating in the major historical and literary shift that was to place prose at the heart of modern written culture.

NOTES

1. That incunabula, *The Boke of St Albans* (1486), an early work of instruction, partly in verse, partly in prose, is attributed, at least in part, to a shadowy woman, Dame Juliana Berner.
2. See Catherine Belsey, *The Subject of Tragedy: Identity and Difference in Renaissance Drama* (London and New York: Methuen, 1985).
3. There is space here only for mention of a few manuscript materials,

although these seem by far to exceed the number of printed works by women; see the discussion of women and manuscript culture in chapter 7 of this volume. Examination of archival holdings constantly brings new manuscripts by women, including private letters and journals, to light. The following are some print collections of such materials: *The Lisle Letters*, ed. Muriel St Clare Bryne (6 vols.; Chicago: University of Chicago Press, 1981–3); *Letters of Royal and Illustrious Ladies of Great Britain*, ed. May Anne Everett Green [Wood] (3 vols.; London: Henry Colburn, 1846) (the authenticity of some of the material has been questioned); *The Letters of Queen Elizabeth*, ed. G. B. Harrison (London: Cassell, 1935); *The Letters of Lady Arbella Stuart*, ed. Sara Jayne Steen (Oxford: Oxford University Press, 1994). For short excerpts from a wider range of manuscript materials, see Charlotte F. Otten, ed., *English Women's Voices, 1540–1700* (Miami: Florida International University Press, 1992).

4. Gerda Lerner, *The Creation of Feminist Consciousness From the Middle Ages to Eighteen-Seventy* (New York: Oxford University Press, 1993), p. 47.

5. See chapters 1–3 of this volume for discussion of women's education, cultural frameworks, speaking and silence.

6. See Janel Mueller, 'Autobiography of a New "Creatur": Female Spirituality, Selfhood, and Authorship in *The Book of Margery Kempe*', in Mary Beth Rose, ed., *Women in the Middle Ages and the Renaissance* (Syracuse, NY: Syracuse University Press, 1986), pp. 155–71.

7. Gerda Lerner, *The Creation of Patriarchy* (New York: Oxford University Press, 1986), p. 6.

8. On Roper, see Elizabeth McCutcheon, 'Margaret More Roper: the Learned Woman in Tudor England', in Katharina M. Wilson, ed., *Women Writers of the Renaissance and Reformation* (Athens: University of Georgia Press, 1987), pp. 449–80. On printing, see Maureen Bell, 'Women Publishers of Puritan Literature in the Mid-Seventeenth Century: Three Case Studies' (Ph.D. dissertation, Loughborough University, 1987).

9. Virginia Blain, Isobel Grundy and Patricia Clements, eds., *Feminist Companion to Literature in English: Women Writers from the Middle Ages to the Present* (New Haven: Yale University Press, 1990), p. 466; Charlotte Kohler, 'Elizabethan Woman of Letters, the Extent of her Literary Activities' (Ph.D. dissertation, University of Virginia, 1936).

10. Hilda L. Smith, *Reason's Disciples: Seventeenth-Century English Feminists* (Urbana: University of Illinois Press, 1982), especially pp. 117–39.

11. The most recent biography, Michael K. Jones and Malcolm G. Underwood, *The King's Mother: Lady Margaret Beaufort, Countess of Richmond and Derby* (Cambridge: Cambridge University Press, 1992), devotes only a few lines to Beaufort's literary work.

12. See the discussion of humanist education in chapter 1 of this book; also Retha M. Warnicke, *Women of the English Renaissance and Reformation* (Westport, CT: Greenwood Press, 1983).

13. See chapter 1, note 5 of this volume; see also Charity Cannon Willard, 'A

Fifteenth-Century View of Women's Role in Medieval Society: Christine de Pizan's *Livre des Trois Vertus*', in Rosemarie Thee Morewedge, ed., *The Role of Women in the Middle Ages* (Albany: State University of New York Press, 1975).

14. Foster Watson, ed., *Vives and the Renascence Education of Women* (London: Edward Arnold, 1912), p. 14.

15. Arthur W. Reed, 'The Regulation of the Book Trade before the Proclamation of 1538', *Transactions of the Bibliographical Society*, 15 (1917–19), 157–84; Henry R. Plomer, *Wynkyn de Worde and his Contemporaries From the Death of Caxton to 1535. A Chapter in English Printing* (London: Grafton, 1925).

16. See Anne Lake Prescott, 'The Pearl of the Valois and Elizabeth I: Marguerite de Navarre's *Miroir* and Tudor England', in Margaret P. Hannay, ed., *Silent But For The Word: Tudor Women as Patrons, Translators, and Writers of Religious Works* (Kent, OH: Kent State University Press, 1985), pp. 61–76.

17. E. J. Devereux, 'The Publication of the English *Paraphrases* of Erasmus', *Bulletin of the John Rylands Library*, 51 (1969), 348–67; 'Queen Mary', in George Ballard, *Memoirs of Several Ladies of Great Britain* (1752; reprinted Detroit, MI: Wayne State University Press, 1985), pp. 147–55.

18. *Writings of Ed. VI, William Hugh . . .* (Philadelphia: Presbyterian Board of Publication, 1862), pp. 173–85.

19. Janel Mueller, 'A Tudor Queen Finds Voice: Katherine Parr's *Lamentation of a Sinner*', in Heather Dubrow and Richard Strier, eds., *The Historical Renaissance: New Essays on Tudor and Stuart Literature and Culture* (Chicago: University of Chicago Press, 1988), pp. 15–47, and 'Devotion as Difference: Intertextuality in Queen Katherine Parr's *Prayers or Meditations* (1545)', *HLQ*, 53:3 (Summer 1990), 171–97; see also John N. King, 'Patronage and Piety: the Influence of Catherine Parr', in Hannay, ed., *Silent But For The Word*, pp. 43–60.

20. Elaine V. Beilin, 'Anne Askew's Self-Portrait in the *Examinations*', in Hannay, ed., *Silent But For The Word*, pp. 77–91; Leslie P. Fairfield, 'John Bale and the Development of Protestant Hagiography in England', *JEH*, 24:2 (April 1973), 145–60.

21. For extended discussion of Anne Askewe, see chapter 2 of this volume.

22. Pearl Hogrefe, 'Anne Cooke, Lady Bacon', in *Women of Action in Tudor England* (Ames: Iowa State University Press, 1977), pp. 39–56.

23. The translation remained in manuscript (BL MS Reg. 15.A) until this century. It was discussed by Margaret Arnold in 'Jane Lumley's *Iphigeneia*: Self-Revelation of a Renaissance Noblewomen to Her Audience' (unpublished paper presented at the Shakespeare Association of America conference in 1990).

24. On such representations see, for example, Louis A. Montrose, '*A Midsummer Night's Dream* and the Shaping Fantasies of Elizabethan Culture: Gender, Power, Form', in Margaret W. Ferguson, Maureen Quilligan and Nancy J. Vickers, eds., *Rewriting the Renaissance* (Chicago: Chicago University Press,

1986), pp. 65–87, and A. L. Rowse, *Sex and Society in Shakespeare's Age: Simon Forman the Astrologer* (New York: Scribner's Sons, 1974), pp. 20–1.

25. Allison Heisch, 'Queen Elizabeth I: Parliamentary Rhetoric and the Exercise of Power', *Signs*, 1:1 (1975), 31–55; Frances Teague, 'Elizabeth I: Queen of England', in Wilson, *Women Writers of the Renaissance and Reformation*, pp. 522–47; Leah Marcus, 'Shakespeare's Comic Heroines, Elizabeth I, and the Political Uses of Androgyny', in Rose, *Women in the Middle Ages*, pp. 135–53; and, more generally, Steven W. May, 'Recent Studies in Elizabeth I', *ELR*, 23:2 (Spring 1993), 345–54. For some speeches by Elizabeth, see Teague, 'Elizabeth I'; and George P. Rice, ed., *The Public Speaking of Queen Elizabeth* (New York: Columbia University Press, 1951); for proclamations, see Paul L. Hughes and James F. Larkin, ed., *Tudor Royal Proclamations* (3 vols.; New Haven: Yale University Press, 1969).

26. P. E. Hallett, ed., *St Thomas More's History of the Passion, translated from the Latin by his granddaughter ... edited in modern spelling with an introduction* (London: Burns, Oates and Washbourne, 1941).

27. Susanne Wood, 'The Body Penitent: a 1560 Calvinist Sonnet Sequence', in Anne Lake Prescott, ed., *Renaissance Studies*, a special issue of *ANQ*, NS 5:2/3 (April, July 1992), 137–40; William L. Stull, '"Why Are Not Sonnets Made of Thee?" A New Context for the "Holy Sonnets" of Donne, Herbert, and Milton', *MP*, 80:2 (November 1982), 129–35.

28. John Foxe, *Actes and Monuments* (Jane Grey: VI, 418–24; Askew: V, 537–50). A famous anecdote on Jane Grey's love for learning was told by Roger Ascham in his *Scholemaster* (1570).

29. In our own day, C. S. Lewis has praised the work highly: 'If quality without bulk were enough, Lady Bacon might be put forward as the best of all sixteenth-century translators.' (*English Literature in the Sixteenth Century* (Oxford: Oxford University Press, 1954), p. 307.

30. Wendy Wall, 'Isabella Whitney and the Female Legacy', *ELH*, 58 (Spring 1991), 35–62; Betty S. Travitsky, 'Isabella Whitney (flourished 1566–1573)', *DLB*, vol. CXXXVI, ed. David Richardson (Columbia: Bruccoli-Clark Layman, 1993), pp. 341–4.

31. Tina Krontiris, 'Breaking Boundaries of Genre and Gender: Margaret Tyler's Translation of *The Mirrour of Knighthood*', *ELR*, 18 (1988/9), 19–39; Louise Schleiner, 'Margaret Tyler, Translator and Waiting Woman', *ELN*, 29:3 (March 1992), 1–7.

32. For Tyrwhit, Abergavenny and Martin see Elaine V. Beilin, *Redeeming Eve: Women Writers of the English Renaissance* (Princeton: Princeton University Press, 1987), pp. 81–6; for Stuart, *Queen Mary's Book, A Collection of Poems and Essays by Mary Queen of Scots*, ed. Mrs P. Stewart-MacKenzie-Arbuthnot (London: George Bell, 1907); for Mildmay, Linda Pollok, *With Faith and Physic: The Life of a Tudor Gentlewoman Lady Grace Mildmay, 1552–1620* (London: Collins and Brown, 1994).

33. Colin B. Atkinson and William P. Stoneman, '"These griping greefes and

pinching pangs": Attitudes to Childbirth in Thomas Bentley's *The Monument of Matrones*, 1582', *SCJ*, 21:2 (1990), 193–203.

34. Beilin, *Redeeming Eve*, pp. 51–5; Betty Travitsky, ed., *Paradise of Women: Writings by Englishwomen of the Renaissance* (Westport, CT: Greenwood Press, 1981; rpt. 1989), pp. 146–7.

35. See Roland H. Bainton, *Women of the Reformation: From Spain to Scandinavia* (Minneapolis: Augsburg Publishing House, 1977).

36. Elaine V. Beilin, 'Writing Public Poetry: Humanism and the Woman Writer' *MLQ*, 51:2 (1990), 249–71.

37. Helen Andrews Kahin, 'Jane Anger and John Lyly', *MLQ*, 8 (1949), 31–5; Linda Woodbridge, *Women and the English Renaissance* (Urbana: University of Illinois Press, 1984); Katherine Usher Henderson and Barbara F. McManus, eds., *Half Humankind* (Urbana: University of Illinois Press, 1985).

38. See the now standard biography of Mary Sidney, Margaret P. Hannay's *Philip's Phoenix, Mary Sidney, Countess of Pembroke* (New York and Oxford: Oxford University Press, 1990), and Diane Bornstein, 'The Style of the Countess of Pembroke's Translation of . . . de Mornay . . .', in Hannay, ed., *Silent But For The Word*, pp. 126–48. For further discussion of this major figure within this volume, see chapters 2 (religion and self-expression), 8 (her courtly tradition), 9 (her Psalms in English verse) and 12 (her drama).

39. See chapter 2 of this volume, and Retha M. Warnicke, 'Eulogies for Women: Public Testimony of Their Godly Example and Leadership', in Betty S. Travitsky and Adele F. Seeff, eds., *Attending to Women in Early Modern England* (Newark: University of Delaware Press, 1994), pp. 168–86.

40. Mary Ellen Lamb, 'The Cooke Sisters: Attitudes toward Learned Women in the Renaissance', in Hannay, ed., *Silent But For The Word*, pp. 107–25. The same amalgam of prose styles can be demonstrated in the manuscript journals of two women who straddled the Elizabethan and Jacobean periods, Margaret Hoby (1570–1633), MS 1599–1605, and Anne Clifford (1590–1676), MSS at intervals between 1603 and 1676, parts of whose writings have been printed in this century. See Sarah Mendelson, 'Stuart Women's Diaries and Occasional Memoirs', in Mary Prior, ed., *Women in English Society, 1500–1800* (London: Methuen, 1985), pp. 181–210, and Helen Wilcox, 'Private Writing and Public Function: Autobiographical Texts by Renaissance Englishwomen', in S.P. Cerasano and Marion Wynne-Davies, eds., *Gloriana's Face: Women, Public and Private, in the English Renaissance* (Hemel Hempstead: Harvester Wheatsheaf, 1992), pp. 47–62.

41. The critical and facsimile texts edited by Susanne Woods, *The Poems of Aemilia Lanyer, 'Salve Deus Rex Judaeorum'* (New York: Oxford University Press, 1993) and A. L. Rowse, ed., *The Poems of Shakespeare's Dark Lady* (London: Jonathan Cape, 1978) both include the prose preface.

42. See chapter 3 of this volume, and Christine W. Sizemore, 'Early Seventeenth-Century Advice Books: The Female Viewpoint', *South Atlantic Bulletin*, 41 (January 1976), 41–8.

43. The pamphlet texts are reprinted in Henderson and McManus, eds., *Half Humankind*. See also Ann Rosalind Jones, 'Counter-attacks on "the Bayter of Women"': Three Pamphleteers of the Early Seventeenth Century', in Anne M. Haselkorn and Betty S. Travitsky, eds., *The Renaissance Englishwoman in Print: Counterbalancing the Canon* (Amherst: University of Massachusetts Press, 1990), pp. 45–62; Betty Travitsky, '"The Lady Doth Protest": Protest in the Popular Writings of Renaissance Englishwomen', *ELR*, 14 (Autumn 1984), 255–83; Barbara K. Lewalski, 'Defending Women's Essential Equality: Rachel Speght's Polemics and Poems, in *Writing Women in Jacobean England* (Cambridge, MA: Harvard University Press, 1993), pp. 153–75.

44. The trial of Swetnam is further enacted in the anonymous *Swetnam the Woman Hater Arraigned by Women* (1620). See Constance Jordan, 'Gender and Justice in *Swetnam the Woman Hater*', *RD*, NS, 18 (1987), 149–69.

45. Two additional anonymous pamphlets, published in 1620, are *Hic Mulier* and *Haec Vir*. On the controversy, see Woodbridge, *Women and the English Renaissance*, and Travitsky, 'The Lady Doth Protest'.

46. The texts, edited by Josephine A. Roberts, are being published by the Renaissance English Text Society. For a sense of the burgeoning scholarship on Wroth, see chapter 8 of this volume, and Elizabeth Hageman's bibliography in Kirby Farrell, Elizabeth Hageman and Arthur Kinney, eds., *Women in the Renaissance* (Amherst: University of Massachusetts Press, 1990), pp. 301–4; a good review is provided in Lewalski, *Writing Women*, pp. 243–307.

47. Betty Travitsky, 'The New Mother of the English Renaissance: Her Writings on Motherhood', in C. N. Davidson and E. M. Broner, eds., *The Lost Tradition: Mothers and Daughters in Literature* (New York: Ungar, 1980), pp. 33–43.

48. Beilin, *Redeeming Eve*, pp. 280–2, and Travitsky, *Paradise of Women*, pp. 57–60.

49. *DNB*, vol. XI, 1262. Livingston was guardian of Princess Elizabeth, daughter of James I and VI.

50. See Tina Krontiris, *Oppositional Voices* (London: Routledge, 1992), pp. 78–101; and 'Style and Gender in Elizabeth Cary's *Edward II*', in Haselkorn and Travitsky, eds., *Renaissance Englishwoman in Print*, pp. 137–53; and the introduction to Barry Weller and Margaret W. Ferguson, eds., *The Tragedy of Mariam* (Berkeley: University of California Press, 1994), especially pp. 12–17.

51. Travitsky, *Paradise of Women*, pp. 209–33.

52. Elaine Hobby, *Virtue of Necessity: English Women's Writing, 1649–1688* (London: Virago, 1988), p. 26. See also Ester Cope, *Handmaid of the Holy Spirit* (Ann Arbor: University of Michigan Press, 1992).

53. Ruth Hughey, 'Forgotten Verses by Ben Jonson, George Wither, and Others to Alice Sutcliffe', *RES*, 10 (1934), 156–64; Travitsky, *Paradise of Women*, pp. 157–8, 47–8, 158–9.

54. Travitsky, *Paradise of Women*, pp. 159–62.

55. Simon Shepherd, ed., *The Women's Sharp Revenge* (London: Fourth Estate, 1985), p. 170.
56. Patricia Higgins, 'The Reactions of Women with Special Reference to Women Petitioners', in Brian Manning, ed., *Politics, Religion, and the English Civil War* (London: Edward Arnold, 1973), pp. 177–222.
57. For a list of the tracts, see Cope, *Handmaid of the Holy Spirit*, pp. xiii–xvi. See also Hilda L. Smith and Susan Cardinale, *Women and the Literature of the Seventeenth Century* (New York: Greenwood Press, 1990), pp. 37–49.
58. George Ballard, *Memoirs of Several Ladies of Great Britain* (1752; reprinted, ed. Ruth Perry, Wayne State University Press, 1985), pp. 264–5; Ethyn Morgan Williams, 'Women Preachers in the Civil War', *Journal of Modern History*, 1:4 (1929), 561–9.
59. See excerpts in Otten, ed., *English Women's Voices*, pp. 283–4, 301–9.
60. Keith Thomas, 'Women and the Civil War Sects', *Past and Present*, 13 (1958), 42–62.
61. See chapter 2 of this volume, and Hobby, *Virtue of Necessity*, pp. 31–6; Champlin Burrage, 'Anna Trapnel's Prophecies', *English Historical Review*, 26 (1911), 526–35.
62. Phyllis Mack, 'Women as Prophets in the English Civil War', *Feminist Studies*, 8 (1982), 19–45; See also chapter 2 of this volume, and Hobby, *Virtue of Necessity*, pp. 26–53.
63. According to Margaret Ezell, 'of the nearly two hundred first editions by women published between 1651 and 1670, ninety-three of them were by Quaker women; between 1651 and 1660, twenty-eight Quaker women published more than four works each' (*Writing Women's Literary History* (Baltimore: Johns Hopkins University Press, 1993), p. 134, and see pp. 132–60).
64. B. G. MacCarthy, 'The Pastoral Romance,' in *Women Writers: Their Contribution to the Novel, 1621–1744* (1944; reprinted Cork: Cork University Press 1948), pp. 47–70. See also Patrick Cullen, ed., *A Continuation of Sir Philip Sidney's 'Arcadia'* (Brown University Women Writers Project; Oxford: Oxford University Press, 1995).
65. Moira Ferguson, 'Margaret Lucas Cavendish: a "Wise, Wittie and Learned Lady"', in Katharina Wilson and Frank Warnke, *Women Writers of the Seventeenth Century* (Athens: University of Georgia Press, 1989), pp. 305–40.
66. Bernard Capp, *English Almanacs 1500–1800: Astrology and the Popular Press* (Ithaca: Cornell University Press, 1979).
67. Another of the writings of Dorothy Pakington (died 1679), *Causes of the Decay of Christian Piety*, appeared in 1667. For More, see Dorothy Latz, ed., *'Glow-Worm Light ... ': Writings of Seventeenth-Century English Recusant Women From Original Manuscripts* (Salzburg: Institut für Anglistik und Amerikanistik, Universitat Salzburg, 1989).
68. Joyce L. Irwin, 'Anna Maria van Schurman: Learned Woman of Utrecht', in Wilson and Warnke, *Women Writers*, pp. 164–85.

69. See Mary Beth Rose, 'Gender, Genre and History: Seventeenth-Century English Women and the Art of Autobiography', in Rose, *Women in the Middle Ages*, pp. 245–78, for a discussion of biographies by Cavendish and three other women. Particularly noteworthy is the biography first printed in 1806, *Memoirs of the Life of Colonel Hutchinson*, by Lucy Hutchinson (1620–80?).

70. Elaine C. Huber, 'A Woman Must Not Speak: Quaker Women in the English Left Wing', in Rosemary Radford Ruether and Eleanor McLaughlin, eds., *Women of Spirit: Female Leadership in the Jewish and Christian Traditions* (New York: Simon and Schuster, 1979), pp. 153–81.

71. Janet Todd, '"Were I Empress of the World": the "German Princess" and the Duchess of Newcastle', in her *The Sign of Angellica: Women, Writing, and Fiction, 1660–1800* (London: Virago, 1989), pp. 52–68: Anthony B. Dawson, 'Mistris Hic & Haec: Representations of Moll Frith', *SEL*, 33:2 (1993), 385–404.

72. Aphra Behn has been commonly, but mistakenly, reputed to be the earliest woman to earn her living by her pen in England. See Hobby, *Virtue of Necessity*, pp. 96–100, 166–75.

73. *Ibid.*, pp. 185–7; and the facsimile of *The Midwives Book* published by Garland in 1985. For Makin, see Frances Teague, 'Bathsua Makin: Woman of Learning', in Wilson and Warnke, pp. 285–304.

74. For Fanshawe, see Rose, 'Gender, Genre and History', pp. 245–78; Charlotte Otten views Fanshawe quite differently (*English Women's Voices*, p. 131). The text is available in John Loftis, ed., *The Memoirs of Anne, Lady Halkett and Ann, Lady Fanshawe* (Oxford: Clarendon Press, 1979). For Wentworth, see Hobby, *Virtue of Necessity*, pp. 49–53. See extracts from Wentworth's *Vindication* in Elspeth Graham, Hilary Hinds, Elaine Hobby and Helen Wilcox, eds., *Her Own Life: Autobiographical Writings by Seventeenth-Century Englishwomen* (London: Routledge, 1989), pp. 180–96.

75. Catherine F. Smith, 'The Feminist Mind and Art of a Seventeenth-Century Protestant Mystic', in Ruether and McLaughlin, eds., *Women of Spirit*, pp. 183–203.

76. Otten, *English Women's Voices*, pp. 58–9, 79–80. See also Rosemary Foxton, '*Hear the Word of the Lord': A Critical and Bibliographical Study of Quaker Women's Writing, 1650–1700* (Melbourne: Bibliographical Society of Australia and New Zealand, 1994).

77. *Ibid.*, pp. 206–11; Hobby, *Virtue of Necessity*, pp. 21–3, 187–9.

78. Margaret Ferguson, 'Juggling the Categories of Race, Class, and Gender: Aphra Behn's *Oroonoko*,' in *Women in the Renaissance: an Interdisciplinary Forum (MLA 1989)*, ed. Ann Rosalind Jones and Betty S. Travitsky, a special issue of *Women's Studies*, 19:2 (1991), 159–81.

79. Otten, *English Women's Voices*, pp. 81–2.

80. Moira Ferguson, *First Feminists British Women Writers, 1578–1799* (Bloomington: Indiana University Press, 1985), pp. 201–11.

81. Smith, *Reason's Disciples*, pp. 117–39.

CHAPTER 12

The first female dramatists

Ros Ballaster

> Then she usurpes upon anothers right,
> That seekes to be by publike language grace't:
> And though her thoughts reflect with purest light,
> Her mind if not peculiar is not chast.[1]

The woman playwright's accession to 'public language' is, as this quotation from the first original published play in England by a woman, Elizabeth Cary's *The Tragedie of Mariam* (1613), illustrates, almost inevitably attended by animadversions on her chastity. It is not language itself, but specifically its 'publicity' (the refusal to keep the mind 'peculiar', that is private or to itself) that is at issue here for women as writers. Yet, despite this consistent equation of public display with public shame, the state and status of women's playwrighting undergoes dramatic transformation between the beginning of our period, the early sixteenth century, and its close, the late seventeenth century. The earliest play discussed, Jane Lumley's *Iphigenia in Aulis*, is a manuscript translation of Euripides, probably produced as a schoolgirl's exercise around 1550 by an aristocratic daughter and available as part of a manuscript volume of writings, otherwise in Latin, which appear to have been presented to her father, Lord Arundel, through her husband, Baron John Lumley.[2] The latest, *The Beau Defeated; or, the Lucky Younger Brother* by Mary Pix is a satirical city comedy based on Dancourt's *Le Chevalier à la Mode*, performed at a public theatre, Lincoln's Inn Fields, in 1700 and printed in the same year; its author, a clergyman's daughter and merchant tailor's widow, was a professional playwright and author of six tragedies and six comedies.[3]

What conditions, then, enabled women like Mary Pix to enter the 'public language' of the stage at the end of the seventeenth century, but which were not available to women in the earlier great flowering of the public theatre, the late sixteenth century? The determining factor appears to be the advent of print culture in late seventeenth-century England, in tandem with increased literacy among women of the middle classes who had less to lose in public display than their aristocratic predecessors. What is remarkable about the proliferation of plays by women on the Restoration public stage is the willingness, indeed eagerness, to announce their female authorship and to make equations between the spectacle of a play and what Sophie Tomlinson has referred to, in the context of the Caroline court masque, as the 'staging of women'.[4] The act of female authorship in the drama need not, of course, be understood as necessarily an act of public language; the one figure who is emphatically *not* physically present on the stage in performance is the author herself, who appoints surrogates in the shape of actors to present prologues and epilogues on her behalf. Pix and her most famous predecessor, Aphra Behn, as well as her contemporaries, Susannah Centlivre, Catharine Trotter, 'Ariadne' and 'Ephelia', even where they do not disclose their names, make certain that their audience is aware of their sex. Seventeenth-century aristocratic women (with the notable exception of Margaret Cavendish, Duchess of Newcastle) whose plays were published either concealed their sex or revealed it only to disclaim their involvement in the decision to publish the text.

Despite these radical class-related differences between women's entry into the public language of the drama, a consistent and gender-specific negotiation of the equally public and equally taboo (for women) terrain of political debate can be traced across the spectrum of the plays under discussion. Sixteenth- and seventeenth-century political discourse consistently deploys analogies of sexual and marital love to explore the power relations of proper government, and women dramatists are no exception to this rule. The importance of this analogy has been acknowledged in the analysis of plays, particularly the tragedy, by male dramatists from John Webster's *Duchess of Malfi* to Thomas Otway's *Venice Preserv'd*.[5] However, plays by women continue, in the main, to be interpreted through the exclusive filter of their presumed concern for women's sexual freedom. An attention to the state–political, as opposed to sexual–political, preoccupations of women's drama entails an acknowledgement of the difference within that drama. A study of the politics of women's drama requires that we question the category 'female dramatist' itself. For the women writers under discussion here, loyalty in state or party politics does not by any means come second to their loyalty to their sex; indeed, one might go so far as to argue that the ostentatious 'staging' of female authorship in late seventeenth-century drama by women provides cover for a far more dangerous presumption on the part of these writers to enter the wider stage of state–political controversy.

The twin concerns of 'staging' femaleness (turning the body of the woman, whether that of the dramatist or female character, into a spectacle for visual and verbal contemplation) and 'staging' a female perspective on government and power are a consistent and complex unifying factor in the work of women dramatists throughout the period. However, a chronological and formal division can be made between two periods, from 1550 to 1668 and from 1669 to 1700 (see discussion in chapter 5 of this volume). An interesting phenomenon emerges in comparing these two periods, that of the problematic status of the female body in plays authored by women. Women's public drama flowers with the appearance of women playing women's parts. Women, most famously the queen herself, had acted in the court theatre of Henrietta Maria during the reign of Charles I, but the Renaissance and Jacobean public theatre had used young boys to play female parts.[6] Charles II's exiled sojourn in France had accustomed him to women acting in public theatres, and a patent issued to Thomas Killigrew on 25 April 1662 required 'all of the woemen's part' to be acted by women due to the 'offence' caused by the 'prophane, obscene, and scurrulous passages' in plays that used men 'in the habit of women'.[7] Ironically, the performance of their plays with women acting female parts seems to have forced a constraint on women playwrights that the aristocratic women writers of 'closet' drama rarely had to confront; they explore in print the question of their 'difference' from two proximate professions for women, that of the actress and that of the prostitute. In all three professions women display their talents for material profit.[8] While the presence of the female body on stage might be understood as a useful analogy for the woman playwright, in fact, she more often sought to distinguish her own image from that of the actress.

CLASSICS AND CLOSETS: WOMEN DRAMATISTS, 1550–1668

The earliest plays by women are translations. Jane Lumley's *Iphigenia in Aulis* translates Euripides' play from the Greek; Mary Sidney Herbert's *Antonius* translates the French Senecan play by Robert Garnier, *Marc-Antoine*, and was published in 1592 in the same volume as her translation of the Stoic treatise by Philippe Mornay, *Discourse of Life and Death*. Unlike the professional women playwrights of the Restoration stage who drew freely on sixteenth- and seventeenth-century plays from France, Spain and England for their plots, these translators were anxious to be as exact and faithful as possible to their original, in Mary Herbert's case to the detriment of poetic elegance itself. Critical interpretation of these plays rests less on their specific treatment of material and language than on the choice of play itself and what function the act of translation served for the writer.

Lumley's *Iphigenia* seems a particularly speaking choice for a daughter to produce for her father, since the play concerns itself with Agamemnon's decision to sacrifice his daughter to the goddess Diana of Aulida, at the instigation of the prophet Calchas, in order to gain a wind for the Greek fleet to reach Troy and win back his brother Menelaus' bride Helen (twin sister to Agamemnon's wife Clytemnestra), after her abduction by Paris. Agamemnon lures his wife and daughter to Aulis through the device of a projected marriage between Iphigenia and the Greek hero Achilles. Achilles, discovering the plot, defends Iphigenia, but she finally and heroically embraces her destiny, only to be taken up by the goddess at the scene of her sacrifice to be replaced by a white hart. *Iphigenia* dramatically identifies the importance of the exchange of women in the masculine sphere of military glory and state politics and the struggle of the daughter to acquire a voice in that exchange culture.[9] When Iphigenia hears that Achilles is in danger for his life as a result of taking her part, she finds her voice, but directs it to her mother Clytemnestra, rather than the men she is being encouraged to address, presenting an eloquent defence of the rightness of her own death:

if this wicked enterprise of the Troians be not revenged, then truly the grecians shall not kepe neither their children, nor yet their wives in peace: And I shall not onlie remedie all these thinges withe my deathe: but also get a glorious renoune to the grecians for ever. Againe remember how I was not borne for your sake onlie, but rather for the comodite of my countrie. (lines 1178–87)

The acquisition of agency for women in the play is then paradoxically only asserted through the assent to the status of object of exchange in the politics of state. Clytemnestra complains that Iphigenia's sacrifice is for 'a naughtie woman's sake' (line 983), that is, for the adulteress Helen. Iphigenia here identifies the exchange, her life for Helen's, as nothing to do with the intrinsic 'value' of women, but with their status as 'comodite' of a country that will be ruined if men's property relations are not secured. Helen's chastity, or not, is precisely 'naught' in this exchange.

Over a century later the same tension between familial love and duty

to country is the focus of Katherine Philips's choice of plays for translation, Corneille's *Pompey* and *Horace*, this time in the far more powerful
and, for Philips, personal, context of the divisions between families of the
civil war and its aftermath.[10] Both plays centre on female figures who are
divided, through marriage, in their loyalties to their country and their
husbands or lovers, a predicament they share with their author, the
Royalist sympathiser Katherine Fowler, who was married at the age of
sixteen to her stepfather's kinsman, the Parliamentarian soldier and later
politician Colonel James Philips.

Cornelia, heroine of *Pompey*, is the widow of the Roman general
Pompey, whose disagreement with Caesar resulted in civil war, Pompey's defeat in the battle of Pharsalus and flight to Egypt where he was
murdered. Her loyalty to her dead husband obliges her, while conceding
Caesar's nobility, to support her sons in making war against him in
revenge for their father's death. Similarly, in *Horace*, Sabina of Alba finds
her native country at war with that of her husband, the Roman Horace.
This civil war (Romulus was born in Alba) is to be resolved through
hand-to-hand combat in which her husband and his two brothers must
fight her Alban brothers, including Curtius, who is himself in love with
Camilla, Horace's sister. The attraction of this play to Charles II's
Restoration court in the late 1660s, still struggling to reach a peaceable
settlement after the civil war and commonwealth years, is obvious. Its
focus is, however, firmly on the female protagonists' sense of their own
impotence and a validation of their compassion as a representative mode
of judgement in political conflict. For their partners, including the spirit
of Pompey who visits Cornelia in her sleep, there should be no conflict.
Horace's 'rough Virtue' (II.iii.83) demands that his wife's loyalties should
be with the state she has married into, that of Rome. Sabina in soliloquy,
however, finds it impossible to vanquish her internal divisions of loyalty
and love:

> my griev'd heart from no one wound is free'd.
> At which a Husband, or a Brother bleed;
> Which sad reflection so much terrour draws,
> I onely view the Actors, not the Cause:
> Nor can the Conquerours fame salute my thought,
> But to remember with whose Blood 'twas bought;
> The vanquish't Family claims all my care,
> Here I'm a Wife, and am a Daughter there,
> And to each party am so strictly ty'd,
> That I must be on the unhappy side.
>
> (*Horace* III.i: *Poems*, p. 93)

The sentiments of the heroic embrace of self-division on the part of the female protagonist expressed in both *Iphigenia*, *Pompey* and *Horace* are as far from the stoic Senecan domestication of women's state role in Mary Herbert's *Antonius* as are Philips's elegant transposition of Corneille's alexandrines into heroic couplets and Lumley's attractively simple prose version of Euripides from Mary Herbert's ponderously accurate translation of Garnier.[11] Herbert's choice of translation, as Tina Krontiris has outlined, is, however, a significant one in that Garnier's play represents Cleopatra as a virtuous wifely force for justice and loyalty in relation to a vacillating Antony whose heroism is continually questioned.[12] *Antonius* is best understood in the context of Mary Herbert's considerable status as patron and practitioner of humanist arts. Sister of the poet Philip Sidney, and dedicatee of his *Arcadia*, Mary led a coterie circle of artists and writers at her stately home, Wilton House in Wiltshire. Herbert's interest in rewriting and reinterpreting the masculine tradition of Renaissance humanist literature appears to have been in the attempt, as Mary Ellen Lamb puts it, to 'fashion a constant heroine', Cleopatra, as a constant lover of the vacillating man who falls short of a heroism for which she compensates through her powers of poetic discourse.[13]

Mary Herbert's poetic achievements in print were celebrated by John Davies, another member of the Pembroke circle, in his dedicatory poem to his 1612 *Muse's Sacrifice, or Divine Meditations*, along with those of Lucy, Countess of Bedford (now best known for her patronage of the poet John Donne)[14] and Elizabeth Cary (née Tanfield), to whom he had acted as writing master. Davies chides all three women because they 'presse the Press with little' that they have written (as discussed in chapter 7 of this book; see p. 157). The next year Cary, who married Sir Henry Cary at the age of fifteen in 1602 and appears to have commenced writing her play in the same year, published the *Tragedie of Mariam*. Like Lumley and Mary Herbert before her, and Katherine Philips after her, Cary's plot centres on a woman divided between familial loyalty and national duty. Her play is based on a narrative rendered in Josephus' tenth-century *Jewish Antiquities*, available in English since Thomas Lodge's translation of 1602, which recounts Herod's execution of his second wife, the Jewish Mariam, sister to the rightful Jewish king whom Herod had murdered. Herod is rumoured to have been executed by Caesar for his association with Mark Antony; Mariam is angered to discover that he has ordered his second, Sohemus, to kill her in the event of his own death and is unable to respond with the required joy when he returns home unexpectedly. His sister Salome, attempting to engineer her own freedom from one marriage to enter another, builds on this suspicious behaviour to persuade Herod of Mariam's infidelity with Sohemus. After her execution, her innocence is discovered to Herod's despair and regret. Cary's choice and rendering of this plot is, as Lumley's was, peculiarly appropriate to her own biographical circumstances; the Protestant Sir Henry Cary, later Viscount Falkland, married her when she was fifteen for her dowry. In 1626 the couple separated due to Lady Falkland's conversion to Catholicism; *Mariam*'s criticism of arbitrary and absolute reign on the part of a loved husband in the figure of Herod seems to be peculiarly proleptic.[15]

The play follows the Senecan closet mode of Mary Herbert's *Antonius*, employing a chorus which, like Herbert's, frequently expresses a more conservative position on marriage and mortality than the characters express within the action. As Margaret Ferguson has deftly illustrated (see chapter 7 of this volume), *Mariam* sets in train a complex debate about the effectiveness of speech and silence, reading and writing, as modes of resistance for aristocratic women in the face of tyranny.[16] The play establishes a sophisticated network of allusion and metaphor regarding the instability that results in trying to establish the veracity of the visual and verbal signs that women produce. Mariam's assumed verbal licence (Herod complains 'Her mouth will ope to ev'ry strangers eare' (iv.vii.1707)) is explicitly contrasted with Salome's verbal caution (she does speak, but always selectively and to the appropriate interlocutor, where Mariam's complaints seem to be heard by everyone but her husband). The verbal power of both is contrasted with the silence and, hence presumably, chastity of Graphina, a slave girl whom Herod's brother Pheroras hopes to marry. Graphina's name invokes writing as a source of truth where speech, in *Mariam*, appears to fail so dramatically for its female protagonist. The 'closet' play, then, becomes its own speaking metaphor for the aristocratic married woman's access to public language, a form of verbal power that appears to sidestep the problem of women's speaking in public precisely because the play is not designed for performance.

If aristocratic women appear to have positively chosen modes of dramatic writing not designed for performance prior to the civil war and Commonwealth years (1642–60), during those years the closure of public theatres by edict of the Commonwealth and the transformation of Royalist stately homes that had previously served as sites of private performance into places of siege and dereliction (Cavalier heads of household found themselves in exile with the princes Charles and James), made performance itself a fantasy space for aristocratic women writers. Although both Katherine Philips and her contemporary Margaret Cavendish, Duchess of Newcastle, published their plays in the decade following Charles II's restoration to the throne in 1660, they are perhaps best understood as products of the paradoxical limbo in which aristocratic women with Royalist sympathies found themselves in the interregnum. As Royalists, they too wished to see the 'restoration' of an aristocratic culture as the centre of power. Yet, as women they had experienced new agency and power in the Commonwealth years. Margaret Cavendish visited England in 1652 to petition the parliamentary committee for compounding with a wife's share in her husband's sequestered estates; in London she wrote and paid for the publication of her *Poems, and Fancies* and *Philosophicall Fancies* (both 1653), taking advantage of the advances in print culture. Katherine Philips, as the wife of a leading Parliamentarian, had access to political knowledge that her lowly origins as daughter of a merchant would not have allowed her prior to the civil war. Their response to this ambiguity is an attempt in the early years of the Restoration to produce (fractured and unstable as it is) an art that understands female artistry as an important ideological *agent* in the work of 'restoring' a Royalist culture. In this process we find women writers developing a fantasy of a Royalist return to Renaissance values in which women figure the possibility of a 'restored' economy of literary–social relations without the underpinning of a patriarchalist belief (in the divine 'fatherhood' of sovereign power) as an exclusively masculine circuit of patronage and power.

This new attention to fantasy (or what Cavendish terms 'fancy') and fictionality as a source of power for women and an environment into which they can now enter on equivalent terms to the male artist, is most powerfully demonstrated in a consideration of Margaret Cavendish's two volumes of published plays of 1662 and 1668, alongside a manuscript closet drama written by her stepdaughters Jane Cavendish and Elizabeth Brackley, entitled 'The Concealed Fansyes' and written sometime between 1642 and 1649.[17] The sisters were resident at their father's country seat, Welbeck in Nottinghamshire, in July 1644 when their father William Cavendish and two of his sons, Charles and Henry, went into exile. In August of that year Welbeck surrendered to Parliamentary forces. It was briefly recaptured in July 1645, but by November it was back in Parliamentarian hands. In France, the 52-year-old William Cavendish met and married 23-year-old Margaret Lucas, maid of honour to Henrietta Maria, in 1645. Despite the fact that his daughters had not met his new wife and do not appear to have been prejudiced in her favour, there are striking similarities between the political sentiment and verbal fancifulness of the sisters' play and that expressed in their stepmother's later published plays.

'The Concealed Fansyes' concerns itself with two sisters, Lucenay and Tattyny, who playfully withhold their consent from their two suitors, Courtly and Presumption, until the men have learnt not to expect absolute wifely subservience from their partners. This amiable courtship is interrupted by a siege and the sisters are obliged briefly to enter a convent and watch powerless as their family home is appropriated by enemy forces. A combination of divine intervention and the return of their father, the widowed Lord Calsindow, liberates them from their retirement and the play concludes with a series of marriages, with the notable exception of Calsindow himself (possibly a veiled criticism of his second marriage). The play raises questions as to what 'fansy' is being concealed and why. Its concluding address from the sisters to their father implies that the Cavendish sisters had conceived it as a fanciful gift for their own father in which they expressed their 'concealed' reactions to their own experiences under siege and the news of his marriage in France. Tattyny's epilogue declares:

> Have you now read my Lord, pray doe not speake
> For I'm already grown, soe faint and weake
> Not knoweing how you will now sensure mee
> As rash to thinke, noe witt a present bee
> But if you like not, I pray lett mee knowe
> The Pen and Inke shall have a fatall blowe.   (v.836)

The concealed fancies, however, that are explored in this elegant play, which with its use of song, dance and fantasy resolution owes more to the Caroline court masque than the Elizabethan and Jacobean Senecan drama previously discussed, may also be the comic exploration of the possibilities for aristocratic women to defer and dictate the conditions of their own marriage relations in the absence of a patriarchal presence that might ensure their concession to their lovers' 'siege' before they have ensured that they will, as Tattyny puts it, 'contynew [their] own' (II.816). The play, of course, powerfully affirms the importance of that patriarchal figure in the resolution – the lovers' siege is displaced by a martial siege against which the sisters are powerless and their father, like the monarchical figure in the court masque, enters as a 'deus ex machina' to set all to rights. Yet, the brief space of 'fansy' (a space the Cavendish sisters appear to have been carving out for themselves in the very act of writing the play while their family home was seized, liberated and retaken around them) is affirmed as a space peculiar to and peculiarly powerful for women.

This recognition is equally central to Margaret Cavendish's numerous published plays, and the term 'fancy' is her most frequently cited aesthetic category.[18] The 1668 volume of *Plays* opens with a declaration 'To the Readers', that '*having pleased my Fancy in writing many Dialogues upon several Subject, and having afterwards order'd them into Acts and Scenes, I will venture, in spight of the Criticks, to call them Plays*' (n.p.). Her plays do not appear to have been performed on the London stage, and the comment here suggests that Cavendish herself wished to present them as singularly different from other forms of drama. Many of her plays are, in fact, little more than discourses or dialogues arranged into scenes; *The Female Academy*, published in the 1662 collection, is only the most notable example, comprising twenty-nine scenes arbitrarily divided into five acts. The play takes the form of a series of 'discourses' delivered by the aristocratic women who live cloistered in an academy of women instructed by older matrons, which, ostensibly, prepares them to become wise and worthy wives. The women in the female academy discourse on a variety of subjects (whether women are as capable of wit and wisdom as men, friendship, the proper behaviour of women, discoursing itself), where the rival neighbouring male academy offers nothing but a repetitive stream of mock-Puritan invectives against the dangers of cloistering women and their duty to marry, procreate and serve their husbands. In scene 21 two gentlemen discuss the relative merits of the two institutions:

1 GENT. Methinks the womens Lectural discourse is better than the mens; for in my opinion, the mens discourses are simple, childish, and foolish, in comparison of the womens.
2 GENT. Why, the subject of the discourse is of women, which are simple, foolish, and childish.
1 GENT. There is no sign of their simplicity or folly, in their discourse or Speeches, I know not what may be in their Actions. (III.21; *Plays* (1662), p. 669)

Verbal wit is here reconfigured as a specifically female capacity. The play is resolved when the men, despairing at defeating the women through language (or indeed being heard), disrupt their activities through playing trumpets; a matron visits the male academy and persuades them that the academy is not designed as a cloister or convent but as a space in which noble women will be instructed in how to become wise and worthy wives.[19] Male action then becomes the only means of competing where women's superior linguistic fancy defeats them.

Cavendish's most actable play, *The Sociable Companions; or, the Female Wits* (in *Plays* (1668)) takes a similar approach to women's capacity to imagine resolution through verbal wit in the face of crisis. This intelligent comedy of intrigue engages directly with the financial difficulties that faced cavalier soldiers on the Restoration and, as such, it interestingly presages Aphra Behn's better-known and most successful play, *The Rover* (1677). Like Behn's cavalier soldiers in Madrid, Cavendish's cavaliers (Captain Valour, Will Fullwit and Harry Sencible) are a rascally impoverished band who retreat into drink and lechery. The army is disbanding and their property and estates have been sequestered, with little hope of return on the Restoration. Their friend, Lieutenant Fightwell, comments in the opening scene that 'all the Cavalier Party lost their Wits when they lost their Estates' (i.i.8). It is their sisters, Peg Valourosa, Jane Fullwit and Anne Sencible, who provide that purpose:

HARRY. Why what would you have us do?
ANNE. Not to sit drinking in a Tavern most of your time; but to seek and endeavour to get some good Offices and Employments that may help to repair your ruins, and to maintain us according to our births and breedings. (ii.ii.30)

When the men show no sign of taking this sound advice, the women set about winning themselves wealthy marriage partners from those men who have profited from the wars and their aftermath, a lawyer, a doctor and a usurer. Peg, Jane and Anne embark on complicated confidence tricks, trapping their husbands (drawn by lot) through mock paternity suits and cross-dressing disguises. In the process they win a wealthy wife for another cavalier, Dick Traveller, one Lady Riches whom the three men they appoint to be their husbands have been courting. In this play, then, Cavendish trenchantly locates educated and nobly born women (however impoverished) as a vital source of regeneration and restoration in a culture that has lost and mourns the imagined securities of an earlier male authority.

That this privilege (of female agency through the exercise of fancy) is exclusive to upper-class women is equally clear. Cavendish's Female Academy only admits women of the gentry, the Female Wits vindicate their duplicity by virtue of what is owed to their 'birth and breeding'. Not only is this freedom restricted to the nobly born, but it is also firmly confined to the 'fancy' itself, which appears to be the property of that class. Fascinated as she is by the splendid and extravagant display of a powerful aristocratic femininity, reminiscent of her former mistress Henrietta Maria's appearances in the court masque, Cavendish remains deeply suspicious of performance itself. The word 'act' in the title 'actor' clearly resonates for Cavendish as a suspicious privileging of materiality over the world of imagination. Actors turn the playwright's fanciful words into action. For Cavendish it appears a play, or the free play of fancy, is a play only when it is not played, turned into a performance; the female body as icon of absolute monarchical authority is only splendid when it is invoked in words not materially embodied.

POETESSES AND PUNKS: WOMEN DRAMATISTS, 1669–1700

> Punk and Poesie agree so pat,
> You cannot well be *this*, and be not *that*.[20]

Only a year after the publication of Cavendish's plays, the professional female playwright dramatically announces her presence in one of the two public London theatres, the King's Company at Bridges Street, and 1670 saw the production of two new plays by women at its rival, the Duke's Company at Lincoln's Inn Fields. Frances Boothby's tragicomedy *Marcelia: or the Treacherous Friend* was presented by the King's Company in 1669; Elizabeth Polwhele's tragedy *The Faithful Virgins* and Aphra Behn's *The Forced Marriage* were presented by the Duke's Company in 1670.[21] There can be no doubt that these plays were written for performance; Boothby, about whom nothing is known beyond her play, provides a prologue that already has all the ingredients of the 'woman's defence' of her play in public performance. The prologue, delivered by a male actor, announces:

> I'm hither come, but what d'ye think to say?
> A Woman's Pen presents you with a Play:
> Who smiling told me I'd be sure to see,
> That once confirm'd, the House wou'd empty be.[22]

The prologue balances self-deprecation and aggression, not neglecting a special plea for support from the 'ladies' ('she hopes the Ladies out of Pride / And Honor, will not quit their sexes side'). This structure becomes the distinctive mark of the woman dramatist's prologue in Restoration drama, whether tragic or comic, providing a specifically female twist to the male prologue, which also addresses and attempts to invoke the interest of specific sectors of the audience.

The stature and significance of Aphra Behn in the early years of Restoration drama cannot be underestimated. From 1671 to her death in 1689 (with the exception of a lost play by the mysterious 'Ephelia', *The*

Pair-Royal of Coxcombs, which appears to have been presented at a dancing school in *c.* 1678[23]) she is the only female dramatist to be writing plays for, and having them performed on, the public stage (a total of fifteen plays were printed and produced during this period). A manuscript of Elizabeth Polwhele's lively comedy of intrigue *The Frolics*, which was evidently written for performance and dates from 1671, seems never to have been performed, and Boothby appears to have produced no further plays for the public stage.[24] Not until 1695, with the production of Catherine Trotter's tragedy *Agnes de Castro* at the Theatre Royal and a comedy by 'Ariadne', *She Ventures and He Wins*, at Little Lincoln's Inn Fields were any other women dramatists introduced to the London stage. The following year saw the production of four plays by two new women writers, Delarivier Manley (*The Lost Lover* and *The Royal Mischief*) and Mary Pix (*Ibrahim* and *The Spanish Wives*).

Both *Agnes de Castro*, the plot drawn from Aphra Behn's novella of the same title first published in 1688, and *She Ventures and He Wins* firmly locate themselves as successors to Behn. Trotter's play, when published in 1696, was accompanied by a commendatory poem from Delarivier Manley which hailed Trotter as ushering in a new reign for the women dramatist with '*Orinda* [Katherine Philips] and the Fair *Astrea* gone' and 'Not one . . . found to fill the Vacant Throne' until Trotter herself (Greer *et al.*, eds., *Kissing the Rod*, p. 398).[25] In the preface to *She Ventures and He Wins*, 'Ariadne' speaks of 'the inclinations [she] had for scribbling from [her] childhood' and admits:

> when our island enjoyed the blessing of the incomparable Mrs Behn, even then I had much ado to keep my muse from showing her impertinence; but, since her death, has claimed a kind of privilege; and, in spite of me, broke from her confinement.[26]

However, we cannot ascribe the singularity of Behn and the corresponding silence of other women dramatists over this period as wholly the effect of Behn's dominance as a playwright (and there can be little doubt, in comparing her plays with those of Polwhele and that of Boothby, of the aesthetic superiority of her work). The 1690s saw the transformation of the London stage, culminating in Jeremy Collier's pamphlet *A Short View of the Immorality and Profaneness of the English Stage* (1698), into a far more sentimental and less rumbustious environment with a corresponding refinement of both tragedic and comedic content. This shift in the cultural expectations of theatre may be ascribed to a number of causes, not least the declining interest in the stage on the part of the English monarchy. Mary and Anne were far less enthusiastic theatre-goers than their father James II and his brother Charles II; their courts were also, at least publicly, far more decorous, reserved and familial than those of their father and uncle and the notorious immorality of the theatre world, as a centre and source for mistresses of royalty and aristocracy (of which Nell Gwynn is only the most famous example), came into question. The decline of royal patronage appears to have been attended by increasing access for the middle classes, resulting in a slow 'reformation' of the stage. This appears to have made it more attractive for the apprentice female writer, who wished to maintain a reputation of morality.[27]

This debate and transformation in the stage was *not necessarily* conducted in the interests of women, nor did the advent of sentimental comedy inevitably lead to female ascendancy in playwrighting. As with the novel in this period, it could be argued that what is at stake here is rather an evolution of a particular ideological construction of a new class identity, displaced into a discussion of female virtue.[28] It is the centrality of the motif of sexual intrigue as a mode of political analogy, and its changing character from the 1670s to the 1690s, to which the remainder of this chapter will attend. In doing so, I have chosen to concentrate on eight plays in the two dominant modes of Restoration drama, the comedy of intrigue and the Oriental She-tragedy (a version of the heroic tragedy which centres on the erotic figure of the virtuous, suffering female protagonist). In each case, a better-known play by a male playwright, Congreve's *The Way of the World* (1700) and Dryden's *All for Love* (1678), is employed in order to highlight the slight but perceptible differences in women's treatment of the ideological and linguistic resources of the public stage.

The most common complaint made by students of Restoration drama (tragedy or comedy) is the confusion that results from a certain sameness in plot structure and the difficulty of differentiating one character from another (Willmore from Wouldbe from Willful from Fainwood, etc.). This sameness is not the result of a poverty of imagination on the part of the playwrights, but what might be described as a shared 'artillery' of themes and tropes that are drawn upon by Tory and Whig playwrights.[29] These themes and tropes function as an artillery precisely because they are being 'fought over' from different political positions in the late seventeenth century. The recurrence of rape as a political motif may serve as an example. For the Tory Royalist it figures the 'mob' excesses associated with the civil war and the execution of Charles I. For the Whig Parliamentarian it figures the dangers of popery associated with a monstrous feminine desire that instigates the abuse of an idealised Englishness in the body of the embattled bourgeois heroine. Despotic reign is associated for the Whigs with tyrannous kings in an implicit critique of the Catholic James, Duke of York and later James II; for the Tories it signals the usurpation of rightful inheritance on the part of illegitimate sons in an implicit attack on the rebellions in the 1680s led by the illegitimate James Scott, the Duke of Monmouth, against his father Charles II, or William of Orange's displacement of his father-in-law James II from the throne in the 'Glorious Revolution' of 1688. Party and sexual politics are closely, virtually inseparably, intertwined in these plays. 'Plots' in the drama are constantly equated with the political 'plots' that dogged the later Stuart kings, most famously the supposed 'Popish Plot' of 1678–82 which led to the 'Exclusion Crisis' (a rumoured Catholic plot to murder Charles II and place his Catholic brother on the throne, supposedly headed by James, the Pope and the French king Louis XIV).

Women playwrights, Whig and Tory, were placed in a complex position in this process because they might be expected to be as concerned with sexual as with party politics. In other words, sexual conflict does not work for them *simply* as a process of *analogy* for party conflict. Their focus must be double, representing both the difficulties of being female in a patriarchal culture and the difficulties of being an 'honest' Whig or Tory in a minefield of political duplicity (plots and counter-plotting). It is not the case, of course, that their male contemporaries do *not* have sexual political agendas as well as party political ones; one of the successes of women playwrights in this period is that they manage to enter the field of party political debate *on the same terms* as their male contemporaries. However, it can be argued that they succeed in developing a model of female sexual political activity which, by analogy, suggests their capacity to enter the (masculine) field of party political activism. The differences between male and female playwrights of the Restoration are slight, but not less significant for that.

THE COMEDY OF INTRIGUE

Aphra Behn, *The Lucky Chance* (1686), 'Ariadne', *She Ventures and He Wins* (1695), Mary Pix, *The Beau Defeated* (1700), William Congreve, *The Way of the World* (1700).

Behn and Congreve both open their plays with a male couple (Bellmour and Gayman in *The Lucky Chance*, and Fainall and Mirabell in *The Way of the World*) who are discussing their different difficulties in love, a device which calls our attention to the structural 'homosociality' of Restoration culture in which women figure as exchange tokens between men as a measure of their political–social alliance. Gayman is seeking to prevent his friend's mistress Leticia from marrying Sir Feeble Fainwood, who has deluded her that Bellmour has been executed for murder in Holland, while Gayman pursues his attempt to cuckold Sir Cautious Fulbank, who has married the woman he was previously courting, Julia. In Congreve's play the men are in a position of rivalry, although they appear at first to be co-conspirators, both engaged in the attempt to release the inheritances that Lady Wishfort controls of their respective partners, Mrs Fainall and Millamant, whom Mirabell is courting.

By contrast, 'Ariadne' and Mary Pix both open their plays with female negotiations to win the men of their choice. Charlotte Frankford and her cousin Juliana enter dressed in men's clothes (and hence mimicking the conventional opening of the paired male co-conspirators in the comedy), intending to seek a lover for Charlotte, who will court her for her self rather than for her money, settling on the melancholy Lovewell, an impoverished younger brother. Mary Pix's play opens in the boudoir of the frivolous cit-widow (a reference to her lowly 'citizen' origins) Lady Rich, who aspires to marry an aristocrat, interrupted in her plotting with a maid by her guest Lady Landsworth; the latter, like Charlotte in *She Ventures*, is in love with an impoverished younger brother, Clerimont, whom she is pursuing in disguise to test whether his love is mercenary or genuine. In all three plays by women, despite Behn's privileging in her opening of the homosocial context of male plotting over female friend-ship, the 'managerial' or 'plotting' capacity of the men is quickly surmounted by the manipulative wit of their female counterparts, who engineer their freedom to marry the man of their choice.

That freedom, in three of the four plays, has to be won at the expense of an older generation, which is cozened by a younger: that older generation takes the form of two old men in *The Lucky Chance* (Feeble Fainwood and Sir Cautious Fulbank, who are explicitly identified as Whig city worthies), and two older women in *The Beau Defeated* and *The Way of the World* (Lady Wishfort and Mrs Rich, who are both presented as *arrivistes* whose status is bought rather than inherited). 'Ariadne's play concerns itself with a younger generation, who seem to be entirely free of such constraints, offering an almost pastoral and certainly mythic image of companionate marriage as established purely through their own agency, a strategy in keeping with the prefatory declaration of the freeing of her muse with the death of a powerful originating model in Aphra Behn.

This sense of a displacement of an old order to make way for a new is compounded in Restoration comedies by a focus on the importance of contractual rather than arbitrary or patrilineal duty. Contracts and documents that must be obtained and verified proliferate in these plays. In *The Way of the World*, Mirabell, as well as famously negotiating a premarital verbal contract of the provenance of the roles between himself and his future wife, Millamant, resolves the play's crisis by revealing a contract made before her marriage to Fainall between himself and Mrs Languish that conveys her estate to him in trust. Bellmour in *The Lucky Chance* insists on the legitimacy of the verbal contract between himself and Leticia to marry that predates her contract with Sir Feeble Fainwood, as well as seeking and obtaining the written pardon for the murder he has committed in a duel that Fainwood has been hiding in order to keep him in exile. Not only is this a mark of a society moving toward a culture of 'paper', but also one that is increasingly conceiving of relations (political, financial and sexual) in terms of mutual consent and contract between two parties rather than pre-given obligations of power and ownership on the basis of status.[30]

Women playwrights reveal both the potential for women's freedom in this new conception of consenting relations over given relations of dominance, but also limitations that are set on them if these relations of contract and consent are only established *between men*. Behn's Julia Fulbank expresses her displeasure at her exclusion from the agreement between her lover Gayman and her husband Sir Cautious, that the former should spend a night with her in exchange for a £300 debt incurred by Sir Cautious from gaming with his rival. Despite Millamant's wit and playfulness and her future husband's concession that she has a right to negotiate over the sexual–political dynamics of their marriage, it is worth noting that she is not *structurally* in the same position in this play as her female counterparts in plays by women; Julia Fulbank, Lady Landsworth and Charlotte Frankford are all considerably more active and independent in engineering their own freedom to elect their future husbands, if their displays of verbal wit are less sparkling.

THE ORIENTAL SHE-TRAGEDY

John Dryden, *All For Love* (1678), Aphra Behn, *Abdelazer; or the Moor's Revenge* (1676), Mary Pix, *Ibrahim, The Thirteenth Emperor of the Turks* (1696), Delarivier Manley, *The Royal Mischief* (1696).

Dryden dedicated his play to Thomas, Earl of Danby, Treasurer to Charles II. The dedication expresses pity for him being attacked by jealous rivals and praises Danby for his loyalty to his master. Presumably we are meant to equate Danby's actions with those of the play's virtuous general Ventibius, who tries to disengage Antony's affections from Cleopatra and direct them back to his wife, to Rome and to the pursuit of victory over Caesar for his own sake rather than that of his mistress. In the dedication, Dryden announces: 'my nature, as I am an Englishman, and my reason, as I am a man, have bred in me a loathing to that specious name of a republic, that mock appearance of a liberty, where all who have not part in the government, are slaves.'[31] Dryden then makes quite explicit the allegorical and political framework of his (Royalist) play about the importance of virtuous council in directing the aberrant desires of rulers, male (Antony and Caesar) or female (Cleopatra). By contrast, Delarivier Manley in her preface simply defends her play from charges of excessive 'warmth':

in all Writings of this kind, some particular Passion is describ'd, as a Woman I thought it Policy to begin with the softest, and which is easiest to our Sex; Ambition & c. were too bold for the first flight, all wou'd have condemned me if venturing on another, I had fail'd, when gentle love stood ready to afford an easy Victory, I did not believe it possible to pursue him too far.[32]

Now, Manley's play is quite as political as Dryden's and from a similar, if more extreme, ideological position. Her anti-heroine Homais is married to an impotent prince, known as a 'Protector', and seeks her sexual pleasure elsewhere with an honourable prince who is his nephew. This Tory Royalist play comes close to advocating absolutism as the only way of controlling the riotous desires of the state figured as a woman.

The She-tragedy traditionally counterpoints virtuous women and lustful tragic queens or courtesans: Queen Isabella and her daughter, Leonora, in *Abdelazar*, Cleopatra and Octavia in *All for Love*, Sheker Para and Morena in *Ibrahim*, Homais and Bassima in *The Royal Mischief*. Sheker Para and Homais are both attached to powerful men but lusting after younger flesh. Homais is married to an old and impotent 'Protector', whose title invokes the English 'Protector', Oliver Cromwell; analogically, the play suggests the attractions of virile and honourable young Toryism in contrast with faded Commonwealth men. Pix, as a Whig writer, deploys a reverse strategy, demonising the woman who, in alliance with self-interested ministers, corrupts the head of state. Cleopatra is corrupting, despite herself, in Dryden's *All for Love*. Her love is genuine but the interference of desire with matters of state is bound to divide loyalties, a representation typical of Dryden's ambiguities about the sexual license of the Stuart princes but desire to defend their "divine right" and his preference for monarchy over Commonwealth.

At the centre of the Oriental She-tragedy is the attraction of dramatic scenes of suffering womanhood, whether embodied in the sentimental power of the virtuous heroine or the erotic vision of a ranting queen driven by lust to destruction. Women playwrights exploit this eroticism as much as their male counterparts. However, as with the comedy, female playwrights remain more preoccupied than their male counterparts with the question of female political agency rather than simply employing femininity as a figure of the embattled state or the dangers of popery (depending upon which side of the political fence they stand on).

For the women playwrights this means questioning which is the more politically efficacious role for women, that of lascivious queen or suffering princess. This contrast is particularly clear in Pix's *Ibrahim*. The Mufti (High Priest of Turkey) has raised his virtuous daughter Morena to eschew the duplicities of the feminine sex:

> Heaven not blessing me with a Male, I have try'd
> To mend the Sex; and she, instead of (coining looks)
> And learning little Arts to please him, hath Read
> Philosophy, History, those rough Studies.[33]

By contrast, Sheker Para, the courtesan, uses her feminine wiles to gain political power, procuring virgins for the perverted and dissipated tastes of Ibrahim, forging alliances with his male counsellors to advance her own interests. She wins Azema the Grand Vizier to her cause against the Mufti by asserting:

> On whom is't thou art studying revenge,
> Old Statesman! wouldst though have it bitter,
> Deep and secure; take a Woman with thee!
> —Or Bloody, as thy remorseless Heart can frame,
> Still take a Woman's Counsel! (III.15)

Sheker Para engineers the rape of Morena by Ibrahim out of jealousy; she lusts after the noble Amurat, Morena's suitor. Both women die by their own hands, but the play is quite clear about the contrast between Sheker Para's duplicitous agency and Morena's passive valour, her suffering without return.[34] Women's political agency or success in the heroic tragedy by women is more often than not achieved *at the expense of* their opposite, the virtuous woman. To be political agents in the drama, female characters in Restoration drama by women are required to play with and manipulate the ideologies of femininity that constrain them, rather than eschew them completely. That way, the tragedy argues, lies madness.

The self-conscious slippage between the figure of the prostitute and the witty bourgeois woman (in the comedies), or the sexually driven Oriental queen (in the tragedies), can be paralleled with that between the actress/prostitute and the female playwright. The key issue for all these figures is that they are 'playing a part'; they are mistresses in the art of disguise. The part they play might best be described as that of 'subversive mimesis'. They mimic femininity successfully so as to persuade their male audience, fellow writers and actors, that they are solely motivated by the proper province of women, sexual desire. But the mimicry is also a form of subversion; its very extravagance (whether ranting or engaged in repartee) indicates another agenda for the woman performer. Just as the prostitute simulates sexual pleasure for material gain, the actress and the playwright display their bodies/works simultaneously to conceal and reveal their other agenda, to demonstrate their capacity to be agents in their culture, whether politically (the playwright) or financially (the actress). Aphra Behn is the past mistress of this particular art.

Women's only political instrumentality is, then, to be achieved solely by playing the role of seductress. Not only does the woman writer receive approval rather than scorn for her confinement of her 'interest' to the sphere of love, she also receives financial remuneration. In fact, in her prologue to her first play, *The Forc'd Marriage*, Behn goes further, and identifies the woman playwright as exceeding both the prostitute and the actress in her strategies of securing power. Where the actress is trapped in the typecast (Restoration actresses, as Elizabeth Howe demonstrates, consistently played the same 'type', with little variation, throughout their careers), and the prostitute has only one chance at financial gain in each transaction with her customer, the female playwright succeeds in constantly reconfiguring herself for her audience, retaining their attention by virtue of her enigmatic concealment rather than ostentatious display. With reference to the new phenomenon of women adopting the role of the playwright, Behn argues:

Women those charming victors, in whose eyes
Lie all their arts, and their artilleries
Not being contented with the wounds they made,
Would by new stratagems our lives invade.
Beauty alone goes now at too cheap rates
And therefore they, like wise and politic states,
Court a new power that may the old supply,
To *keep* as well as gain the victory:
They'll join the force of wit to beauty now,
And so *maintain* the right they have in you.[35]

The association between prostitute, actress and playwright is only invoked to be disentangled through the key factor of the playwright's 'wit'. Unlike the numerous Witwoulds, Wouldbes and Willmores of her plays, the female playwright uses her 'wit' to secure rather than merely aspire to the capacity to speak publicly about the public issues from which she is, supposedly, debarred.

NOTES

1. Elizabeth Cary, *The Tragedie of Mariam, the Fair Queen of Jewry* (London, 1613), III.iii.1243–6. Reprinted by the Malone Society (Oxford: Horace Hart for the University Press, 1914). There is now an edition of *Mariam* available in paperback, edited by Barry Weller and Margaret Ferguson (Berkeley: University of California Press, 1994).

2. BM MS Reg. 15.A.ix. The first leaf bears the inscription 'The doinge of my Lady Lumley dowghter to my L. Therle of Arundell', followed by the autograph signature of Lord Lumley. The text of *Iphigenia in Aulis* is available in Malone Society Reprint (London: Chiswick Press, 1909).

3. Mary Pix, *The Beau Defeated* (London, 1700), reprinted in Paddy Lyons and Fidelis Morgan, eds., *Female Playwrights of the Restoration: Five Comedies* (Everyman Library; London: J. M. Dent, 1991), pp. 161–234.

4. Sophie Tomlinson, 'She that Plays the King: Henrietta Maria and the Threat of the Actress in Caroline Culture', in Gordon McMullan and Jonathan Hope, eds., *The Politics of Tragicomedy: Shakespeare and After* (London and New York: Routledge, 1992), pp. 189–207, p. 190.

5. See, on Renaissance drama, Jonathan Dollimore, *Radical Tragedy: Religion, Ideology and Power in the Drama of Shakespeare and his Contemporaries*, 2nd edn (London: Harvester Wheatsheaf and University of Chicago Press, 1989). On Restoration drama, see Laura Brown, *English Dramatic Form, 1660–1760* (New Haven and London: Yale University Press, 1981); Robert Markley, *Two Edg'd Weapons: Style and Ideology in the Comedies of Etherage, Wycherley, and Congreve* (Oxford: Oxford University Press, 1988).

6. For Henrietta Maria's important role in Caroline drama and politics, see Tomlinson, 'She that Plays the King', Eric Veevers, *Images of Love and*

Religion: Queen Henrietta Maria and Court Entertainments (Cambridge: Cambridge University Press, 1989), and Martin Butler, *Theatre and Crisis, 1632–1642* (Cambridge: Cambridge University Press, 1984).

7. Quoted in Elizabeth Howe, *The First English Actresses: Women and Drama, 1660–1700* (Cambridge: Cambridge University Press, 1992), p. 25.

8. See Catharine Gallagher, 'Who was that Masked Woman? The Prostitute and the Playwright in the Comedies of Aphra Behn', in Heidi Hutner, ed., *Rereading Aphra Behn: History, Theory and Criticism* (Charlottesville and London: Virginia University Press, 1993), pp. 65–85.

9. On the rhetorical mechanisms of this exchange culture, see Lorna Hutson, *The Usurer's Daughter: Male Friendship and Fictions of Women in Sixteenth-Century England* (London and New York: Routledge, 1994).

10. Katherine Philips's translation of Corneille's *Pompey* was performed in Dublin in February 1663; a Dublin edition of 500 copies quickly sold out. Her translation of Corneille's *Horace* was completed by Sir John Denham after her premature death at the age of thirty-two of smallpox, and was produced at court on 4 February 1668. It ran in public performance at the Theatre Royal from 16–21 January 1669. Both plays were published in her collected works, entitled *Poems*, of 1667.

11. On the centrality of Seneca for Renaissance closet drama, see Rebecca W. Bushnell, *Tragedies of Tyrants: Political Thought and Theater in the English Renaissance* (Ithaca, NY: Cornell University Press, 1990).

12. Tina Krontiris, 'Mary Herbert: Englishing a purified Cleopatra', in her *Oppositional Voices: Women as Writers and Translators of Literature in the English Renaissance* (London: Routledge, 1992), pp. 64–78.

13. Mary Ellen Lamb, *Gender and Authorship in the Sidney Circle* (Madison: University of Wisconsin Press, 1990), p. 133.

14. See Barbara K. Lewalski, 'Lucy, Countess of Bedford: Images of a Jacobean Courtier and Patroness', Kevin Sharpe and Steven Zwicker, eds., *Politics of Discourse: the Literature and History of Seventeenth-Century England* (Los Angeles: University of California Press, 1987), pp. 137–58.

15. Elizabeth Cary's biography is given by her daughter who became a Catholic nun in France. See Richard Simpson, ed., *The Lady Falkland, her Life from an MS. in the Imperial Archives at Lisle* (London: Catholic Publishing and Bookselling Co., 1861). The biography is also included in the Weller and Ferguson edition of *Mariam*.

16. Margaret Ferguson, 'The Spectre of Resistance: *The Tragedy of Mariam* (1613)', in David Scott Kastan and Peter Stallybrass, eds., *Staging the Renaissance: Reinterpretations of Elizabethan and Jacobean Drama* (London and New York: Routledge, 1991), pp. 235–50.

17. '"The Concealed Fansyes": a Play by Lady Jane Cavendish and Lady Elizabeth Brackley', ed. Nathan Comfort Starr, *PMLA*, 46 (1931), 802–38. The text is now available in S.P. Cerasano and Marion Wynne-Davies, eds., *Renaissance Drama by Women: Texts and Documents* (London: Routledge, 1996).

18. See Sophie Tomlinson, '"My Brain the Stage": Margaret Cavendish and the Fantasy of Female Performance', in Clare Brant and Diane Purkiss, eds., *Women, Texts and Histories 1575–1760* (London: Routledge, 1992), pp. 134–63, and Susan Wiseman, 'Gender and Status in Dramatic Discourse: Margaret Cavendish, Duchess of Newcastle', in Isobel Grundy and Susan Wiseman, eds., *Women, Writing, History, 1640–1740* (London: Batsford, 1992), pp. 159–77.

19. This is by no means an uncommon strategy in late seventeenth-century feminist argument. Both Bathsua Makin in her *An Essay to Revive the Antient Education of Gentlewomen* (1673) and Mary Astell in her *A Serious Proposal to the Ladies* (1694) make the same case.

20. Robert Gould, *Satirical Epistle to the Female Author of a Poem* (London, 1691). Quoted in Gallagher, 'who was that Masked Woman', p. 69.

21. Polwhele's play is only available in manuscript with the legend 'This Tragedy apoynted to be acted by the dukes Company of Actors only leaving out what was Cross'd by Henry Herbert' at its head (Bodleian Library MS Rawlinson. Poet. 195). Boothby's *Marcelia* was licensed in October 1669 and published in 1670. Behn's *The Forced Marriage* was published in 1671.

22. Frances Boothby, *Marcelia; or the Treacherous Friend* (London, 1670), NP. For a full discussion of women and theatrical performance in early modern Britain, see chapter 5 of this volume.

23. Four poems, the prologue, the epilogue and two songs from *The Pair-Royal of Coxcombs* are given in *Female Poems on Several Occasions* (London, 1679), pp. 16–21. The 'Prologue' is reprinted in Germaine Greer, Jeslyn Medoff, Melinda Sansone and Susan Hastings, eds., *Kissing the Rod: an Anthology of Seventeenth-Century Women's Verse* (London: Virago, 1988), p. 275. The identification of 'Ephelia' as one Joan Phillips by Samuel Halkett and Catherine Laing, in their *Dictionary of Anonymous and Pseudonymous Literature* (Edinburgh: W. Paterson, 1882–8) seems to have no foundation.

24. Elizabeth Polwhele, *The Frolicks or The Lawyer Cheated* (1671), eds. Judith Milhous and Robert D. Hume (Ithaca, NY, and London: Cornell University Press, 1977). For the theory that Polwhele was the daughter of a nonconformist minister, Theophilus Polwhele, vicar of Tiverton and wife to another Cornish divine, the Reverend Stephen Lobb, and the hypothesis that her marriage may have brought an end to her writing, see the editors' introduction to the aforementioned volume.

25. In reciprocation, both Trotter and Pix contributed commendatory verses to Manley's tragedy *The Royal Mischief* (1696), and Trotter provided an epilogue for Pix's *Queen Catherine* (1698) (Greer *et al.*, eds., *Kissing the Rod*, p. 410, pp. 414–15, p. 411). Pix's poem to Manley also cites Behn describing Manley's poetry as 'Like *Sappho* Charming, like *Afra* Eloquent, / Like Chast *Orinda*, sweetly Innocent' (*Ibid.*, pp. 414–15).

26. 'Ariadne', *She Ventures and He Wins*, reprinted in Paddy Lyons and Fidelis Morgan, eds., *Female Playwrights of the Restoration: Five Comedies* (Everyman's Library; London: J. M. Dent, 1991), p. 105.

27. See David Roberts, 'The Ladies and the Change in Comedy', in his *The Ladies: Female Patronage of Restoration Drama 1660–1700* (Oxford: Clarendon Press, 1989). For Collier, see 'The Collier Controversy', Scott McMillin, ed., *Restoration and Eighteenth-Century Comedy* (New York: W. W. Norton, 1973), pp. 391–419, p. 393.

28. With regard to the novel, see Nancy Armstrong, *Desire and Domestic Fiction: a Political History of the Novel* (Oxford: Oxford University Press, 1985) and Michael McKeon, 'The Gendering of Ideology', in his *The Origins of the English Novel, 1600–1740* (Baltimore and London: Johns Hopkins University Press, 1987), pp. 255–65.

29. This argument is outlined in more detail and sophistication by Susan J. Owen in 'Interpreting the Politics of Restoration Drama', *SC* (Special Issue: Forms of Authority in Restoration England, ed. Paul Hammond), 8:1 (1993), 67–97. Much of my own more general reading is built upon her groundbreaking work in the area.

30. For a political reading of 'plotting' along these lines, but which pays little attention to the ambiguous positioning of women writers, see Richard Braverman, *Plots and Counterplots: Sexual Politics and the Body Politic in English Literature, 1660–1730* (Cambridge Studies in Eighteenth-Century Literature and Thought, 18; Cambridge: Cambridge University Press, 1993).

31. John Dryden, 'To the Right Honourable Thomas, Earl of Danby', *All for Love or the World Well Lost*, reprinted in *Restoration Plays* (Everyman Library; London: J. M. Dent, 1932), p. 3.

32. Delarivier Manley, *The Royal Mischief* (London, 1696), A3r.

33. Mary Pix, *Ibrahim, The Thirteenth Emperor of the Turks* (London, 1696), act 3, p. 19 (the printed play gives no scene divisions).

34. Susan Owen notes, however, that this passive valour as an analogy for political quietism is valued by Tory playwrights, as a means of averting the repetition of the trauma of civil war ('Interpreting the Politics', pp. 84–5).

35. Aphra Behn, 'Prologue', *The Forced Marriage; or, the Jealous Bridegroom* (London, 1671), NP.

Further reading

A large number of primary texts and critical works are referred to during the course of the preceding chapters. All these references may be found in the notes to individual chapters, and primary authors and texts may be further located by means of the index. The following guide lists a selection of anthologies, critical and historical works with which to begin further study of women and literature in Britain during the sixteenth and seventeenth centuries.

ANTHOLOGIES

Aughterson, Kate (ed.) *Renaissance Woman: a Sourcebook*. London: Routledge, 1995.

Cerasano, Susan and Marion Wynne-Davies (eds.) *Renaissance Theatre by Women: Texts and Contexts*. London and New York: Routledge, 1996.

Goreau, Angeline (ed.) *The Whole Duty of Woman: Female Writers in Seventeenth-Century England*. New York: Dial Press, 1985.

Graham, Elspeth, Hilary Hinds, Elaine Hobby and Helen Wilcox (eds.) *Her Own Life: Autobiographical Writings by Seventeenth-Century Englishwomen*. London: Routledge, 1989.

Greer, Germaine, Jeslyn Medoff, Melinda Sansone and Susan Hastings (eds.) *Kissing the Rod: an Anthology of Seventeenth-Century Women's Verse*. London: Virago, 1988.

Henderson, Katherine Usher and Barbara F. McManus (eds.) *Half Humankind: Contexts and Texts of the Controversy about Women in England, 1540–1640*. Urbana: University of Illinois Press, 1985.

Keeble, N. H. (ed.) *The Cultural Identity of Seventeenth-Century Woman: a Reader*. London: Routledge, 1994.

Klein, Joan Larson (ed.) *Daughters, Wives and Widows: Writings by Men about Women and Marriage in England, 1500–1640*. Urbana: University of Illinois Press, 1992.

Lyons, Paddy and Fidelis Morgan (eds.) *Female Playwrights of the Restoration: Five Comedies*. London: J. M. Dent, 1991.

Otten, Charlotte F. (ed.) *English Women's Voices, 1540–1700*. Miami: Florida International University Press, 1992.

Prescott, Anne Lake and Betty S. Travitsky (eds.) *Rereading the Renaissance*. New York: Columbia University Press, 1996.

Purkiss, Diane (ed.) *Renaissance Women: the Plays of Elizabeth Cary, the Poems of Aemilia Lanyer*. London: William Pickering, 1994.

Salzman, Paul (ed.) *An Anthology of Seventeenth-Century Fiction*. Oxford: Oxford University Press, 1991.

Shepherd, Simon (ed.) *The Women's Sharp Revenge: Five Women's Pamphlets from the Renaissance*. London: Macmillan, 1985.

Travitsky, Betty (ed.) *The Paradise of Women: Writings by Englishwomen of the Renaissance*. Westport, CT: Greenwood Press, 1980; rpt. 1989.

N.B. Two major publication series are currently making texts by early modern women writers in English more widely available: The Early Modern English-woman, a facsimile series from the Scolar Press, and Women Writers in English, 1350–1850, published by Oxford University Press in co-operation with the Brown Women Writers Project.

CRITICAL AND HISTORICAL STUDIES

Ammusen, Susan Dwyer. *An Ordered Society: Gender and Class in Early Modern England*. Oxford and New York: Basil Blackwell, 1988.

Beilin, Elaine V. *Redeeming Eve: Women Writers of the English Renaissance*. Princeton, NJ: Princeton University Press, 1987.

Bell, Maureen, George Parfitt and Simon Shepherd (eds.) *A Biographical Dictionary of English Women Writers, 1580–1720*. Hemel Hempstead: Harvester Wheatsheaf, 1990.

Belsey, Catherine. *The Subject of Tragedy: Identity and Difference in Renaissance Drama*. London and New York: Methuen, 1985.

Benson, Pamela Joseph. *The Invention of the Renaissance Woman*. University Park: Pennsylvania State University Press, 1992.

Brant, Clare and Diane Purkiss (eds.) *Women, Texts and Histories, 1575–1760*. London: Routledge, 1992.

Cerasano, S. P. and Marion Wynne-Davies (eds.) *Gloriana's Face: Women, Public and Private, in the English Renaissance*. Hemel Hempstead: Harvester Wheatsheaf, 1992.

Cotton, Nancy. *Women Playwrights in England c. 1363–1750*. London: Associated University Presses, 1980.

Crawford, Patricia. *Women and Religion in England, 1500–1720*. London and New York: Routledge, 1993.

Davies, Stevie. *The Idea of Woman in Renaissance Literature*. Brighton: Harvester, 1986.

Evans, Robert C. and Anne C. Little (eds.) *'The Muses Females Are': Martha*

Moulsworth and Other Women Writers of the English Renaissance. West Cornwall, CT: Locust Hill Press, 1995.

Ezell, Margaret J. M. *The Patriarch's Wife: Literary Evidence and the History of the Family*. Chapel Hill: University of North Carolina Press, 1987.

Writing Women's Literary History. Baltimore: Johns Hopkins University Press, 1993.

Farrell, Kirby, Elizabeth H. Hageman and Arthur F. Kinney (eds.) *Women in the Renaissance: Selections from 'English Literary Renaissance'*. Amherst: University of Massachusetts Press, 1990.

Ferguson, Margaret W., Maureen Quilligan and Nancy J. Vickers (eds.) *Rewriting the Renaissance: the Discourses of Sexual Difference in Early Modern Europe*. Chicago: University of Chicago Press, 1986.

Gent, Lucy and Nigel Llewellyn (eds.) *Renaissance Bodies: the Human Figure in English Culture, c. 1540–1660*. London: Reaktion Books, 1990.

Grundy, Isobel and Susan Wiseman (eds). *Women, Writing, History, 1640–1740*. London: Batsford, 1992.

Hackett, Helen. *Virgin Mother, Maiden Queen: Elizabeth I and the Cult of the Virgin Mary*. London: Macmillan, 1994.

Hannay, Margaret P. (ed.) *Silent But For the Word: Tudor Women as Patrons, Translators, and Writers of Religious Works*. Kent, OH: Kent State University Press, 1985.

Harvey, Elizabeth D. *Ventriloquized Voices*. London: Routledge, 1992.

Haselkorn, Anne M. and Betty S. Travitsky (eds.) *The Renaissance Englishwoman in Print: Counterbalancing the Canon*. Amherst: University of Massachusetts Press, 1990.

Hendricks, Margo and Patricia Parker (eds.) *Women, 'Race', and Writing in the Early Modern Period*. London: Routledge, 1994.

Hinds, Hilary. *Strength in Weakness Manifest: Seventeenth-Century Womens' Writing and Feminist Literary Criticism*. Manchester: Manchester University Press, 1996.

Hobby, Elaine. *Virtue of Necessity: English Women's Writing, 1649–1688*. London: Virago, 1988.

Howe, Elizabeth. *The First English Actresses: Women and Drama, 1660–1700*. Cambridge: Cambridge University Press, 1992.

Hull, Suzanne W. *Chaste, Silent, and Obedient: English Books for Women, 1475–1640*. San Marino, CA: Huntington Library, 1982.

Jardine, Lisa. *Still Harping on Daughters: Women and Drama in the Age of Shakespeare*. Hemel Hempstead: Harvester Wheatsheaf, 1989.

Jones, Ann Rosalind. *The Currency of Eros: Women's Love Lyric in Europe, 1540–1620*. Bloomington: Indiana University Press, 1990.

Jordan, Constance. *Renaissance Feminism: Literary Texts and Political Models*. Ithaca, NY: Cornell University Press, 1990.

Kelso, Ruth. *Doctrine for the Lady of the Renaissance*. Urbana: University of Illinois Press, 1956.

King, Margaret L. *Women of the Renaissance*. Chicago: Chicago University Press, 1991.

Krontiris, Tina. *Oppositional Voices: Women as Writers and Translators of Literature in the English Renaissance*. London: Routledge, 1992.

Laurence, Anne. *Women in England, 1500–1760: a Social History*. London: Macmillan, 1994.

Lewalski, Barbara K. *Writing Women in Jacobean England*. Cambridge, MA: Harvard University Press, 1993.

Lucas, Caroline. *Writing for Women: the Example of Woman as Reader in Elizabethan Romance*. Milton Keynes: Open University Press, 1989.

MacCurtain, Margaret and Mary O'Dowd. *Women in Early Modern Ireland*. Edinburgh: Edinburgh University Press, 1991.

Maclean, Ian. *The Renaissance Notion of Woman: a Study in the Fortunes of Scholasticism and Medical Science in European Intellectual Life*. Cambridge: Cambridge University Press, 1980.

Paster, Gail Kern. *The Body Embarrassed: Drama and the Disciplines of Shame in Early Modern England*. Ithaca, NY: Cornell University Press, 1993.

Pearson, Jacqueline. *The Prostiuted Muse: Images of Women and Women Dramatists, 1642–1737*. Brighton: Harvester, 1988.

Prior, Mary (ed.) *Women in English Society, 1500–1800*. London and New York: Methuen, 1985.

Rose, Mary Beth (ed.) *Women in the Middle Ages and the Renaissance: Literary and Historical Perspectives*. Syracuse, NY: Syracuse University Press, 1986.

Smith, Hilda L. *Reason's Disciples: Seventeenth-Century English Feminists*. Urbana: University of Illinois Press, 1982.

Smith, Hilda L. and Susan Cardinale. *Women and the Literature of the Seventeenth Century: an Annotated Bibliography Based on Wing's Short-Title Catalogue*. New York: Greenwood Press, 1990.

Todd, Margo. *Christian Humanism and the Puritan Social Order*. Cambridge: Cambridge University Press, 1987.

Travitsky, Betty S. and Josephine A. Roberts. *English Women Writers, 1500–1640: A Reference Guide (1750–1996)*. New York: G. K. Hall, 1997.

Travitsky, Betty S. and Adele F. Seeff (eds.) *Attending to Women in Early Modern England*. Newark: University of Delaware Press, 1994.

Wall, Wendy. *The Imprint of Gender: Authorship and Publication in the English Renaissance*. Ithaca, NY: Cornell University Press, 1993.

Wiesner, Merry E. *Women and Gender in Early Modern Europe*. Cambridge: Cambridge University Press, 1993.

Woodbridge, Linda. *Women and the English Renaissance: Literature and the Nature of Womankind, 1540–1620*. Brighton: Harvester, 1987.

Index